THE GHOST WARRIORS

INSIDE ISRAEL'S UNDERCOVER WAR AGAINST TERRORISM

SAMUEL M. KATZ

DIVERSION
BOOKS

Diversion Books
A division of Diversion Publishing Corp.
www.diversionbooks.com

First Published by Berkley Caliber
Copyright © 2016, 2025 Samuel M. Katz

Diversion Books and colophon are registered trademarks
of Diversion Publishing Corp.

For more information, email info@diversionbooks.com

First Diversion Books Edition: April 2025
Paperback ISBN: 979-8-89515-010-8
e-ISBN: 979-8-89515-016-0

Cover design by Jen Huppert
Design by Neuwirth & Associates, Inc.

Printed in the United States of America
1   3   5   7   9   10   8   6   4   2

Diversion books are available at special discounts for bulk purchases in
the US by corporations, institutions, and other organizations. For more
information, please contact admin@diversionbooks.com.

CONTENTS

To Sigi—
I have learned everything there is to know about courage
from the one closest to me.

AUTHOR'S NOTE

The seventh of the nine Arab–Israeli wars* was fought between October 1, 2000, and April 30, 2008. It was the longest protracted conflict in Israel's brief and bloodstained history, and it was waged inside the West Bank and the Gaza Strip, as well as inside most of Israel's towns and cities. The battlefields weren't barren stretches of no-man's-land where two armies clashed. They were cafés and city buses, shopping malls, and even children's bedrooms. Palestinian terrorist groups—Hamas and the Islamic Jihad, together with forces allied with the Palestinian Authority—perpetrated hundreds of suicide bombings and active shooter attacks against Israel's population centers; thousands more attacks were foiled before the terrorists could reach their targets. The bloodshed resulted in 1,053 Israeli dead and nearly 5,000 wounded. The majority of Israel's casualties were civilians. There were 4,789 Palestinians killed during the war. The vast majority of the Palestinian casualties were combatants.

The seventh of the nine Arab–Israeli wars was the third bloodiest in Israel's brief but all too bloody history—only the 1948 War of Independence and the 1973 Yom Kippur War resulted in more killed and wounded in action. Yet these years of carnage were never actually called a war. The tense and terrifying reality that was those horrible eight years was known simply as the intifada, the Palestinian colloquial term for "uprising" or "shaking something off." This, the second such uprising, eventually earned a name: the al-Aqsa intifada.

Wars are generally fought to achieve political objectives or to conquer swaths of territories held by others. Yet there was no realistic Palestinian endgame to the violence of the second intifada, just as there was no end

---

* The ninth war—the October 7 conflict—that began with the Hamas invasion and ended being a seven-front conflict (Gaza, Lebanon, Yemen, Syria/Iraq, and Iran) is still ongoing at the time of this book's writing.

game to the unprecedented carnage of October 7. There was no master plan, either by Palestinian Authority president Yasir Arafat or the Hamas leadership, to achieve political concessions from Israel or to create new fact-on-the-ground territorial realities as a result of the endless killing. The only tangible Palestinian military objective of the intifada, it appeared, was to make Israel bleed.

The suicide bombings and massacres were never going to force Israel into making political concessions. The opposite, in fact, occurred. The intifada emboldened Israel's right wing and all but diluted the political strength of the left wing in Israel, who believed that peaceful coexistence with the Palestinians was achievable. The intifada also destroyed Yasir Arafat's post-Oslo political legitimacy as a responsible peacemaker in the eyes of the West and many Arab states who, following the September 11, 2001, attacks against the United States, found themselves on the right side of history in the global war on terror.

The intifada was by no means a spontaneous eruption of violence. For months, throughout peace negotiations with Israel, Arafat had planned for it as the means to support his political standings. He positioned his resources accordingly. Yet the eruption of the violence caught Israel by surprise. The two Israeli intelligence services responsible for counterintelligence and counterterrorist operations against the Palestinians—A'man, or Military Intelligence, and primarily the Shin Bet, the internal security and counter-terrorist agency—had misjudged Palestinian intentions, underestimated their capabilities and rage, and dismissed the level of outside money—primarily from Iran and Hezbollah—that would ultimately fuel the bloodshed. But Israeli intelligence was operating in the dark for several years: When Israel withdrew from the West Bank cities and from the Gaza Strip as part of the Oslo Accords, Israeli intelligence services had lost their traditional bases of operations and day-to-day access with their agents and sources in the field. Israeli intelligence agents could no longer overtly run human intelligence sources inside the Gaza Strip and in the West Bank. Both A'man and the Shin Bet were forced to rely on electronic and signals intelligence and coop-eration with their U.S.-funded and CIA-trained Palestinian counterparts in Arafat's numerous security services; all of these sources had great limitations. Exacerbating the situation, Israel's security apparatus—primarily its citizen army, the Israel Defense Forces (IDF)—was not ready, nor was it mobilized, for a war inside cities and villages that it had once controlled.

Peace, perhaps, was never really a possibility between Israel and the Palestinians: two enemies so entrenched in unimpeachable stances. Four different Israeli prime ministers from four different political camps were voted in and out of office during the span of this intifada. Political debate in Israel, as fractious and opinionated as can be found in any democracy, was always a mix of surviving today and thriving tomorrow, and thoughts of survival were difficult to think of on days when buses were being ripped apart at the frame by suicide bombers. Survival meant destroying the Palestinian terrorist infrastructure by any and all means.

To Israel, this intifada was nothing short of total war—there were no rules in this war, no invisible lines in the sand that the Palestinians wouldn't cross out of the fear of international condemnation. There were never any calculations by the Palestinians to call off operations in order to spare civilian casualties: The Palestinian groups purposely mounted attacks that would result in catastrophic loss of life, and they were incredibly effective and relentless in perpetrating this campaign. In its fight against the Palestinian terror campaign, the State of Israel mustered all of its military, intelligence, technological, and law enforcement capabilities in a singular mission. The campaign was driven by intelligence and directed by two parallel paths: preventative deterrence—the nonstop law enforcement effort to buttress Israel's cities with layer upon layer of security, making it difficult for the bombers to reach their targets—and proactive deterrence—the dynamic effort of Israel's aerial and military might and counterterrorist forces to capture, kill, and destroy the Palestinian commanders who directed the intifada and dispatched the terrorists into Israel. Ultimately, much of the proactive deterrence fell on the shoulders of Israel's special operations units.

Israel's counterterrorist and commando units were some of the most experienced and highly specialized in the world, and they found themselves overwhelmed by the unimaginable volume of work. There was no shortage of locations to raid, bomb factories to destroy, suicide bombers to intercept, and high-value targets to capture and kill. These units—such as the Ya'ma'm, the Border Guard police counterterrorist and hostage-rescue unit, and Flotilla 13, Israel's naval commando force—executed lightning strikes deep inside the Palestinian cities and fought pitched battles against determined forces of terrorists who often fought to the death; many of the Israeli military and law enforcement casualties during the conflict were from these tip-of-the-spear units. The enemy did not wear uniforms and they did not operate in the open. The terrorists hid among the civilian population, using innocents as human shields. The operations were never easy and always fraught with peril.

The most specialized of Israel's counterterrorist forces were the Mista'arvim,* or Arabist undercover units. These squadrons of commando-capable Arabic-speaking operatives infiltrated Palestinian areas dressed as the local inhabitants. The undercover operators would dress as laborers, old men, and even women in order to stealthily enter territories under Palestinian control and then search for high-value targets who were wanted by Israeli intelligence. The mission of these units was to walk between the raindrops, to be invisible, and dissolve into Palestinian areas where the terrorists felt safe and at ease, and then attack with stealth and surprise. An IDF undercover unit, known as Duvdevan, Hebrew for "Cherry," operated in the West Bank; Duvdevan was made up of conscript paratroopers, some of whom had Arabic-language training.

Yet Israel's primary undercover force—full-time, professional, and with a steady stream of experience in this form of warfare—belonged to the Border Guard, the paramilitary arm of the Israel National Police. Known as the Ya'mas, the Hebrew acronym for undercover unit, three separate forces operated in different regional sectors: one unit worked the West Bank, another worked the areas in and around Jerusalem, and a third fought in the Gaza Strip. Each unit was made up of a small number of conscripts mentored by a much larger force of professional specialists. The Ya'mas units were built around NCOs and officers from Israel's minorities—Druze and Bedouins primarily—who were native Arabic speakers and who understood the customs, mindset, nuances, and vulnerabilities of the Palestinian community. Many Ya'mas operators were Jews whose parents or grandparents hailed from the Arab Diaspora—they had heard Arabic spoken in their homes and they were accustomed to the cultural nuances and mannerisms. Other

---

* Also pronounced Mista'arvim in the Israeli operational vernacular.

operators, including some of the most decorated fighters that the State of Israel would produce, were born in the Soviet Union and in the former republics of Central Asia.

To this Tower of Babel of religions and backgrounds, undercover counterterrorist warfare was not a brief assignment, but rather what they did for a living. Many of the veterans had already been at war for a decade when the al-Aqsa intifada erupted; they had earned their battle scars during the first intifada. Remarkably, many of these men are *still* at war—they are as of this date still venturing into Hamas and Islamic Jihad strongholds in disguise years later.

The three Ya'mas units fought a very close-up-and-personal type of war. There was nothing clean and inside-the-lines about it. These units didn't launch a missile from high in the sky and obliterate a target by pushing a button. Their war was one of long-range insertion and concealment, face-to-face skirmishes and hand-to-hand combat. Everything about the Ya'mas was done at point-blank range. The Ya'mas undercover operators walked straight up to the men that they would capture or kill—always outnumbered and surrounded—and used every trick in the book, every tactic honed on a range or in a classroom where Arabic was the only language spoken, to get the job done and make it out alive.

The Ya'mas units operated in small teams, sometimes consisting of a handful of men, and other times in groups of a dozen. It was a very Israeli type of commando warfare that relied on audacity, courage, and professional confidence. Veteran Israeli military officers, men who had spent their fair share of dark nights in precarious situations deep behind enemy lines and who were unimpressed by most exploits of courage, could not believe the daunting dare that these men displayed day in and day out in some of the most dangerous areas, trip wires, of the Arab-Israeli battlefield.

Each of the three Ya'mas units fought their own type of war during the intifada; inside their own unique terrain, on very diverse battlefields. The unit in the West Bank, or Judea and Samaria as the Israelis refer to it, fought a high-stakes undercover campaign of cat and mouse, hunting terrorists responsible for some of the most horrific suicide bombings in the intifada. Some of these operations were lightning swift and the masquerade so convincing that the terrorists were captured without the operators even having to remove their weapons from their concealed holsters. Other times, though, Ya'mas raids resulted in full-scale combat. Unit personnel were killed and scores wounded. The Jerusalem unit, operating inside Israel's capital and in the Palestinian areas that surrounded it, waged a classic undercover campaign, where guile, disguise, and innovative determination stopped many suicide bombers from reaching the city limits. In Gaza, the Ya'mas unit found itself engaged in full-scale combat inside the fortresses of Hamas-controlled territory. To the unit, every day was Mogadishu—a day of full-scale combat where a handful of special operations professionals routinely found themselves fighting for their lives while outnumbered one hundred to one. Each of the three units never numbered more than a hundred men or so, yet *each* unit carried out more than fifteen hundred operations during the intifada. They killed some of the top terrorist commanders who led the intifada, and they apprehended thousands more.

The undercover units decapitated and dismantled the Palestinian terror command structure responsible for the intifada. The Ya'mas units played a pivotal role in ending it. Their relentless raids destroyed much of the Palestinian field command, rendering the organizations worn out and too feckless to continue. Undercover operations so unnerved the psychology of the Palestinian terror infrastructure that the Palestinian Authority ultimately entered into an agreement with Israel, in effect ending the conflict—the terrorists would put down their arms and promise to cease operations in exchange for Israel's Special Forces agreeing to not go after them. A senior Ya'mas commander said that he knew that the intifada was coming to an end when the men on their most-wanted list were twenty-three years old and inexperienced; the hardcore leadership, the men in their thirties who had launched the war, were either dead or in prison.

The success of Israel's undercover unit campaign was a combined effort of intelligence, technology, and audacious special operations strikes. The combination of intelligence tradecraft and technological means to intercept communications, along with apprehension operations by tactically proficient men who spoke Arabic and who masqueraded as indigenous civilians, turned the tables on terror. The terrorist chieftains responsible for the daily onslaught of suicide bombing attacks—some that were intercepted before damage could be done and others that resulted in the death and maiming of scores of men, women, and children—were denied a moment's sanctuary inside their traditional safe havens. The end result was that the terrorist commanders who so brazenly carried out a war on Israel's civilians were either dead, captured, or too scared to rear their heads out into the light for long enough to remain effective. The Israeli campaign did not rely on any one singular tool; the effort was not carried out by remote control. Rather, the combination of all the resources at the disposal of Israel's security services, relentlessly applied and audaciously executed, is now a template for defeating terror and one that can be used by the West for campaigns against groups like ISIS, al-Qaeda, Hezbollah, Boko Haram, and countless others. The audacity of the undercover units was part of their mystique—a measure of their effectiveness. "Anywhere we want by any means we choose" was the motto of the undercover force that operated in Jerusalem, and it captured the confidence and determination of those who ventured daily into the most treacherous of confines. That in-your-face approach to special operations was very Israeli, a part of each operator's DNA, and embodied the determination of their fight. They ventured day in and day out into hostile terrain rife with threat because this was their calling.

A senior Israeli intelligence commander who fought in the trenches of the intifada likened the undercover operators to the Royal Air Force pilots who defeated the German efforts to bomb London and other cities into submission during the Battle of Britain. The Ya'mas units were small bands of stubborn and resilient specialists who were instrumental in breaking the back of the enemy's capabilities and crippling its resolve. In doing so, they saved the lives of a great many Israeli citizens who, as a result of their actions, always carried out at great peril and sacrifice to themselves, were not killed or maimed. This was their finest hour. This is their story.

CAST OF CHARACTERS

Primary Characters

WEST BANK (JUDEA AND SAMARIA) YA'MAS

*Abu Ahmed** One of the unit's most experienced and decorated speakers, operators, and combat medics.

Eli Avram The first commander of the West Bank Ya'mas. A former Ya'ma'm operator, Avram was killed in August 1992 while leading an operation in Jenin.

Yaakov Berman A highly decorated member of the unit, Berman was a team leader from 1998 to 2002; a squadron commander from 2002 to 2006; the commander of the Jerusalem Ya'mas unit from 2006 to 2010; and the commander of the West Bank Ya'mas unit from 2010 to 2013.

Uzi Levy A veteran Ya'ma'm operator who commanded the Ya'mas from 2000 to 2006.

Nasser A Druze officer (a veteran of the Golani Brigade's Egoz counter-guerrilla unit) and decorated Ya'mas officer.

Sa'ar Shine One of the most decorated soldiers/policemen in Israeli history, Shine served in the unit from 2001 to 2010.

JERUSALEM YA'MAS

Yossi Aberfeld The unit commander at the outbreak of the intifada, Aberfeld was a highly experienced officer.

Alex Ya'mas operations officer and veteran team leader who served in both the Gaza and Jerusalem units.

Hayim The unit commander from 2004 to 2006.

---

* Names in italics are pseudonyms or partial names.

Shai A veteran of IDF special operations, and a long-active member of the unit who served throughout the second intifada.

Yoni One of the unit's veteran team leaders and officers.

GAZA YA'MAS

Yaakov "Kobi" Shabtai A former paratroop officer who served as the commander of the Ya'mas Gaza unit during the Oslo Peace Accords. He is the former commander of the Border Guard police force (2016–2021) and the commissioner of the Israel National Police (2021–2024) who led the force during the October 7 attack and the immediate aftermath.

Shimon Joined the unit in 1991, Shimon went on to serve his entire career in Gaza (he was in the Border Guard stationed in the Strip before becoming an undercover operative), going from new recruit to, ultimately, the unit commander.

Yaron A veteran Ya'mas officer in Gaza who served as operator, NCO, officer, team leader, operations officer, and deputy unit commander.

Yehonatan A former naval commando and operator in Duvdevan, Yehonatan went on to serve in the Ya'ma'm and in the Gidonim before being appointed commander of the Gaza Ya'mas unit in 2003.

Israeli Military and Police Leadership

Ami Ayalon A former commander of Flotilla 13 and the IDF/Navy who served as director of the Shin Bet from 1996 to 2000.

Ehud Barak One of the founding fathers of the Sayeret Mat'kal commando unit, Barak became the most decorated Israeli soldier in IDF history. In the IDF he served as the head of military intelligence, the head of Central Command, and as the chief of the General Staff. He has also served as Israeli foreign and defense minister and ultimately prime minister.

Major General (INP) Uri Bar-Lev IDF officer who was the first commander of the Duvdevan undercover unit, Bar-Lev was also founder and the first commander of Unit 33, the elite undercover and intelligence force of the INP in Jerusalem and later nationwide.

Major General (INP) Yitzhak "Jack" Dadon Commanded the INP Border Guard from 1998 to 2001.

Meir Dagan A veteran paratroop officer and the man who created the Sayeret Rimon undercover unit that fought in Gaza from 1970 to 1971. Dagan ultimately reached the rank of major general and served two prime ministers as counterterrorism and national security advisor. Prime Minister Ariel Sharon appointed him Mossad director in 2002, and he remained at the post until 2011.

Avi Dichter A veteran Sayeret Mat'kal officer, Dichter served as the Shin Bet director from 2000 to 2005.

Yuval Diskin A veteran reconnaissance officer during his service in the IDF, Diskin enjoyed a lengthy career in the Shin Bet and served as the agency's director from 2005 to 2011.

Major General (IDF) Yitzhak Eitan IDF Central Command officer in charge from 2000 to 2002.

Major General (INP) Hasin Fares Commander of the INP Border Guards from 2004 to 2007 and the first Druze to reach that rank in the police.

Major General (INP) Yaakov Ganot Commander of the INP Border Guard from 2001 to 2002.

Major General (IDF) Moshe Kaplinsky IDF Central Command officer in charge from 2002 to 2005.

Major General (IDF) Amos Malka Head of Israeli military intelligence from 1998 to 2001.

Major General (IDF) Yair Naveh IDF Central Command officer in charge from 2005 to 2007.

Ariel "Arik" Sharon A veteran of the 1948 War for Israeli Independence and one of the founding fathers of Israeli Special Forces, Ariel Sharon became one of the most successful generals in IDF history. He commanded the paratroopers that landed at the Mitla Pass in Sinai in 1956; led a division that punched Egyptian defenses in Sinai in 1967; and, as a general in 1973, saved the Sinai front with an audacious crossing of the Suez Canal. As defense minister in 1982, he was the architect of Israel's disastrous foray into Lebanon. In 2000, as head of the opposition Likud Party, he visited the Temple Mount, providing the Palestinians with the casus belli to launch the al-Aqsa intifada. He was subsequently elected as prime minister and served during most of the violence, spearheading Israel's unilateral withdrawal from the Gaza Strip in 2005.

Major General (INP) David Tzur A former commander of the Ya'ma'm (1991 to 1995), David Tzur served as INP Border Guard commanding officer from 2002 to 2004.

Moshe ("Bogie") Ya'alon A veteran reconnaissance and commando officer, Moshe Ya'alon commanded the IDF's Paratroop Brigade reconnaissance force as well as Sayeret Mat'kal; he also commanded A'man. He was the Central Command officer in charge from 1998 to 2000 and served as deputy chief of the General Staff and chief of the General Staff during the second intifada. At the time of this book's writing, he is the Israeli defense minister.

Major General (IDF) Aharon Zeevi-Farkash Head of Israeli military intelligence from 2001 to 2006.

Key Palestinian Figures

Yasir Arafat The president of the Palestinian Authority, the Egyptian-born Arafat founded Fatah, an Arabic acronym for the Palestinian liberation movement, in Kuwait in 1959 and developed it into the most dominant of the Palestinian nationalist groups that employed terror against Israel and against other interests around the world. Kicked out of Jordan in 1970, Lebanon in 1982, and rumored to never sleep in the same bed twice, he was forced to enter into U.S.-led negotiations with Israel in the wake of his support for Saddam Hussein during the first Gulf War. Arafat won the Nobel Peace Prize after shaking hands with Israeli prime minister Yitzhak Rabin on the White House lawn on September 13, 1993. Arafat returned to Gaza in 1994 as part of the Oslo Accords and presided over the Palestinian Authority from West Bank headquarters in Ramallah and an office in Gaza. In the fall of 2000, he launched the al-Aqsa intifada following the failed Camp David summit earlier that summer. Trapped inside his Ramallah fortress following Israel's Operation Defensive Shield, Arafat ultimately ceded his post to Mahmoud Abbas (the PA president at the time of this book's writing) in 2003. Arafat died in 2004, ostensibly from natural causes.

Yehiya Ayyash A West Bank native and Hamas military commander who became the organization's first "engineer," or bomb-builder, and developed inexpensive and highly lethal explosive vests and devices used in the first campaign of suicide bombings against Israel (1994 to 1996). Ayyash was killed by a booby-trapped exploding telephone in Gaza in January 1996; Israel has never taken responsibility for his death.

Marwan Barghouti Fatah operative and founder of the Fatah Tanzim, Barghouti was apprehended by Israeli special operations units in 2002.

Mohammed Deif Military commander of Hamas who topped Israel's most wanted list in the year's following Ayyash's killing. Deif was behind many of the suicide bombings and terror attacks during the second intifada and the years that followed; he survived numerous Israeli assassination attempts. Deif was one of the masterminds of the October 7 Hamas invasion of Israel, and was killed in an Israeli airstrike in Gaza on July 13, 2024.

Dr. George Habash The Greek Orthodox founder of the Marxist Popular Front for the Liberation of Palestine (PFLP), Habash introduced terrorist hijackings into the international vernacular.

Mahmoud Abu Hanoud Hamas military commander in the West Bank who, in August 2000, was the target of a failed Duvdevan raid that resulted in three soldiers killed from friendly fire. He was killed in November 2001 by a helicopter strike.

Khaled Mashal Hamas political leader who survived an Israeli assassination attempt in Amman, Jordan, in 1997.

Ramadan Abdallah Shalah A former University of South Florida (Tampa) professor and the commander of the Damascus-based Palestinian Islamic Jihad.

Salah Shehada One of the founders of the Hamas military wing, Salah was killed in an Israeli air strike in Gaza in 2003.

Saleh Jaradat Jenin PIJ (Palestinian Islamic Jihad) leader in Jenin, killed during a Ya'mas arrest operation in 2003.

Ahmed Yassin The quadriplegic founder and spiritual leader of Hamas, killed in an Israeli air raid in 2004.

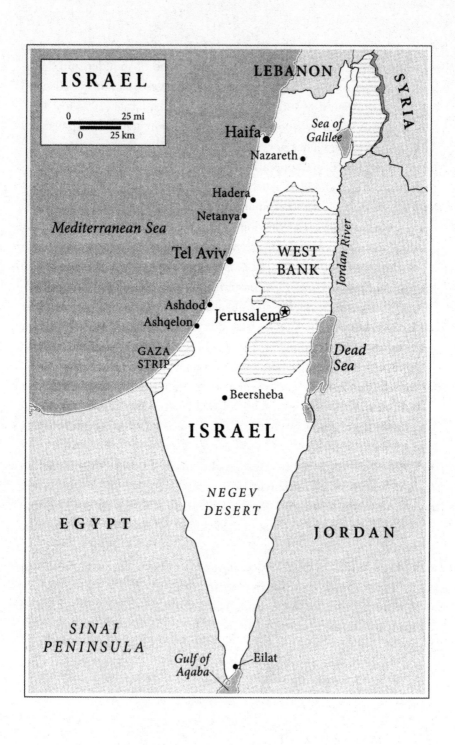

The 1993 Oslo Accords divided the West Bank into three administrative areas that were known as Area A, Area B, and Area C. Area A, consisting primarily of the largest Palestinian cities (Hebron, Bethlehem, Jericho, Ramallah, Nablus, Salfit, Qalqilya, Tulkarm, and Jenin) and some rural areas, was administered fully by Palestinian Authority security and civil control. Area B, consisting of nearly one-quarter of the West Bank, consists of areas that were under Palestinian civilian (with some police) administration, but under Israeli security control. Area C consists of areas that are under both Israeli security and civilian control.

PROLOGUE

An Apprehension in Beit Ummar

Salah* was all of twenty-one years old when he walked into the Palestinian town of Beit Ummar on a mission of such strategic importance and risk that several generals and a deputy director of Shin Bet, Israel's internal security agency, had had to authorize it. It was midday and cold; Decembers were always chilly in the Judean Hills. Sometimes, once a winter, it even snowed in the rocky slopes that cut across the biblical landscape that separated Jerusalem and Bethlehem to the north and the city of Hebron to the south. Beit Ummar was home to some fourteen thousand inhabitants—nearly five thousand of whom happened to be under the age of eighteen. Beit Ummar had historically been a farming town that was famous throughout the West Bank for its grape vines, its olive trees, and its plentiful apple orchards. The city had at one time been a Christian outpost in the region, but the only vestiges of that dwindling community's presence in the town were the ruins of a church. It was December 1999, and for four years, ever since the implementation of the Oslo Accords, Beit Ummar had been part of Area B—Palestinian civil administration and Israeli security control. (Area A was territory under full Palestinian security and civil control, while Area C encompassed territory under full Israeli security and legal administration.) That was on paper. In reality Beit Ummar was a stronghold of the Harakat al-Muqawamah al-Islamiyya, the organization known by the acronym Hamas. Hamas, and the AK-47-wielding masked men of the Izzedine al-Qassam Brigade, the organization's military wing, owned the town.

---

* A pseudonym—true identity withheld for security considerations.

Salah was a sergeant in the Ya'mas, the Israel National Police Border Guard undercover unit, and a two-year veteran of the dangerous cat-and-mouse game of hunting terrorist fugitives in the West Bank. Salah had grown up in northern Israel, in a small Druze village in the Galilee hills. His childhood was spent in and out of delinquency. He was both cunning and defiant; few had expected much of him other than a lifetime of run-ins with the law. But Salah was determined to defy the expectations of his family and his village elders. He was conscripted into the Border Guard, the paramilitary arm of the Israel National Police where Israel's Druze minority flourished, and he specifically requested a chance to serve as an undercover specialist. His path to being an operator in the unit was an arduous one. There was the stringent selection process to overcome along with the Herculean physical stamina tests that each candidate had to master in the prescribed time. There were the many months of basic counterterrorist special operations training to see if he had what it took to be a member of an operational team.

Salah had all the precious qualities sought after by Ya'mas commanders. He was a native Arabic speaker who possessed the stubborn mettle of someone who could survive any pressure-packed moment. Salah was also very cool and determined under fire. Less than a year earlier, on January 13, 1999, Salah's team had been ambushed by Hamas terrorists in the Hebron Hills near Beit Ummar. The battle was fierce and waged at close range. Before the terror squad was killed, Master Sergeant Joshua Gabriel, Salah's team leader, was killed in the firefight. Joshua had been a medic as well as something of a mentor to Salah when he first joined the unit, and when his sergeant was killed in the terrorist cross fire, Salah volunteered to take a tactical paramedic course to become the team's combat medic. But still, Salah's skill—and importance to the team—was as someone who could easily masquerade as a Palestinian. The entire operation in Beit Ummar, the arrest of the local Hamas commander, centered on the intimacy that Salah—and his partner, Sergeant Fares*—possessed with Arabic and Islam.

Salah's target had topped the Shin Bet's most-wanted list for months. He was a middle-aged man of religious significance whose cover as a cleric

---

* A pseudonym—true identity withheld for security considerations.

and a political leader in Hamas concealed his clandestine role as a recruiter for the organization's military arm. He spent most of his time inside the Hamas-affiliated mosque and was often accompanied by sturdy men, all heavily armed, who protected his every move. He was known to spend most of the day—and often much of the night—at the Islamic cultural center; his gray kurta robe was wrinkled from the endless wear. If the target was to be apprehended without the operations resulting in a full-blown battle, the snatch would have to be executed with pure audacity laced with incorrigible guile. The decision had been made to strike in December, in the middle of Ramadan, with a daring plan.

It was a chilly afternoon when a sedan dropped Salah and Fares off near the Islamic center in the middle of town. The vehicle was German-made, slightly battered, and sporting the green-and-white license plates of the Palestinian Authority. The two Israelis wore jeans and the green nylon flight jackets that had become the favorite of those in the territories who belonged to one of the resistance groups. Each man wore a tight-fitting dark T-shirt that revealed the martial outline of his frame. Salah's beard was unkempt and long. His mustache had been trimmed to slight stubble. Fares wore aviator glasses and sported five days' worth of facial hair. Both men walked into the religious center without asking for the directions to the target's office; neither man felt any need to announce his presence. The two walked downstairs, past a series of velvet murals depicting Hamas founder Sheikh Ahmed Yassin, the quadriplegic founder of the organization, amid a backdrop depicting the shiny gold vista of the Dome of the Rock mosque. The downstairs consisted of several meeting halls, a few classrooms, and some offices; space heaters tried to fight the winter chill, but they made the air stuffy. Men spoke on their mobile phones inside the corridors, and young students shuffled to a seminar. The target was sitting in his office, engaged in a deep conversation on a mobile phone.

Both Salah and Fares moved toward the target's office but respectfully stopped. There were too many people around for them to try to snatch him. But the cleric had caught a glimpse of the two solid figures, each of whom looked like he could impressively beat the shit out of the most capable Israeli commando in the hand-to-hand combat of a street fight, and he summoned them to come into his office. Both men looked as if they might be armed.

The target was sure that the two men were messengers from Hamas. They just had to be.

Salah and Fares walked straight toward the target and presented themselves with the blessings and salutations that a young man would bestow on a religious leader who was so respected inside the organization. The target hugged each man and blessed him. Salah explained that they needed help with a car. "I knew you guys were here for me," the target said with a broad smile, now convinced that the two men were his escorts to a meeting somewhere, perhaps in the nearby al-Arroub refugee camp, to discuss important matters. After all, Israeli special operations units, the dreaded *qawat al-hasa*, as the Special Forces were called in Arabic, had recently launched some lethal strikes against the most senior of Hamas commanders, and the organization's command echelon had been scrambling to somehow respond.

The target deserved reverence, and both Salah and Fares followed the man's pace with the respect owed to a teacher. The three men walked through the center and outside the main glass doors, engaging in small talk about the monthlong holiday. Fares walked to the curb and onto the street, where the driver of the German sedan inched the vehicle forward. Fares opened the door for the target and made sure that he entered the car without difficulty. Fares then sat down next to the target on his left side. Salah rushed around the rear of the car and sat next to the target on his right side. Once the doors closed, the sedan's driver pushed down on the accelerator and tore through the narrow Beit Ummar streets toward the outskirts of town. The sudden burst of speed alarmed the target, yet before he could voice his concern, he heard the squelched bursts of Hebrew coming over a military radio hidden underneath the driver's seat. The target went limp in his chair. The color evaporated from his bearded face and he closed his eyes in absolute resignation.

The target was one of the fifteen terrorist commanders who were wanted by the Shin Bet throughout the entire West Bank in December 1999. In less than a year there would be more than two hundred high-value terrorist suspects in the West Bank city of Jenin alone. The semblance of a pretend peace was about to detonate into the fiery shrapnel of all-out conflict.

BOOK ONE

THE WEST BANK

(Judea and Samaria)

CHAPTER ONE

By Strength and By Guile

The first tires were set alight after morning prayers that sunny May morning—Monday, May 15, 2000. Within hours, a wall of flames and a menacing thick cloud of black acrid smoke engulfed the junction leading into Nablus outside the Balata refugee camp. Like clockwork, every May 15, Palestinians around the world marked the *Naqba*, or Great Catastrophe, recalling the fateful day in 1948 when the State of Israel was established with fits of rage fueled by unimaginable sorrow. There were *Naqba* demonstrations wherever Palestinians lived in large numbers. In Lebanon, in Damascus, and in refugee camps in Jordan where the misery was allowed to fester, the day on which the State of Israel declared its independence was one of mourning and burning tires. Many of the *Naqba* commemorations were orchestrated by the various resistance groups and religious factions dedicated to Israel's destruction. This was the seventh *Naqba* event since PLO chairman Yasir Arafat and Israeli prime minister Yitzhak Rabin had shaken hands in an epic moment of history to launch what was hoped to be a forever and lasting peace for two people locked in inextricable conflict. The newly formed Palestinian Authority was the embryo of a future Palestinian State that would declare its independence through negotiations—and not violence—to live side by side and in peace with the State of Israel. There was hope that the shattered pride of the Palestinian people would soon be rewarded with the independence and self-determination they craved. The path to peace, it was hoped, would render the *Naqba* rage into a joyous celebration of statehood.

This was the seventh *Naqba* for Inspector Yaakov Berman, an officer in the undercover counterterrorist unit in the West Bank, the Ya'mas, responsible for

Judea and Samaria.* From an observation post on a nearby hill, Berman and
a small team of operators scanned the large-scale demonstrations through
field glasses and the telescopic scopes of their rifles. There was something
different this year, the men felt. Some of the veteran operators, men who had
served in regular Border Guard companies in the West Bank for years before
volunteering in the new undercover unit a decade earlier, had never felt the
hatred as such a tangible force—not even during the uprising years earlier. The
size of the crowd chanting death to Israel was larger. The rage displayed was
electric, and amplified to voltages never felt before. The men were all veteran
enough to know that there was something foreboding on the terrain before
them. Berman knew that some sort of conflict could not be far behind.

Born in the Soviet Union, Berman was a compact package of rough-and-
tumble stubbornness. What he lacked in height he compensated for in sheer
defiance; his hard-as-nails armor was a by-product of growing up inside the
state-sanctioned and culturally rabid anti-Semitism of the old Soviet system.
In 1991, he immigrated to Israel as a teenager and had hopes of becoming a
commando once conscripted into the ranks of the Israel Defense Forces (IDF).
He dreamed of serving in Sayeret Mat'kal, the General Staff Reconnaissance
Unit and absolute top tier of all Israeli commando units. Mat'kal had captured
the world's imagination with the legendary Entebbe rescue in July 1976; the
unit produced Israel's most famous—and most decorated—officers, men
like Ehud Barak, and Yonatan "Yoni" Netanyahu. But Berman's Hebrew was
sluggish and Mat'kal, which monitored sixteen-year-old boys while they
were still in high school so that they could recruit and select the very best
of the best, was reticent about taking a chance on a newcomer to Israel who
still required a basic Hebrew-language refresher class. Undaunted, Berman
demanded that the conscription officer place him wherever the action was.[1]
He was conscripted into the Border Guard, the paramilitary arm of the Israel
National Police.

---

* Although the areas between the 1967 War demarcation lines with Jordan and the Jordan River are
universally known as the West Bank, that term is rarely used in Israel and almost never by its security
services. Instead, the areas of the West Bank are referred to by their Old Testament names of Judea and
Samaria, or *Yehuda ve'Shomron* in Hebrew; and, because Israeli security arms, like military and law
enforcement entities around the world, love using acronyms, the area is simply known as *A'yo'sh*, for
Aizor Yehuda ve'Shomron, or Judea and Samaria Area.

The IDF might have been the great assimilator of Israel's many ethnic groups and new immigrants, but the Border Guard was Israel's true melting pot. New immigrants, members of Israel's Arab, or minority, communities—the Druze, Bedouins, Circassians, and Christians—all served together in the only true professional combat force in Israel; the IDF, after all, was built around the notion of the citizen soldier: eighteen-year-old conscripts completing their three years of mandatory service (two years for females) and reservist formations that constituted as much as three-quarters of Israel's overall military strength. The *Mishmar Ha'Gvul*, or Border Guard, was formed in 1953 and was a mix between a cadre of professional paramilitary policemen and conscripts drawn into its ranks. The Border Guard was the only service in Israel where Jewish, Christian, Muslim, and Druze holidays were honored with equal reverence and opportunity.

The Border Guard was a true melting pot of cultures and ethnicities with a culture of acceptance. In the Border Guard, it was said, there was no religion or language, just the calling card of their characteristic green beret. Many inside the ranks of the Border Guard made police work their profession. As a result, the average age of the men inside the Border Guard's ranks was older than that of the IDF, where for the most part the conscript army consisted of kids out of high school completing their mandatory three years of national service. The professional element to the Border Guard's rank and file was popular with the new immigrants who craved a regimented and highly disciplined existence and the opportunity to advance themselves inside Israeli society with status and salary.

Israel's minorities excelled in the ranks of the Border Guard, with many enjoying long and illustrious careers inside the service. The minorities were ideally suited for security operations inside the "territories." They spoke the language of the Palestinians and they understood their religion, mentality, and customs.

Yaakov Berman might have been disappointed when his commando dreams were dashed, but once inside the framework of the Border Guard command he made it known to everyone within earshot that he intended to volunteer in the best and most dangerous special operations unit inside the Border Guard's order of battle.

The Border Guard fielded two of Israel's top counterterrorist units. The first was the Ya'ma'm—Israel's national counterterrorist and hostage-rescue unit. The Ya'ma'm, the acronym for the *Yechida Mishtartit Meyuchedet*, or Special Police Unit, was formed in 1974 after Sayeret Mat'kal failed to rescue scores of children held hostage by Palestinian terrorists in a schoolhouse in the northern city of Ma'alot. At the time, hostage-rescue responsibilities in Israel were the domain of the IDF and Sayeret Mat'kal, even though that unit's primary mission was long-range and intelligence-gathering operations deep behind enemy lines. Nearly thirty dead children in Ma'alot convinced Israeli leaders that the nation needed a full-time unit dedicated to full-time counterterrorism. This new unit, the Ya'ma'm, was placed inside the Border Guard order of battle and would ultimately become one of the top direct action counterterrorist strike forces in the world.

The Ya'ma'm was also the most selective unit in Israel—accepting less than 1 percent of the thousands who tried out for it. And the Ya'ma'm was *only* open to IDF combat veterans—off-limits to new conscripts. So Berman volunteered for a spot in the Ya'mas instead. The Ya'mas—the Hebrew acronym for *Yechidat Mista'aravim*, or Undercover Unit—was the Border Guard's second elite force; the literal translation of the word *Mista'aravim* is "those who masquerade as Arabs." Although the Ya'mas was a professional unit—made up of career policemen—it was also open to conscripts. It was here, inside an odd assortment of Druze, Bedouins, Christians, Circassians, and Jews—all sons of the Arab Diaspora—that the son of the Soviet Union would not only find a home carrying out some of the most dangerous assignments in Israel's covert war on terror, but become one of Israel's most decorated combatants in the process.

The State of Israel had been disguising its soldiers and spies as the enemy for as long as Arabs and Jews had fought over the tiny slice of land between the Mediterranean Sea and the Jordan River. The Haganah, Israel's pre-independence underground army, had many in its ranks who spoke Arabic and who had learned the language and customs of the Palestinian Arabs; many in the Haganah originally came from Arab lands. In 1941, as the Axis powers pushed forward in the Middle East, British intelligence and the

Haganah forged an alliance of necessity in the war against Hitler. One of the by-products of that cooperation was the Pal'mach, or Strike Companies, a special operations sabotage and surveillance force that was to help defend Palestine from Axis invasion. The Pal'mach attracted the elite of the future Jewish state's military icons, including men like future prime minister Yitzhak Rabin.

One specialized Pal'mach unit went by the code name of *Shachar*, or Dawn, though it was more commonly known as the Arab Platoon.* The unit's expertise was Arabic, Arab customs, and the Arabic way of life.[2] Unit personnel were primarily drawn from a cadre of Syrian-born Jews, mainly men whose families were originally from Damascus and Aleppo, though some of the unit's deep cover operatives had lesser Middle Eastern pedigrees. The men of the Arab Platoon underwent extensive tradecraft instruction to learn the intricacies of Arabic slang, Arabic accents, basic life in the areas where they might operate; all learned how to develop cover stories and maintain the masquerade if ever challenged by a policeman or an enemy agent. British intelligence supervised the sabotage element of their training, including a very intense explosives course.[3]

The unit adopted Arab dress as its uniform, and Arab customs, and the Arab language was incorporated into the basic fibers of the Hebrew language; in fact, the Arab Platoon, it would be discovered, was responsible for instilling countless Arabic-laced slang words and expressions in today's modern Hebrew spoken by Israelis.[4] Arab Platoon operatives adopted Arab names, and they were never caught without the traditional Arab headscarf, wrapped around their neck.

The masquerade, and the mystique of going native like the men in the Arab Platoon, became the source of Israeli legend. In June 1941, Moshe Dayan lost his eye in Lebanon while masquerading as an Arab and leading a commando strike. During Israel's War of Independence, the Arab Platoon fought

---

* A German Platoon was also created from new immigrants to Palestine from Germany and Austria. These men, most with fairly Germanic appearances, masqueraded as Afrika Korps troops on long-range intelligence-gathering operations in North Africa (and elsewhere in the Mediterranean theater of operations), and they infiltrated German POW camps on intelligence-gathering assignments. Units like the Arab and German Platoons would serve as a nucleus cadre for the Israeli intelligence services that would emerge following independence.

many small encounters against invading Arab armies and bands of irregulars that attempted to attack Jewish settlements. Following the war, many of the deep cover men of the Arab Platoon who had been positioned in the Arab capitals throughout the Middle East played an instrumental covert role in facilitating the migration of Jews from the Arab Diaspora to the newly formed Jewish State. In August 1948, the men of the Arab Platoon were officially incorporated into the IDF's Intelligence Branch—the unit was known as Shin Mem 18.[5] Other unit veterans went to work for the newly formed foreign intelligence service, the Mossad, and in Israel's domestic counterintelligence and counterterrorist agency, the General Security Service, better known simply by its Hebrew acronym of Shin Bet.

Immigrants to the fledgling Jewish State from Arab lands provided top-flight material for Israel's intelligence services. The Arabists of old didn't just appear in a village, or a city, in disguise, in order to carry out a specific operation. They were deep plants who lived like Arabs, in an Arab environment, and established long-term Arab identities—complete with a house, a wife, and even children.[6] Eli Cohen, the legendary Mossad spy who would provide Israel with a wealth of intelligence on the Syrian military in the mid-1960s, was an Egyptian-born Jew of boundless espionage talent. He had so embedded himself inside the Syrian political and military hierarchy that he was being considered as a possible candidate for the post of defense minister. Uncovered by Soviet counterintelligence specialists, Cohen was ultimately arrested and hanged in central Damascus, but the intelligence he relayed back to Tel Aviv was vital in Israel's lightning-fast victory over Syria, Jordan, and Egypt in the June 1967 Six Day War.

Israel captured the Golan Heights from Syria and the Sinai Peninsula from Egypt in its remarkable six-day victory, but more significantly, it captured the West Bank of the Jordan River and 850,000 Palestinians in the process. In the south, at the northwest lip of the Sinai Desert, was the Gaza Strip, home to 422,000 Palestinians.[7] The Jordanian and Egyptian secret services had fostered the fedayeen (Arabic for "men who sacrifice") from the various Palestinian guerrilla movements; the fedayeen were subservient to the Arab powers, and when the territories were lost in June 1967, they became a proxy force in a war of attrition that would follow. Several Israeli reconnaissance commando units battled Palestinian guerrillas in the West

Bank. In the Gaza Strip, Israeli forces faced a full-scale terrorist insurrection. A more specialized approach was needed to prevent this uprising from turning into a full-fledged war.

Major General Ariel "Arik" Sharon, the head of Southern Command, was the man responsible for pacifying Gaza. Known as the "Bulldozer," Sharon was a no-nonsense hurricane of a man who had forged a lethal reputation among Israel's Arab enemies. One of the founding fathers of Israel's paratroopers and special operations units, Sharon had commanded a counterterrorist commando force that was known as much for its no-questions-asked violence as it was for its daring and effectiveness. Known as Unit 101, the force was a maverick counterterrorist retaliatory formation that operated wherever targets were identified and whenever it chose to strike. On October 14, 1953, the unit spearheaded Operation Shoshana, a retaliatory strike against the Jordanian village of Qibya in the West Bank that had been a base of operations for guerrillas attacking Israel. The raid killed and wounded sixty-nine civilians. The international outcry was loud and vocal; the Israeli public was equally as shocked by the brutality of the operation. But the guerrilla raids stopped, and Sharon was ultimately promoted. His legend was sealed. In 1967, when he commanded a division that punched an armored fist through Egyptian defenses in Sinai, Sharon was considered one of Israel's most innovative and successful military leaders.

Sharon was not the kind of commander interested in winning hearts and minds, and in crushing the terrorist presence in Gaza, he demanded immediate results. He summoned an old friend from the paratroopers, Captain Meir Dagan, and gave him command of a new reconnaissance unit that would use the disguised intelligence-gathering capabilities of Israel's first generation of undercover operatives and add the dynamic reality of direct action bloodshed. The new unit was named Sayeret Rimon—Grenade Recon.

Born Meir Huberman, Dagan* was another forged-into-steel son of the Soviet Union who never forgot the impact that the Holocaust had on his family. Dagan was a no-nonsense officer of unquestioned courage, and

---

* Meir Dagan served as the Mossad director from 2002 to 2010 and was considered one of the organization's most dynamic leaders, specializing in direct action operations to eliminate threats—terrorist and existential—to Israel's security.

for this mission he handpicked soldiers similar to himself whom he could depend on in a dangerous fight with an Uzi submachine gun and a dagger. Some of his volunteers were Arabic speakers, or those who thought they could master the language in a crash course; others weren't. Everyone in this new force underwent a crash course in Arabic and Palestinian cultural keys. Dagan knew that it would be street talk, the melody of marketplace and café chitchat, that would either secure or compromise the operator's masquerade.

The commandos used disguise and cunning to infiltrate every corner of the terrorists' world. They ate in restaurants where guerrilla commanders held court; they shopped in markets controlled by the various terrorist groups. Dagan's commandos assembled highly detailed and far-reaching dossiers on the men and women they hunted. They knew where the guerrillas lived, and where they slept. An elaborate intelligence network provided the names of wives, lovers (male, female, or both), and even compromising details of their finances and personal proclivities. Dagan's commandos were a direct action force—the sheer volume of terrorists killed by this mysterious squad of Arabic-speaking operators sent shock waves throughout the Gaza Strip. Ultimately, Palestinians on the most-wanted list turned themselves in to the Shin Bet rather than face Dagan's men.

The Palestinians called Dagan the *ibn zana*—"the bastard" (or, as it translated into the Palestinian colloquial, "the son of a whore"). Dagan's personal courage, especially when the Russian-born officer was masquerading as a Palestinian, became legendary. On January 29, 1971, in an encounter with a wanted terrorist named Abu Nimer, Dagan personally wrestled a hand grenade with its pin already pulled from the wanted man during an arrest operation in the Jebalya refugee camp.[8] The operators, the rank and file who terrorized the terrorists, were known as *Abu Ali*, or Violent Men. But the violence worked. Sayeret Rimon neutralized the fedayeen presence in Gaza in less than a year. The quiet in Gaza would last for twenty years.

In 1986, Major General Ehud Barak, the head of IDF Central Command that was responsible for the West Bank, had a notion about re-creating the success of an IDF undercover unit with a singular counterterrorist mission. Barak was the most decorated soldier in IDF history and the man who personified the daring of the Israeli commando. On May 8, 1972, as commander of Sayeret Mat'kal, Barak and his men donned white airport mechanic's coveralls to convince four Black September terrorists that they were going to ready a hijacked aircraft to ostensibly take off from the tarmac at Lod Airport in Israel; Barak's commandos, including a young lieutenant named Benjamin Netanyahu, stormed the aircraft, killed two of the terrorists, and executed the first tubular hostage-rescue assault in military history. A year later, on April 9, 1973, Barak and his commando officers dressed in platinum blond wigs, 36DD bras, and tight miniskirts to conduct a joint strike against Black September's leadership in Beirut.

A growing Palestinian terrorist infrastructure had developed in the West Bank, and Barak was determined to fight it. He summoned Captain Uri Bar-Lev, a reconnaissance paratroop officer with a reputation for unorthodox practices and a disdain for the rigid trappings of command, with an idea: to create a special commando force, an undercover team, with a singular counterterrorist mission for the command. Bar-Lev was known as a rogue thinker, and although he would have probably been court-martialed for myriad offenses in any other army in the world, the IDF approved of men who possessed an innovative streak even if it was laced with insolence. Bar-Lev had lost part of his left leg below the knee during his service as an engineering officer. He refused to allow his handicap to impact his military career. He marched faster than conscripts in his battalion who were ten years his junior, and he never let any of his detractors see him sweat.

Barak ordered Bar-Lev to create a small and highly mobile counterterrorist force that could initiate preemptively pinpointed strikes and operate inside areas with a large indigenous population. The unit would masquerade its operators as Palestinians to infiltrate areas that were denied to IDF and police units in order to apprehend terrorist commanders and gather eyes-on-target intelligence in a way that couldn't be gathered through other means. Bar-Lev recruited officers and NCOs that he knew and trusted, and not necessarily those whose parents came from the Arab Diaspora. Many of those whom Bar-Lev selected for the unit had blond hair and blue eyes. Their family backgrounds might have been German or Eastern European, but their attitude, arrogance, and flair was definitively Levantine.

The physical masquerade was easy to achieve. Some of the operators had dark complexions and dark hair and could easily disguise themselves as locals from Nablus or Hebron, or anywhere else in the West Bank. If the operation required that the undercover operator impersonate a *raza-leh* ("beautiful woman"), or anyone else, then makeup and props could expedite the transformation. The unit developed a costume wardrobe that would have been the envy of a theatrical ensemble. To complete their disguise, makeup artists were summoned to prepare the men for under-cover forays into the heart of Palestinian areas. This new unit's name was Duvdevan: "Cherry."*

By July 1986 four Duvdevan squads worked the confines of the West Bank. The unit's capabilities were tiny; each squad consisted of a command-ing officer, two combat medics, two team leaders, two snipers, and several handfuls of men. Uri Bar-Lev's objective was simple: to make the terrorists so unnerved by the possibility that their safe havens were infiltrated by Israeli forces that they could not operate freely and openly. Bar-Lev wanted every terrorist clandestinely planning an attack to be wary of the three men across the street sitting inside a battered sedan, as well as to be equally wary of the old woman across the street carrying bags of produce who could be a twenty-year-old soldier with a Mini-Uzi submachine gun under his dress. "The premise of the undercover unit was simple," Bar-Lev explained. "To make the terrorist so scared and so preoccupied about the Israelis masquer-ading in his midst that he wouldn't have the ability to work on attacks against Israel. We were designed to get under their skin and inside their central nervous system."[9]

Bar-Lev had built something unique out of absolutely nothing. He went from a dozen men to a force that numbered more than 150. One evening in 1987, before a major operation, Major General Barak, newly appointed to the position of deputy chief of staff, made a surprise visit to Duvdevan. He decided that he would undress, don a local disguise, and join the forces going into a village in upper Samaria. The raid was a success and was carried out

---

* Special operations units were always referred to in the Israeli vernacular as *ha'katzefet*, or "the cream." Duvdevan, the unit founders rationalized, was different, the icing on the cake, like the "cherry on top." The name stuck. Inside its operational circles, of course, Duvdevan is known by its numeric designation.

without incident—six terrorist suspects were arrested in the operation and a cache of weapons seized.[10]

Duvdevan would soon find itself on the front lines—and behind hostile lines—in a bitterly fought conflict. In December 1987, a large-scale Palestinian uprising erupted in the Gaza Strip and the West Bank. The protests quickly turned violent and metastasized into an armed confrontation with terrorist factions instigating the rioting and hurling of rocks and Molotov cocktails against Israeli forces, and using the chaos and political upheaval of the uprising to target Israeli civilians—and security personnel—in terrorist strikes. The violence was known as the intifada, an Arabic word that meant "shaking off" but soon stood for any popular uprising of Palestinian resistance. Israel responded to the rioting with force; images of Israeli soldiers shooting at Palestinian protesters—kids and women—with rubber bullets became a public relations nightmare for Israel, even though these youths and women were hurling rocks and petrol bombs. Palestinian factions in exile realized an enormous military and political opportunity in what had been a spontaneous explosion of protest and anger, and Arafat seized control of the uprising. The PLO wanted to increase the tempo of the violence and to show the world—and especially Palestinians inside the territories—that they alone controlled the fate of the Palestinian people. From their plush villas in Tunis, Arafat and his lieutenants directed cells inside the territories into action. Some of the attacks were primitive yet bloody; others were more elaborate and resulted in Israeli civilians killed and wounded.

The intifada afforded Bar-Lev and his cadre of innovatively audacious officers with a laboratory for Duvdevan's undercover brand of no-rules counterinsurgency warfare. Bar-Lev had the enthusiastic support of Ehud Barak in carrying out the most daring of operations, even though many in the IDF General Staff—and the higher echelons of Israeli political power—felt that Bar-Lev improvised too freely. One case in point involved a Palestinian terrorist suspect working for Yasir Arafat's Fatah faction, who had given an interview to Israeli television. In 1988, after reporters from Israel's Channel One television filmed an interview with a West Bank Fatah commander that the Shin Bet had not been able to arrest, Bar-Lev's men masqueraded as an American television crew. The operators stenciled the first three letters from a decal set, "ABC," to the side of a van and then drove to the village requesting assistance, in flawless English, to interview the Fatah operative. The bait of being seen on American television was too great to resist. The Fatah operative emerged wearing his Sunday best and not only agreed to be interviewed, but disclosed the extent of his terror network. The Duvdevan news crew asked the suspect if he'd mind being interviewed at the studio in Jerusalem, and he boarded their van and headed toward the city. A day later, the young man's family called ABC News in Jerusalem and wanted to know when the he would be returning home. An investigation ensued, and Roone Arledge, the president of ABC News, called Prime Minister Shamir to voice his protest. Shamir was outraged and summoned half of the general staff—as well as Bar-Lev—to his residence in Jerusalem to chew them out. But Bar-Lev had a magnanimous charm to him and convinced Shamir, a short, squatty statue of stubbornness, about the tradecraft necessities of using every trick in the book. Shamir had served in the Mossad and realized the importance of the deception. Bar-Lev wouldn't be chastised again.

One of the most lethal gangs operating on behalf of Fatah during the intifada was the Black Panthers. Named after the feared jungle predator, the Black Panthers were formed around a cadre of violent criminals that Fatah had funded so that it could abduct, torture, and murder Palestinians suspected of being Shin Bet informants. The mutilated bodies of men—and women—soon began to appear throughout the West Bank; the gang's favorite tool in dealing with suspected traitors was the hatchet. The Black Panthers didn't shy away from armed confrontation with Israeli forces either—in fact they welcomed the chance to kill Israeli soldiers or policemen. Hunting down the Black Panthers became a full-time—and overwhelming—endeavor for the Shin Bet and units like Duvdevan.

In 1990, Brigadier General (also known as an assistant commissioner in the British-based Israeli police rank structure) Yitzhak "Jack" Dadon, the Border Guard police officer in charge of Judea and Samaria in the West Bank, wanted to create a new undercover unit—one specifically designed to deal with the challenges of the intifada; a start-up Border Guard undercover force, as an experiment, had started working in the Gaza Strip months earlier. Originally, this new unit was never meant to compete with Duvdevan but rather to augment its overloaded operational requirements.[11] Conceptually, Dadon knew the type of unit he wanted to create—the only question was who would command it.

Night after night, Dadon and his staff of officers reviewed personnel files looking for the man with the right stuff. They interviewed thirty-nine officers, but none had the vision, charisma, and pedigree that they were looking for. Finally, the name of Inspector Eli Avram entered the mix. Avram had been an operator in the Ya'ma'm for several years, though when he passed his officer's qualification course, he was promoted out of the unit and placed in charge of a narcotics unit working in central Israel. Routine police work, even dangerous investigations against drug dealers, wasn't in Avram's blood. When asked if he'd like to return to the world of counterterrorism, he jumped at the opportunity.

Major General Danny Yatom,* the head of IDF Central Command, wasn't impressed with Avram when the two met for the first time. Yatom had grown up inside Sayeret Mat'kal, alongside Ehud Barak and others whose reputations were hard as steel and sharp as a razor. Avram was skinny with an endearing smile, Yatom would later recall; he looked like he was only twenty years old.[12] But Inspector Avram won the job, and he won over Yatom. Avram was determined to make it work. The *Yechidat Mista'aravim* for the West Bank had been created. The Border Guard undercover units, like many units in the Israeli military and security vernacular, would come to be known by their Hebrew acronym—Ya'mas.

On May 20, 1990, the first Border Guard undercover unit counterterrorist course began: The class consisted of thirty men, including Avram himself.[13] The class lasted all of four weeks and consisted of fast-moving assault tactics, evasive driving, marksmanship proficiency with 9mm pistols, M16s, and Mini-Uzi submachine guns, and basic undercover skill sets and operational procedures. Slowly but surely the ragtag force of hopefuls developed into the nucleus of a skilled and highly specialized unit. Tactics that hadn't existed

---

* Yatom served as the director of the Mossad from 1996 to 1998.

previously were invented straight out. Standard operating procedures for infiltrating areas known to be terrorist strongholds were conceived of and perfected on the fly.

Avram borrowed men, materials, and weapons from his old unit, the Ya'ma'm. Ya'ma'm commander Chief Superintendent David Tzur saw great dividends in what Avram was attempting to build and offered the Ya'mas commander whatever assistance he could. Avram recruited carefully, creating a balance of manpower that had tactical expertise as well as an intimate lay of the land. These men were seasoned and highly experienced police officers who could read a person's pantomime and assess with uncanny accuracy who was guilty and who might be innocent. These veteran patrolmen knew every chop shop, underworld social club, brothel, and drug den in the territories; they knew all the thieves, pimps, prostitutes, weapons sellers, and drug pushers by sight and by name. Criminal enterprises financed a nice piece of the intifada campaign against Israel.

The secret ingredient enabling Avram to build a turnkey unit ready to hit the field running was the open recruitment of Druze, Bedouins, Circassians, and Christian Arabs. Traditionally, the minorities had not been eyed for service in elite units, but the Border Guard defined multiethnic egalitarianism; and, for the sake of logistics and bureaucracy, these men were already inside the system, on the payroll ledgers, and their courage and dedication was well documented in Border Guard files. The minorities didn't have to be schooled in the intricacies of undercover work inside the Palestinian population. They didn't have to learn about what was an Arab and what it was like to be a Muslim. These men knew a thousand-and-one basic facts about the Palestinians that it would have taken twenty years to teach a soldier in Duvdevan—a unit that did not recruit from Israel's minority population. The minorities didn't have to rely on makeup to effect the masquerade: They were the genuine article.

Some of the minority operators served as the Speakers—Ha'Dovrim. The Speakers were the first element of any operation. They drove the unmarked vehicles, they reconnoitered the Palestinian towns and villages, and they would be the ones to talk if challenged on the street. To minimize the risk of giving away their true identities, the Speakers had to be schooled on the local dialects; the slang used in Jenin, after all, was diametrically different than the accent common in East Jerusalem. But their Arabic wasn't forced or textbook taught. It was legitimate and it flowed with absolute authenticity.

The Speakers were, of course, also full-fledged operators. And they were supported on missions by the remainder of the unit—the men who would provide tactical backup in plain clothes and in full tactical kit—during the explosive moments of an arrest or a hostile engagement. The tactical vehicle was a Sus, or Horse—the unit's name for the unmarked vehicle used to transport the operators to their missions. Some of the operators would assume the secondary tasks of personnel trainers, snipers, weapons specialists, intelligence officers, and even hand-to-hand combat specialists. Each member of the embryonic force assumed two or three tasks. The primary Ya'mas mission was the interdiction of terrorist activity and the apprehension of terror suspects wanted by Israeli intelligence. In fulfilling this mission, the Ya'mas—like all military and police units—was directed by the ethics of *Tohar Ha'Neshek*, or Purity of Arms, the directive that dictated how and when a soldier or a member of the police and security services could use his or her weaponry, and that all measures be taken to avoid harming civilians, and protecting their honor and property. But rules also applied to the use of deadly force, and Israeli soldiers and policemen were to use the required force when confronted by armed suspects who had the ability to resist arrest and endanger the lives of unit personnel and civilians.

The Ya'mas quickly forged a unique esprit de corps that was common for units loaded with alpha-type personalities. The Arabic speakers went by guerrilla noms de guerre; operators, even some blond-haired and blue-eyed former members of the Ya'ma'm, earned their bona fides by buying their own costumes from shops in Nablus, Ramallah, and Hebron. Everything the unit needed was attended to in-house. They were never issued with high-impact body armor that could be worn underneath clothing, so operators simply sewed surplus bulletproof vests into indigenous Palestinian clothing; armored vehicles, for undercover assignments, were rigged using ingenuity and some artistic skill. Whatever couldn't be acquired through channels was borrowed or stolen.

The only measure that could be used to judge the unit's capabilities was to see how it performed in the field. Avram relentlessly lobbied the top brass for assignments. He went to every battalion and brigade commander that would agree to see him, even if just to introduce himself and share a cup of coffee. The unit was constantly putting on a dog-and-pony display for this colonel or that general. He constantly promised the top brass that his men would successfully accomplish any assignment if they were only given the chance.

The first assignments given to the Ya'mas were small-scale and routine: the arrest of someone throwing a Molotov cocktail, and the apprehension of low-level Fatah suspects in Ramallah or Bethlehem. But with each mission accomplished came another Shin Bet request for assistance. Within weeks of becoming operational, Avram and his officers found themselves huddled inside the smoke-filled room of the ops center scanning aerial photographs and reviewing maps before putting together a plan for a general's approval. Days began at dawn and then continued without rest until well past midnight.

In addition to lobbying the commands for work, Avram and the unit's officers had placed a determined emphasis on learning the topography of the land, in order to successfully navigate their way in—and out—of any location in Judea and Samaria. Before—and even after—every mission, Avram and his two platoons of operators would reconnoiter the back roads of rural farmland and the bustling centers of refugee camps in order to learn the landscape better than their own homes. It was a job requirement that good Shin Bet case agents undertook from day one of their assignment and that Avram was resolved to instill in his men. Yaakov Peri, who joined the Shin Bet in 1966 and would rise up the ranks to command the organization, once recounted: "I served in Nablus for almost two years. I learned to know every street and alley, every roof that connected to another roof in the Kasbah, every hole that led to another escape hole, every neighborhood and sheikh's grave, every stream, every grove and abandoned field. I could walk around the area in total darkness."[14] Such intimacy with the landscape became one of the Ya'mas calling cards, as did blending into the landscape like an alley cat. The work required endless preparation. The work that went into most undercover assignments—from the smallest reconnaissance sorties to unit-size raids—was as exhaustive as the actual missions themselves. Intelligence-gathering reconnaissance sorties of the target had to be conducted. The complete disguise, to include costumes and vehicles, had to be selected. "The name of the game in undercover work," a Ya'mas commander stated, "was to assimilate into the surroundings. Not to attract attention. Not to stand out. And Jerusalem was different than the territories. You had to know the language and the very specific slang, style of clothing worn, and you had to know how the landscape looks and feels during the day. Who drives what kind of car, and who [gangs and their leaders] rules the street. You had to know the names of the dominant families in town and on a particular block. You had to know the mood on the street."[15]

Because of their familiarity with the terrain, the Ya'mas began to operate in areas where other units—even Duvdevan and some of the other top IDF units—preferred not to work. Jenin was one such place. The Black Panthers ruled the city and the adjacent village, as did new and more fanatic gangs, belonging to the new fundamentalist Islamic groups of Hamas and the Islamic Jihad. But the Ya'mas wanted to work here, and Avram pleaded with brigade and division commanders, who had to approve all high-value operations inside their areas of responsibility.

One such operation was on the night of March 12–13, 1992, when the unit embarked on the high-risk apprehension of Khaled Shaker Fahmawi, a twenty-year-old Black Panther commander, who was known to move about freely in the Jenin refugee camp and to be armed, and was considered extremely dangerous. Other Israeli special operations units would have brought four of five platoons to the camp and closed everything down as they searched for the elusive suspect, but the Ya'mas operated differently. The undercover operators conducted an up-close-and-personal reconnaissance of the area and noticed that the suspect was in the bathroom of a three-story block of flats that was connected to a series of other buildings. Fahmawi was a wanted man, high on the Shin Bet list, and he lived an existence of lurking in the shadows and moving about at night. His one Achilles' heel was his teenage bride, a woman considered to be the prettiest in all Jenin. The Ya'mas operators burst into the flat while the two were having sex. Fahwami kept a pistol under his pillow and shot at the Israeli operators as he attempted to flee. He was shot and killed before he could escape.[16]

Dozens of terror suspects were killed by the Ya'mas in its first two years; hundreds more were arrested. Some of the terrorists that the Ya'mas pursued

were targets of opportunity, names that popped up during a Shin Bet investigation. Other names, men with blood—Palestinian and Israeli—on their
hands, had been on the Shin Bet most-wanted list for weeks, months, and
sometimes years. Some of the most dangerous fugitives were in and around
the Jenin area, and Eli Avram wanted his unit to capture or kill them all. In
August 1992, Ahmed Awad Kamil, the head of the Black Panthers in Jenin,
topped Avram's list.

Kamil had been on the run for well over a year, and he was known to
hide in and around the area of Qabatiya, a city of twenty thousand inhabitants four miles south of Jenin. Avram had spent enormous time and effort in
blueprinting an operational plan that the new division commander, Brigadier
General Moshe "Bogie" Ya'alon,* would authorize. But two months earlier, on
June 8, 1992, a force from Duvdevan attempted to capture the elusive terror
chief in Barta'a, a village that straddles Israel on one side and the West Bank
on the other. Kamil escaped, but a Duvdevan operator, First Sergeant Eli Isha,
was killed in a blue-on-blue friendly fire incident. Many Shin Bet case agents
lobbied that the Kamil file go to the Ya'mas, but Ya'alon was determined to
keep the mission within the IDF framework. Instead, the Ya'mas received
the files of Ibrahim Zariqi and Ibrahim Saliman Salim Jalamneh, two Black
Panther assassins who hid deep inside Jenin.

Avram's men pursued every Shin Bet lead in the pursuit of the Black
Panther tandem. In August 1992, a Shin Bet informant had painted a building,
House No. 211, in the eastern part of the city, where the two men were known
to be every night; according to the intelligence, the two slept in a makeshift
hut they had built on the rooftop of the building.[17] Ya'mas teams reconnoitered
the area and trained on a model of the location that had been prepared at a
nearby military base. The unit waited for the intelligence to verify that the two
men had returned home. Weeks passed without any additional information
on the two. The unit moved on.

On the night of August 25, 1992, Eli Avram was on his way home to see
his wife, Anat, and their infant son after working with one of his platoons

---

* Lieutenant General Moshe Ya'alon served as IDF chief of staff during the height of the al-Aqsa intifada
and, at the time of this book's writing, is the Israeli defense minister (during Operation Protective Edge
in Gaza during the summer of 2014).

operating in Jenin, when the call from the Shin Bet came in: Zariqi and Jalamneh had just been seen entering the building at No. 211 and had retired for the night. Eli turned his vehicle around and headed straight for the brigade HQ to set up the operation.

An advance team of Avram's men was ordered to Jenin once the Shin Bet intelligence was received. The operators, dressed as local Jenin laborers, moved into the city under the cover of darkness and positioned themselves against the outer wall at No. 211, monitoring the location from deep inside the shadows. The remainder of the unit reached the building a short time later. The main strength of the Ya'mas force had parked their vehicles down the road and then moved toward the targeted location silently on foot. But the terrorists had hired the services of an old woman to stand guard of the building at night. When she saw suspicious men in the street down below, she began to scream, "*Jesh, Jesh*," the Arabic for "Army." Gunfire soon erupted. With the element of surprise lost, Avram rushed toward the roof, using terraces to launch his climb, in order to surprise the terrorists engaging his men on the first floor. Avram reached the roof, and then attempted to make his way down a staircase to engage the terrorists from behind. But he was met by a burst of automatic fire as he peered down the flight of stairs. He was shot in the head and killed instantly. The Ya'ma'm was summoned, and following a lengthy and pitched battle, both Zariqi and Jalamneh were shot and killed.

On November 4, 1994, Israel's leading newspaper, *Yediot Aharonot*, published an article that revealed the existence of the Border Guard undercover unit. The headlines were provocatively sensational: "Revealed for the First Time: The Border Guard Undercover Unit Has Killed Fifty Terrorists."[18] The article spoke in glowing terms of the unit's capabilities, and how the men of the Ya'mas felt more at home masquerading as Palestinians in the Kasbah of Nablus than they did in their own homes. The reporter had accompanied Israeli president Ezer Weizman as he visited the unit's base and was witness to an impressive display of disguise and firepower. The news scoop came more than a year after the historic handshake between Israeli prime minister Yitzhak Rabin and PLO chairman Yasir Arafat on the White House lawn, sealing into reality the peace deal that would become known as the

Oslo Accords. There was a feeling—a prayer—in Israel that the intifada had come to an end and that the violence between Arab and Jew would once and for all subside. "We are all happy about the peace process," Superintendent Nechamia, Eli Avram's replacement, said, "but we will continue to fight terror without compromise."[19]

A new terrorist threat to Israel had emerged. Hamas, an offshoot of the Egyptian Muslim Brotherhood, and the Palestinian Islamic Jihad (PIJ), opposed the peace deal that Arafat had sealed with his hand reaching out to the Israeli premier. Hamas had made a name for itself by kidnapping Israeli soldiers and brutally torturing and murdering them before dumping their remains in undisclosed graves. Hamas and the PIJ had strong roots in the Palestinian Diaspora in North America, and they had support and funding from both Syria and the Islamic Republic of Iran; both groups were cunning and resourceful organizations, driven by religious fanaticism that fueled unstoppable hatred and bloodlust. In April 1994, Hamas launched two suicide bombing attacks in northern Israel, killing thirteen people. By the time the article exposing the existence of the Ya'mas appeared in the newspapers, another twenty-two Israelis would be killed in a suicide bombing, this time of a bus in the heart of Tel Aviv. The politicians worked feverishly for peace, but on the ground, in the trenches of the West Bank, a new and much bloodier war was beginning. It was the onset of a new terrorist strategy—a war on civilian Israel.[20]

Sergeant Yaakov Berman had been one of the Ya'mas NCOs dazzling the Israeli president that sunny autumn day. He had joined the Border Guard in 1993 and excelled in the Ya'mas training course: sixteen weeks of basic training; a selection process to determine which volunteers were suitable for Ya'mas training; and specialized training for the life as an undercover agent (weapons proficiency, hand-to-hand combat, counterterrorist tactics, and undercover operations in urban terrain). Only a miniscule percentage of those who try to earn a spot in the unit pass the rigorous process. Berman was a natural—he possessed the required mental doggedness and tactical proficiency to excel as a Ya'mas operator.

After a few years in the unit, Berman lost some of his heavy Russian accent. He had grown a scruffy beard and had even mastered enough Arabic slang to pass—from a distance—as Palestinian. Berman had been in the unit for more than a year and had been involved in his fair share of close-quarter firefights with the new Islamic fundamentalist armies that were now fighting for the soul of Palestine. He would breeze through his sergeant's exam and spend the next six years fighting Hamas and the Islamic Jihad as an NCO in the unit; his commanders sent him to officers' school. As a freshly commissioned sub-inspector, Berman had led operations against Hamas bomb dens, and he had engaged PIJ gunmen in close-quarter battles. He had watched as the Israeli military withdrew its forces from the major West Bank cities to allow the newly formed Palestinian Authority—and its many intelligence and security forces—to take control.

By May 15, 2000, Chief Inspector Berman commanded one of the two Ya'mas operational teams. Together with some of his men, veteran Bedouin and Druze Speakers alongside native-born Israeli Jews and even a few new immigrants from the Caucasus, Berman watched the *Naqba* demonstrations with an uneasy sense of foreboding. He had seen enough of these displays to know that this year's rage was virulent. AK-47s were fired into the air, as demonstrators flooded the road out of Nablus and threatened to move on the thoroughfares that led to nearby Jewish settlements. Some of Berman's men grabbed their M4 assault rifles, in case the Palestinian mob pushed forward, across the barriers, toward Israeli lines.

The tires continued to burn in the blue spring sky that sunny day in May. The scuttlebutt was that the Ya'mas was living on borrowed time. Prime Minister Ehud Barak would be launching a new peace initiative at a conference that would be held with Arafat and U.S. president Bill Clinton shortly, in which Israel would make the Palestinians an offer they couldn't refuse. If peace was imminent, as the rumors hinted, there would be no need for a unit like the Ya'mas to continue in the West Bank. There were, after all, only a handful of names that remained on the Shin Bet list of wanted terror suspects. Berman and his men watched the fires and knew that the rumors were nothing more than wishful thinking. Where they stood, thoughts of peace were always dashed by spasms of uncontrolled violence.

CHAPTER TWO

The Fuse

Superintendent Uzi Levy first learned that he would be the next Ya'mas commander in the summer of 2000. Levy, a tall and gregarious officer whose wild hair stood out in the crowd of counterterrorist officers who always wore theirs close-cropped, had spent four years in the IDF's 35th Paratroop Brigade before volunteering for the Ya'ma'm. He spent nineteen years as an operator in the Israeli counterterrorist unit, first as a team sergeant and then as an officer. He rose up the chain of command inside the insular force to the rank of Ya'ma'm's deputy commander. The Ya'ma'm had been pretty much all that Levy had known about the world of counterterrorism, and he had mixed feelings and an emotional conflict about assuming the position as Ya'mas commander.

Eight years earlier, on the night of August 26, 1992, Levy had been the on-call Ya'ma'm squadron commander when the unit received an emergency call for assistance to rescue Ya'mas commanding officer Eli Avram, who had been shot in a house in the eastern neighborhood of Jenin. By the time Levy and his Ya'ma'm operators reached Jenin, it appeared as if the entire IDF was there, including elements from a half-dozen commando units. But with two heavily armed terrorists held up inside a fortified location, the operation to rescue Avram, or to retrieve his body, was given to the Ya'ma'm.

Levy recalled the ferocity of the room-to-room battle inside No. 211. The two Black Panther terrorists made the Ya'ma'm fight for every inch of the building. The flash of hundreds of rounds being fired at close range illuminated the thick cloud of plaster debris and smoke that injected itself into the darkness. The two Palestinians had fortified themselves with enough ammunition to hold off an army, and they sprayed magazine-emptying bursts of M16 fire at the advancing members of the Ya'ma'm team trying to reach the mortally wounded undercover commander. The Ya'ma'm had to pull the residents out of the building and out of the kill zone, while at the same time pushing deeper into the apartment block to try to get to the staircase where Avram's body lay. A surgical team, the best that the IDF had, was rushed to Jenin just in case Avram was still alive. But the Ya'mas commander was dead—just getting to Avram's body took hours of sustained fighting. Ya'ma'm's K9 handlers dispatched two highly trained assault dogs toward the rear rooms of the second floor where the two Palestinians had barricaded themselves, but the terrorists shot both animals dead.[1] It would be just before dawn, after four hours of incessant combat, that the two Palestinians were killed and a Ya'mas team could retrieve the body of their commander. Avram was brought out on a stretcher as the first hint of dawn cast its orange embers over Jenin. A woolen olive-drab blanket covered his face.[2]

That night in Jenin forever changed the procedural approach to how Israel's special operations units assaulted locations during terrorist arrest operations. A new tactic, the *Seer Lahatz*, or Pressure Cooker, was introduced whereby forces would surround a location with significant firepower. An Arabic-speaking operator would call for all women and children to remove themselves from any location where a terrorist had barricaded himself; if the civilians refused to leave, they would be removed from harm's way. In case the barricaded suspect refused to surrender, a D9 bulldozer would be on standby within eyeshot of the area; the IDF's fleet of Caterpillar D9R dozers were heavily armored to make them blast- and bullet-resistant in order to work under fire against entrenched and fortified military targets. The IDF D9, known as the *Dubi*, or Teddy Bear, was modified with an indigenously designed and produced armor system, consisted of both transparent and opaque components that provided bullet and blast protection to the mechanical systems and to the operator cabin. The D9's two-man crew, an operator and a commander, were protected inside an armored cabin shielded from blasts and machine gun and sniper fire by thick panels of armored steel and bulletproof glass; other armor, throughout the vehicle and adding fifteen tons to its overall weight, protected the D9 from RPGs, land mines, and IEDs. If the terrorist resisted, or if the situation became too dangerous to continue with the siege, the D9 would be summoned and flatten the building. The lives of Israeli soldiers and policemen were deemed too valuable to risk in assaults against adversaries determined to die. Levy had seen this new protocol implemented in the Ya'ma'm playbook many times in the years after Avram's death.

When Levy arrived at the unit's headquarters, memories of the night that Eli Avram was killed filled his mind. Avram's legacy was iconic. It was an unenviable position to be in, especially as the peace talks between Israel and the Palestinians would dictate the future of the unit—now his unit.

The summer of 2000 was one of the hotter seasons on record in Israel. The *Sharav*, the harsh desert winds that brought temperatures above and beyond 100°F, made too many appearances in July and August, and it was more than many Israelis—and Palestinians—could bear. There was unease in Israel—the almost forbidden desire to hope played on the nerves of those who were optimistic about the future.

U.S. president Bill Clinton was in regal glory as he shuttled from cottage to cottage in the shady summer breeze at Camp David, buried deep inside Maryland's Catoctin Mountain Park. He and his staff rushed after him, hoping to bring Palestinian Authority president Yasir Arafat and Israeli prime minister Ehud Barak ever so close to a historic breakthrough. Clinton was at the end of an eight-year presidency where, beyond scandals and bitter fights with his political opponents, the one lasting image of his legacy was standing between Arafat and Yitzhak Rabin on the White House lawn as they shook hands on September 13, 1993. With only months left in his second term, Clinton was determined to outdo himself and once and for all end the bitter conflict between Palestinian and Israeli. The best-laid plans of outsiders, though, have a long and bloody history of backfiring in the no-man's-land of Arab–Israeli logjams.

Because Ehud Barak, like his mentor Yitzhak Rabin, had been an IDF chief of staff and was a man with unimpeachable defense credentials, it was thought that he—and, perhaps, he alone—could succeed in selling finalized peace deals to the Israeli electorate. In May 2000, Barak had seen to it that the last of the Israeli forces departed Lebanon after eighteen long and bloody years of conflict and loss. Barak's political opponents, primarily the head of the right-wing Likud opposition, Ariel Sharon, viewed the unilateral Israeli withdrawal as a sign of defeat. Barak didn't care. Israel's presence in Lebanon had produced more misery than security. Barak wanted to end the Palestinian stalemate with pragmatic vigor.

For two weeks, from July 11 to July 25, President Clinton; his secretary of state, Madeleine Albright; and special Middle East negotiator Dennis Ross made a Herculean effort to bring the Palestinian and Israeli leaders to agreement. The tension between the two distant sides was impassable. In one of the more memorable scenes from the marathon that was captured by news film crews, Clinton, Barak, and Arafat faced an etiquette tussle to see which one of the leaders—Israeli or Palestinian—would politely allow his counterpart through a door first. Like all matters Palestinian–Israeli, politeness soon gave way to a tugging match, and it appeared in the end as if Barak manhandled Arafat and shoved him to the negotiating table; and, in the eyes of many Palestinians, since Barak had played a part—either directly pulling the trigger or commanding the operation from afar—in the killing of many of Arafat's deputies along the way, the move struck a resonant chord of coercion. But perception mattered little. The two weeks of haggling were for naught. Both the Israelis and the Americans would later claim that Arafat wasn't ready, willing, or perhaps able to make the final deal with Israel. The Palestinians claimed that the Israelis and Americans weren't ready to make full-blown concessions. The Israelis, with American support, went for an all-or-nothing approach; Barak even offered what was for him a political knife to the jugular—to divide Jerusalem so that the eastern part of the city could serve as the capital of a future Palestinian state. Arafat balked.

The talks ended in abysmal failure. Mont Blanc pens, specially prepared for the signing of a document, were returned to their hardened cases.

President Clinton never achieved his dream of ending the Palestinian–Israeli conflict. Barak achieved little other than to spark a fire under the looming bulldozer of Ariel Sharon, the head of the right-wing Likud Party, who now sensed that his political opponent was vulnerable. Arafat and the Palestinian Authority felt humiliated by the equation of a conference where two superpowers—one global and the other regional—attempted to force him into a final deal when he needed nothing more than a minor success of his brinksmanship. The Palestinians prepared for the violence that would inevitably follow.

Uzi Levy wasn't the only Israeli security commander being promoted that volatile season. On May 4, 2000, Avi Dichter was appointed the new Shin Bet director. A former protégé of Ehud Barak's in Sayeret Mat'kal, Dichter began his Shin Bet career as a sky marshal for El Al Israel Airlines, and then in 1974, after completing an extensive Arabic-language immersion and training, he began to serve in a variety of counterterrorist postings, primarily in a regional command responsible for the Gaza Strip; his special operations skills were unique, though, and he remained unofficially attached to the commando unit for many years.[3] He had played, according to accounts, a critical role in the January 1996 operation in which a booby-trapped cellular phone was handed off to Yehiya Ayyash, the original Hamas engineer, as he hid from Israeli forces in Palestinian Authority–controlled Gaza. Ayyash's targeted killing, by way of true Le Carre deception, sparked a wave of retaliatory suicide bombings, but was considered a master stroke of Israel's domestic intelligence service. Dichter, along with most of his senior commanders, grew up during the first intifada, and they had persevered—some truly excelled—in the war against Hamas and the PIJ during the terrible three years of suicide bombings. They knew the importance of relentlessly targeting high-value terrorist targets—both during times of relative quiet and when buses were blowing up in downtown Jerusalem.

In August 2000, a handful of high-value targets populated the Shin Bet most-wanted lists, but one name made it to the top: Mahmoud Abu Hanoud. Abu Hanoud was born in 1967 in Asira ash-Shamaliya, a village near Nablus. The fourth of seven children, he dreamed of studying the Quran and becoming the village imam. But he was shot by Israeli forces during disturbances in 1988, at the height of the first intifada, and he joined the ranks of Hamas. Following the kidnapping and murder of an Israeli policeman in 1992, Abu Hanoud and 414 other top Hamas commanders were deported from their homes in the West Bank and Gaza and dumped in the no-man's-land of southern Lebanon in between Israeli and Hezbollah forces. The "415," as the Hamas deportees became known, forged links with Hezbollah operatives and

Iranian Revolutionary Guardsmen who taught the Palestinians the A-to-Zs of bomb-building and suicide bombing tactics. Shortly after Israeli prime minister Yitzhak Rabin allowed the 415 to return to their homes—President Clinton[4] had demanded it—the first Hamas suicide bombing campaign began. Abu Hanoud led much of the Hamas infrastructure in and around Nablus.

On July 30, 1997, Abu Hanoud dispatched two suicide bombers to Jerusalem's bustling Mahane Yehuda Market at lunchtime, when it would be the most crowded. The bombers were dressed in black ties and white shirts, posing as lawyers, and they wore yarmulkes to masquerade as Orthodox Jews. The first bomber, equipped with five kilograms of TATP homemade explosives, triggered his device near a food stand. The second bomber detonated his package of ten kilograms of high explosives wrapped up with nails and screws three minutes later, targeting the first responders he knew would arrive. Sixteen people were killed and 178 critically wounded. A month later, Abu Hanoud dispatched three suicide bombers on a simultaneous assault on Jerusalem's trendy Ben Yehuda Street shopping promenade. Five people, including three teenage girls, were killed in the bombings; two hundred people were critically wounded. The bombers had all come from Asira ash-Shamaliya.

Mahmoud Abu Hanoud understood just how high a priority a target he was and he acted accordingly. He rejected traveling with the large signature entourage of heavily armed bodyguards, and preferred to rely on one trusted man, always a relative, to watch his back. He changed his mobile phone daily, and he never used the same SIM card more than once. He trusted his wits and the thirty-round magazine of his always handy AK-47 assault rifle, and carried two hand grenades on his body at all times. On more than one occasion, the Israelis came close to cornering him in one of his safe houses, but when commandos kicked in the door, all they found was a hot kettle on the stove and a half-eaten plate of warm food on the kitchen table. His penchant for always being one step ahead of Israel special operations units had earned him the nickname of *rajol bi saba' arwah*: the "man with seven lives." The Shin Bet invested enormous resources to try to ascertain his location.

Asira ash-Shamaliya was a ten-minute drive from Nablus and was quite affluent by West Bank standards—historically, the nearby forests had provided a lucrative lumber trade. More recently, though, the village had become a desired location for Palestinians who had immigrated to the United States years ago and now had come back to build second homes. Only one road, the 5715, entered and exited the small village. But it was no longer really small. Numerous new multi-story buildings and multi-family apartment blocks, built with wealth from the American Diaspora, had transformed the once-rural landscape into an urban bottleneck ideal for use as kill zones. Asira ash-Shamaliya was also a Hamas stronghold.

Asira ash-Shamaliya was in Area B, an administrative zone created by the 1993 Oslo Peace Accords that granted the Palestinians civil control over certain locations near major West Bank cities. In Area B, the security was handled by the Palestinian police, with overall Israeli security control still the responsibility of the Israeli military. Area A consisted of the towns and cities of the Palestinian Authority in which Arafat's security services and his civil servants maintained full control; and Area C was under complete Israeli civil and security administration.

In late August, Mahmoud Abu Hanoud surfaced—or, more accurately, the Shin Bet gained a lead on his whereabouts. Sensitive operations, those with genuine military repercussions, had to be approved by the head of a regional command, a major general, or even the IDF chief of staff. Operations that could swing the political pendulum into a crisis had to be approved by either the defense minister or even the prime minister. The various special operations units that worked the counterterrorist beat inside Israel's order of battle presented their plans to be approved by the military hierarchy—as was standard practice. Brigadier General Shlomo Oren, the commander of the Judea and Samaria Division, was a veteran paratroop officer and he favored utilizing Duvdevan. Oren argued that because any operation in Asira ash-Shamaliya had the potential to develop into a pitched battle, only an army unit, with full army support, could handle any escalation of hostilities. There had been a perception in the unit that there was too much focus on the undercover piece and that it should expand into a more diverse focus on special operations—in 1994, then-Duvdevan commander Ram Rotberg, a naval commando veteran, commented that the "undercover work alone was limiting the unit."[5]

Duvdevan was, of course, the larger force and it had greater specialized resources than many of the other specialized units for counterterrorist operations in the West Bank, including the Ya'mas, which was a smaller unit, but professional in design. Oren also had a close-knit relationship with Duvdevan commander Lieutenant Colonel Miki Edelstein, himself a highly decorated special operations officer with a stellar combat record. Sometimes all it took to decide one unit over another was the personal relationships that existed between generals and the unit commanders that lobbied for work. The IDF brass decided to use a chain saw over a scalpel to seize Abu Hanoud. Duvdevan was entrusted with the assignment and the operation was code-named "Symphony of Life."

Operation Symphony of Life was planned for Saturday, August 26, 2000. H-Hour was set for 2130. A large piece of the Duvdevan unit, backed by para-troopers, snipers, K9 personnel, and combat engineers, would be in support. With their gargantuan D9 bulldozer, the engineers were particularly good in case of any standoff. The massive D9s could flatten any building and its armed inhabitants. The D9s epitomized psychological terror, and so did the dogs. It was said that the Hamas foot soldiers hated the K9 units because the Quran said dogs were dirty. Between the dogs and the prospect of being crushed by fifty-four tons of Caterpillar steel, even hardcore Hamas commanders usually opted to surrender.

Two Israeli Air Force Cobra attack helicopters would be on standby, as would choppers from the elite paramedic unit, just in case casualties needed to be medevaced to a nearby trauma unit. A drone was launched over Asira ash-Shamaliya to monitor the operation and broadcast it back, via live feed, to the top brass assembled nearby at a makeshift command post.

The Duvdevan operation was split into four interlocked components. Force A, an undercover team of operatives masquerading as locals, was to position itself outside the house where it was suspected Abu Hanoud was hiding. Force B would conceal itself behind a wall connected to a nearby apartment building and cover the rear exits of Abu Hanoud's hideout. Simultaneously, Force C, several Duvdevan sniper teams, would take rooftop positions on the tallest buildings around the targeted location. Finally, Force D, the tactical backup, consisting of more than fifty Duvdevan operatives and additional paratroopers, in tactical reserve, was in position some three hundred yards away in their armored jeeps, prepared to roll forward in force to assist should a general firefight develop.

Once the undercover element surrounded Abu Hanoud's house, Force D would close all access to and from the village. The undercover operators would call upon Abu Hanoud to surrender or, failing that, allow any non-combatants to leave his compound. If Abu Hanoud decided to surrender, the troopers would take their prize and return to base by 2300. But there was always the chance for the incident to develop into a Pressure Cooker.

2130 hours, Saturday, August 26, 2000: The Duvdevan vehicles pushed ahead, though slowly, through the main village road and negotiated the throngs venturing out to shop and mingle in the cool of darkness. Young men were everywhere—sitting inside the village's two coffeehouses, its hummus eateries and religious clubhouses, and just hanging out on the street corner smoking cigarettes. About thirty men, all in soccer jerseys, hovered around the stoop of a storefront, arguing about a match. Women, some leading a procession of six kids or more, were out, as well, shopping for the next day's meals. Yellow taxi vans, the life's blood of travel inside Areas A and B, were double- and triple-parked everywhere.

The streets in Asira ash-Shamaliya had no official names, and none of the houses had numbers—such was this Byzantine world. Several streets, though, had been named and labeled prominently in honor of village sons who had been killed battling the Israelis or martyred as suicide bombers. Posters of these men hung everywhere. It took the vehicles several minutes to slink their way toward the affluent section of Asira ash-Shamaliya, situated north of the main mosque; the vans were known as "toaster ovens" because the windows were always sealed and the heat inside was stifling—especially for operators in full tactical kit and constricting body armor. The vans pushed into parking spots twenty-five meters from Abu Hanoud's two-story home and silently unloaded the men. From the darkened cover of a pine forest a kilometer out-side of town, the Duvdevan commander and his men prepared to enter the village. When the main force arrived, a loudspeaker would be used to demand that Abu Hanoud surrender. The entire village would become a closed army zone until Mahmoud Abu Hanoud was either in custody or killed. In keeping with the protocols of the Oslo Peace Accords, a liaison officer would need to visit the Palestinian police station in the village, located in the northeast outskirts, and inform them of the operation once the mission began. There were fifty armed Palestinian policemen representing ten of Arafat's police and intelligence services in the village. Some were Hamas sympathizers; others were full-fledged operatives.

The undercover operators spread out around the house and quickly took aim with their M4s; their ACOG sights illuminated a red dot on each of the windows and doorways to cover the escape routes. They listened for any signs of life from inside the house, but the building was dark. A television was on. Someone was cooking, banging pots and pans. The teams closed in.

Abu Hanoud and his bodyguard, Nidal Dagles, had taken advantage of the cool mountain breeze and were enjoying the evening in a rooftop lounge they had recently constructed under hanging blankets—blankets that shielded them from any intruding overhead surveillance. Suddenly, they heard the cries of small children yelling "*Jesh*," for "Army," in Arabic. The Hamas chief had employed neighborhood children as lookouts, paying them ten shekels a day, and his force of small trip wires had been worth the modest investment. A grenade exploded near the Duvdevan team positioned in front of the house. The blast was followed by dedicated bursts of small arms and AK-47 fire. The Duvdevan operation had been compromised.

First Sergeant Niv Ya'akobi and Staff Sergeants Ro'i Finsteiner-Even and Liron Sharvit, conscripted NCOs in the unit, reacted instinctively when the sounds of gunfire pierced the night's calm. At the pre-raid briefing, the operators had been ordered not to change their locations—or rush to the rooftops of the surrounding homes and buildings—under any circumstances unless directed to do so. The three Duvdevan sergeants knew that the unit's snipers had yet to establish their firing positions and were not in a position to engage Abu Hanoud. They felt that they had to act and act immediately. The three made a dash into a three-story building fifteen yards from the target house, and then made their way to the roof. Testosterone and adrenaline had proven to be a more powerful potion than instructions and restraint.

The three sergeants seized the corners of the building's first floor, and then each landing of the staircase. As one operator turned a corner, he stopped and provided cover while the other two rushed up. Each move had been rehearsed over and over again in tactical exercises. It was second nature to them: deliberate tactical choreography.

As the three sergeants pushed up the staircase, they heard the full-auto bursts of AK fire from Abu Hanoud and his partner. The three reached the rooftop and identified Abu Hanoud and Dagles some twenty-five meters away. The two Palestinians fired at them—the ricochets of near misses sparkled in the dark night sky. Ya'akobi, Sharvit, and Finsteiner-Even immediately engaged the two Hamas targets with a dedicated response. Tracer rounds careened into the darkness in what looked like green laser beams. The Israelis' shooting was disciplined and accurate, but not fatal. Abu Hanoud took a bullet to the right shoulder. His sudden movement threw off the Israeli's aim and kept the round from his punching into his heart. Dagles was hit several times in the left leg and thigh.

Then, without warning, the Duvdevan sergeants were hit by an explosive burst of fire from a nearby rooftop and killed. Unit snipers, fearing that their comrades from Force A on the ground were trapped under fire, had rushed to their rooftop positions and unleashed a barrage of automatic weapons fire. The snipers didn't know that the three operators had taken the high ground themselves.

Chaos and confusion erupted. The overloaded radio frequency was interrupted by cries coming from the soldiers demanding that their comrades respond and acknowledge. Helicopter gunships were summoned, as was the chopper belonging to the paramedics. The backup forces rushed frantically toward their preplanned positions in and around the targeted house—and the village.

Mahmoud Abu Hanoud, bleeding heavily from a 5.56mm round that punched clean through his right shoulder, took advantage of the Israeli confusion by jumping out a rear window and making a dash for safety; his bodyguard was ordered to hold off the Israelis for as long as he could in order to facilitate the escape.

Duvdevan search teams found a blood trail leading from the targeted house to the west, in the direction of dried brush and the outskirts of town. By now, dozens of flares hung in the night's sky, turning the darkness into daylight. IDF jeeps equipped with loudspeakers rolled up and down the main road ordering the residents to remain in their homes.

A team of Duvdevan operators followed Abu Hanoud's blood trail to a small house at the southern outskirts of Asira ash-Shamaliya. They had radioed their position to Lieutenant Colonel Edelstein and requested permission to gain entry, when they heard rustling in the nearby brush and the clanking sound of a sling banging against a weapon. The soldiers swung their weapons toward the new threat and squeezed off several three-round bursts. The rounds lit up the darkened backdrop, and several ricocheted off rocks, which added to the confusion and chaos. But their target, they discovered to their horror, was a member of the unit: Staff Sergeant Avi Yosef was shot in the thigh and arm.

Duvdevan combat medics worked feverishly to resuscitate Ya'akobi, Sharvit, and Finsteiner-Even, but the three were ultimately pronounced dead. News of the friendly-fire tragedy spread quickly over the communications gear worn by each operator.

Throughout the night Duvdevan operators, as well as commandos from a paratroop reconnaissance unit, scoured the village in search of Abu Hanoud or anyone who might know where he went. Young villagers who wandered outside once the gunfire started were quickly rounded up by Duvdevan operators and detained. Dozens of men, blindfolded and hands cuffed behind their backs, were thrown to their knees and readied for Shin Bet interrogation. Arabic-speaking Shin Bet agents pressed those detainees for any news of the Hamas chieftain's whereabouts.

Abu Hanoud had made it through the brush and into a thicket of pine trees to reach the outskirts of Nablus. He ventured to the safest place for him inside the West Bank—the headquarters of Arafat's notorious Preventative Security Service—and demanded shelter. He was treated like a conquering hero rather than a man whom the Palestinians had sworn they would arrest on sight. A prominent surgeon was brought to attend to his shattered shoulder, and he was allowed to recuperate inside what was referred to as a jail cell, but in reality was a comfortable VIP guest room equipped with satellite TV, secure phone lines, and computers.

Outside Abu Hanoud's home, his bodyguard had managed to buy the terror chief time to make good his escape, holding off the Israeli forces for nearly eight hours. Parleying with Duvdevan hostage negotiators, he claimed that there were women and children inside the home and said that he wanted to make sure he would be handled under the guidelines of the

Geneva Conventions and not tortured or killed. When Israeli commanders finally determined that Dagles was alone, they summoned the D9. The dozer's two-man crew fired up the 474-horsepower engine and guided the fifteen-foot-wide armored behemoth up an incline toward the targeted house. Inching forward at seven miles per hour, the D9 crushed an outer stone wall and then moved toward the house. Dagles begged for his life and surrendered moments later.

IDF officers embarked upon the heartbreaking task of notifying three sets of parents that their sons had been killed. Some of the parents were awoken at four thirty in the morning[6] by the dreadful knock in the predawn darkness and the silhouettes of men and women in the uniform aiming their eyes at the ground. Duvdevan, and the Israeli task force, did not leave Asira ash-Shamaliya until 0800 the following morning.

The following day, Lieutenant Colonel Edelstein gave the eulogies at all three funerals. He spoke of what a terrible responsibility of securing the country Israel burdens its eighteen-year-old conscripts with.

Asira ash-Shamaliya came close to being a mortal wound for Duvdevan. As so often happens when thousands of man hours and the most ambitious of intentions fail to yield dividends because of human error and poor luck, everyone who could began to point fingers. The politicians blamed the generals. The generals, of course, blamed the men in the field. The parents of the fallen soldiers gave interviews to the voracious Israeli press, critiquing the planning and execution of the operation. In one scathing exposé, embittered Duvdevan operators claimed that they had warned of the risk of friendly fire incidents in the past, and that in the unit, there were many instances where the "colorful" force, in disguise, came under fire from the "green" force.[7]

The viciousness of the infighting was par for the course in Israel, a nation where mandatory military service elevated many to the rank of armchair general. But the nature of special operations—especially the ultra-dangerous world of undercover work—was one of risk and peril, where an operation that has been a year in the planning can self-destruct in seconds because of

human error or poor luck. Lost in the blame game was the fact that Duvdevan had executed some two hundred successful counterterrorist operations
in the months previous to Asira ash-Shamaliya.[8]

Both Brigadier General Oren and Lieutenant Colonel Edelstein submit-
ted their resignations to IDF chief of staff Lieutenant General Shaul Mofaz.
Only Oren's was accepted.*

When the raw intelligence on Abu Hanoud first emerged, some inside
Israel's counterterrorism community wanted the Ya'mas to handle the target
because of their deft touch and small signature. Indeed, one of the initial
findings of the investigation into what went wrong that night in Asira ash-
Shamaliya was that too many soldiers were involved in the raid and that
overload of the unit's communications systems added to the confusion and
chaos once gunfire erupted.[9]

Ya'mas operators, working at their base near where the friendly-fire incident
transpired, mourned the young soldiers killed that night and prayed for
their families. They knew, perhaps better than anyone else involved in Israel's
unending war on terror, just how dangerous undercover work was; these
men, some of them in their late thirties, with a decade's worth of experience
in the fight, knew just how precarious and explosive these operations could
be. The operators—the young men in Duvdevan and the older and more
experienced specialists in the Ya'mas—were highly skilled and full of motivation, but Murphy's Law, or the Palestinian variant, was always a factor that
could turn a spectacular operation into a debacle. And the generals—and
the politicians—were ill-equipped to deal with debacle. Duvdevan would be
taken off the line following the friendly-fire debacle, as teams of investigators

---

* Lieutenant Colonel Edelstein continued to serve as Duvdevan commander until the end of 2001. He
was promoted to colonel and commanded an infantry brigade that fought some of the toughest battles of
the 2006 Lebanon War against Hezbollah. He was promoted to brigadier general in 2010 to serve as the
chief paratroop and infantry officer and, in 2012, was named as the commander of the Gaza Division.
During Operation Protective Edge, the 2014 war in Gaza, Brigadier General Edelstein directed much of
the ground effort against Hamas.

tried to determine what had gone wrong that awful night near Nablus in Asira ash-Shamaliya.

The arrival of fall is a joyous time in Israel. The weather cools slightly as the harsh summer heat dissipates in greeting the arrival of the Jewish New Year. Rosh Hashanah launches a month of holidays and celebrations that bring the country to a virtual halt. Families gather for gut-busting feasts, schoolchildren receive what to parents appear to be an endless number of days off, and the main national focus seems to be on grocery shopping in preparation for the festive meals and last-minute travel deals for those wishing to spend their religious-inspired time off overseas.

September 2000 went by quickly, some of the Ya'mas veterans thought. The Duvdevan incident reinforced the sense of doom, that of a lit fuse about to ignite an unimaginably explosive force that would engulf the landscape shortly. Intelligence officers who were regulars at the Ya'mas base spoke of increased chatter among the terrorist factions and a lot of "fortifying the nest" on the Palestinian Authority side. There was a tangible tension that was felt everywhere in the terrain—the villages and roadways of Area B where the Ya'mas operated—where the Ya'mas worked. Unit members began to use armored jeeps when leaving base to run an errand, rather than their own vehicles; few traveled the roadways of the area without an M4 close at hand.[10] The violent electricity that Yaakov Berman and his most experienced operators felt during the *Naqba* demonstrations was now high-voltage. Some of the operators had a sixth sense that they wouldn't be home for the holidays. They hoped that their wives and children would understand.

On the morning of Thursday, September 28, 2000, a day before the eve of the Jewish New Year, Likud Party leader Ariel Sharon—along with a large force of police and security—ventured to the Temple Mount and the al-Aqsa mosque in a grandstanding display that torpedoed the very notion of Ehud Barak's offer to divide Jerusalem. Sharon's gesture was designed to illustrate that the city of Jerusalem, including the third holiest site in Islam, was sovereign Israeli territory and would always remain so. Sharon's much publicized media event was a political opportunity for Arafat to respond to Camp David and the impasse over Barak's overture the only way he knew. Palestinian rioting throughout East Jerusalem erupted shortly thereafter. The rioting soon spread to the West Bank and Gaza. Rocks and petrol bombs would soon be replaced by automatic weapons and grenades.

Few Ya'mas operators would be home for the New Year. In fact, the unit's personnel would miss most of the holiday celebrations for the foreseeable future.

CHAPTER THREE

Intifada

Early in the morning of Friday, September 29, 2000, rioting erupted inside the Balata refugee camp in Nablus just as morning prayers came to an end. The demonstrations soon spilled onto main roadways that fed into the Israeli-administered territory, and the main highways that connected the West Bank settlements and the Palestinian cities of Area A were suddenly besieged by violence. Palestinian demonstrators launched rocks and Molotov cocktails at Israeli forces. The Israelis responded with troops and policemen in full riot kit, to break up the disturbances with less than lethal measures. Ya'mas units were ordered into the knuckle-scraping front lines, as well. Breaking up violent riots by infiltrating the demonstrations was, after all, the classic mission of the undercover units, with tactics fine-tuned during the first intifada. Ya'mas operatives injected themselves deep inside the rage-filled cauldron to apprehend the ringleaders who were directing the violence. But rocks and petrol bombs were soon replaced by AK-47 and M16 fire. Ya'mas squads, in and around Nablus, as well as the other cities of the West Bank, soon found themselves overwhelmed and outgunned in lethal close-quarter fighting. In many cases, Palestinian police units that should have put a stop to the violence joined into the bullet-strewn chaos. The Oslo Accords were dead.

The rioting was particularly fierce in Qalqilya, a West Bank city that straddled a thin frontier line next to the Kfar Saba, a fairly affluent suburb in the greater Tel Aviv area. Superintendent Yosef Tabeja, a veteran officer with the Border Guard, had never seen Palestinian disturbances this violent before. The twenty-seven-year-old commanded a joint patrol with his Palestinian counterparts to safeguard the frontier separating the two cities. The joint security patrols were one of the more promising signs of the Oslo Accords: one of the genuine statements of Palestinian and Israeli cooperation, which Palestinian policemen and Israeli Border Guards conducted outside the cities of Area A.

Like the patrols, Tabeja's story was one of promise. He had come to Israel as a child in 1984 as part of Operation Moses, a Mossad-led effort to rescue Ethiopian Jewry. He served in the paratroopers and then the Border Guard, where he excelled working with his Palestinian counter-parts in operating the joint patrol program. On the first day of the intifada, Tabeja led a patrol of two jeeps—one Israeli and one Palestinian—along the lines near Qalqilya, but the force had to pull over so that the offi-cers could take a break from the stones and tear gas. Some of the Border Guards removed their helmets to wipe the sweat from their foreheads; the Palestinian policemen grabbed a quick smoke and some water. One of the Palestinians, Nabil Suliman, walked toward Tabeja's jeep and shouted "*Allahu Akbar*" ("God Is Great"), before shooting Tabeja dead in the back of the head at point-blank range. Moments later, Palestinian policemen began to fire at Israeli forces.

The violence throughout the West Bank—and Jerusalem and Gaza—quickly escalated into an uncontrollable force of its own. There were acts of untold barbarity, including the lynching of two IDF reservists who acciden-tally wandered into Ramallah and sought refuge at the Palestinian police station; there was loss of life on both sides. Overall, the Israeli response to the opening chaos of the intifada was disorganized—Israel's security services were unclear what the conflict actually was or what the national response should be. The IDF, one undercover unit officer reflected, was woefully unprepared. It took weeks, sometimes much longer, for armored fighting vehicles and tanks to be positioned along key routes and junctions that were often attacked. The army didn't know whom to target because the Shin Bet and the military intelligence units did not have the assets in place. "We were not ready. The army wasn't ready; the security establishment wasn't ready."[1]

Superintendent Uzi Levy received a tumultuous baptism of fire to launch his command of the unit. Instead of lobbying Shin Bet and IDF commanders for work, he now had to manage his small band of men to respond to multiple flashpoints of violence that erupted throughout the area.

The popular narrative concerning the intifada always has been that the Palestinian violence was spontaneous, an explosion of frustrated dreams of statehood that boiled over because of Israeli pertinacity; that was, of course, what the Arafat narrative pushed to his own constituents and to the West. But Arafat had been preparing for a conflict for quite some time. There were reports of food hoarding (including sheep and milk-fed calves from Australia coming into Gaza).[2] The telephone chatter between Arafat and his security heads spoke of raising the tempo of the violence. Hamas and PIJ commanders who had been held inside Palestinian prisons on security charges were suddenly released or the terms of their incarceration so relaxed that these masterminds became de facto VIP guests rather than security threats serving out lengthy sentences. Street thugs, used by Arafat's lieutenants to deal with political opponents, were now unleashed against Israeli targets.

The Israeli intelligence assessment was that once forced into a corner by the failed Camp David summit, Arafat would use bloodshed to attain goals he did not want to achieve at the negotiation table.[3] In the autumn of 2000, Arafat clearly controlled the street, and he could have turned off the violence should he have deemed it strategically advantageous. Violence became a duplicitous weapon in Arafat's jockeying for a political stance. He could claim that he had no control of the street, and then declare himself the victim of Israeli retaliation. "Early on in the fighting," a U.S. diplomatic security agent stationed in the country at the time commented, "it was possible to put the genie back into the bottle." But Arafat found it impossible to issue the order to cease hostilities without being able to boast a military victory of his own. The elusive quest for this achievement became an unstoppable ailment that fed off of absolute misery.

Israel faced a multitude of underground armies during the intifada. Some were lavishly financed and equipped; others were fueled by ideologies and newfound fanaticism. The Islamic Republic of Iran had become a seismic eruption influencing the Palestinian march toward full-fledged conflict. When the IDF withdrew its force from southern Lebanon in May 2000, Iran and Hezbollah needed a new front for the war against Israel and the Palestinian struggle took center stage. Sheikh Hassan Nasrallah, Hezbollah's secretary-general, changed the thrust of his rhetoric-laced sermons to focus on the West Bank and Gaza.[4] Tehran, through Hezbollah, had become a key financier to Hamas and the PIJ, as well as to the Palestinian Authority. A mysterious figure named Qais Obeid, an Israeli-Arab from the village of Taibe that straddled a pocket just south of Tulkarm on the Israeli side of the pre-1967 frontier, became a key facilitator of funding the al-Aqsa intifada. Obeid was a low-level con artist, loan shark, and swindler, who had fallen into financial trouble following several failed business ventures; his business partner had been imprisoned in a Shin Bet sting, for selling arms and ammunition to West Bank gangs, and Obeid had also served time for gun possession. Clan contacts put him in touch with Hezbollah agents who lavished him with financial freedom. Obeid served as a recruitment officer for Hezbollah's intelligence wing, locating operatives that could be on the Lebanese Party of God's—and Iran's—payroll from both inside Israel and the West Bank and Gaza. Obeid had played an integral role in Hezbollah's October 2000 kidnapping of an Israeli colonel in the reserves, Elhanan Tennenbaum, who had been lured to Abu Dhabi for a cocaine deal.

Obeid, from his offices in Lebanon, served as an intifada ambassador, funneling cash and material from Hezbollah to Hamas and the PIJ. Arafat's lieutenants, interested in siphoning off some of this money for themselves, created new terror factions that could give Hamas and the PIJ a run for their money in the competition to see who could strike at Israel the hardest.

Arafat had created no less than eleven separate arms, including a coast guard for the West Bank (a slice of land that had no bodies of water). The most feared of all these services was the *al-Amn al-Wiqa'i*, or Preventive Security Force, a plainclothes intelligence service with a despicable human rights record. Force 17, Arafat's Praetorian Guard, constituted his special operations arm. Many members of these heavily armed factions had fought with Arafat and the other factions in Lebanon and had become guardians of the Arafat regime; many of these men were experts in countersurveillance and counterintelligence operations. Although diplomatic accords were intended to limit the number of men under arms and the type of weapons they were permitted to carry, Arafat had assembled more than fifty-five thousand such men.[5]

Arafat did not openly employ the services of his security forces during the intifada—he had also nurtured underground formations that could be summoned to carry out dirty work. The Tanzim, or Organization, was an unofficial enforcer to make sure that anti-Arafat forces never gained traction on the Palestinian street. The Tanzim leader was Marwan Barghouti, a veteran Fatah operative who had learned Hebrew inside an Israeli prison; Barghouti was the only Tanzim leader given a seat at the Fatah table. Most of the Tanzim commanders were men who had earned their combat scars fighting in the first intifada, and the majority of the men they commanded were top-notch thugs. The Tanzim employed thieves, extortionists, career criminals, rapists, murderers, and men who perpetrated violence with glee. These street warriors earned hefty paychecks stirring the pot and killing Israelis. The Tanzim paraded with weapons, such as M16s, but liked to be photographed with axes and daggers. There were believed to be some three thousand Tanzim on a full-time war footing; another three thousand could be summoned if needed. The Tanzim were most prominent in places like Ramallah, Qalqilya, and Tulkarm—cities that straddled the pre-1967 Israeli frontiers.

The al-Aqsa Martyrs Brigade was another one of Arafat's deniable creations. Just as the notorious Black September Organization in the 1970s had been a deniable special operations element of Arafat's Fatah, so, too, did the al-Aqsa Martyrs Brigade provide Arafat with a force of Islamic-fueled operatives who would carry out the most heinous of terrorist attacks without ever officially being linked to the Palestinian Authority president.[6] The al-Aqsa Martyrs Brigade was well represented in the cities of Ramallah and Bethlehem in the Jerusalem areas, and Nablus and Jenin in upper Samaria. The al-Aqsa Brigade operated in small, highly secretive, and highly compartmentalized cells. Well equipped and fanatically charged, they would quickly develop into a group that helped unite the other factions in common strikes against Israel.

Both Hamas and the Palestinian Islamic Jihad (PIJ) were offshoots of the Egyptian Muslim Brotherhood, which was dedicated to the destruction of the Jewish State and the establishment of a fundamentalist Islamic state. Hamas, the Arabic acronym for *Harakat al-Muqawamah al-Islamiyya*, or Islamic Resistance Movement, also meant "zeal," "courage," and "bravery." The Hamas nerve center was Gaza—the group's founder, the quadriplegic Sheikh Ahmed Yassin, had spent most of his entire life in Gaza, and Gaza connected the Palestinian Islamists with their spiritual mentors in Egypt. Hamas was well funded at first by wealthy Palestinians living in the diaspora of the United States and the Persian Gulf.

Hamas was divided into a political and a military wing, though the separation of the two was profoundly invisible; the foot soldiers of the armed resistance (initially the Abdullah Azzam Brigade in the West Bank and, ultimately, the Izzedine al-Qassam Brigade that would assume the military spotlight for the entire organization) operated at the behest of the political hierarchy. A similar symbiosis existed between the PIJ and its military arm, the Jerusalem Force. The PIJ was strongest in the northern West Bank—upper Samaria—regions, as it was closely aligned with Islamic political organizations inside Israeli-Arab towns that bordered the post-1967 frontiers. Even though both Hamas and the PIJ were fundamentalist Sunni organizations, the two groups maintained close operational links—what could even be considered subservience—to Hezbollah, Syria, and the Islamic Republic of Iran.

There were tens of thousands of Palestinian gunmen and suicide bombers poised for war against Israel. The Palestinian groups had built highly sophisticated and ultra-secretive networks inside Area A and throughout much of Area B. The Shin Bet and Military Intelligence had not been able to truly grasp the depth of the terrorist infrastructure inside the West Bank and Gaza since the implementation of the Oslo Accords. Israel's intelligence services—the forces that directed the military and police component—had not operated inside Palestinian areas since 1995.

The terrorist activity continued throughout the fall of 2000. Israel's brief winter and rainy season was punctuated by incessant violence. The darkening clouds and bone-numbing drizzle foretold a growing sense of frustration that Oslo was a failure and that the hopes of peace with the Palestinians had evaporated into the post-blast concussion of full-scale warfare. Elections were held in February 2001, and Ariel "Arik" Sharon's Likud Party trounced incumbent Ehud Barak on a platform of security. Sharon's supporters rallied outside Likud headquarters in Jerusalem and sang, "Long Live Arik, King of Israel." The intifada, though, continued unabated.

The Palestinians relentlessly probed Israeli resolve: roadside shootings, the odd car bomb, and even a few small-scale suicide bombings. Some acts were desperate yet still shook Israel's fleeting sense of security. On February 14, 2001, a bus driven by a Palestinian terrorist slammed into a crowd of commuters at a bus stop in the Tel Aviv suburb of Holon, killing eight and injuring twenty-five. And then the suicide bombings began in earnest.

In 2000, according to Shin Bet records, there were four suicide bombings perpetrated by Palestinian terrorists against Israeli targets. In 2001, there were fifty-three such incidents.[7] The suicide bombings began on March 4, 2001, when three people were killed and sixty injured in an attack against a shopping mall in Netanya. Two suicide bombings that summer were catastrophic. On June 1, 2001, twenty-one teenagers were killed by a suicide bomber outside a discotheque on the Tel Aviv shore. Throughout July and August 2001, the bombings were weekly—almost daily—occurrences. The worst of the summer strikes was the August 9 suicide bombing of a pizzeria in Jerusalem; fifteen people were killed in the Hamas attack, including seven children and five members of the same family. The bombings briefly stopped after September 11, 2001. The Palestinians—masters at manipulating the CNN battlefront—had been lumped together as an integral piece of the global jihad following the 9/11 attacks against the United States; the video feed of Palestinian women, ululating their tongues in glee as the towers fell, did not enhance their image around the world. Palestinian Authority president Arafat donated blood to be sent to New York. He declared his unwavering commitment in the war on terror. Yet weeks later, at the United Nations General Assembly gathering in New York City, U.S. president Bush refused to meet with him.

Prime Minister Sharon used the Palestinian time-out to go on the offensive. An Israeli targeted killing campaign launched in the late autumn of 2001 was designed to eradicate the operational leadership of the terrorist factions without launching large-scale ground incursions into the PA. On October 23, 2001, Ayman Halaweh, the number three commander in the Hamas military wing, was killed when a Hellfire missile launched from an AH-64 Apache gunship ripped into the car he was in near Nablus. On October 31, 2001, Jamil Jadallah al-Qawasmeh, one of the heads of Hamas in Hebron, was killed when a missile was fired through the living room window of his home. And on November 23, 2001, Mahmoud Abu Hanoud finally met the justice that

Duvdevan had failed to exact—he was killed when a missile turned the sedan he was driving near Nablus into a flaming heap of molten steel.[8]

Before 9/11 (and before Iraq and Afghanistan and the U.S. entry into drone warfare), the United States had expressed vocal opposition to the targeted killings. Only two months before the attacks against the Twin Towers and the Pentagon, U.S. secretary of state Colin Powell stated, "We continue to express our distress and opposition to these kinds of targeted killings, and we will continue to do so."[9]

Aerial targeted killing was considered a tactically safe response. On a technicality, as well, Israel wasn't throwing an invasion force into Area A and therefore was not, on paper, violating the Oslo Accords. "We didn't go into Area A," a Ya'mas officer remembered. "For us Area A was as if we traveled to Lebanon or to Syria even though we had all been there before Oslo. The operational necessity warranted that we go in closer. Little by little we overcame the mental obstacle. We went one hundred meters deeper inside one day, two kilometers deeper the next. Our confidence increased, and Shin Bet intelligence became stronger. The intelligence and tactical piece went side by side. It was a slow process, but an effective one."[10]

The Ya'mas maintained a heavy workload throughout the first year of the intifada. Operators infiltrated gangs of demonstrators and gunmen and arrested hundreds of terrorist operatives. One operation that brought the unit its fair share of headlines and controversy was the November 7, 2001, killing of Issa Halil Dababse, a wanted Fatah fugitive who had killed Dov Drieben, an Israeli settler, in April 1998 over a land deal gone wrong. Dababse was one of the key Palestinian arms dealers in the Hebron Hills, and he was a facilitator, a man who helped turn terrorist intentions (from all the groups) into actual operations. Dababse hailed from the city of Yatta, located eight kilometers south of Hebron. With a population of nearly fifty thousand inhabitants, Yatta was one of the West Bank's largest cities, but it was also one of those places where everyone knew everyone else and everyone was suspicious of outsiders.

Although there was plenty of work for both Duvdevan and the Ya'mas—even in the early part of the intifada—Duvdevan generally operated in the southern portion of the West Bank, in Judea, and the Ya'mas in the north, in Samaria. But, in fact, both units worked everywhere and anywhere there was work. When the Shin Bet came to Uzi Levy with word of Dababse's whereabouts, the unit jumped on the opportunity.

Yatta was built around a series of hills that dominated the incoming roadways from all directions. Hamas lookouts perched themselves on the rooftops of five-story apartment blocks that were already atop the high ground on hilltop cliffs. These men, fueled by thermoses of strong mud-like coffee laced with cardamom, watched the cars come in and out of IDF checkpoints several kilometers down the road. Vehicles that were deemed suspicious were stopped inside the city by armed men with AK-47s. Whoever couldn't answer the questions satisfactorily was taken to a Hamas detention center for additional questioning; a bullet-peppered wall behind a rear courtyard was used as a last stop for those even suspected of being Israeli agents. Beyond the Hamas obstacles, there were always Palestinian Police checkpoints and roadblocks, as well as other Palestinian elements that would have to be dealt with: Months earlier, several Ya'mas operators had encountered heavily armed gunmen from Force 17 during an arrest ambush; the Ya'mas operators killed several of Arafat's elite guard in a close-quarter firefight. An undercover unit that was compromised in Yatta would have to face off against an overwhelming number of gunmen before help could arrive.

There was a required process in turning a Shin Bet file into an operational plan. Intelligence files were reviewed and aerial reconnaissance video analyzed. An assault plan had to be articulated into a proposal that could be presented to the local brigade commander for approval. Once the plan was approved, elements of the raiding force would train on a model of the target. Operators participating in the assault, especially the Speakers and the officers, would venture into Palestinian territory on a reconnaissance sortie—an undercover probing action that in and of itself was a full-blown mission requiring air support and tactical backup to be on standby. On the morning of November 7, the task force departed the staging area where the Hebron (Judea) Brigade commander, Colonel Dror Weinberg, was waiting with Uzi Levy at a forward command post with a sizable contingent of armored infantrymen ready to rescue the undercover squad should they encounter stiff resistance. The Ya'mas team traveled to Yatta in vehicles bearing white-and-green Palestinian plates. In keeping with the masquerade, a Ya'mas liaison officer made sure that they were scrutinized properly at the checkpoint by Israeli forces—just in case Palestinian spotters were looking. What the Ya'mas contingent had to do was to pierce two kilometers into Yatta and then, once they made it past the twisting roads surrounded by Hamas gunmen at their cinder-block positions, head east toward the Dababse clan homes on the fringe of town.

The temperature was seasonal that November morning. It was cold enough to notice the harsh winds slicing through the hills south of Hebron but not enough to force everyone indoors; the past few days had seen a constant drizzle. The Dababse clan had assembled in grand numbers to dig a sewage line. They had rented a small excavator to cut through the rain-softened earth, and relatives and children looked on in amusement; the women brought the men working on the project kettles of piping hot sweet tea. The Ya'mas plan was to positively identify Dababse and muscle him into one of the Horses that would pull up in a hurry. If all went well, the snatch and grab would take a few seconds and the Ya'mas operators would be safely back behind Israeli lines before the local Fatah headquarters was alerted.

The Horse pulled up to fifty meters from the dig, so that Berman and a few of his men could inch their way toward the crowd on foot. As Berman moved closer, the Horse rolling slow enough for it not to be noticeable, the Soviet-born team commander scanned the faces, looking for the facial characteristics he had studied so closely by staring at a Shin Bet photo of Dababse. Berman tried to appear naturally curious as he examined the people watching the diesel-powered tractor claw a hole through the moist ground. Dababse was in the center of the mix directing the dig and acting very much like the family patriarch, but a checkered keffiyeh covered his face and it was hard for Berman to make a positive identification of the wanted suspect. Berman's heart rate was steady; his hands moved slowly toward his concealed holster. Dababse sensed danger. He quickly removed a pistol clipped to his trousers in the small of his back and tried to aim it at Berman at point-blank range. Dababse drew first, but Berman was quicker on the trigger. Dababse was shot and killed in a sudden flurry of violence. Several of the men in the crowd attempted to pummel Berman; one swung a shovel at him, others attempted to overcome the undercover team and seize their weapons. One of Dababse's sons was shot in the leg during the melee.[11] Operators in full tactical kit emerged from the Horse to secure the withdrawal. Dababse's listless body was tossed into the rear of the Horse, and Berman and his squad raced back to Israeli lines. The Horse headed straight for a field trauma unit, but Dababse died en route to the triage center.

Later that evening, Uzi Levy received a phone call. The Ya'mas commander was expecting to be chewed out by this general or that one because the suspect had died. But the caller, Prime Minister Sharon, was happy enough to offer a job well done to the unit chief.[12] Sharon knew, better than most perhaps, that this particular war would be ugly and would have to be won by any means necessary.

Israeli commanders knew that the intifada would have to be defeated by intelligence-driven precision: targeted killings and lightning-fast direct action raids to arrest or eliminate the men who directed and facilitated the carnage on Israel's streets. The use of special operations forces would be a critical element of this strategy, and the very best of Israel's commando units found themselves behind Palestinian lines on a dangerous mission to chip away at the Palestinians' ability to wage the intifada.[13] The commanders of every one of the IDF's special operations units, more than a dozen in all, including the most secretive and selective forces designed to operate far from Israel's shores on top-secret missions of the highest order, understood that the fight would require an imaginative and relentless campaign of unnerving the enemy. Each of these units, all highly specialized, possessed the bravest and the brightest of Israel's military; some of them, like the Flotilla 13 naval commando force and Sayeret Mat'kal, were considered so prestigious that Israeli high school students were known to pay for preparatory conditioning courses just so that they could be ready for the grueling selection process that had to be overcome to earn a spot in the commando basic training course (from which, more than 90 percent of applicants ultimately washed out). These commando formations could shoot better, climb higher, and deploy farther from Israel's shores, but they weren't full-time forces of professionals capable of deploying at a moment's notice inside enemy terrain and outside it.

The undercover units assumed their spot as the tip of the spear of the Israeli commando effort to deter and detain terrorist commanders from dispatching their legions of bombers against Israel's civilian population. Duvdevan recovered from the blue-on-blue tragedy in 2000 to sustain a loss of a different kind. On the night of February 14, 2002, Duvdevan's commanding officer, Lieutenant Colonel Eyal Weiss, was killed in a freak accident in the village of Zaita after a wall collapsed on him following a Pressure Cooker operation to apprehend PIJ terrorists.[14]

The battlefield reality required that the Ya'mas increase the scale and scope of its behind-enemy-lines forays—both to apprehend suspects and, because of its fluid molecular structure, to respond to an immediate break in intelligence from the Shin Bet, to stop suicide bombers en route to their targets. On the afternoon of March 5, 2002, an urgent call came to Inspector Ronen Goresh, one of the more experienced unit officers, concerning an urgent breaking tip that a Shin Bet case officer had received about a suicide bomber. Goresh had been in the unit for nearly a decade and had climbed up the chain of command, going from new recruit to operator to team sergeant, junior officer, and ultimately commander of one of the unit's two teams. The call he received at headquarters that Tuesday was one of absolute urgency.

Israel's security doctrine was built around layers—each layer being more difficult to penetrate—and it was always best to engage a threat at the outermost layer. This was one of the pillars behind Israel's reliance on dynamic proactive deterrence to strike out preemptively rather than absorb a preventable blow. News of a possible suicide bomber en route toward a target, perhaps one in Jerusalem, sounded an alarm that required an immediate and decisive response. The Ya'mas headquarters was a few miles down the road from where the terrorists—the bomber and his transporter—were believed to be traveling. Ya'mas operators raced into their vans and armored jeeps. They got dressed on the way.

Finding a vehicle on a busy thoroughfare is like locating a needle in a haystack—a haystack traveling at ninety kilometers per hour—and the Ya'mas armada traveled in between hastily-thrown-together checkpoints it had established. The suspect vehicle, a late-model sedan with yellow Israeli license plates, was discovered traveling south on Route 60 en route toward a junction that split two ways—one going to Tel Aviv, and the other heading to Jerusalem.

The most important part of neutralizing the bomber was isolating the vehicle. Veering a sedan off the road was one of the basic skill sets that every Ya'mas operator learned in undercover school, but the lanes of traffic had to be closed simultaneously to make sure that commuters heading home from their offices in Jerusalem weren't hit by bomb fragments. One of the Bedouin Speakers* who was also one of the most skilled drivers in Goresh's team followed the sedan in one of the undercover Horses, one with Palestinian license plates, followed closely behind by other elements of the undercover convoy. The Speaker closed the distance with the sedan and then swerved sharply to the left to knock it to a sand-and-gravel embankment at the side of the road. The rest of the armada raced in to close the sedan in a hermetic circle of unmarked military vehicles.

"Both of you come out with your hands up," one of the Speakers demanded in an authoritative Arabic laced with the accent of a man from northern Galilee. "Lift your shirts over your heads and turn around."[15] The Israeli protocol identified anyone wearing a bomb as a threat, and lethal firepower could then be used; wires wrapped around a device worn on someone's torso were considered ample probable cause in wartime. Anyone refusing the command was, under Israeli statutes, also deemed a threat. The driver of the vehicle seemed apprehensive and stuttered in his step as the veteran Speaker yelled his orders through the high-volume roar of a police loudspeaker. The passenger was even less compliant and far more hesitant; he held a small satchel. Once again the Speaker demanded that the passenger raise his arms skyward and drop the bag, otherwise he would be killed. The passenger hesitated, and then jerked, trying to make a sudden movement. The driver then attempted to trigger the device, prompting the Ya'mas operators to open fire. The fusillade of fire was brief. Before the driver could escape or the passenger push a toggle switch or press the button activating his device, both men collapsed in a spray of automatic weapons fire. The driver was killed; the passenger was hit multiple times, but his wounds were not life-threatening.

Route 60 was closed for hours after the incident. The area was evacuated in order to allow Border Guard and Israel National Police EOD experts

---

* Identity withheld for security considerations.

the opportunity to examine the body—and the bag—and to neutralize any explosive components. The EOD specialists worked with six-wheeled Wheelbarrow robots, and with wire cutters and raw nerve. Shin Bet investigators who worked the case long into the night couldn't assess what the bomber's final target was. It was hard for them to calculate how many lives had been saved by the interception on Route 60.

The Ya'mas began to carry out a dozen or so missions a week; each success brought on more and more work. Even by Israeli standards, the unit's operational responsibilities were becoming intensive. The unit's reputation grew, as word of this small yet incredibly cohesive band of fighters spread through the security services. Officers serving in the IDF soon requested transfers into the Border Guard in order to volunteer into this force. Eighteen-year-olds who had dreamed their entire childhoods of serving in the paratroopers now requested the chance to try out for the Border Guard undercover unit.

The fires of the intifada intensified that cold and rainy March. The war was already eighteen months and running, with no letup in sight. Shin Bet intercepts of terrorist chatter indicated that the conflict was intensifying.

CHAPTER FOUR

The Deadly Spring

Holidays are important to Israelis—all-important, in fact. The Israeli calendar consists of four seasons: before and after the New Year, and before and after Passover. Holidays enable Israelis to take a breath and slow down from a self-imposed stomach-acid churn of a lifestyle. The New Year and the high holidays are a solemn time for Israelis. Passover, the weeklong holiday of freedom and redemption that commemorates the Jewish exodus from slavery in Egypt, initiates the start of spring and a joyous time of valleys turned green by the winter's rain before the harsh reality of summer sizzles in.

Yet there was nothing joyous about this approaching spring. March 2002 had been a brutal month for suicide bombings. The month had yet to come to an end, and already there had been seven suicide bombings resulting in thirty-three deaths and more than three hundred wounded. One of the worst attacks was carried out in Jerusalem's Rehavia section only one hundred meters from Prime Minister Sharon's official residence. At 10:30 p.m. on the night of March 9, 2002, a Hamas suicide bomber blew himself up inside the crowded Moment Café on the corner of Gaza and Ben-Maimon Streets. The force of the blast destroyed the popular night spot and killed eleven people and wounded fifty. A sense of unrelenting peril gripped the nation. People still said "Yihye Beseder" ("It'll be OK") to one another as they passed, though fewer and fewer actually believed it to be true.

There was little good news that March offering the hint that things would be OK. The ferocity and scope of the conflict intensified daily. Some inside the Palestinian Authority's security apparatus, some who had been trained by the CIA[1] as well as Jordanian and Egyptian intelligence, went off the reservation—they took their tradecraft and weapons and openly fought Israel. Others, primarily from the blue, or regular patrol, police, haplessly watched from the sidelines: If they intervened and arrested terror suspects, they would be branded as collaborators; if they openly assisted the terror factions, then they became legitimate targets for the Israelis. Arafat controlled the street, and he used the lawlessness for his own political objectives.

There was a sense in Israel that the intifada had become a total war—a war that had to be won. At Ya'mas headquarters, they knew that the uprising was a full-scale conflict. Still, the operators and officers were relieved that the Passover break was approaching. The workload in recent months had been overwhelming and the level of terrorist activity was mind-boggling. The men needed a break.

Holidays were sacrosanct inside the Israeli security establishment. Unit commanders went to great lengths to allow as many soldiers and policemen as possible to be home with their families for religious celebrations. Uzi Levy was always sensitive to the need of his men to go home, a team leader said of the unit commander. He was very sensitive to their mental and physical makeup and realized that if he could give his men a break, he demanded that they go home and be with their parents, wives, and girlfriends.

The conscript operators who were given leave slept late the morning of March 27. Their fathers took care of the last-minute shopping and preparations; their mothers had woken up before dawn to fire up the stove and take care of the many courses of what promised to be a stomach-filling feast. The older operators couldn't sleep late. They were woken up by the greatest alarm clock known to man—children jumping in bed hugging their long-absent fathers and not letting go. Before daring to return their children's hugs, though, the operators checked their Motorola pagers. The West Bank was under full military lockdown for the holiday, but there was an Arab League summit in Beirut, and it was rumored that the Saudis would suggest some drastic proposal that would recognize the State of Israel. Overtures of peace were always met by acts of senseless violence.

On the night of March 27, somewhere near Nablus, at the IDF base where the Ya'mas was headquartered, those on duty made their way to the dining hall for the military Seder. The Ya'mas Seder table personified the mosaic that was the Border Guard: The men seated around the festively decorated table, complete with white tablecloth and police-issued Haggadah prayer booklets, consisted of Jewish, Muslim, and Christian policemen.

Abdel Aziz Baset el-Odeh was deep inside Tulkarm when the IDF military curfew was enforced over the million-plus inhabitants of the West Bank for the Passover holiday. His handlers were not concerned by the closures; there were always ways around them. Odeh was a critical cog in a Hamas operation that had been planned, paid for, and implemented by Abbas al-Sayyid, an American-educated biomedical engineer with a round face and a full head of salt-and-pepper hair, who commanded one of the most ambitious and lethal terror cells in the West Bank, which operated in both Nablus and Tulkarm. Abbas al-Sayyid was both a political and military leader, and he maintained communications with Hamas offices in Lebanon and Syria through which money and instructions were funneled to the territories.[2] Wherever al-Sayyid traveled, he was protected by a phalanx of heavily armed Hamas gunmen. The man who would wear the explosive vest was, of course, disposable.

Abdel Aziz Baset el-Odeh had been secreted in a remote part of town, where he was ushered into a safe house far from prying eyes and possible Shin Bet informers. A light meal, from one of the city's takeout stands, was brought to him along with some condiments and yogurt. He prayed. As preparations were made for his busy day ahead, he was taken to a room with a pillow and a woolen blanket folded on top of a mattress. The window to Odeh's room was gated shut. He slept under heavy guard his last night on earth.

The day's work began early, just after dawn, on the morning of Wednesday, March 27, 2002. Odeh washed and prayed. He ate a light breakfast. Dressed in a pair of blue jeans and a long-sleeve white shirt, he put on a brown leather vest and a green Hamas headband. One of the Hamas representatives handed him an M16; the thirty-round magazine had no bullets in it. A photographer snapped a hundred or so photos against a white wall backdrop as Odeh struck combat poses aiming the weapon. Then he was videotaped issuing his final manifesto. Officially, he had already ceased to exist. He already had one foot in paradise.

A Hamas operative shaved Odeh's mustache and beard. Another applied the makeup, including generous layers of lipstick and mascara; a straight store-bought wig was fastened to Odeh's closely cropped hair. An explosive vest with pockets, filled with more than ten kilograms of high explosives and a lethal payload of tightly packed ball bearings, screws, and nails, was placed around Odeh's torso. Hamas commanders watched as Odeh dressed: He put on a pair of women's shoes, blue feminine-cut jeans, a silk blouse, and a brown leather jacket with a leopard-print collar. A forged Israeli Teudat Zehut, or ID card, in a woman's name completed the disguise.[3] The man who would drive Abdel Aziz Baset el-Odeh to his target, Fathi Khattib, had purchased a sedan with yellow Israeli license plates using cash given to him by al-Sayyid.

Odeh was very familiar with the day's target—Netanya. The coastal city, a mix of a resort and an industrial town, boasted pristine beaches that had become popular with British and French expatriates seeking retirement with beach access. During more peaceful times, Odeh had made a living by stealing cars from the city and driving them to chop shops in the Palestinian Authority. The drive from Tulkarm to Netanya, even via the back roads and smuggler paths, was quick. Odeh and his driver crossed an invisible point separating Israel from the Palestinian Authority and into the Israeli-Arab city of Baqa el-Gharbiya. Once inside Israel proper, it was an effortless journey along Israel's interconnecting roads and highways to reach any location in the country. The two drove to the Ha'Sharon Mall located just off the coastal highway, but the shopping plaza was virtually empty. Perplexed, the two drove around the city looking for crowds, but the streets were empty. Everyone had gone home to prepare for the Seder. Hamas operational planners had failed to realize just how early in the day Israel shut down for the holiday.

Odeh and his driver feared returning to Tulkarm without having carried out their mission, so they drove south—first to Herzliya, and then to Tel Aviv. Both cities looked liked ghost towns. The sun was already beginning to set, and Odeh ordered his driver back to Netanya. There were hotels along the beach that Odeh remembered. They were usually full during the holiday.

The drive from Tel Aviv to Netanya took less than twenty minutes. Khattib headed toward the seaside and pulled into a quiet area near the beachfront hotels. He let Odeh out of the car and then drove back to Baqa el-Gharbiya to get rid of the car. Odeh stumbled slowly away from the car, walking clumsily in his costume and weighted down explosive vest. The Mediterranean waves crashed to his right as he walked to 7 King David Street—the Park Hotel.

The Park Hotel had managed to fill its rooms and banquet halls with Israelis—and some tourists—eager to celebrate a grandiose Passover feast with their large and extended families together without having to cook and clean at home. Some 250 people, including children and the elderly, were already sitting inside the hotel's main banquet room. Many more were in front of the hotel, dressed in their holiday finest, slowly filtering their way inside. A lone security guard stood watch at the hotel entrance. Simply overwhelmed by the number of people trying to get in, he waved his magnetometer around whoever he could stop; most walked through without being searched. Odeh walked into the hotel without even a summary glance. He walked calmly past the check-in desk and straight for the banquet hall where the sounds of families conducting several private and joyous Seders could already be heard. Odeh calmly made his way toward the center of the room. Mothers snapped photographs as the young children asked the traditional Four Questions. Older men raised their wineglasses; many of those who were in attendance were Holocaust survivors.

A blinding flash was followed by an ear-crushing thud. Acrid black smoke quickly filled the room. The force of the blast was so powerful that computer screens in the reception area were obliterated by the ball bearings turned indiscriminate warheads. The destruction froze time for a brief second.

It was seven thirty in the evening when the Motorola pagers began to vibrate in the homes of the security commanders throughout Israel.

The Pereg family was deep into a discussion at the Seder table. The large extended family, consisting of brothers, four sisters, brothers-in-law, and their children, were talking about food, sports, and the decaying security reality inside Israel. Patrick, whose jovial smile always served as cover for the dangerous world he lived in, was more vocal this night than on most others. Chief Inspector Patrick Pereg had recently been promoted to be the Ya'mas operations officer.

Known to just about everyone solely by his first name, Patrick hailed from Ofakim, a desolate poor town built for Jewish immigrants from North Africa and India following the establishment of the State of Israel, located southwest of the Gaza Strip, near the Egyptian border. He was conscripted into the Border Guards in 1990 and served as a combat platoon commander. Patrick joined the unit shortly before Eli Avram was killed, and he grew up inside the Ya'mas during the vicious firefights against the embryonic emergence of a hardcore Hamas presence in Judea and Samaria. Patrick was, according to many, a natural for the dangerous yet cunning world of Ya'mas operations. He was soft-spoken yet courageously confident; his personality was ideal for being integrated into a team of very similar-minded men. Patrick, some of his teammates commented, oozed charisma, yet he fit seamlessly into the social melting pot of his Ya'mas team. His teammates—including Druze operators and newcomers to Israel from the former Soviet Union—took a protective liking to him. He was always smiling and his full head of black hair was recognizable from a mile away. "Patrick was confident and capable," one of his teammates commented. "Anyone who worked with him, regardless of the complexity of the operation, always felt a sense that it was going to be OK in the end. When he was with you on an operation, you simply had a sense of reassurance."[4]

Patrick fit the casting call as an operator—muscular, athletic, and capable of erupting into explosive action in a flash. But he was cerebral in his approach to special operations warfare and was inherently always consumed by the minutiae of operational detail that was often the difference between life and death on a dark night in the West Bank. Patrick rose quickly through the ranks—first sergeant, then newly commissioned officer, and then team leader. The promotion to operations officer was recognition of his skill and his promise. Uzi Levy's deputy, Erez Yefet, said that if he was ever commander of the unit, Patrick would be his number two.[5]

But the promotion created newfound responsibilities and concerns. There seemed to be a burden weighing heavily on Patrick's mind; at the Passover table, his newfound seriousness was evident to his closest family members. Before his pager buzzed with the official police communiqué concerning the Passover bombing, Patrick told his brother-in-law, "I am willing to die for my country."[6]

Shortly following the news from Netanya, Patrick, like many of the Ya'mas operators who had been home for the holidays, was already making his way back to the Samarian hills to suit up and await operational orders. The magnitude of the suicide bombing had yet to sink in; the fact that the bomber had struck on a holiday, and that his target consisted of many senior citizens who had survived Hitler's death camps, made this crime even more egregious. The Ya'mas operators listened intently to *Galei Tzahal*, the IDF radio station that was the nation's most popular music and news service, as the first reports from Netanya came through. The first-person accounts of the carnage, broadcast live from the crime scene, were absolutely chilling. Witnesses spoke of the horrible cries from the maimed and wounded. One fireman described the white walls and white marble floors covered inch deep in blood and flesh. The death count was already high. Fifteen were confirmed dead an hour after the attack. Hundreds were reported to be critically wounded. Scores more were expected to die, the radio reports warned. March 2002 had already been the deadliest month since the eruption of the intifada. This latest attack, the Passover Massacre, would ultimately claim the lives of thirty-one victims.

Throughout Israel, family heads had stopped conducting their Seders and sat glued to their television sets. The "Breaking News" from Netanya filled hours of live feed coverage on Israel's Channel One, the BBC, and CNN. At Ya'mas HQ, inside the operations center, the remote control worked overtime as officers channel surfed to see if anyone was reporting anything new. The telephone lines rang without stop. The military radio frequencies were hopping with back-and-forth traffic. Everyone knew what was coming next, but first Israel mobilized for war. The IDF called up twenty thousand reservists. Special operations units rushed to brigade and division HQs in the West Bank to ready their forces for the inevitable combat assignments.

It wasn't until dawn the day after Netanya that the gravity of the Passover Massacre was truly felt. World leaders condemned the attack in unequivocal horror. Kofi Annan, the United Nations secretary-general, called the attack "morally repugnant"; United States president George W. Bush said that "this callous cold-blooded killing must stop." The bombing in Netanya unified the usually fractious Israeli government, though there was little need for Israel's television ambassadors to hit the airwaves and plead their case. Throughout Israel, tank transporters, towing the state-of-the-art of Israel's armor might toward forward staging areas, moved along the country's roadways toward the West Bank cities.

On the night of March 28, the Ya'mas was placed on alert to serve as an on-call rapid deployment force in case of a terrorist attack somewhere in the area. The unit shared this duty with other special operations and reconnaissance units in the divisional command. Usually being days on alert came and went without incident; a response to a report of a ticking bomb traveling on this road, or an unidentified man with a weapon seen near a settlement. But the terrorist groups liked to strike in rapid succession to illustrate that although an Israeli response would be harsh and swift, they would not be deterred. Sometimes a follow-up attack was perpetrated out of jealousy. A rival terror faction would often launch a quick strike following a major suicide strike in order to grab some headlines of their own. It was 2100 hours when the emergency request came through the divisional command. Patrick was the on-call duty officer.

A Hamas gunman armed with an AK-47 and as many thirty-round ammunition magazines as he could carry had infiltrated the settlement of Elon Moreh, situated in the Samarian hills near Nablus, on the slopes of Mount Kabir. Elon Moreh, founded in 1980, was home to some 1,250 residents, most of them Orthodox Jews; in the Old Testament, Elon Moreh is the location where God said to Abraham, "To your descendants I will give this land." The lone wolf terrorist cut a hole in the settlement main security fence and proceeded to break into a target of opportunity: the home of the Gavish family. He was uninterested in seizing hostages in order to negotiate some sort of exchange. He had no political agenda. His mission was to kill as many people as he could until he was cut down in a hail of gunfire. The terrorist shot and killed David and Rachel Gavish, both fifty, and their daughter-in-law's father who was visiting for the holiday. The Gavishes' son, Avraham, a veteran of the Sayeret Mat'kal commando unit, was also shot and killed after he chased the terrorist upstairs; Avraham's wife, Na'ama, and two-year-old daughter, Daria, hid under the kitchen table in terrified silence. The settlement's security contingent responded to the Gavish home, but the terrorist kept them at bay with dedicated bursts fired from an upstairs window.

Elon Moreh was very close to Ya'mas headquarters. Patrick heard of the attack on the regional emergency frequency and assembled the unit. The Ya'mas was the first force to respond to the barricade.

Patrick and his Ya'mas force reached the outer perimeter, raced through the gunfire toward the embattled home, and began to engage the terrorist by firing at the window where he was returning fire. Patrick was poised to order the assault, when Colonel Yossi Adiri, the commander of the Samaria Brigade responsible for the sector, ordered the Ya'mas to stand down. The Ya'ma'm, the national counterterrorist and hostage-rescue team, had been summoned. They were the hostage-rescue specialists—they would handle the call.

Patrick stood outside the door immobilized by anger. Members of his force were perplexed and angry. "We were outside the door and we could have resolved the situation quickly and effectively," one of the operators reflected. "So what if the regional commander ordered us to stop? Patrick should have simply pulled his earpiece to the ground and gone in anyway. He could have always said that he didn't hear the order to stand down."[7]

The Ya'ma'm arrived shortly, as did elements of Sayeret Mat'kal. The intervention specialists deployed and quickly burst into the Gavish family home, killing the gunman as they methodically cleared the house room by room. Patrick ordered his men back to base—the men felt insulted and full of rage. There is no standing down when there is an active shooter, they argued, some mumbling under their breath as they passed the colonels and generals who had arrived on scene. The operators swore to themselves that they would never again let anyone tell them to stop when a terrorist was on the other side of the door.

Few Ya'mas operators slept the night of Elon Moreh. The operators lay in their bunks and stared toward the ceiling, trying to keep the stomach acid from racing up their airways. The rotor thrust of helicopters flying in every direction added to the anxiety and anger of the night. Patrick changed that night, some of the Ya'mas veterans recalled; they thought the decision to obey the order had troubled him.

Prime Minister Sharon was a man known for impulsive decisions of destruction, but the military action against Arafat's Palestinian Authority was a fuse that burned slowly inside him for a year. Sharon, reportedly, wanted to go in and eradicate the Palestinian terrorist infrastructure following the Tel Aviv Dolphi Disco bombing in June 2001, when a sixteen-year-old West Bank teenager blew himself up at the entrance to a seafront discotheque in southern Tel Aviv, killing 21 teenagers and wounding 132 more; most of the victims were recent newcomers to Israel from the former Soviet Union who probably did not understand the complexities of the security threats connected to a Friday night out. The attack, one specifically targeting youngsters, was particularly abhorrent, and many expected Sharon to act immediately and decisively against the Palestinian Authority and its safe havens for terror. But the Israeli prime minister reined in his instinctive impulses, perhaps wary of an American reaction. The September 11, 2001, attacks against the United States changed the equation for good. Palestinians in the West Bank were televised dancing in the streets celebrating the deaths of so many Americans. As the world wept for the thousands killed that horrible day, the Palestinian cause was inextricably becoming linked to al-Qaeda and the bloodthirst of the Jihadist movement. Yet still Sharon waited. The Israeli response to the ramping up of Palestinian violence had been surgical and special operations–focused. Sharon waited. He waited for Israel's 9/11 before authorizing the large-scale military effort he believed was required.

In the early morning hours of March 29, 2002, the IDF launched Operation Defensive Shield—the largest Israeli military incursion into the West Bank since the 1967 Six Day War. The objective of the operation was to confiscate and destroy illegal weapons and bombing materials; destroy bomb-building and rocket-production facilities; choke the freewheeling environment in which the terrorists planned, prepared, and executed their attacks; and, most important, neutralize the terrorist commanders and operatives behind the suicide bombings. It was an ambitious undertaking; IDF commanders were concerned that the casualties on both sides would be horrific. Some senior intelligence officers warned that hundreds of Israeli soldiers would be killed.[8] But the killing of Israeli civilians had to be stopped.

The IDF quickly reentered and recaptured the cities in Area A. Ramallah, with Arafat's *Muqata* compound, was a primary objective. Marginalizing Arafat as a mere prisoner inside a besieged fortress was a strategic play. Sharon knew that Arafat would become a martyr should Israeli forces kill him, so they destroyed much of his West Bank presidential palace, shut off the power, and let Arafat and his commanders live inside his Ramallah lair without running water and toilets that flushed. Israeli armor and infantry pushed quickly and decisively into Bethlehem, Nablus, Tulkarm, and Jenin. The battles for many of these cities were fierce. The combat was street-to-street, house-to-house, and room-to-room; in many instances, especially inside the old Kasbahs, the fighting was hand-to-hand. The combat was particularly bloody in Jenin, the city that the Palestinians themselves touted as the suicide capital of the world; nearly half of the suicide bombers that had attacked Israel during the intifada hailed from this northern West Bank town. The battle for Jenin would last twelve days and result in twenty-three Israeli combat fatalities. In one battle, a force of paratroopers was led into an ambush and thirteen soldiers were killed; naval commandos fought a pitched battle to retrieve body parts that had been seized by Palestinian militants.

Israeli forces captured tons of Palestinian weapons and bomb-making materials during Operation Defensive Shield. Hundreds of terrorists were killed in the fighting and scores more captured. But the suicide bombings continued. March, in fact, continued to be one of the bloodiest months in Israel's history. On March 29, two people were killed—including a teenage girl who had gone to the market for her mother—when a female suicide bomber belonging to the al-Aqsa Martyrs Brigade blew herself up in a supermarket in the Kiryat Yovel neighborhood in Jerusalem. A day later, a suicide bomber blew himself up inside a Tel Aviv café. And, on March 31, fifteen people were killed and more than forty critically wounded when a Hamas suicide bomber blew himself up inside the Matza Restaurant, adjacent to a gas station near Haifa's Grand Canyon shopping mall. In all, 133 Israelis were killed in March 2002; more than 500 had been seriously wounded. As fighting raged inside Ramallah, Bethlehem, Nablus, Tulkarm, and most ferociously in Jenin, many Israelis wondered when—if at all—would the killings end?

Operation Defensive Shield was something of a time-out for the Ya'mas—the unit was used to operating in the shadows, immersing itself in the hostile landscape, and not marching forward alongside columns of armor and mechanized infantry. Uzi Levy welcomed the break. It allowed him to send some of his men home so that they could reconnect pieces of the shattered holiday with their families. Leaves were granted in shifts. Levy tried to maintain a sizable force ready to respond when needed. Chief Inspector Patrick Pereg took the call on the night of April 3. Inside the operations room at Ya'mas headquarters, the intelligence and operations staff reviewed aerial photographs and read through the lengthy Shin Bet files. Too many cigarettes were smoked to the filter those chilly spring nights, chased down by gallons of strong, bitter coffee.

The target assigned to the Ya'mas was Mohammed Kapisha, one of the top-ranking facilitators in the Hamas military hierarchy. Kapisha was the man who controlled the flow of weapons and explosives, and his business was acquiring AK-47s, sniper scopes, RPGs, and high-grade military explosives for terror cells that attacked Israel's cities. His smuggling networks were extensive and connected surplus and black market tools of war from the Palestinian Authority's arsenals, from Jordan, and from the lawless frontiers in Sinai. The extended Kapisha clan was well represented in all the terrorist factions throughout the Hebron region. On June 29, 1995, Tahar Kapisha, a high-ranking Hamas commander, was killed in a firefight with the Ya'ma'm who were out to arrest him for his role in attacks that killed six Israelis; Master Sergeant Doron Ben-Zachari, a Ya'ma'm team leader, was killed in the shoot-out. Tahar Kapisha's cell had been responsible for the deaths of nine Israelis and the wounding of dozens more.[9]

Like his cousin, Mohammed Kapisha lived on the run. He moved from safe house to safe house in the attempt to stay one step ahead of Israeli intelligence. He traveled with one bodyguard, one man who would have his back—his brother. His immediate family lived in the Abu Sneina neighborhood in southern Hebron, notorious for being a Hamas stronghold, and that's where the Shin Bet located him.

Hebron was a remarkable city of great contrast* and conflicting religious claims; many of the city's landmarks were where massacres had been committed. Situated in the Judean Hills, Hebron is the largest city in the West Bank, with a population of approximately 250,000 Palestinians and approximately 1,200 Israelis; Israeli settlements, such as Kiryat Arba, west of the city, had grown from extended neighborhoods to full-fledged cities of their own. Everything connected to Hebron revolved around conflict. Any incident in the city had the potential to ignite an international incident.

Abu Sneina was a congested neighborhood dominated by multistory dwellings that had illegal additions built atop illegal additions. Narrow alleys connected winding streets that interconnected to dead ends. Many of the residents were allegiant to one terror faction or another and weapons were everywhere. Ya'mas had spent several days working on Kapisha, and on April 3, S., the Ya'mas team leader, placed his outline of the operation on Patrick's desk. Patrick, as unit operations officer, would have to approve the assault plan before taking it up the chain of command. Uzi Levy would have to sign off on it, and then bring it to the Hebron Brigade commander, Colonel Dror Weinberg, for his ultimate approval.[10]

Colonel Weinberg had a unique pedigree to oversee the complexities and risks concerning the arrest operation for Kapisha. Weinberg had grown up in the ultra-secretive Sayeret Mat'kal and Sayeret Maglan reconnaissance commando units before rising up the senior ranks of command in the paratroopers. Weinberg understood the dangerous intricacy of such operations, and he knew the complexity of the landscape better than most. Hebron was considered the most difficult sector in the West Bank—only officers destined for the top echelons of command received that posting.[11]

Inside the brigade ops center, the Ya'mas command team utilized an old overhead projector to transmit the hand-scribbled clear slides to the canvas screen that had been weathered to a light shade of brown by years of nicotine. The Ya'mas officers sold their plan of attack, as Colonel Weinberg—and senior

---

* Hebron—under the guidelines of the 1995 Oslo Agreement and the subsequent Hebron Agreement—was divided into two sectors. Sector H1 was controlled by the Palestinian Authority and Sector H2 was controlled by Israel; H1 constitutes roughly 80 percent of the city's total area and H2 consists of approximately 20 percent. The division was an accommodation to secure the approximately seven hundred Israeli settlers that lived in the city.

Shin Bet agents—listened intently. Each element of Kapisha's arrest had to be articulated, while Weinberg and his officers reviewed the intelligence and the step-by-step assault plan. Weinberg also had to coordinate the backup force and mobilize the rescue assets—including tanks and D9s—in case something went wrong.

As operations officer, Patrick's place was at the CP with the unit's commanders coordinating the flow of intelligence and manpower into a decisive attack force. This was a large operation, and the assault force was comprised of members from both teams put together into one cohesive assault element. But Patrick wanted to be on the line, with the operators. No one in the unit questioned his decision to participate in the assault.

Patrick made it home on April 3—the drive from the field to his front door took approximately an hour. His wife, Ela, had dated Patrick for eight years and had accompanied him throughout his journey up the ladder of command in the unit; the two married on March 23, 2000, six months before the intifada erupted. Their young son, Elay, was ten months old. As devoted as Patrick was to the unit and his men, his wife and son quickly became the meaning of his existence. Ela, like all the Ya'mas wives, had worried in silence on those dark nights when Patrick was inside Jenin or Tulkarm, under fire from all corners, so far away in another world yet in reality so close to home. It was one of the haunting complexities of the war that was difficult for people outside the Israeli–Palestinian conflict to fathom. The comforts of home and a firefight in a Hamas-controlled neighborhood were usually separated by nothing more than a sixty-minute drive.

On the morning of April 4, Patrick asked to be awoken at five thirty, so that he could take his time and spend a few moments of quality time at home before embarking on the Kapisha raid. But he overslept. When he finally dragged himself out of bed and dressed, he quickly grabbed his car keys and his pistol and kissed Ela goodbye. As he headed out the door, he stopped himself and returned to give his wife a proper kiss.[12]

Drones were dispatched over Abu Sneina late in the morning of April 4, 2002. The drone, known by the Hebrew acronym *Ma'z'lat*, or light unmanned aircraft, was one of the Israeli contributions to modern warfare. It flew silently over the target and high enough so Hamas sentries that patrolled the neighborhood would be unlikely to notice it overhead. The images that the drone returned to the forward operational command post were grainy, but still clear enough to identify the targeted location and to provide the raiding party with real-time intelligence feeds. Several vehicles moved in a convoy from the brigade staging area toward Kapisha's hideout. The entire West Bank was under a military curfew; the streets that the convoy moved through were empty. The stores along the roadways were all shuttered with metal gates; many of the shutters were littered with graffiti supporting the local armed factions. The weather was crisp. The bright blue skies were deceiving. The low clouds hinted that a storm was close at hand.

The house where Mohammed Kapisha was hiding out was a light stone multistory square of a building that sat at the base of a hill. The plan called for the unit to surround the location and for one of the Speakers to call for Kapisha and his brother to surrender.[13] The hope was that the presence of the *qawat al-hasa*, or Israeli Special Forces, would be enough to convince Kapisha and his brother to surrender.

Patrick relayed the instructions the assault force received from the command post to his operators, and then relayed the convoy's progression back to the high-ranking officers watching the events in real time. The vehicles moved deep inside Abu Sneina, passing the Wadi al Haria valley to the west along a winding road that ran north to south, from the bottom of the hill toward the congested apartment buildings where it was believed Kapisha was hiding. The vehicles pulled up in front of his building and the operators emerged and rushed it. In the command post, several of the officers took deep drags on their Time cigarettes. Some of the officers nervously bit their nails.

The Ya'mas moved silently around the building to make sure all points of escape were covered. With the perimeter sealed, Patrick removed a stun grenade from a pouch on his load-bearing gear and threw it toward the building. The Speaker then grabbed the microphone in the armored jeep and called for Kapisha to surrender. There was silence. The Speaker summoned the two men to remove themselves from the premises, hands in the air, and to surrender. Again silence.

But then gunfire erupted. At first the shots were isolated; lone rounds dispatched from somewhere in the periphery. The sporadic gunfire was followed by dedicated bursts of AK-47 and M16 fire coming from multiple concealed locations. The operators moved forward and sought cover, attempting to pinpoint the sources of Palestinian fire and to engage the threats. But the gunfire intensified. Patrick took aim with his M4 carbine, toward windows and openings where a threat could be hiding, and he located a gunman bearing down on the Ya'mas force. Patrick fired a short burst. "I hit him," he said, letting his partner know that one of the Palestinian targets had been taken out; the wounded man was Kapisha's brother and bodyguard. The operators held their ground around the besieged building. Patrick ran approximately fifty meters to the left in order to connect with Abu Ahmed,* a veteran Speaker and medic, and told his squad to push tighter around the building. Patrick peered through his field glasses, attempting to figure out where the additional sources of Palestinian gunfire were coming from. Abu Sneina had suddenly turned into a war zone. Dozens of weapons now opened up on the Ya'mas task force as the neighborhood was awoken to the presence of the Israeli commandos in the area. One of the Ya'mas sergeants yelled to Patrick to take cover, seeing that he was exposed. Rounds were now bouncing off the Ya'mas vehicles, pinging as they impacted. Palestinian snipers, some firing from significant distances, had begun to engage the Ya'mas raiding force. The shots were pinpoint and improving in accuracy.

A lone shot whipped in the wind into the Israeli lines. Patrick buckled before he hit the ground, falling in a sort of slow motion. Ron,† a Ya'mas operator from a Druze village in northern Israel, didn't even think that Patrick had been shot. "There was no blood, no wound, and no cry for help indicating that he was hit," Ron remembered. Ron crawled to Patrick to see what had happened; he tried to talk to him and hoped to see some sort of reaction. Patrick looked up, but the expression was vacant and fleeting. Patrick's mouth moved

---

* A pseudonym—true identity withheld for security considerations.

† A pseudonym—true identity withheld for security considerations.

slightly, but no words came out. "Patrick is hit! I repeat, Patrick is hit!" the mission commander screamed into his radio, interrupting the matter-of-fact transmissions that the officers were used to sending over the airwaves, even when taking incoming fire. "Patrick is hit," he repeated several more times.[14] At the command post, a numbing silence overtook the men watching the drone feed.

Abu Ahmed, one of the more experienced combat medics in the raiding force, rushed to Patrick's aide. The operators pummeled the apartment block with fire in order to cover Abu Ahmed as he rushed across the open ground under a hail of gunfire. Abu Ahmed immediately opened Patrick's body armor to see where the bullet might have entered, but he found no traumatic injury—there was no evidence of an entry wound or even any signs of trauma.

Yefet, the Ya'mas deputy commander, rushed toward Abu Sneina the moment he heard that Patrick had been shot. He grabbed several Ya'mas officers from the CP and loaded them up into his armored jeep. Yefet drove directly into the Palestinian fire and positioned his vehicle right in front of Patrick to shield the wounded officer and the men who attended to him from the Palestinian fire. Patrick was loaded into the rear of Yefet's jeep to be rushed to the brigade aid station, and that's when Abu Ahmed located a small entry wound in the lower left side of Patrick's back. The bullet had penetrated a spot less than a centimeter below the lower edge of his body armor.

Chief Inspector Patrick Pereg was declared dead shortly after he was examined by the divisional surgeon in Hebron. He was the third Ya'mas operator to be killed in the line of duty in the twelve years that the unit had been operational.

The battle in Abu Sneina raged until dark. The Ya'mas force grappled with the gut-numbing news that their comrade had been killed as they maintained the siege of the Kapisha stronghold. The operation was supposed to have been a hit-and-run arrest, but it ended up becoming a series of close-quarter battles against entrenched gangs of heavily armed gunmen who never seemed to run out of ammunition. Mechanized infantrymen from the Hebron Brigade joined in the fight. Heavily armored Puma APCs, vehicles designed to withstand RPGs and antitank rounds, pushed forward amid endless hails of gunfire. Night-vision goggles were removed from bins inside the armored jeeps. A Merkava main battle tank that had rumbled into the neighborhood unleashed a 120mm high-explosive round into the building, resulting in a thunderous explosion. The walls of the building crumbled into debris and dust after the massive five-inch shell punched a mighty hole through the foundation; the flames from the ensuing fires illuminated the sky in an eerie orange glow. Finally, as was the case in so many of these battles, the D9 was summoned. Two operators, soldiers from the Engineering Corps, directed the fourteen-foot-wide bulldozer over Kapisha's home. The fifty-four-ton monster churned the pavement as it crushed the smoldering remnants of the building into rubble.

A search of the rubble yielded nothing. The Ya'mas team searched the building and the nearby alleys and hiding spots for Kapisha, but he had vanished in the confusion and chaos of the battle. His wounded brother was left behind, though. Abandoned to fend for himself and to buy time enabling Kapisha to flee, the brother had been taken into custody by the Ya'mas during the battle. Kapisha would remain a fugitive for another month.*

Yuri had been at home when his pager buzzed. The Soviet-born operator, like the old-timers in the unit who started in 1990 and had been around when Eli Avram was killed in Jenin, looked at Patrick as one of the anchors of the force. Patrick mentored many of the operators, especially those who were new immigrants—from the former Soviet Union and many of its far-reaching former Asian republics—and he had served as a reassuring presence when newcomers to the State of Israel also became newcomers to the world of undercover counterterrorist operations.

---

* Kapisha was ultimately apprehended by reconnaissance elements from the 1st Golani Infantry Brigade during Operation Another Wind, a large-scale sweep of Hebron by infantry and armored units. More than 150 terrorist suspects were arrested in the dragnet, and hundreds of assault rifles, antitank weapons, thousands of rounds of ammunition, and enough bomb-building materials to equip a battalion of suicide bombers were seized. Kapisha had hid in the city's hospital, and attempted to talk his way out of the Israeli operation dressed as a surgeon, but the twenty-one-year-old fugitive proved to be a better man on the run than medical doctor impostor. Kapisha had used the hospital, including patient rooms, as a warehouse space for part of his arsenal.

The notion that something could happen to Patrick was inconceivable to Yuri. When word came over the unit's internal communications network that he had been killed, Yuri grabbed his car keys and crossed the thirty miles from his front door to the main gate of the unit headquarters in Formula One time. He arrived at the Ya'mas base to see some of the unit's support staff openly weeping. The operators, still in their combat gear, sat outside their quarters with their heads bowed down in sorrow. The post-mission briefing had been tear-filled.

There were discussions under way in the open-air courtyard about what had happened. Some of the operators said that Patrick didn't have to be on the operation, but that the events at Elon Moreh had changed him.[15] Others wondered why he hadn't sought cover. He had been fired upon enough times to know the risks. The operators sat in the soothing spring air under the West Bank stars and talked among themselves, as they chain-smoked cigarettes at a wooden picnic table. There was a numbing seriousness to the back-and-forth as the hours dragged on into the predawn of a night when few slept. The discussions were sobering. Patrick's death made the operators realize just how routine the extraordinarily dangerous had become for them.

Yuri walked past Patrick's office and went inside. He rubbed his eyes to deflect the effects of his weeping, but the tears still ran down his face. He couldn't believe that Patrick was gone.

There were enormous psychological pressures at work inside the minds of each operator; most of those who did not make the cut didn't fail because they weren't strong enough or couldn't shoot straight—they failed because they couldn't withstand the turning of the vise tightening around their heads incessantly. The men in the unit often referred to their lives as one of internal switches being flipped on and off. There was the concentration and analytical evaluation switch that had to be applied before an operation. There was the patience and guile switch that had to be flipped en route to a target. There was the adrenaline and adrenaline-fueled courage switch during the actual arrest and the more-than-likely shoot-out that would ensue. There was the pressure switch when word came to headquarters of an active shooter somewhere within reach and the unit had to drop whatever it was doing. There was also the heads hanging low switch when word of an attack came over their pagers, and the men were unable to prevent the carnage. There was also the switch that turned off all the other switches when they went home to be with their wives and children. And, of course, the unit being on-call without letup, the disappointment and apology switch when a call-out required that they leave their wife and kids hours after returning home from being in the field for weeks or longer.

Most operators candidly admitted that the backbone of the unit was the support that they received from their families. There were very few divorces inside the unit during this desperate period. Children were born without truly having their fathers at home for the first few years of their lives, but the families survived. And when there was a member of the extended family killed in the line of duty, the unit pulled together to show a united front.

Throughout the night, elements of the unit headed to assist Patrick's widow and family in making the necessary arrangements. A Border Guard rabbi and Uzi Levy made the call to the Pereg household to notify Ela of the tragic news. Other unit personnel, some of whom were deployed elsewhere throughout the West Bank, rushed back to base to ready themselves for the next day's funeral.

Superintendent Patrick Pereg was laid to rest at the military cemetery in his hometown of Ofakim. Hundreds of mourners, policemen, soldiers, and citizens joined the procession to pay their last respects to the fallen young officer. Cabinet ministers, generals, and unit commanders eulogized him. Men who had fought with Patrick stood in stoic silence as his younger sister, Rachel, said, "Brother, where are you now? You always told Mom that it would be OK."

Many of the officers participating in the operation in Abu Sneina attended the funeral, as well; a sizable contingent of Shin Bet agents were also there. These men had worked with Patrick and the other Ya'mas officers in putting together the intricate pieces needed to mount the Kapisha raid. Some in attendance, like Colonel Dror Weinberg, would soon be eulogized at their own funerals in the months to follow—casualties of the hard-fought conflict.

Virtually the entire Ya'mas came to pay their final respects to Patrick that sun-soaked morning in southern Israel. White clouds hovered high overhead in the picture-perfect blue skies. Members of the unit wore their dress uniforms, many already adorned with medals of valor for daring counterterrorist operations both before and after this intifada's eruption. They were joined by members from the other two Ya'mas units operating in Jerusalem and in Gaza. Some of Patrick's comrades shed tears as the rabbi led the prayers. Others stood with their heads down and their minds overwhelmed by deep concern. News photographers were asked not to take photographs of the men in attendance for security reasons.

The spring of 2002 had begun with a bloody launch. Many of the operators wondered where the conflict was heading and how many more funerals they would have to attend. The unit went right back to work after Patrick's death—the men weren't taken off the front line, nor were they attended to by a staff of clinical psychologists. There was no time, though, to think too much—the unit was too busy. All of Israel's counterterrorist units were busy.

Shortly after Patrick's death the Ya'mas was back in Hebron. On May 14, 2002, the unit apprehended Ali Qawasmeh in a predawn raid on his residence. Qawasmeh, a mid-level commander of the Hamas military wing in the city, had been wanted for numerous attacks and attempted attacks in the area.[16]

Morale in the unit was tenuous following Patrick's death, but the workload only increased. The teams were deployed on what seemed to be the pursuit of an endless list of high-value terrorist targets who now emerged to engage in all-or-nothing warfare. At first, during the early phases of the intifada, there were five operations a week—then a dozen a week, and then the unit simply stopped counting. Operation Defensive Shield had opened up the West Bank and enabled the Shin Bet and A'man to explore terrain they had not seen in nearly seven years. The war was entering an interesting phase and a period when the Ya'mas would be tested like never before.

CHAPTER FIVE

Itamar

Late on Thursday, June 20, 2002, on the night before the Sabbath, Rachel Shabo was busy preparing her house for the festive meal her family of nine always enjoyed together. The mother of seven, Rachel was a full-time mother who took pride in the task of keeping a house filled with hustle and bustle. Only a year earlier she had been a working mom, and she truly cherished the time at home with the family. The traditional work of a Jewish mother—cooking, cleaning, and shepherding her young children from morning to lights out—was noble, and Rachel immersed herself in her family's wellbeing. Thursdays were precious at home, as the entire family prepared for the Shabbat dinner, and a day to pray and rest. Families waited all week for Thursday night so that they could appreciate the quiet of the weekend.

Even though there was a lot of work to be done in the house, Rachel didn't mind that two of her oldest children, Yariv, seventeen, and Atara, fifteen, had gone to visit friends nearby. Young people had to enjoy being young, she knew. In the cities, Thursday was a night to party and to embody the live-for today manner by which Israelis coped with the pressure of being on a constant war footing. In the West Bank, families found solace inside their own communities, together, and safe in their fortified settlements under the shield of the Israeli military.

The Shabo family's five youngest children—Neria, sixteen; Avia, thirteen; Zvika, thirteen; Asa'el, eight; and little Avishai, five—were home helping Rachel prepare the house for the Sabbath. Rachel was most concerned about Neria. A month earlier, while he was sleeping over at his high school, three of his friends had been killed in a terrorist attack; bullets had grazed the pillow on which he slept.

Life in Itamar didn't offer the conveniences and excitement of Tel Aviv, but its compensations were in many ways divine: the crisp air, carried on winds whipping briskly across valleys and hilltops, just as they had done for a thousand years, and mountain vistas breathtaking enough to convince almost anyone that there was an all-knowing deity connected to every stone, wildflower, and grain of sand. Living in one of the settlements wasn't for the faint of heart and certainly not for all Israelis. The threat of terror attack was integral to daily life. Some settlements were located adjacent to Palestinian villages, and were fortified by rings of concertina wire, guard booths and watchtowers, and electronic sensors. Virtually everyone carried a pistol or a rifle for protection, because the settlements, isolated and vulnerable, were a favorite target of Palestinian terrorists.

Rachel and her husband, Boaz, had been among the original families to settle in Itamar. They had lived there in times of peace, when Palestinian men and women from the nearby villages worked inside the community, and during times of open hostilities. As a regional ambulance driver and paramedic, Boaz had been a first responder to terrorist shootings and bombings in which settlers had been critically wounded. It was part of the world in which they lived. Boaz Shabo always looked forward to the Sabbath. The festiveness and calm were bliss. Thursday nights, though, were generally busy for the ambulances on call. There was no shortage of reckless drivers on the West Bank's roadways, and there were always accidents to respond to.

Situated atop a hill in the Samarian Mountains, some five kilometers southeast of Nablus, Itamar was one of the larger West Bank settlements. It sat adjacent to a cluster of Palestinian villages that dotted the endless stretches of brown sandy hills. The settlement's residents were Orthodox, primarily, and found employment in cities. Itamar's houses, stucco and split-level, had proliferated into a very suburban sprawl that few could have expected—or believed they could afford. Still, many worked the land. Pens with livestock were situated to the far corners of the community. In spite of the terrorist threat, people left their doors unlocked and children played outdoors without worry.

The hills around Itamar were draped in absolute darkness at night, and that June night in particular, the darkness provided ample cover to one sole figure, wearing jeans and a T-shirt, who slowly and silently moved up the side of the hill, avoiding any trip wires or sensors. Many of the trees up the hillside had been cut down to provide lookouts with a better view of anyone encroaching up the rocky slopes, but in the darkness the one man was virtually invisible as he made it to Itamar's outer perimeter. The terrorist, armed with an AK-47 and a satchel full of ammunition, crawled through an opening to pass inside. Itamar's residents had for ideological reasons opposed a plan to build a security fence all around the settlement.[1]

From there, it was barely one hundred meters to the Shabo residence, up a rocky slope covered in bushes and flowers and then to a neatly paved street.[2] It was close to 9:00 p.m. when the shooting began.

Several miles away from Itamar, at the Ya'mas home base, Yaakov Berman's team was on call. The team was the area's rapid reaction force, the first responders to any critical incident in the area, to be summoned at a moment's notice, like firemen, racing to save the lives of their countrymen and fellow settlers. Usually, though, being assigned as the readiness force was something of a break for the team—especially considering the never-ending workload they had day in and day out. Berman wasn't there, though. For the first time since the intifada began, he had taken a night off; he was trying to advance his studies and earn a degree, but the endless cycle of raids made it impossible for him to attend class or even take the time on days off—if there were any ever—to sit and study. For weeks he had told his NCOs that he would need to take one night off to cram for an exam, but that promise was always delayed by developing Shin Bet leads and operations being carried out. Yet Berman's professor threatened to throw him out of the course if he didn't take at least *one* test during the semester.[3] Chief Inspector Ronen Goresh, the tall and charismatic unit veteran, was the duty officer that night.

As the afternoon hours pressed into the evening dusk, news of an operation came to the unit's op center. There was a chance that the Shin Bet had something brewing in the village of Beit Furik, a Palestinian town located some six miles southeast of Nablus and just across the valley, to the east, of Itamar. Beit Furik had a population of a little more than ten thousand inhabitants, and it was a known Hamas and Popular Front for the Liberation of Palestine stronghold. Members of the unit who were on leave or at home were summoned back to base. First Sergeant Mordechai,* one of the unit's senior men and a team NCO, was called in from home that afternoon. Mordechai had joined the Border Guard and had served in both Bethlehem and Hebron following the creation of the Palestinian Authority and then joined the Ya'mas in August 1998; a day after he graduated the grueling undercover counterterrorist course, Mordechai found himself masquerading as a local operating around Jenin. Mordechai had a knack for dressing as a Palestinian and became an integral element in countless operations of high risk deep inside terrorist-controlled terrain. After a brief period outside the force, he was brought back to the Ya'mas in July 2001 following the Dolphinarium discotheque bombing when the unit mustered as many veterans as it could find for the war at hand. On this warm summer's evening, Mordechai was working the phones liaising with his Shin Bet counterparts and trying to get some intelligence on the individual they would be after so that the force could prepare for a possible raid. Weapons had already been signed out for; Kevlar body armor and other tactical kit were pre-positioned for the green light from the Shin Bet. It was all routine, Mordechai thought to himself.[4] There had been so many operations, so many raids, it was all par for the course. Sa'ar Shine, Berman's team sergeant, was watching television in the unit lounge, drinking cup after cup of "mud," the Israeli derivative of instant Turkish coffee, and chain-smoking. Sa'ar and his teammates knew that if they fought the urge to sleep for too long, just for one more night, the chemical compound of stress, adrenaline, caffeine, and nicotine could keep them awake for days on end; staying awake and alert in an undercover unit was an occupational necessity. Sa'ar and his teammates had just completed a heavy round of physical training, or PT, to remain fresh. Yuri had seen it happen too many times: A simple call-out turned into a three-day ordeal of nonstop combat. Yuri wanted to prepare himself with a cup of coffee with a generous tablespoon of Hawaij, a blend of Yemeni spices that had become a staple of the Israeli palate and a calling card of Yuri's caffeine habit. But before he could design the perfect cup of Ya'mas rocket fuel, Yuri was determined to hit the shower. If he was going to

---

* A pseudonym—true identity withheld for security considerations.

be summoned on a call-out, one that could last a few days, at least he wanted to be clean.

The team was exhausted, both physically and mentally. For weeks without letup they had gone from mission to mission. Each operation, no matter how big the target was or how routine the movement of men looked on paper, required planning, coordination with the backup forces and the IDF commands that controlled them, and intricate counterintelligence tradecraft with the Shin Bet. No operation was ordinary, even those that seemed routine. Sometimes, the arrests were done on the fly and the unit was out of the base gate after lunch and back before dinner. Some of the operations were small in scale and involved no more than a couple of vehicles, six to eight men at the most. But sometimes, those small ops ended up yielding enormous bounties of intelligence—more than just terrorist suspects taken off the Shin Bet most-wanted lists, but critical cell phones obtained, SMS message histories to harvest, revealing that the Hamas operative was en route to a meet, inside a café, or expected there in thirty minutes. In such instances, there was seldom time to prepare; no time to call in the cavalry. Sa'ar, Mordechai, Yuri, and the other members of the unit were out the door, changing quickly into Palestinian attire while on the move, entering a targeted location undercover, loaded up with full tactical kit. The hours often turned into days, and the days lasted forever.

Throughout May and June the unit operated nonstop. The names and faces of the terror suspects they hunted all became a blur. The streets and narrow alleys of each town and village morphed into a single image. It was a most difficult period for the unit, and it appeared as if there was no sunshine on the horizon. This war, they all knew, was very far from over.

All along the boundaries of the large army base that served as their home, powerful night-lights, positioned in and around the sprawling eucalyptus trees, basked the base with an orange glow. The Ya'mas operators went through their paces. Some worked out in an improvised outdoor gym built from discarded plumbing pipes soldered together; they were listening to the sounds of *Muzika Mizracheet* ("eastern music"), a Hebrew hybrid of love songs and the blues composed to Arabic-style rhythms that were both soul and hip-hop for Israelis from the Arab Diaspora. Runners had just completed their laps and were slowly stretching before heading to the showers.

The soldiers serving in the base's operations center were primarily conscripts. Many were female soldiers, all teenagers, who would be heading home
the next morning for the Sabbath leave, and the festive meal with parents and
siblings. Thursday nights were when rooms were scrubbed, weapons cleaned,
and last-minute details attended to in the hope of passing the morning's
inspection.

Mordechai had sent one of his conscripts to the unit's armory to get a certain
kind of communications gear that would be suitable for a nighttime foray
inside the deep valleys around Beit Furik, where reception was always a challenge. The soldier had overheard some soldiers talking about an incident in
Itamar, and they had used the code words for an active shooter attack. The
confirmation came moments later. Still, details remained sketchy: one heavily armed terrorist and multiple casualties. Single-gunman missions were a
favorite tactic of the Palestinians against Jewish settlements in the West Bank
and Gaza. It was 2100 hours.

The report set the base into motion, and it was soon a blur of Ya'mas
operators rushing to their lockers to get dressed and assemble their tactical
kits. On went the body armor, the load-bearing equipment, and weapons.
Yuri dressed soaking wet and was one of the first to muster outside and pile
into the two armored jeeps and a GMC Savana passenger van that the readiness force had at its disposal. Intelligence reports, instructions, and any other
relevant piece of information that would be needed would be disseminated
and assembled on the fly. Just outside the unit's home base, the convoy linked
up with a jeep belonging to Goresh for the short race toward Itamar. Goresh
briefed them on what little he knew at that point, but there were so many
unanswered questions concerning the incident: Was there really only one
terrorist? How many casualties? How many homes were overtaken?[5]

Sixteen men in all set out for Itamar in several vehicles. The operators
were sandwiched inside the vehicles, with barely enough room to move their
limbs, their M4s jammed between their cramped legs, squeezed in by their
body armor fortified with an extra ceramic plate worn across their chests.
The twists and turns of the high-speed convoy made the journey all the more
uncomfortable for the operators; each time a right or left turn was negotiated,

the force propelled the helmeted heads to impact. There was no small talk inside the vehicles that raced toward Itamar—there was none of the chitchat that the operators usually exchanged with one another while en route to a raid. Sa'ar jammed his earbud tighter in order to listen to the brigade frequency. The radio bursts talked of everyone being dead. The silence inside the vans now became more noticeable.

Goresh drove the lead vehicle toward Itamar, pushing his armored jeep to speeds in excess of one hundred miles per hour. After heading north through the dark roads of the West Bank, Goresh led the convoy in making a sharp turn onto Route 555 and the path toward the settlement. The operators inside held on tight as the vehicles banked on their sides and skidded. They knew that they were near. A white road sign with black Hebrew, Arabic, and English lettering pointed to the entrance to Itamar.

Itamar had been built atop a hill and the twisting road toward the main entrance was lined with trees and brush. A young man in a blue T-shirt, a hand-knitted yarmulke on his head, was waiting in the middle of the road to guide the Ya'mas team toward the besieged house, and the caravan full of commandos sped there while multiple army and police radios hissed with static and chatter and several guard dogs barked hysterically.

The Ya'mas force was met by Colonel Yossi Adiri, commander of the Samaria Brigade, already in Itamar, along with his deputy and the brigade's operations officer. Colonel Adiri informed Goresh and the operators that there was a terrorist, perhaps two, inside a house a hundred meters down the road and that initial reports were that everyone inside was already dead. The operators positioned their vehicles several houses down from the Shabo family home. There were no words spoken and no instructions issued. The men split into two parallel five-man formations and moved cautiously behind the stucco homes and the neatly kept gardens. The operators raised their M4s to eye level as they moved forward, butt stocks tight in on their shoulders, peering through the orange prism of their Meprolight day/night illuminated reflex sights. They were careful not to trip on garden hoses and children's toys that were strewn about, and not to be surprised by a sudden burst of gunfire.

Their movements were quick and fluid, reflecting choreography that had been written by highly skilled instructors and drilled into them time and time again.

Boaz Shabo was working his evening shift when he checked in with the regional operations center to see if there were any ambulance calls that he needed to respond to. An eighteen-year-old female soldier picked up the phone and said, "Boaz, we've been looking for you, there is a terrorist infiltration at Itamar. There are dead and wounded. We need you." Overcome with dread, he asked, after hesitating, "Do you know the name of the family? Is it Shabo?"

The reply nearly buckled his knees: "How did you know?"[6]

As Boaz gunned the engine of his ambulance and turned on the road back to Itamar, he said to himself, "I have seven children. Just let *one* of them live so I'll have a reason to wake up in the morning."

Goresh and his men moved quickly toward the Shabo home. Two bewildered reservist soldiers, who had been stationed in Itamar as part of their annual military duty, stood frozen at the entrance to the house, making sure that no one escaped the premises. They stood over the body of a young man with fair skin and a short and neatly trimmed beard lying in a thick pool of blood; an M16 rifle was near his hands. Yuri at first thought the mortally wounded man to be a terrorist, but he then noticed the white cloth fringes of a pair of tzitzit, the specially knotted ritual fringes on an undergarment prayer shawl worn by Orthodox Jews, and understood that he was a local resident killed in the assault. The dead man was, in fact, Yosef Twitto, thirty-one years of age, volunteer member of the community's guard force. When he heard the shooting come from the direction of the Shabo residence, he'd responded but was cut down by a burst of rifle fire.

Sa'ar kicked in the door and his entry team streamed inside a vestibule area toward the first floor. At the first opening one operator turned right and secured the area so that two other men could dart across the space and take cover on the left side; a fourth operator, on his knees, scanned the area with his weapon in the ready position. "There was no need for verbal commands," First Sergeant Mordechai recalled. "The men had been with one another in enough tight tactical spots before to instinctively communicate with one another and know who had to push right, and who had to move left as we turned corners."[7] The entry team turned sharply behind each side of the wall to make sure that there were no surprises waiting for them at the other end. The operators flooded the first floor and scanned the living room and open kitchen with the flashlight attachments mounted below the barrels of their M4s. Cooked food was thrown all around and everywhere. The place was a shambles. Shrapnel damage and bullet holes had punched through the walls and ceilings. Dozens of shell casings, too many to count at the moment, littered the white marble floor.

Suddenly, the operators heard footsteps racing up a flight of stairs toward the second-floor landing. They paused and prepared to head up there, hoping to move silently and not let the terrorist know that they had been alerted. But then a cell phone rang somewhere in the house and didn't stop ringing. Boaz Shabo was calling Rachel's mobile telephone, desperate to know who in his family was still alive.

The closed staircase leading up to the second floor was unusually narrow and encased by thick concrete walls. The entry team gripped their weapons tighter and moved cautiously up the stairs. When they reached the second-floor landing, Yuri scanned around an open space, and then found a room to the left from where, they believed, the terrorist had fired at them moments earlier. With his teammates covering him, Sa'ar removed a fragmentation grenade from his pouch, kicked in the door, and tossed the grenade inside. The earsplitting blast smashed a bookcase and threw its wreckage into the entrance to the room. Pushing past it, Sa'ar scanned the room with his M4, while Yuri crouched on one knee and turned to cover the corner to his right. Through the smoke and dust, they found, to their horror, a boy, no more than thirteen, dead underneath his bed. It was Zvika. Another child was lying on the bed, alive, but in a frightened state of shock. His right leg had been blown off beneath the knee and he was bleeding profusely. It had never dawned on Sa'ar that there might be people still alive in the house.

The child was conscious and responsive. Sa'ar slung his rifle over his torso, wrapped the child in a blanket, and carried him to a window where First Sergeant Eran* was waiting. The child was held securely and brought

---

* A pseudonym—true identity withheld for security considerations.

to the awaiting ambulance and a hastily set up triage center for emergency medical care. Eran radioed the command post outside that they had found a survivor. "What's your name?" Eran asked. "My name is Asa'el," the young boy replied.[8]

Boaz Shabo had made it back to Itamar moments after the Ya'mas rescue assault began. He was rushed to the wall, near where much of the Ya'mas backup and support force had mustered. Boaz prayed for the lives of his family; prayers he thought would go unanswered when he heard the muffled blast of Sa'ar's grenade. Seconds later, though, one of the operators nearby told him that Asa'el was alive, though wounded, and that he was going to be brought out. Boaz's hands trembled. He slowly removed a piece of paper from his trouser pocket and he wrote down the name "Asa'el." He prayed for the chance to add names to the list of children who were still alive.[9] As Sa'ar and Yuri scoured the room and closets in the second-floor landing, the rest of the team pushed on.

The perspective of the mission—not the objective—changed. They had entered the Shabo home to kill the terrorist, but now they had to be careful because there was the possibility, clearly the hope, that there were other members of the family alive and still inside. But first and foremost the men were determined to kill the terrorist and then remove the dead and wounded.

Goresh and Mordechai continued searching the floor at the foot of the staircase leading up to the third floor, as the two operators pushed forward, clearing the rooms quickly. "I missed the room where the youngest child, Avishai, had been killed," Mordechai remembered. "The terrorist had apparently covered the baby with his blanket after killing him."[10] Rachel's body was found in the next room. Goresh and Mordechai looked at Rachel's lifeless body; her eyes were open and her glasses were still on. The two men paused in their tracks, frustrated that there was nothing they could do to save the life of the woman, and angered that they hadn't been able to arrive five minutes sooner.

For the men entering the house, it was still hard to know if there was more than one terrorist inside. It was still not known how many terrorists there actually were. There was no way of knowing how many more dead they would locate. Could anyone inside still be alive? But the gunfire continued. The Ya'mas operators were forced to seek cover from magazine-emptying bursts of AK fire emanating from the third floor.

Sa'ar took over on point. He moved toward the staircase with Goresh on his right and Mordechai on his left. Mordechai had to expose himself slightly in order to take aim inside the constricting area, and he saw the terrorist leap across the opening, firing as he moved. The terrorist had dark curly hair and an olive complexion. He wore a turquoise short-sleeve T-shirt and blue jeans; dozens of AK-47 thirty-round magazines were held inside a homemade olive-green vest that adorned his torso. Mordechai raised his weapon and took aim using the mounted flashlight attachment for illumination, but all he saw was the barrel of an AK-47. In the split second before Mordechai could pull the trigger, the terrorist unleashed a lengthy burst of 7.62mm fire down the staircase before he disappeared behind the thick concrete slabs supporting the walls. Mordechai tried to slink into position to gain something of a tactical advantage, but as he exposed himself the terrorist opened fire again. A 7.62mm round tore through Mordechai's forearm and stopped in his bicep. He threw his body back, but he felt complete paralysis in his right arm. Protected from the terrorist fire by a wall, Mordechai saw that his entire arm had been split open by the AK fire. He could see shattered bone through the blood.

"I'm hit," he radioed on the team frequency, and Yuri assumed Mordechai's position in the stick and followed Sa'ar as the team rushed the narrow staircase, tossing a grenade in the opening to cover their movement. Mordechai removed himself from the house and rushed to an ad hoc aid station set up behind a stone wall. An IDF medic wanted to apply a tourniquet to Mordechai's gaping forearm wound, but the Ya'mas sergeant refused. He barked at the medic and ordered him to use a field dressing. Mordechai inserted a fresh thirty-round magazine into his M4 and then returned to the house, to assist with perimeter work.

The response force continued its work. Halfway up the stairs, Goresh suddenly saw the unmistakable forward sight of an AK-47 barrel sticking out from behind a wall at the top landing. He grabbed Sa'ar by his vest and pulled him out of the line of fire. The terrorist sprayed the staircase with a burst of fire, and four rounds slammed into Goresh's front chest plate at close range. He fell back, the wind completely knocked out of him, but none of the bullets had penetrated his body—they were all stopped by the body armor he wore and the extra ceramic plate thrown in for good measure. Saʾar checked his body for hits; the rounds had grazed his helmet and pierced his coveralls near the thigh, but none of the bullets penetrated flesh.[11]

The staircase was too narrow for the Yaʾmas team to negotiate together, so Yuri took the lead and propelled his body forward. He conquered the staircase in a blind dash and secured the landing so that the others could follow. Saʾar was right behind him.

Methodically, the team scoured the top floor in their search for the gunman. They cleared corners and moved toward the parents' master bedroom in a precise procession forward. The darkened hallway was covered first, and several hand grenades were tossed in areas where the terrorist could be hiding behind a cinder-block wall. The smell of cordite and burning plaster began to fill the top floor of the house, as the grenades and gunfire soon set the house on fire.

A narrow wooden staircase led to an attic crawl space, and Saʾar took point making his way up the steps just in case the terrorist had sought shelter there. The crawl space was already on fire and engulfed in smoke. Carefully maneuvering his frame up the narrow stairs, Saʾar made it inside just enough to reach with his arms and upper torso to see if anyone was up there. The flames singed his coveralls and burned his hands and forearms, but he continued his search; the burning wooden house frame and combustible insulation created a toxic mix of smoke and carcinogens that laced his eyes with the sense that acid had been thrown into his face.

As he slowly and painfully lowered himself from the attic, Saʾar realized that the terrorist had to be in the parents' master bedroom down the hall. The Yaʾmas team moved forward, realizing that they had the terrorist cornered. Saʾar went in first, made a quick glance to the left, and then looked toward the right. The room was empty, and he realized that the terrorist had to be trapped in the adjacent bathroom. He raised his weapon higher, holding it ever so tight as he inched his way closer inside the room to get into firing position. Then, out of the corner of his eye, he saw a young face emerge from underneath the bed. It was Avia, the Shabos' thirteen-year-old daughter. Avia had been shot several times, and even though she was wounded she had managed to find shelter underneath her parents' bed. Saʾar stood still, frozen. He signaled the rest of the operators to enter the room, and then he urged Avia to stay where she was. "Don't move, don't move." He motioned to her with his hand. But the terrified teenager wanted to go to the men in the sage-green fatigues. Avia struggled to twist herself out from under the bed, and the Ya'mas operators leapt forward to unleash a dedicated barrage of fire on the bathroom door to keep the terrorist from shooting back and hitting Avia.

Sa'ar rushed in toward the girl and locked his hands underneath her arms to support and protect her from the close-range muzzle blasts, bullets, and shrapnel. With Avia firmly in his grip, he twisted her around so that he could shield the girl with his body armor. Outside the door, elements of the Ya'mas backup team created a human chain to evacuate the wounded girl out of the kill zone. She was handed off from one operator to another and whisked out of the house and to an awaiting stretcher.[12]

Boaz Shabo rushed to his daughter. Although he was a trained medic, he knew that others had to render the emergency care to her. He held her hands and looked into her eyes. He found himself incapable of uttering a word. "Mommy's dead," she told her father. "Everyone's dead. It hurts me, help me." Holding back his tears, Boaz held her hand as she was triaged and placed inside an ambulance.[13]

Sa'ar, Goresh, Yuri, and the other members of the team trained their weapons on the third-floor bathroom door. Other operators waited in the third-floor landing and on the staircase in case more men would go down and they were needed. Sa'ar had lost his patience with this one tenacious terrorist, and he was eager to end the ordeal now. "Let's get this over with and now." Yuri moved in first, firing his M4 at the door as he closed the gap between the bedroom entrance and the bathroom. He heard what sounded like the groans of a wounded animal coming from the bathroom. But the terrorist had enough fight left in him to unleash another volley. The fusillade threw Yuri on his back. He felt a terrible burning sensation in his hands, as if he were gripping molten steel. He glanced down and saw that one bullet had entered his right wrist and shattered the bone; another had taken off his left pinkie. Two operators from the rear brought Yuri out of the line of fire.

Sa'ar pulled the pin from a hand grenade and tossed it into the bullet-riddled bathroom. The antipersonnel grenade, so lethal in room-to-room clearings, landed inside the cast iron bathtub and exploded in an earsplitting crack. The bathtub absorbed the force of the blast and all of the shrapnel, leaving the gunman unscathed. The terrorist continued to fire from his AK-47, spraying the bedroom with a dedicated burst. And then there was silence. The entry team moved in. It was then that their earpieces buzzed with word from the outside that a solitary figure, armed, had just leapt from the bathroom window down to the grassy area behind the house. "Is this guy for real?" Sa'ar thought to himself. "This bastard refuses to go down!"[14]

Goresh and Sa'ar immediately raced down the stairs after him. They saw the gunman run through the garden and past a palm tree, around a corner to the side of the house, where he found cover near some propane tanks. In a quick exchange of gunfire, the propane tanks exploded into a blinding flash of bright light and orange glow. The heat from the blast was so intense that it blew both Goresh and Sa'ar off their feet. For some unexplained reason, the explosion did not kill the terrorist.

The house was soon engulfed in a fireball of an inferno. The two Ya'mas operators, undeterred by the heat of the fire, continued their pursuit of the terrorist. Scouring the area, they noticed, near the rear of the house, a silhouette of a man that appeared to be crawling away. The two operators didn't know if this was the terrorist or, perhaps, another victim seeking shelter, so they moved in to close range to make sure. The terrorist had been attempting to flee through the gap in the fence that had been cut for him, but when he saw the Ya'mas operators moving in he decided to fight to the end. He raised his AK-47 and aimed at both Sa'ar and Goresh, but before he could fire a shot, he was cut down in a flurry of fire.

In a spasm of violence that night in June 2002, Yosef Twitto, Rachel Shabo, and three of her children—Neria, age sixteen; Zvika, age thirteen; and Avishai, age five—had been killed; two other Shabo children had been critically injured. The bloodshed had been perpetrated by one lone Palestinian terrorist gunman.

The nightmare in Itamar was finally over. Nighttime operations in the West Bank were only just beginning.

Yaakov Berman reached Itamar just as the incident had come to an end. He had been paged from home and was furious for having missed the incident. He raced toward the West Bank from his home near Tel Aviv and had managed to talk to Mordechai, who had to be forced away from the perimeter and tied to a stretcher.* Berman raced into Itamar at full speed and maneuvered his olive-green Toyota Hilux past the narrow roadway toward the forward perimeter, virtually barreling the other vehicles out of his path. The entrance to the West Bank settlement was clogged by an endless parking lot of armored jeeps, trucks, and staff cars. It was as if half the State of Israel had rushed to the settlement, he thought to himself, and they all arrived before him.[15] He grabbed his M4 and unfastened the holster for his Glock 17C 9mm semiautomatic pistol. He rushed toward his men.

Colonel Adiri was walking about the perimeter, as were other colonels, generals, and Shin Bet officials. Investigators and intelligence personnel were everywhere. Medics scurried about to attend to the wounded. Several rabbis and military chaplains attended to the dead and to the grieving Boaz Shabo. The night's sky was painted an eerie shade of orange by the fire that had engulfed the Shabo home. The orange sky was a backdrop for a relentless assault of red flashing lights belonging to ambulances and fire trucks, and blue flashing lights bouncing from police and army vehicles. There was no escaping the squelched hiss of Motorola radios and orders being barked in the heavy Hebrew of command. The grinding thud of army boots, hundreds of them, pounding on the paved sidewalks, was heard everywhere.

News trucks arrived at Itamar prepared to broadcast the breaking news of the latest act of bloodshed. Massacres had become all too common during the intifada; even in a nation where everyone knew everyone else, the victims of this war became faceless statistics. Covering a massacre became less

---

* The two seriously wounded Ya'mas fighters, Mordechai and Yuri, were flown by helicopter to Tel Hashomer hospital. Mordechai had to be resuscitated on the short flight due to massive blood loss, though he recovered. Yuri returned to active duty minus a finger shortly after the incident; Mordechai's path to recovery was longer. He returned to the Ya'mas in a support role, though he continuously worked to learn how to shoot and fight using his left arm, so that he could once again be classified as operational.

shocking and more matter-of-fact—especially in the aftermath of the Park Hotel bombing. There were families slaughtered before and there would be families who would be killed later. Still, the ever voracious Israeli press knew the limitations of decency and military security when covering these terrorist attacks in real time, but the army kept the cameras far away nonetheless.

Police crime scene investigators began photographing the entire area and assembling forensic evidence for future cases that would evolve around the massacre. Shin Bet agents scoured the entire area, as well. It was highly doubtful that the terrorist had his *Batiqat Hawiya*, or identity card, on him; if the terrorist dropped his mobile phone, a bus ticket, or even a piece of paper that indicated where he worked or went to school, it would help the Shin Bet in its efforts to identify the dead gunman. One of the Shin Bet agents, a case officer who had worked this part of the West Bank for a long time, stared at the dead man's face in the odd shot that he would recognize him from an earlier arrest or interrogation. An agent pushed an ink roller over the dead man's fingers. His body would be removed to the national forensic lab in Abu Kabir in south Tel Aviv for further examination.

Berman checked on his wounded operators, and made sure that they were attended to. He wanted his men far from the lights and sirens, and he wanted the unit to be back at headquarters. Berman ordered his men to return to their base and reload their ammo, check their gear, and stand by. One by one the men piled into the two vans for the quick ride back to base. Many of the operators were covered in soot. Some of their combat overalls were charred brownish black from the fires inside the house. Some of the men were sprayed with the blood of their wounded comrades. The operators sat in silence while the drivers tried to figure out how they were going to negotiate their way past all of the response vehicles that had boxed them in. The operators thought of the Shabo children shot at close range. They needed a few moments to themselves and several cups of rocket fuel coffee.

The team returned to base just after midnight. The vans stopped in front of the unit armory, where fresh loads of ammunition were distributed to each man. Weapons were checked, radios recharged, and canteens filled. But before the tin of Turkish coffee could be opened and the water set to boil, a Shin Bet case officer contacted the unit. There would be raids that night. The hunt was on for the masterminds of the massacre and the random murders of virtually an entire family.

The Shin Bet understood that an entire network, an indigenous Palestinian industry of sorts, surrounded each attack; the architects of these operations, as well as those who perpetrated the acts, would all shoot to the top of the Shin Bet most-wanted list. The man in custody possessed links to a matrix of accomplices, handlers, financiers, and liaison officers to Damascus and beyond. Every layer of the network uncovered and neutralized revealed new layers. This was the never-ending chess match of counterterrorist operations during the intifada.

The morning after Itamar, Dr. George Habash's Popular Front for the Liberation of Palestine claimed responsibility for the attack; the communiqué, revealed to news agencies in the West Bank and Damascus, was brief and boastful. The PFLP, the Marxist Pan-Arab group that had introduced aircraft hijacking to the terrorist lexicon thirty years earlier, was opposed to both Fatah and Hamas; both groups, the PFLP's Greek-Orthodox Christian chieftain argued, were not truly revolutionary in spirit. The PFLP had used the violence of the intifada as a vehicle by which to attract new recruits and new legitimacy. The Shin Bet didn't have to wait for a communiqué to know that the PFLP was responsible for the Itamar murders. The entire Ya'mas unit was on the hunt that night, and operations in the villages of Beit Djan and Awarta revealed that the shooter's name was Iyad Ramahe, a member of the PFLP's Abu Ali Mustafa Brigade, a small and obscure terror cell belonging to a Marxist Syrian-based group that had tried very hard to compete against the fundamentalist forces of Hamas and the PIJ.[16] Ramahe was a throwaway, a rock star for a day; his commanders were the ones that the Shin Bet was interested in. Their names would rush to the top of the agency's most-wanted list.

The Ya'mas operators who returned from Itamar and the subsequent arrest operations in the villages around Nablus that night and early morning felt that the West Bank battlefield was deteriorating into a free-for-all of unchecked violence. The men sensed that the ground on which they stood had fractured into a fiery chaos. So the operators removing their body armor from the tired and aching torsos did what they had done since the intifada erupted: They reloaded their ammo, drank cup after cup of Turkish coffee, and smoked the better part of a pack until the phone rang and the Shin Bet gave them their inevitable next assignment.

CHAPTER SIX

The Hunters

Undercover warfare was often described—in the unique Hebrew military slang that emanated from Israel's many conflicts—by the term *avoda pintzeta*. Roughly translated into functional English, the phrase meant "tweezers' work"; it was a reference to the fact that plainclothes counterterrorist operations required precision, delicacy, a steady hand, and ultimately the proper amount of force to yank and pull a wanted terror suspect into custody quickly and silently. When conditions were right, an undercover operation could locate, neutralize, apprehend, and evacuate a terror suspect in seconds with the minimum of force. Zakaria Zubeidi, a former Palestinian policeman, notorious car thief, and head of the Fatah's Tanzim force of thugs and al-Aqsa Martyrs Brigade in the northern West Bank, once gave an interview in which he spoke of how the explosive surprise and speed of the undercover units made him nervous. Although he was on the run, one of the top names on the Shin Bet's most-wanted list, Zubeidi loved granting interviews to the press, and in one such exchange he stated that every stray cat jumping on a garbage can made him jump; every old lady that walked across the street warranted a second look from him and his bodyguards.[1] The Ya'mas was everywhere, Zubeidi and his comrades thought. It was precisely what the unit wanted the terrorists to think.

The entire Palestinian terrorist infrastructure was centered in the cities of Area A—the cities, protected in principle by the Oslo Accords, the PA's security and intelligence services—and the abundance of weapons and gang control of neighborhoods made it possible for Hamas, the al-Aqsa Martyrs Brigade, and the PIJ to operate with absolute impunity in Area A. In many parts of Area A, the terrorist groups were yielded more control than the

PA; this was especially the case after Defensive Shield when many PA security men shed their uniforms and disappeared into the chaos. "Operation Defensive Shield rearranged the furniture," a retired Israeli special operations officer said, reflecting on how both the Palestinians and the Israelis attempted to rebuild their operational infrastructures inside the West Bank, "and it took a while for everyone to get used to the new layout. Once the dust settled, everyone went back to work. The terrorist attacks continued as did the Israeli response."[2]

In the six months after Operation Defensive Shield, between April and September 2002, Palestinian terrorists succeeded in sending fourteen suicide bombers into Israel's cities, killing eighty-one people and wounding nearly three hundred more. One of the worst attacks was the Hamas bombing of a crowded game room in the Tel Aviv suburb of Rishon Le'Tziyon that killed fifteen and wounded fifty-five.

Israel's campaign of targeted killings—and targeted arrests—continued, as well. One of the most significant targeted killings was the IAF's July 22, 2002, dropping of a 2,205-pound bomb on the Gaza City home of Salah Shehada, the Hamas leader. Israel's counterterrorist and reconnaissance units were also operating around the clock, attempting to apprehend the most dangerous Palestinian commanders who were directing the intifada. On April 5, the Ya'ma'm attempted to apprehend Qeis Adwan, one of the chief Hamas engineers and a man the Shin Bet linked to the deaths of seventy-seven Israelis, in the West Bank town of Tubas. Adwan and his four bodyguards resisted the call to emerge from their hideout and were ultimately killed in an exchange with the Ya'mam operators and the D9 dozer that supported the operation. On April 15, in Operation Bright Light, a special operations task force of several units led by Duvdevan captured Marwan Barghouti, the head of Fatah's Tanzim and one of the architects of the intifada; Barghouti was seen by many as Arafat's heir apparent.[3]

Another high-value target was Samir Farid Ziad, the Hamas commander for Tulkarm. Tulkarm had been one of the more prosperous of West Bank cities—before and after the arrival of the Palestinian Authority. Conveniently situated within eyeshot of Netanya, Tulkarm straddled an area called the Lower Triangle: several Israeli-Arab towns that buttressed the Palestinian city of more than ninety thousand inhabitants along the invisible Green

Line. These border towns included Qalansawe, Tayibe, Kfar Qasm, Tira, Kfar Bara, and Jaljulia. Tulkarm boasted a flourishing trade, ranging from spices and hummus, to stolen cars, pirated DVDs, and smuggled weapons. There were parts of Tulkarm that were pure affluence; the city even boasted two professional soccer clubs—Thaqafi Tulkarm and Markez Shabab Tulkarm. During more peaceful times, Israelis flocked to the city for low-cost weekend shopping.[4] There were, though, two refugee camps inside Tulkarm—Nur Shams, with some nine thousand residents, and the Tulkarm camp, with approximately twenty thousand inhabitants.

Because of its proximity to Israel's coastal cities, Tulkarm was a natural springboard for terrorist activity. Hamas, in particular, boasted a strong footprint in the city—primarily because of Samir Farid Ziad. On paper, Ziad ran the Tulkarm Zakat Committee, a Hamas charitable organization that laundered funds secreted from Damascus and Tehran into banks around the region and ultimately to terror cells in the West Bank. The Zakat Committee paid stipends to the families of suicide bombers and paid for the chemicals and hardware used in the manufacturing of explosives and suicide belts; the charitable foundation paid the monthly rent checks to safe houses and explosive laboratories. The Zakat paid the salaries of the men in the field, and the monies the committee controlled paid off Israeli-Arabs who would help secrete suicide bombers into Israel. Ziad's checkbook was responsible for feeding an entire army.

Ziad was all of twenty-four years old, but his youth hid a wealth of clandestine and combat experience. He was ten years old when the first intifada raged. He was sixteen years old when the Palestinian Authority assumed control of his native Tulkarm. By the time the al-Aqsa intifada erupted, Ziad had risen up the chain of command to control a fortune in cash.

Samir Farid Ziad was a top-priority target for Shin Bet case agents. Besides being the Hamas financier in the area, and a walking data center of invaluable intelligence on the organization's intricate networks in the West Bank, Ziad was, the Shin Bet had learned, assembling the moving parts to launch a suicide bombing attack. He had become a ticking bomb.

Ziad was a cautious man, however. He rarely traveled anywhere without armed guard and he moved about mainly at night. A contingent of Hamas fighters trailed his every movement; AK-47-toting guards were posted around his home and where he prayed. In fact, his known movements limited him to two primary locations: the mosques where he prayed and the offices of the Tulkarm Zakat Committee, where, indoors and protected by a steady flow of local inhabitants, he felt invulnerable. Ziad always surrounded himself with a human shield of noncombatants—just in case.

Throughout the summer of 2002, Uzi Levy's men spent many days—and nights—hunting Ziad. The intelligence tips that the Shin Bet received were either faulty, or they came in too late to be effective; in several instances, the intelligence was spot-on, but the Ya'mas task force arrived to the location where Ziad was believed to be hiding only to find out that they had missed him by minutes. But as August progressed into September, the urgency to apprehend Ziad intensified. The Shin Bet wanted Ziad taken alive.[5] Ya'mas officers were determined to apprehend Ziad in a *sawiya* sort of way, the Arabic term for "smooth"—no fuss and no gunfire.

On the morning of September 5, 2002, the Shin Bet case agent handling the Ziad file received the call he had been eagerly anticipating for days—Ziad would be at his desk inside the Zakat offices, all day. His itinerary involved handling a mountain of overdue paperwork and listening to a long list of locals—many in dire need of money for medical care and home construction—that always seemed to be waiting in line for an audience with the Hamas official who doled out the generous stacks of cash; the poor always knew that there was a price to be paid, perhaps not immediately, for the Islamic generosity. Many of those who came seeking help were ashamed to be at the mercy of the man behind the desk. They tended to place their heads low and look at the floor and look away from the others. It was a perfect setting for a raid.

Midday was chosen as the most suitable time to launch the audacious arrest. People tried to avoid moving about outdoors under the relentless summer's sun; certain days in September, especially during the late summer heat waves known in Arabic as *hamseen*, were better spent indoors in close proximity to a Siemens air conditioner. There would be fewer guards outside the building at the height of the September sun. Not even the most hardcore

Izzedine al-Qassam gunman enjoyed baking under the merciless Middle East sun.

The operation was handed to a native Arabic speaker and IDF combat veteran, who had come up with a novel solution to face the least possible resistance in their push inside the city—the entry team would dress in plain clothes and masquerade as local gunmen.[6] In plain clothes and brandishing sidearms with an accompanying arrogance, two Arabic speakers in the unit would simply walk into the building as if they were there to summon Ziad for a sit-down with one of the local warlords, and then walk out with their target. H-hour was set for twelve thirty. The operation was called "Parting Gift."

The drone launched for Operation Parting Gift transmitted clear real-time images—clear enough that the feedback appeared to be a Hollywood film and not a daring mission behind terrorist lines. Ya'mas commander Levy, along with his deputies and intelligence and operations staff, stood inside the command post and watched the small procession of unmarked vehicles move in and out of the city's main avenues and twisting side streets. Colonel Tamir Hayman, the brigade commander responsible for Tulkarm and Qalqilya,[7] along with the various intelligence and military officers represented at the CP, stood silently. There was an intangible apprehension inside the Operation Parting Gift headquarters; Israel Air Force AH-64 Apache helicopter gunships flew above the command post in a circular orbit as they stood by for the call to action.[8] The thumping whirl of their rotor blades was unmistakable and menacing. Nearby was the roar of armored personnel carrier engines being fired up just in case; infantrymen, their body armor and battle rattle already on, awaited the green light to move into the city and rescue the Ya'mas team. Amid the noise and activity, Uzi Levy recalled there being a silence inside the command post that was difficult to describe. Some of the IDF officers, even veterans of commando units, were impressed by the courage displayed by the small Ya'mas contingent en route to their target.

Two nondescript undercover vehicles with authentic plates[9] drove along Tulkarm's crisscrossing avenues and pulled up in front of Ziad's office.[10] Arabic speakers sat in the front seats of both vehicles; heavily armed Ya'mas operators sat in the cargo areas of both vehicles. Five men got out: Three men walked confidently through the front door and entered the building, while the other two taped a sign to the front door indicating that the offices had been closed, then stood outside watching the traffic pass. The remainder of the force then emerged from their darkened seating area to surround the building. All carried sidearms tucked invisibly under their clothing.

The Zakat offices were crowded and narrow. There was a hum of air conditioners struggling to push out the BTUs before blowing their circuitry; the walls were varnished with a stain of slowly applied yellowish-brown nicotine. The three Ya'mas members walked toward the rear offices, passing several secretaries and file clerks. Ziad wasn't in his office, or in any of the nearby rooms. Confusion set in, as did a sense of immense apprehension.

Survival rule number one for an undercover mission—and this even applied to the Speakers who had undergone accent and slang training—was to keep the verbal intercourse with the local Palestinians to an absolute minimum. One slipped "*gh*" instead of an intended "*a'a*" and the masquerade would be compromised immediately. But one of the Speakers went on instinct, realizing that an officer in Arafat's security services could have come from anywhere in the West Bank and might have even been living for years in Lebanon, Syria, or even the Gulf. He pushed their way into a waiting room filled with people—unemployed heads of families needing help to make it to the end of the month, and women, wearing the *niqab* and *hijab* covering their faces, looking for help with the cost of groceries. "We have business with Ziad," the Speaker barked, intent on preempting an argument over cutting the line by displaying the swagger of Arafat's internal security men. "Where is he?"

At a remote corner of the office, near a brand-new photocopier, the three Israeli operators found Ziad trying to collate some paperwork. "We have to talk to you about something important; you need to come with us," one of the Ya'mas operators demanded. Ziad at first thought that the three rugged men were from Hamas, perhaps operatives from another city or representatives of one of the senior political leaders that had just received instructions from Damascus, so he began to comply. Suddenly, one of the operators removed his Jericho 9mm pistol from a holster hidden in the small of his back and shoved it forcefully into Ziad's side. "*Dir Balak* [an Arabic phrase used heavily in Israeli Hebrew slang that means "you should pay attention that this doesn't happen"] if you make a sound or try to resist," the Speaker whispered. "Just walk out with us." Ziad didn't know what to do or what to think. He looked one more time at the Speaker, who now just motioned with his finger and uttered "*Dir Balak*" one final time. As the four men bunched up and walked toward the main entrance, an old woman covered from head to toe in a black *niqab* began motioning toward Ziad and raising a commotion. It was his mother. Careful not to risk any periphery gunfire, the captured Hamas commander gestured that all was well and that he'd be back soon.

The back-and-forth of radio bursts, short and whispered, indicated success. The operators surrounding the building walked inconspicuously back to the vans. Ziad was ushered to the lead vehicle and then wedged in between two operators. Within moments the Ya'mas procession was heading west, twisting in and out of Tulkarm midday traffic toward the no-man's-land shared with Israel.[11] Once the imaginary Green Line had been crossed, Ziad was handed off to the Shin Bet.

At the command post, Uzi Levy brushed his fingers through his thick head of hair and smiled in relief. The colonels and majors who stood with him were in awe by the sheer audacity of it all. As the IAF liaison officer summoned the two attack helicopter pilots, flying a holding pattern over Netanya, to call it a day, the unit headed back to base to prepare for the next mission. There was no time for celebrations.

Operation Defensive Shield not only reestablished—perhaps permanently—an Israeli intelligence presence in the Palestinian cities of Area A, but also sent many of the top terrorist commanders underground—albeit temporarily. There were still hundreds of high-value targets on the Shin Bet radar; each apprehension revealed ten more names of men who were instrumental in the terror networks that had been established before and after the eruption of the second intifada. The suicide bombings would continue in a maddening cycle of seemingly unstoppable violence.

Knowing where a suspect was, what he looked like, where he slept, and what type of firepower he employed was critical to the Ya'mas teams when they had to translate the restrictions of the terrain and the human landscape into operational results. The HUMINT, VISINT, and SIGINT that Israel's services assembled were in the vanguard of this war. This intelligence—nurtured, gathered, processed, analyzed, and disseminated with as fast a turnaround as humanly possible—directed the special operations units that worked around the clock.[12]

The Shin Bet intelligence was, in many ways, ideally suited for the fluid nature and beguiling tactics used by the Ya'mas—a unit whose very effectiveness was the use of the enemy's landscape—and language—to their own advantage. Operation Parting Gift was a classic example of how a small and highly specialized force could apprehend high-value targets without a shot being fired in anger. Many of Israel's top military and intelligence commanders began to take notice.

The special operations campaign mounted by Israel's top-tier units, commando forces designed to attack enemy strongholds and obliterate enemy positions, found it hard to apply that aggressive "type A" DNA to a tedious and often unsuccessful cat-and-mouse reality of hunting the men on the Shin Bet's most-wanted list. The war on terror required patience and imagination and not only a quick trigger finger and uncanny aim. It wasn't a skill set that just any special operations unit could master. Many top-tier Israeli commando formations—units that were masters at deploying at great distances from Israel's frontiers—found the terrain of the territories to be a truly challenging battlefield. On September 26, 2002, three weeks after Operation Parting Gift, Captain Harel Marmelstein, a Flotilla 13 officer, was killed in a firefight with Hamas terrorists in a cave near Tulkarm. The target of the operation was Nisa'at Talatin Jaber, an associate of Samir Ziad's, who was days away, the intelligence reported, from unleashing two suicide bombers against targets in Israel; Jaber was killed by Marmelstein's team. Flotilla 13, like the other commando units, had participated in high-value capture-or-kill missions. Marmselstein, in fact, had replaced a naval commando officer who had been seriously hurt in an operation in Jenin.[13]

Ya'mas commanders were confident that their unit could offer the IDF and senior Shin Bet officials a practical and effective operational solution to the unmanageable amount of high-value terrorist targets that were still operational throughout the command. Instead of dealing with one terrorist on the most-wanted list individually, the Ya'mas proposed, they would deal with a dozen or two dozen names that were concentrated in a single city or area. Whichever one of the names on the list emerged first would be the one they apprehended. The Ya'mas command staff argued that if the unit was already in Jenin looking for one target—with all of the backup and aerial assets that this entailed—they might as well be in the city for an entire day rounding up as many high-value targets as they could.

The tactical details of the arrest operation were relatively unimportant with this strategy. The Ya'mas classified takedowns into three categories—individuals on the street, individuals in vehicles, and individuals in structures. Most of these operations didn't require extensive planning or working for weeks on models of the location. The most difficult element of such an operation was not the tactical part—it was navigating the streets and alleys and being able to maneuver in and out of the hostile environment and remain in the area for hours on end. And this was the unique element to the proposal that was exclusive to the Ya'mas. They were the only unit in Israel's special operations order of battle who possessed Arabic-speaking and territorial fluency. The Speakers and operators were already fluent in the local slang. They had learned the clannish backstories of virtually every neighborhood, and they could navigate down village paths that even locals were unfamiliar with.

Ya'mas familiarity with the landscape inside Palestinian territory became intimate. The unit reconnoitered their assigned targets extensively before a mission; not only was the reconnaissance and terrain-familiarization essential in the pre-operational planning, but entering the Palestinian areas also enabled the operators to gather eyes-on-target intelligence. It was invaluable training, too. The operators who used to struggle memorizing IDF map coordinates and would sometimes fall asleep studying the coded coordinates in their hands now knew the location of landmark restaurants, stores, schools, Internet cafés, and even brothels. After a while the teams knew where they could find the best plate of hummus, and which stands offered the best falafel sandwiches.

Ya'mas intimacy with the surroundings proved invaluable in concocting audacious plans of attack. In one operation, the unit received the Shin Bet file for a PIJ field commander near Jenin. The target worked in a carpentry shop on the outskirts of town, and the plan was for one of the Speakers, an officer, to go inside the warehouse and ask for a computer desk. The masquerade centered on the cover story that the Ya'mas operator was a student,

attending a nearby college, and that he needed a desk for his dorm; significant research was done to establish a cover story, to include a reference from
a family friend (the name of a prominent clan in the area was used) to get a
discount. The operator went into the shop, ordered his desk, and then asked
if the target could help him bring it to his car. As the two men struggled to
fit the wooden table into the back of the car, a Ya'mas van pulled up with
two other men offering to help. Within seconds, the target was in the back
of the van and in handcuffs. A few hours later, as the target sat inside a Shin
Bet facility and waited to be processed, he saw the "student" walk by with a
police-issue sidearm bolstered on his hip. The PIJ commander at first was in
shock, wondering what the college student was doing inside an Israeli holding
area and armed, no less. And then it hit him. He sat there pale-faced, his head
bowed in shame. He couldn't believe that he had been so completely fooled.[14]

In a speech at the noted Interdisciplinary Center in Herzliya, Yoram
Halevy, a former commanding officer of both the Ya'mas and the Ya'ma'm,
addressed these very issues in a think-tank session for the senior Israeli military, law enforcement, and political leadership. In the address, the Ya'ma'm
commander explained that other than the undercover units, Israel didn't
have any specifically trained forces who could initiate operations meant to
undercut the enemy's resolve. Yet the skill and capabilities of the undercover
assets would have no value were it not for the political will to make decisive
and unyielding use of it.[15]

Israel's leadership, and its military and law enforcement command,
were focused on a singular mission—the uprooting and destruction of the
lethal terrorist infrastructure. The Palestinians would be offered no quarter until the terrorist attacks ceased. The Ya'mas proposal to allow them to
add even more to their already overburdened workload was enthusiastically
embraced by the decision-makers in Israel's war on terror. The Ya'mas called
their multi-targeted forays *Yemei Tzayid*, or Hunting Days. The term was
controversial—few in the unit cared.

By late 2002 the Ya'mas had grown in size—two squadrons, each with several teams, replaced the three teams that had existed earlier.* The unit expanded its ranks, and many of the team sergeants and NCO cadre were sent to officers' school so that they could become team commanders and the next generation of undercover leaders. Wartime promotions were sometimes the most effective way to reward those whose courage and leadership under fire could never be measured by aptitude and psycho-technical tests.

There was an in-your-face arrogance in how the Ya'mas executed its missions, but it had nothing to do with swagger; it certainly wasn't from an entitled sense of elitism or bravado. Rather, the Ya'mas wore a defiant suit of armor made of stubborn resolve that was laced together with stitches of *Davka*—a uniquely Hebrew word for "double-spite." On paper the Ya'mas didn't match up to the IDF's elite commando formations. "These men weren't recruited from high school as superstars, monitored by the IAF as a shoo-in to become an F-16 pilot," a Ya'mas officer explained. "They were street fighters and survivalists who were courageous beyond question."[16] Many of the operators grew up in the republics of the former Soviet Union, struggling to survive on the streets of Moscow, or in Tashkent, or Astana. Others grew up in Israel's peripheral development towns where high school test scores mattered little; the streets were their school. According to the IDF, many of these men weren't supposed to amount to much. Some Ya'mas operators, who had served in the IDF as infantrymen or in the armored corps, were not considered by the army to be officer material. Yet in the Ya'mas they excelled and were able to apply pragmatic logic to complex life-threatening challenges. Under fire they displayed leadership qualities that could never be taught in the officers' academy. When they were tested—and when the unit was tested—the operators performed better than the elite of the elite of the IDF special units.[17]

Very close friendships developed between the Shin Bet case officers and the Ya'mas operators they worked with. "We lived with them, ate with them, and went into the Palestinian areas with them," a Ya'mas veteran explained. "This

---

* The exact size of a Ya'mas team and squadron is classified. The name of each squadron is also classified.

was *our* war. They had to manage an enormous workload and they knew that if they failed in locating one of the men on their list, a bus could be blown up in Tel Aviv. We lived under the same pressure, with the same repercussions. Neither of us could live and do what we needed to do without the other."[18] And this symbiotic mutual respect and reliance enabled the Hunting Days concept to work.

Sometimes, the intelligence on a suspect was sketchy—name, face, and his loose network of affiliations. Other times, the file length was more voluminous. The Ya'mas intelligence officers, working closely with their Shin Bet counterparts, assembled extensive dossiers on suspects, listing: where they slept, the names of their family members (immediate and distant), what types of weapons they were known to carry, the name of the mosque where they prayed, and how many people were protecting them.

The more information that the Ya'mas could assemble on a suspect, the more quickly and efficiently they could accomplish their foray inside Palestinian areas; every moment that they moved about inside a town or village while on the hunt constituted risk and danger. A navigational and route map had to be created, as well. If one suspect had twenty-five possible hideouts, then the Ya'mas raiding force would have to know how to get to each one of them. Every street, back road, and footpath needed to reach one of these locations had to be memorized; virtually all of these roads had no names and no markings, just coordinates on master IDF maps. It was a Herculean task. The raiding party, as part of the measures to maintain their masquerade behind enemy lines, could not carry GPS devices with them. On the night before an operation, the team sergeant, the man responsible for navigating the apprehension squad, would need to study reams of paper consisting of maps and coordinates. Often, the sergeant would fall asleep at his desk, overcome by exhaustion. He would wake up when the cigarette in between his fingers burned its way down to the filter.

The first of the Hunting Days was launched against a band of Tanzim operatives, from the villages between Qalqilya and Tulkarm, who had launched a series of deadly shooting and bombing attacks against Israeli soldiers and civilians. The Shin Bet had been after the five for several months, but the young men—car thieves and thugs—had always proved to be one step ahead of IDF efforts to apprehend them. When the files were handed to the

Ya'mas, the results were fairly immediate. Looking at their known hangouts helped the unit intelligence and operations heads to assemble a matrix that pinpointed behavioral patterns and probabilities. The squadron commanders, Yaakov Berman and Ronen Goresh, were able put together a checklist of locations where the suspects were known to be, including outside a girls' school at night where they could watch the girls undress and shower.[19]

The work inside the cities was incredibly dangerous and physically exhausting. The Speakers had to drive for hours on end, maintaining their masquerade and careful to avoid Palestinian police and security service checkpoints; their job was to keep contact with the locals, be they pedestrians or Hamas gunmen armed with RPGs, to its absolute minimum. The Speakers had to drive according to the rules of the road, and be sure not to get into any accidents or altercations. Their sidearms, and their Mini-Uzis and M4s, had to be concealed at all times. The tactical backup that the Speakers ferried, riding inside the concealed and claustrophobic cabin of the Horse, were subjected to stifling heat with no ventilation and absolute darkness; sometimes, the only light available was a small glow from a miniature display transmitting images from a camera located on the vehicle. The men inside the cabin couldn't move and they couldn't make a sound. They sat inside the cramped space wearing more than sixty pounds of gear and body armor. The atmosphere was suffocating and nauseating. The inside of the Horse smelled like farts, dirty socks, gun grease, and mildew growing on wet canvas. The men had to remain statue-like and in silence until they received the coded word on their earpieces to deploy, and then they had to erupt in an explosive moment to engage a target. Often, the operators would fall out of the Horse and on their faces because their legs had fallen asleep during the long drives in and around a Palestinian city looking for a suspect. Emerging from absolute darkness into brilliant Levantine sunshine, the eyes of the men in the Horse often had to adjust under fire as their pupils contracted.

The Ya'mas was the only unit in the IDF special operations arsenal that had the ability to deploy simultaneous arrest squads throughout a landmass of 2,177 square miles with a hostile population of 2.2 million. From a practical perspective, the days dedicated to one particular city were very cost-effective. The brigade or divisional command that had authorized the Ya'mas foray already had the aerial reconnaissance and tactical backup tools at the ready—if a brigade or division commander had assembled several drones and a battalion of paratroopers to deploy for a tweezers' operation that could, from start to finish, last an hour, then those same assets could be readied for dawn to dusk.

The successful pursuit of terror suspects depended on the ability to move invisibly inside Palestinian areas, often for prolonged stakeouts. In one particular operation, in pursuit of Ashraf Safadi, a Fatah commander in Nablus wanted for commanding a cell of terrorists responsible for several suicide bombings inside Israel, the Ya'mas spent days deep inside Nablus looking for their target. In fact, unit operators became such a routine sight in the city that people walking by their vehicles offered them a smile and a *sabah el kheer*, or good morning, as they passed by. On the stakeout, a Palestinian Authority work crew paving a roadway asked the undercover operatives to help them direct traffic while they poured tar onto the street. As the men in the lead car and Horses laughed silently, two veteran Speakers who thought they had done it all and seen it all put on reflective red vests and waved a red flag in the street, directing the morning's commuters past the construction vehicles. The work crew thanked the operators for their kindness and assistance and asked if they could help out with what they were doing. The Ya'mas operators, flattered not by the kindness but at how effective their masquerade had been, respectfully declined the reciprocity. Safadi was arrested in a lightning-flash operation on September 26, 2002.[20] He was in cuffs before he realized what had happened.

The year 2002 had been a truly bloody one for Israel: 452 Israelis had been killed in terrorist attacks, and another 2,284 had been wounded. Not since the 1948 War of Independence had so many Israelis been killed and wounded in conflict. Like the 1948 War, the al-Aqsa intifada threatened every Israeli town and city and every Israeli socioeconomic group with the possibility of indiscriminate carnage. Israeli military doctrine demanded short and clean wars. The intifada was ugly, protracted, and showed no signs of ending.

Technology and supersonic fighter bombers were never going to defeat an asymmetrical enemy that employed unconventional tactics such as terror and hid inside a civilian population, in essence using it as a human shield—not without severe international repercussions, at least. Israel had no choice but to fight this bloody war by removing the Palestinian ability to wage war one high-value target at a time. This was a bare-knuckle street brawl that Israel's generals and spymasters were intent on fighting on their own terms.

The perception that the Ya'mas response to the Itamar attack had put the unit on the map was shortsighted and incorrect. The heroics at Itamar certainly raised the unit's profile and made headlines, but the unit's unrivaled and fluid capabilities had already proved to the skeptics, primarily those in command who had grown up inside the IDF's special operations units, that the Ya'mas was far more than a highly specialized surgical force with Arabic-language capabilities. They were cutting-edge.

The Ya'mas apprehended hundreds of terrorist field commanders in 2002. According to figures published by Major General (also known as a Deputy Commissioner in the British-based Israeli police rank structure) David Tzur, the former Ya'ma'm commander and Border Guard commanding officer, they also killed twenty who resisted.[21] By the end of 2002, the Ya'mas had become the Shin Bet's most important, imaginative, and reliable tool in the fight against Palestinian terrorism in the West Bank; the unit arrested more terror suspects than most of the other special operations units combined, and they killed many high-value targets who were determined to fight to the end in order to avoid being questioned inside a Shin Bet holding facility. Soon, as the intifada entered its third bloody year, Israel would intensify its campaign to catch or kill the terrorist commanders responsible for so much bloodshed. Ya'mas raids would become more daring and far more dangerous.

CHAPTER SEVEN

Hostile Encounters

The first suicide bombing attack of 2003 was an insidiously bloody one. At 6:30 p.m. on the evening of January 5, a young man wearing fifteen kilograms of explosives and shrapnel in a suicide vest hidden underneath clothing blew himself up amid a throng of shoppers near Tel Aviv's old central bus station. The area, in the southern part of the city, was one of Tel Aviv's poorest and most crime-ridden neighborhoods and had become a favorite for foreign workers in the country illegally; the foreign workers, men from Romania, Thailand, and dozens of other countries, replaced Palestinian laborers who traditionally toiled at the menial jobs of Israel's bustling economy but who were no longer allowed to enter Israel because of the security threat. The streets were crowded with many workers returning home from their construction jobs when the first bomb exploded. Bodies were thrown one hundred feet by the powerful blast, and the dying begged for help in a Tower of Babel of languages. Some of the wounded picked themselves up and ran away from the crime scene in a panic—undocumented workers were more concerned about being questioned by the police and deported than they were about being killed. They ran deeper into the narrow streets of the neighborhood and straight toward a second bomber who detonated his lethal payload outside a crowded café thirty seconds after the first blast.

The double-tap suicide strike killed 23 people and wounded 120. The al-Aqsa Martyrs Brigade, in conjunction with the PIJ, had carried out the attack. The bombers originated from Nablus.

The bombing was one of the deadliest to hit Tel Aviv during the course of the intifada, but would also be one of the last major attacks against Israel's largest city. Israel had, three years into the conflict, slowly seized the strategic advantage. Operation Defensive Shield had been successful in disrupting the Palestinian terrorist infrastructure that had been built since the Oslo Accords. The large-scale Israeli military incursion had crippled Arafat's duplicitous security services that often provided manpower, tools, and cover for the terrorist factions. The Israeli invasion put the Palestinians on notice—not with shuttle diplomacy or meetings on the White House lawn but with D9s and commando raids—that the terrorists would pay a dear price for attacks against Israeli cities.

The conventional—and covert—ground campaign coincided with a simultaneous effort to make it far more difficult for suicide bombers to cross into Israel. In June 2002, the Israeli cabinet authorized the construction of a fortified wall separating Israel from the West Bank to physically impede free movement across the jagged frontier. The wall, known as the Separation Barrier, consisted of electronic fencing flanked by security roads, trenches, and concrete walls that were between six and eight meters high. The barrier was a Herculean project and required 440 miles of wall to be erected. Construction of the Separation Barrier was a nightmare for smugglers who crisscrossed the invisible Green Line with black market goods. It was a huge impediment to the terrorists, as well, as it would make infiltrating operatives into Israel far more difficult.

But the wall was not hermetic. And the commandos could not be everywhere all the time. The bombers still made it to their targets.

On March 5, 2003, Mahmoud Amadan Salim Qawasmeh boarded the No. 37 bus in the Carmel section of Haifa. Various handlers and facilitators, all handsomely paid for their efforts, had driven Qawasmeh nearly one hundred miles from his home in Hebron, past checkpoints along a circuitous route, in order to make it to Israel's third largest city and northernmost port. Qawasmeh was a computer student at the Polytechnic Institute in Hebron, and he detonated the fifteen kilograms of high explosives and shrapnel that he wore underneath a jacket on a crowded bus en route toward Haifa University just as the crosstown transport negotiated an intersection along Moriah Boulevard, a tree-lined street of apartment buildings and shops. Seventeen people were killed in the explosion and fifty-three more were seriously hurt; the blast was so powerful that white plastic blinds of nearby apartments were singed black and red from the heat and blood. Haifa was a city where Jew,

Christian, and Muslim lived and worked side by side, but the bomb's lethal payload of shrapnel did not discriminate as it tore through the flesh and organs of the city's citizens.

The Shin Bet was under greater pressure to end the carnage. The special operations units were ordered to do whatever possible to stop the suicide bombers before they could strike yet again.

Qalqilya, a city of forty thousand inhabitants, was the closest West Bank town to Tel Aviv. Qalqilya straddled the affluent suburban town of Kfar Saba, as well as some very exclusive collectives along the plains that separated the Palestinian areas from the pre-1967 lines; former prime minister Ehud Barak lived in Moshav Kochav Yair, which was within walking distance of the Palestinian city. Qalqilya had always been a sort of bridge city caught in the middle of the conflict. In the good days, before the first intifada, Israelis drove to Qalqilya to eat in one of the city's restaurants and to shop in the many stores of the Kasbah. The city was known for its ornate marble. The floors and kitchens of many Israeli homes had come from Qalqilya.

During the al-Aqsa intifada, Qalqilya was a flashpoint. It was in Qalqilya where the dream of the Oslo Accords was executed with the murder of Superintendent Yosef Tabeja on September 29, 2000. Qalqilya was the home of Sa'ed Hotari, a twenty-one-year-old with the face of a cherubic teenager, who had detonated ten kilograms of high-grade explosives and shrapnel outside the Dolphi discotheque on June 1, 2001. Hotari had mingled with a large group of teenagers, mostly new immigrants from the former Soviet Union who lived in and around the Tel Aviv area, who were standing in line to enter the disco. While still in line, he detonated the explosives strapped to his body and killed 21 high-school students and wounded 120 more. The bombing, carried out on behalf of a Hamas cell in Qalqilya, had been planned by the notorious Mahmoud Abu Hanoud.[1] Because of Qalqilya's proximity to Tel Aviv, it took Hotari less than an hour to get from his doorstep in the Third World to his point of detonation in one of the world's hippest high-tech cities.

On March 12, 2003, a Shin Bet case agent knocked on the door of the operations officer at the Ya'mas headquarters. A credible tip had been received that Hamas was planning to carry out a double-pronged suicide bombing against a target in the Tel Aviv area. The tip was vague, but it pinpointed the identities of the two men who would be delivering the devices to a safe house where the bombers were being prepped and readied for their lethal mission. Israeli special operations units traditionally liked to create two or more parallel teams that could compete with one another,[2] and the Ya'mas was no different. The two teams—and later two squadrons—often vied for the same work. Yaakov Berman's squadron jumped at the opportunity. They took the job.

The Ya'mas liked to work in Qalqilya: The West Bank city was easy to get into and, most important, to get out of. There were only three ways in and out. Qalqilya was more or less sealed by geography and walls and fences. "Getting to the target, navigating the roads and the small entrances, was the most difficult part of undercover warfare," an operator explained. "The team sergeant was the man responsible for directing the drivers on where to go and where to turn, and the fear was always there of making a wrong turn that could jeopardize the one small window to apprehend a suspect. Everyone made a mistake at least once, but we appreciated cities like Qalqilya where navigating our way around was so simple."[3]

But Qalqilya's small size also made it a challenge for undercover work. "The city was split by one central boulevard, and all other areas and streets were small and insular. It was the kind of city where everyone knew everyone else," a former member of the unit recalled, "so it was difficult to remain in the lead car, with the team or squadron commander, and remain in character. People suspected you if they didn't recognize your face. The city was intimate and the inhabitants were always very suspicious. You needed to know how to maneuver, navigate, and cruise the city's main drag and its smaller streets in such a way that no one suspected who you were, how you drove, or what your intentions were. Any deviation from what the locals were used to and the operators in the car were compromised. Qalqilya was a difficult place to have to hurry up and wait. The longer you were there, the greater the chance that you might have to shoot your way out."[4] The exfiltration from the target area was always a critical component of any operation. "There were times, many, when we would present a plan to the unit commander, even the brigade and divisional commanders, for approval and we would have it rejected because of the fear that we could get in but we would come out with a few of our own killed," an undercover commander explained.[5]

When news of the ticking bomb reached Berman, the Ya'mas was able to put together an operation—from the first threads of intelligence that came through to the Shin Bet maze to the actual execution—on the fly. Sometimes, the coordination was done in transit. Officers would discuss their ideas and plans over mobile phones with the unit commander, even the regional IDF brigade or divisional commander, get the mission authorized while the unit was en route to the objective, and make sure that the backup plan was in place and all the assets ready. The only other unit that functioned in this way was the Ya'ma'm.

Chief Inspector Berman summoned his men, selected the vehicles, and pre-deployed at a base near the entrance to the city. The tactics were discussed on phones and on police radios en route to Qalqilya. It was a matter of a couple of hours—no more—in between the Shin Bet breaking the news and the IDF brigade commander watching Berman and his men enter Qalqilya from the drone that had been launched over the city. There were no Palestinian police—or terrorist—roadblocks to negotiate. Berman and his men made it inside without any concern.

The Shin Bet knew the make and color of the suspected vehicle, but not the license plate number. The drone was able to pinpoint the target car, and the information was relayed to Berman and his men. The images relayed to the CP were sharp, though it was still impossible to determine just how many men were actually inside the vehicle. The drone's flight path followed the vehicle as it moved in and out of side streets to commercial boulevards. The Ya'mas task force inserted itself into Qalqilya through the main road, and soldiers at the CP directed them toward the targeted vehicle: a white four-door Opel sedan.

For nearly thirty minutes the Ya'mas motorcade followed the car as it weaved in and out of the city's streets. There were at least three people in the vehicle, the operators could see, but they couldn't discern if the wanted suspect was among them. "Everyone wait!" Berman ordered on the communications frequency. The operators limbered their fingers so that they would be ready to rush out of their Horses with their weapons at the ready.

The white Opel pulled up in front of a clothing shop located in the center of town, near the entrance to the Kasbah. One man got out, then another. The driver remained at the wheel. Seconds later, the man whose photo the Shin Bet had displayed at the operations planning session emerged from the store. He was wearing an Israeli military surplus olive-green one-piece winter coverall; a pair of large dark green aviator glasses completed the uniform of the Hamas commander. Berman wanted to order the takedown right then and there, but the suspect entered the Opel and it raced into the labyrinth of narrow stone-paved streets in the Kasbah. Berman knew that the Kasbah was fraught with risk, and the Ya'mas vehicles could find themselves blocked and surrounded in an instant. It didn't matter to him, though. "GO!" he yelled to his driver, one of the more experienced Speakers in the unit. Berman's follow car and the Horses behind him ventured deep into the Kasbah in hot pursuit. The Kasbah was not designed for vehicular chases. Most streets were barely wide enough to accommodate one vehicle.

The Speaker drove through the Kasbah with incredible dexterity, sometimes squeezing into an alley with barely an inch of space on either side. Shopkeepers yelled in anger at the procession of vehicles racing down the narrow streets at Le Mans speeds. In the heart of the Kasbah, Berman's driver noticed a brief opening near a series of shops that would allow his vehicle to overtake the Opel. Berman readied his Glock; the Speaker pressed hard on the gas pedal. Berman could see the Palestinian's face, and he could also see the unmistakable barrel of the AK-47. The Speaker maneuvered his vehicle so that the Opel was cornered. The Palestinian emerged from the vehicle and took aim at the Speaker with his rifle. Berman had rushed out of the vehicle first and took aim. The Ya'mas team leader shot and killed the terrorist at close range. The terrorist's driver was shot and wounded, as well.

The brief shoot-out in the Kasbah invited a throng of onlookers and a barrage of what the unit called "airmail," bottles and rocks tossed from nearby rooftops. Berman ordered the tactical backup to establish a defensive perimeter. The operators leaped out of the vehicles and took up firing positions covering all possible angles of attack. The airmail intensified. Berman examined the body of the dead terrorist to see if he was wearing an explosive vest, and he checked the rear passenger seats in the Opel for grenades and explosives. Berman then proceeded to examine the trunk. Rocks smashed near his head and feet as he flipped open the hood to reveal a thick black nylon tarp covering the cargo hold. Berman placed his hand over the nylon, touching it gently to carefully try to determine what lay underneath. He felt a hard object with a jagged bump. He used a tactical knife to cut the tarp open, and he then froze in a moment of great fear: Two explosive rigs—each consisting of adhesive boards crammed with screws, nails, and bolts that were molded to fit as a chest plate—were attached to cloth vests. Each explosive vest was large—larger than Berman had ever seen before. The Shin Bet tip had yielded a jackpot.

The operators had no intention of leaving the devices in the Kasbah where they could explode; Berman wasn't about to leave them for Hamas, either. He ordered his men to load the wounded driver into the Horse and to follow him toward the outskirts of the city, where the devices could be examined and rendered safe by an army bomb technician. First Sergeant Avi,* an operator from the backup team, got into the Opel to drive the vehicle while Berman made sure that the path ahead was clear of obstacles. Gunfire began to ping around the Israelis as they gathered their gear and followed the Opel out of the city; Berman knew that one stray bullet into the trunk and he could be killed in a thunderous blast.

Avi made a few left turns and then a few right, in the mad dash out of the Kasbah. Hundreds of people, including Palestinian policemen and men in civilian attire carrying M16s and AK-47s, began pushing forward, filling the narrow streets with an impassable flow of humanity; shopkeepers quickly shuttered their gates, fearing there was going to be a large-scale battle inside the confines of the Kasbah. Berman grabbed his Glock and readied his M4. Instead of firing in the air in order to clear the rabble, he rolled down the windows and began to scream, *"Jesh! Jesh!"* in the best Arabic accent the Soviet-born officer could muster, signaling to the crowds that the Israeli Army was chasing them.

Berman brought the Opel to a secluded stretch of mud beyond the IDF checkpoint just outside of Qalqilya. Shin Bet and Israel National Police

---

* A pseudonym—true identity withheld for security considerations.

investigators looked the device over and were rendered speechless. Both devices weighed more than twenty kilograms, and the investigators assessed that they could easily have killed everyone on a packed intercity bus or eviscerated a restaurant full of patrons. The IDF bomb disposal officer who rigged the devices for the controlled explosion could not believe that they had not detonated as Avi and Berman drove the Opel out of Qalqilya. Bullet holes riddled the trunk. News photographers rushed to the no-man's-land to document the controlled explosion. It was dusk by the time the bomb tech issued the "fire in the hole" warning three times to warn of the coming blast. The shutters snapped as the Opel was ripped apart by the powerful detonation. The orange flames illuminated the darkening skies. The thick, acrid black smoke filled the air over Qalqilya for hours.

Chief Inspector Berman returned to the command post hoping to have the adrenaline vacate his system. It had been a good—and productive—day in the field. Many in the IDF hierarchy were furious that Berman had risked the life of the entire force in such an impulsive manner.* Berman shrugged off the lecture—it had become a common routine.

Stopping the intifada was a time-intensive endeavor. Each Shin Bet *Rakaz*, or case officer, spent countless hours cultivating sources and assets inside the Palestinian areas. That information was often checked and double-checked. It was also cross-referenced and checked and double-checked again against SIGINT and VISINT data that had been culled, analyzed, vetted, and disseminated. Sometimes even, in the murky world of counterespionage and counterterrorism tradecraft, data was culled with the help of neighboring intelligence services; these internal security and secret police outfits might not have had Israel's best interests at heart, but they knew that the Middle East—and their country's national security—was best served with these professional terrorists dead or behind bars.

---

* For their heroism above and beyond the call of duty, Yaakov Berman and First Sergeant Avi were awarded the Israel National Police *Itur Ha'Ometz*, or Medal of Courage, for the operation in Qalqilya. The decoration is the second highest police medal for valor.

All of that information was also checked against information assembled from the questioning of terror suspects. Some interrogations were quick and incredibly fruitful. Some even created new assets who would spy on the terror factions on behalf of the State of Israel. Some interrogations, though, lasted days; some lasted longer and yielded very little if anything at all. The entire process warranted great patience and a cold-as-steel temperament. The Shin Bet case officers were like doctors—emotionally detached when needed, and focused on identifying and removing the malignancies that threatened the country. Units like the Ya'mas were the tactical surgeons.

Kassem Iyad (also known as Qawasmeh)[6] was a senior PIJ military operative who was not only wanted for a string of bombings and attempted bombings against Israeli targets, but the intelligence matrix indicated that he was in the process of finalizing a large-scale suicide car-bombing of a city in Israel; according to Israeli assessments, Iyad had even left the territories to receive advanced training in Syria and Iran.[7] Schooled in countersurveillance, Iyad moved about mostly at night. He emerged briefly in daylight sometimes, in order to communicate with his liaisons to the PIJ top political leadership, as well as his subordinates in the field.

In February 2003, following a stint in officers' course, Salah returned to the Ya'mas as a freshly commissioned sub-inspector, the military equivalent of a first lieutenant. Patrick Pereg had recognized many unique leadership qualities in Salah's inexorable makeup, and always recommended that the dedicated Ya'mas sergeant be sent to officers' training. Salah stubbornly resisted. Patrick's death in Hebron had greatly impacted the Druze operator. He had lost his mentor and close friend and he opted to sign up for the command course. The unit changed dramatically during the nine months that Salah was away in officers' training. It had grown in size, and it had proved itself in Itamar and in dozens of high-profile operations where terrorists were captured or killed. The new officer was given command of a team of veteran operators—some of whom had been with the Ya'mas from its very start and had guided Salah when he was a new recruit to the unit years earlier—that was a part of Yaakov Berman's squadron.

It had been nearly a year since Salah participated in an undercover operation. He felt rusty, perhaps a little insecure, and he wanted to reacquaint himself with the unit's modus operandi, especially from the perspective of coordinating the unit's operations from inside the command post. Salah requested that Berman assign him to the CP for an upcoming mission so that he could see how all the moving parts—IDF, IAF, and Shin Bet—worked together along with the unit's hierarchy. That mission was Kassem Iyad's apprehension.

The Shin Bet had learned that Iyad often used the Assil Internet Cafe, located in the heart of Jenin, as an ad hoc office from where he sent emails and communicated with commanders outside of Israel's frontiers. The location was a known PIJ hangout; many of the young men inside the coffeehouse turned computer center were armed.

The Ya'mas plan was brazen and incredibly dangerous. Three Arabic-speaking Ya'mas operators, dressed as locals, would enter the Assil when they knew Iyad to be there and quickly usher him outside, where a van would be waiting. It was hoped that the entire snatch and grab would take a matter of minutes. If everything went according to plan, the arrest operation would happen so fast Iyad's associates would never know what had happened.

The operation was fraught with risk, though. Once inside the internet café, the three Ya'mas operators would have no drone coverage and would be alone and isolated inside a darkened labyrinth of computer terminals and armed men. One wrong move, one wrong phrase, and the compromised mission could go very wrong very fast. But the unit believed that any risk could be overcome with audacity and guile. None of the three Speakers around whom the operation was built felt any fear or foreboding.

But Murphy's Law reared its ugly head early on. The unit's staging area and forward command post was at an agricultural encampment near Jenin; the mission commander was allergic to livestock and suddenly collapsed in pain as his head swelled from working so close to the horses and cows. He was rushed to the emergency room desperately in need of an epinephrine injection. The Shin Bet case agents, along with the IDF majors and colonels who would coordinate the aerial elements and mechanized rescue force, were about to call off the mission when Salah volunteered to take the injured man's place. He ran to the equipment van, grabbed his kit bag, and hurriedly changed out of his tactical coveralls and into one of the outfits he wore when masquerading as a Palestinian. The mission was still a go.

The entry team consisted of three operators—all officers. Chief Inspector Abu Assad* was the operation commander. Sub-inspectors Amal† and Salah would provide tactical backup.[8] Two of the three were members of Israel's minority community, and all were native Arabic speakers and had participated in hundreds of such infiltration masquerades in the past. Each hoped that the intelligence was right and that luck was on their side. The three, along with the men who would be their backup in the Horses, held one final briefing under the warming March sun. They reviewed the latest intelligence, reexamined the tactical plan one last time, and walked confidently to their vehicles.

The unit's senior officers rushed back to the CP to watch the operation unfold. The drone was already flying over Jenin.

March 4, 2003, was a beautiful day in Jenin. A brilliant afternoon sun illuminated the city, but the winter's chill was still evident. The drive crossing into Jenin went smoothly, perhaps too smoothly, the Speakers thought. They had covered this ground before, perhaps a hundred times before since Defensive Shield. The entry points to the city's gate, the "Tank Junction," as well as the avenues intersecting into side streets and alleys, and those that led directly into lethal dead-end kill zones, were all so familiar; each landmark that the two native Arabic speakers passed enhanced their sharpened senses. The men in the lead car wondered how many hours of the last two years of their lives had been spent entering Jenin or another West Bank city to pick up men, too many of them to remember their names and faces, who were still out in the field orchestrating the intifada.

The Assil Internet Cafe in the heart of Jenin was a large, dark room with a dozen or so computers hooked up to internet connections. The establishment, located on a side street that wrapped around one of the main avenues, boasted a varied clientele that ranged from teenage gamers playing *Diablo II* online with complete strangers thousands of miles away, to young men seeking relationships and employment opportunities in the Gulf. It was possible to buy a strong cup of Bedouin coffee or a small glass of sweet tea with

---

* A pseudonym—true identity withheld for security considerations.
† A pseudonym—true identity withheld for security considerations.

mint leaves at the main counter; most of the customers, though, preferred to smoke a narghile water pipe as they sat around or chatted, or chain-smoke pack after pack of East Jerusalem's own Imperial cigarettes. The lights were always dimmed low in the Assil.

Iyad was known to be armed, and he always traveled with at least one heavily armed bodyguard at his side. This was a challenge for the Ya'mas, as the Shin Bet's goal was to capture Iyad alive. The operational plan took into consideration the belief that the PIJ group leader would be less likely to resist inside the claustrophobic and darkened confusion of an internet café than inside a safe house or on the street. The latest intelligence was that the Assil wasn't crowded at the time selected for the arrest.

The convoy of Ya'mas vehicles pushed forward into Jenin without incident. Traffic was heavy and the streets were filled with commercial vehicles trying to weave in and out of lanes clogged by tractors pulling wagons of produce. The undercover vehicles, followed by the Horses, pulled up in front of the entrance of the Assil. Three men emerged from the vehicles dressed in counterfeit jeans and locally made winter jackets. The Horses parked nearby.

The Assil, contrary to the pre-mission assessment, was packed with Web surfers that Tuesday afternoon. The sounds of video-game gunfire and Arabic music bounced off the walls of the darkened hallway. The layout had also changed. Tables had been moved. Chairs weren't where they were supposed to be. The sketches drawn showing the design of the location now appeared to be nothing more than incorrect scribble. A different group of operators from a different type of unit might have walked out of the Assil. But turning back never entered anyone's mind. The three Speakers walked in, their eyes struggling to adjust to the darkness.

The Ya'mas officers walked deeper inside the cavernous café, looking for the face that they had studied so intently at the Shin Bet briefings. It was hard to distinguish the facial features of men illuminated solely by the glow of computer monitors. The three officers looked around cautiously, trying hard to blend in. There were more than a dozen suspicious eyes trained on them. Any stranger who walked into the café was certain to be suspect.

Inspector Abu Assad, a mustache and a carpet of stubble covering his narrow face, noticed Iyad sitting at a desk in the back of the café; his face was immersed in the flashing glow of the computer screen. Abu Assad moved forward, carefully inching his way toward Iyad. In undercover operations, the operator is usually the one who strikes first. Sub-Inspectors Amal and Salah split up and attempted to fit in to the crowd of wary men while trying to maintain contact with their commander—and their target—through the corners of their eyes. It was imperative that they maintain the initiative.

The Ya'mas operators did not see Iyad's bodyguard positioned behind a support beam in the rear of the Assil, watching over as Iyad read his emails. None of the operators heard the bodyguard cocking his weapon and placing a round inside the chamber. All they heard was the sounds of online gaming and teenagers talking loudly under a heavy beat of music from a boom box radio, launching the sounds of the top pop stars hitting the charts in Damascus. The bodyguard fired first. Iyad took aim next, pulling the trigger of a semiautomatic pistol that he kept on the desk next to the keyboard and mouse. Abu Assad and Salah were both shot multiple times in the midsection in the opening fusillade, but all three Ya'mas operators managed to maintain their composure and return fire. The bodyguard was killed first, hit by multiple shots to the head and chest. He collapsed slowly across a bank of computer terminals, his body forcing brand-new monitors to crash to the ground below. Iyad, trying to escape, was also shot and killed. His body, peppered by numerous hits, slumped back in his chair in front of the computer.

Chaos ensued inside the Assil as people raced out the doorway and others inside produced handguns from their coat pockets and from holsters tucked into the small of their backs. Amal fired over the heads of those who remained inside the café, to keep anyone thinking of intervening from looking up. He crawled toward Salah and dragged him behind a desk and wall for protective cover. Bleeding heavily, and barely able to right himself to move, Abu Assad dragged himself out to the curb, where he organized the tactical backup and the rescue attempt.

Word spread immediately that the *qawat al-hasa* were inside the city and outside the Assil. The first bullets to hit the Ya'mas vehicles were sporadic; they were fired from several hundred yards away, what the Israelis liked to call the "periphery." But the gunfire continued and intensified. A full-fledged battle developed to extricate the three officers. The Ya'mas operators were engaging targets one hundred meters away firing from storefronts, third-story windows, and rooftops. A force of operators, including combat medics, rushed into the Assil to rescue Amal and Salah. Some of them slipped on the dozens of 9mm shell casings that now littered the floor.

Armored IDF ambulances were rushed to Jenin, along with APC and reinforcing infantry forces. Abu Assad and Salah were evacuated to a medical center, where they underwent emergency surgery.

When an operator was shot, or suffered a serious in-the-line-of-duty injury, the operator's first thought was always one of relief. "Getting shot meant a few days off," Sa'ar Shine reflected. "We sometimes prayed for that magic bullet that would let us recover for a few weeks and reclaim a little of our lives."[9] But that was the kind of sentiment shared in quarters, over a cup of steaming hot mud coffee laced with *hawayej*, the Yemenite-inspired blend made from aromatic turmeric, cumin, and black pepper. In reality, wounded operators often left their hospital beds early or without their doctors even knowing that they'd disappeared through a rear exit. The operators didn't want to miss the action; no one wanted to hear about a mission after the fact.

Salah's recovery from two gunshot wounds to the gut would require a lengthy—nearly eighteen months—struggle to return to fighting form. The rehabilitation was difficult and painful. Yet Salah's most pressing concern was not his health but rather what would go on in the unit without him. He wondered if, when he returned, there would still be a need for the incessant schedule of working around the clock. His fears were unfounded.

For their courage and dedication to the mission, Inspector Abu Assad and Sub-inspectors Salah and Amal were awarded the Israel National Police Medal of Courage for their role in the events at the Assil Cafe. When Sub-inspector Salah returned to active duty, he was given command of a team of his own, and though he had missed many dangerous forays into Palestinian territories during his recuperation, there would still be many more missions to go on. The war in the West Bank was very far from over.

CHAPTER EIGHT

Clan Warfare

The village of Silat al-Harithiya was a landmark for two types of people—those who were part of the global jihad and those who were fighting it. Everyone else stayed clear away from the hilltop home to slightly under ten thousand inhabitants.

During the British Mandate of Palestine, His Majesty's forces referred to the village as Bandit Country. When the Palestinian village became a West Bank border outpost along the 1949 Armistice Lines, following the establishment of the Jewish State, the Jordanian police and military forces that controlled the area thought it more prudent to ignore the goings-on inside Silat al-Harithiya rather than make the attempt to impose law and order. Israeli forces that assumed control of the West Bank following the 1967 War considered Silat al-Harithiya to be a thorn; the landscape was owned by the hardcore nationalist groups. When Silat al-Harithiya became the northwest-ernmost reach of Area A, fully administered by the Palestinian Authority, even Arafat's security services rarely ventured into the village; it was too dangerous. Some of the best car thieves in the West Bank called Silat al-Harithiya home. Everything from stolen weapons to smuggled cattle passed through the village gates, along with the interconnected bands of brothers and cousins that controlled the black market illicit trade. Even by West Bank standards Silat al-Harithiya was pure outlaw.

Silat al-Harithiya was strategically situated as a bastion for brigands—one could walk from the village to Jenin, as well as to Megiddo Junction inside the pre-1967 boundaries of the State of Israel. Silat al-Harithiya was a stone's throw to the Israeli-Arab city of Umm el-Fahm, the "Mother of Charcoal," that straddled the ultra-important Route 65 artery that connected much of northern Israel along the Mediterranean coast with the Jezreel Valley and points north and south.

Silat al-Harithiya's favorite son was Abdullah Yusef Azzam—the man who created Osama bin Laden. Born in 1941, Azzam was a legendary religious scholar who was trained in Damascus and who taught in a Silat al-Harithiya mosque up until June 1967, when he and his family fled to Jordan after the Six Day War. Targeted by Jordanian intelligence because of his radical views, Azzam fled to the Kingdom of Saudi Arabia, where he joined the faculty at King Abdul Azziz University in Jeddah; Azzam was a professor during the years that Osama bin Laden attended the university. In 1979, when the Soviet Union invaded Afghanistan, Azzam issued a fatwa declaring resistance to the invasion of Muslim lands as an act of faith; both the Afghan and Palestinian struggles, he argued, were holy wars and a personal obligation of all Muslims. He moved to Peshawar, Pakistan, and ultimately founded the Services Office to accommodate Arabs flocking to fight the Soviets, providing them with guest houses and training camps. Azzam traveled around the Middle East and even to the United States to raise funds for his Afghan Arabs. Osama bin Laden became one of Azzam's main benefactors and coordinators; some would say the two men became bitter rivals over the course of a global jihad. Azzam was assassinated in Pakistan on November 24, 1989, by unknown killers. His impact on the global jihadist movement was far-reaching. Azzam's famous phrase of "Jihad and the rifle alone: no negotiations, no conferences, and no dialogues" was spray-painted everywhere in Silat al-Harithiya.

Silat al-Harithiya's favorite family was the Jaradat clan. According to estimates, Israeli and Palestinian, the Jaradat family is one of the largest *Hamulots*, Arabic slang for "clans," in the West Bank. They are certainly the most dominant extended family in the Jenin area, with more than 5,500 family members spread out on both sides of the border. The 1948 War of Israeli Independence split the family in two, with relatives spread out around the northern West Bank on the Palestinian side and Wadi Ara on the Israeli side.[1] The *Hamula* meant everything in the Arab world. The ties to one's extended clan were unbreakable, and they could not be shattered by religion and certainly not nationality. Blood wasn't just thicker than water—it was brewed from impenetrable molten steel. And, even though the extended Jaradat clan was incredibly well represented in the ranks of the various Palestinian terrorist factions, they were always Jaradats first and foremost.

There were some two hundred Jaradat family members in Israeli prisons for security crimes.[2] Some were low-level operatives and triggermen. Others had been elevated to the role of suicide bomber. Others were senior leaders.

On April 10, 2002, Rajab Ahmed Jaradat blew himself up on board the 960 bus en route from Haifa to Jerusalem as it traveled along the eastern slopes of Mount Carmel. Eight people were killed in the bombing; twenty-two were critically wounded. Jaradat carried out the bombing at the behest of Hamas. There were Jaradats who served Arafat's Fatah. One member of the clan, Ali Jaradat, was a high-ranking operations officer in the PFLP; he even served as its unofficial spokesman. Mostly, though, the Jaradats were at the tip of the spear of the Palestinian Islamic Jihad networks in and around Jenin. The PIJ Jaradats, as they were known in Shin Bet circles, were considered to be the most capable terrorists in the entire West Bank. These Jaradats—brothers, nephews, cousins, and in-laws—commanded cells and were responsible for most of the major terrorist attacks perpetrated in northern Israel since the onset of the intifada. Shin Bet agents had no difficulty in alphabetizing their West Bank fugitive files for the West Bank. As one Ya'mas operator said frustratingly, "So many of the Shin Bet's most wanted surnames were Jaradat this or Jaradat that. There was always a Jaradat involved."[3]

The Jaradat clan's code of loyalty was bulletproof, as was the compartmentalized secrecy of the PIJ. The PIJ's core membership was inbred—everyone was related to someone else in the organization. Blood recruited other blood. The area clans provided the PIJ with a very effective veil of armor against attempted infiltration by Israel's security services. Clans like the Jaradats could not be bribed or bullied into cooperating with the Shin Bet: Bribes were ineffective because the Iranians, through the MOIS (Ministry of Intelligence and Security) and Hezbollah, had invested so much money in Silat al-Harithiya that the small village was called "Little Tehran" and the Israeli intelligence services could never compete with the cash that flowed from Iran. But the cash was irrelevant to loyalty. No pressure, physical or psychological, would get a member of the clan to betray another. In this insular world, one was a member of a clan before one was a Muslim or a Palestinian. This airtight loyalty and obstinate defiance enabled the Jaradats to rise quickly up the chain of command of the PIJ's al-Quds, or Jerusalem, Brigade—the military wing of the organization.

Anas Jaradat was one of PIJ's master bomb-builders—an engineer—and one of its most promising commanders. Engineers were always the most important specialists in the Palestinian groups; there was never a shortage of men—and women—who were willing to sacrifice their lives and become *shaheeds*, or martyrs, but they were all harmless unless someone could provide them with an explosive package that was economical yet powerful, reliable yet idiot-proof. Anas had been a prized pupil and protégé of Iyad Sawalhah, the legendary PIJ bomb-builder who had topped the Shin Bet's most-wanted list for years; engineers were always a target of the Shin Bet. Sawalhah, all of twenty-eight years old, had spent the last fifteen years fighting the Israelis or being incarcerated by them. He fought in the first intifada as a member of the Black Panthers, where his trademark skill was that of an executioner; he personally killed dozens of Palestinians suspected of collaborating with the Shin Bet. The Shin Bet arrested him and he served nearly a decade in an Israeli prison. He found religion behind bars, and when in 1998 he was freed as part of a larger amnesty, he joined the PIJ and allowed his prison pedigree to propel him up the chain of command of the West Bank's network of cells and operatives. He was a powerful role model to a man like Anas Jaradat.

Both Anas Jaradat and Sawalhah were behind some of the most lethal suicide bombings of the al-Aqsa intifada—before, during, and after Operation Defensive Shield. Both men were responsible for nearly one hundred dead—their specialty was the bombing of buses that traversed the roadways of northern Israel, just across the Green Line from Jenin. On March 20, 2002, seven people were killed and thirty wounded when a bomber blew himself up on the No. 823 bus traveling from Tel Aviv to Nazareth; the bomber had boarded the bus on Route 65, near an Israeli-Arab town, a stone's throw from Jenin. Anas Jaradat's bomb, handed to a distant cousin, destroyed the No. 960 bus on April 10, 2002, killing eight and wounding twenty-two. On June 5, 2002, seventeen people were killed and thirty-eight people were wounded, when a car bomb, packed with more than one hundred kilograms of home-made explosives, was crashed into the No. 830 bus traveling from Tel Aviv to

Tiberias at Megiddo Junction; the force of the explosion, and the fires caused by the blast, completely destroyed the bus. During the summer of 2002, there were a dozen foiled bombings along Route 65 and in the Wadi Ara area. The carnage could have been worse—some of the bombers were intercepted by aggressive Israeli police patrols.

On October 21, 2002, the No. 841 bus traveling from Kiryat Shmonah near the Lebanese border to Tel Aviv blew up shortly after making a stop to pick up a passenger on Route 65 near Karkur Junction, located just east of the town of Hadera, some twenty-one miles southeast of Haifa. A suicide bomber had driven into the back of the commuter bus a jeep that Jaradat and Sawalhah had fitted with more than fifty kilograms of explosives. The blast resulted in an inferno that engulfed the bus, as well as two vehicles that were nearby. The flames were so intense, so out of control, that first responders could not get close enough to try to rescue any possible survivors; the bus was also full of soldiers and police officers traveling north, and the inferno caused the ammunition they carried to detonate. Fourteen people were killed in the attack and fifty were wounded. One of those killed was Staff Sergeant Liat Ben-Ami, a twenty-one-year-old Border Guard policewoman who was only four months away from completing her mandatory conscripted service. "She had served in combat situations near Jenin," a family friend would say at her funeral, "but now, she gets killed on her way home."[4]

The Karkur Junction attack propelled Sawalhah and Jaradat to the top of the Shin Bet's most-wanted list. The Shin Bet dedicated enormous resources to end the careers of these two ambitious men—especially after an attempt by the PIJ to detonate a massive suicide car bomb underneath the three Azrieli skyscrapers in Tel Aviv was thwarted by alert traffic policemen manning a roadblock. The Ya'mas had spent a good portion of their round-the-clock operational time focused on this tandem of bomb-building engineers. The unit had the files on both men during Yaakov Berman's hunting forays, and the undercover operators had sat in mosques, residences, cafés, and even caves on tips that the Shin Bet received that the men had been located. There was never concrete intelligence about the location of either man, though, only indications. Every special operations unit in the Israeli order of battle acted on those tips in hunting the pair. But Sawalhah and

Jaradat were not even ghosts; they were rumors of ghosts. The raids turned up nothing.

Sawalhah was located first. On the night of November 9, 2002, a Golani Brigade commando task force raided a safe house in the Kasbah of Jenin where intelligence reports believed Sawalhah was hiding. The reconnaissance commandos closed in around the house and ordered Sawalhah to come out and surrender. He sent his wife out to stall, while he hid inside a hollowed-out compartment prepared for him in the home's kitchen. When Israeli forces demanded that he come out and surrender, he threw hand grenades at them and fired at them with automatic weapons. Sawalhah was determined to fight to the end: He kept the Golani force at bay for an hour before the commandos entered the location and ended the ordeal.

Anas Jaradat was now the PIJ commander in Jenin. It was now his turn to be the West Bank's most wanted.

The Shin Bet dedicated enormous resources—and countless man hours—to locating Anas Jaradat. Shin Bet case agents summoned the elite of Israel's special operations arsenal on raids that yielded few results. For six months the Ya'mas acted on tips from the Shin Bet—each squadron and each team was deployed on terrain reconnaissance sorties and actual arrest operations, and each and every time Jaradat was nowhere to be found. To insulate his position, Jaradat made his cousin Saleh Suleiman Jaradat his deputy. Saleh, in turn, recruited other family members to become lieutenants in the al-Quds Brigade, including his cousin Fadi. "When the men in the Jihad or Hamas called one another *Ahi*, or brother, it wasn't a figure of speech," an IDF intelligence officer commented. "It was true."[5] The family connections guaranteed that the only men who knew the whereabouts of the hunted PIJ chieftains were those who possessed clannish blood links that could not be compromised by Shin Bet pressure.

The Shin Bet campaign finally paid off: Anas Jaradat was apprehended on the night of May 11, 2003, in a lightning-fast operation by Duvdevan.*

---

* On December 9, 2003, Anas Jaradat was convicted in an Israeli military court for murdering thirty-one Israeli civilians and sentenced to 735 years behind bars.

The operators from the army's undercover unit descended on the safe house Jaradat occupied and, with a D9 ready to flatten the house, unit commanders convinced the cornered terrorist to surrender. News of the Duvdevan operation was met with grudging admiration at Ya'mas headquarters, though these sentiments were spray-painted with a muted sense of jealousy. The Ya'mas felt very proprietary about Jenin—the city few other special operations units dared to enter and the one that was considered their territory. The Ya'mas knew each intersection and street; the operators had memorized all the landmarks, and they had managed to navigate and circumnavigate through checkpoints, barricades, and other ballistic obstacles often thrown in their way. "Jenin was my favorite place to work," Sa'ar Shine remembered. "It was compact, it was easy to navigate, and it was where we had the most work. Jenin was where we fought some of our toughest battles."[6]

When Anas Jaradat was apprehended, his cousin Saleh became the area's PIJ heir apparent. Shin Bet commanders working Jenin realized that locating a wily target like Saleh would require the skills and stubbornness of a unit that could operate for lengthy periods of time inside Jenin and the surrounding villages. When the Shin Bet contacted Uzi Levy with the Saleh Jaradat file, the Ya'mas pounced on the opportunity.

Saleh Jaradat was not the type of fugitive who languished in one location for days on end inviting a confrontation with the Israeli security services. His legend was that of a ghost, a figure in the shadows who was always one step ahead of forces that hunted him. Everyone in Jenin and the villages around the city—especially in Silat al-Harithiya—was always on the lookout for the *Mistaraboon*, the Arabic word for the undercover commandos. Fugitives would try to move around from location to location during the day and find safe haven at night in order to evade the invisible eyes of the dreaded *Mistaraboon*. Jaradat was constantly on the move. It was a desperate attempt to remain one step ahead of the undercover operatives who hunted him. Pursuing the elusive PIJ commander required patience and tenacity.

Chief Inspector Micha Gafni, the unit's operations officer, had served with the unit since 1991. He joined the unit as an operator in the second platoon when Eli Avram was still building the unit from nothing. He had seen how the unit grew from very Spartan beginnings, when it had to plead for a couple of operations a month to the point, as he put it, "when some of the IDF's top units carried out one raid every couple of months or so, but we carried out two hundred or more a year. When the intelligence came in that a terrorist suspect was at home *now*, not an hour from now, we didn't have to refer to IDF maps to find out where 'Junction X' was and where it intersected with 'Coordinate Y.' We had been to these places so many times we had it all memorized. We had the ability to react to immediate call-outs where we would instruct the elements of the raid on the go, via radio, as we rushed to the target. No other unit had that capability or flexibility."[7]

Chief Inspector Nasser* was one of the Ya'mas officers at the center of the effort to apprehend Jaradat. Tall and lanky, with an infectious smile, Nasser was a Druze from Israel's north; he was a family man. His kind demeanor and endearing good looks camouflaged a hardened soldier who possessed a wealth of combat experience and counterterrorist know-how that had been gained in the treacherous hills of southern Lebanon and inside the narrow confines of Hebron while serving with Egoz, the 1st Golani Infantry Brigade's elite counterinsurgency force. Nasser joined the Ya'mas in 2001 and became one of the unit's most capable officers. Learning every nook and cranny of the West Bank was part of his indoctrination into the unit—a critical element of being able to know how to get in and out of a place like Jenin, let alone maneuver inside the intricate back alleys of the city for hours on end. "Our men knew the terrain like the back of their hands," Chief Inspector Nasser boasted. "They knew each hole and each landmark better than anyone in the Israeli counterterrorist community. The team leaders knew how to deal with any target—house, café, store, alleyway—and the squadron leaders and the intelligence and operational elements knew how to coordinate these activities and operations with the IDF and the support forces that might be needed."[8]

But Nasser's like-the-back-of-his-hand knowledge of the topography alone wasn't going to locate and apprehend a man like Saleh Jaradat; the daily grind of searching haunts where the intelligence believed he might be hiding

---

* A pseudonym—true identity withheld for security considerations.

was time-consuming and physically demanding. On some operations the Israelis found themselves sitting inside the stifling Horse for hours on end. The Horses would have been suffocating even if they were air-conditioned, but they weren't. The heat inside the Horse was oven-like. It was impossible to ventilate the interior cabin where the operators sat, and the Speakers often had to park the vehicles in the sun, cooking all those who sat inside. The effects of the heat were exacerbated by the tactical kit each operator wore—coveralls, body armor, load-bearing gear, communications equipment, and packs with extra ammunition. The entire package often weighed close to thirty-five kilograms. The air inside the small, tight space was heavy and stale; many operators were grateful that they could breathe through their balaclavas and filter out the stench. If a Horse sat on a target for three or four hours, the operators inside had to sit silently still throughout. There were no time-outs for bathroom breaks and little opportunity to stretch one's legs.

The search for Saleh Jaradat took a toll on the entire Ya'mas force. The month of May quickly disappeared into June. There would be no breaks from the daily forays in and around Jenin—no trips home to see the wife and kids, and no free time to catch up on sleep. Any spare time was dedicated to train-ing and the review of Shin Bet intelligence files.

As the long days of surveillance and searching passed into weeks, the intelligence on Saleh became sharper. Ya'mas teams were able to miss their elusive prey by minutes rather than hours. On June 12, 2003, the Shin Bet case officer supervising the Jaradat file came to the Ya'mas forward operating base with the encouraging news the unit had been waiting to hear for nearly a month. Jaradat had been located.

Yaakov Berman gathered the entry team and conducted a quick field briefing. The intelligence of the day was reviewed swiftly, and the operators reviewed photographs of the locations. They had done this so many times before, but nothing was ever left to chance—not even in the seven-minute world of the Ya'mas. The assault team consisted of two vehicles—an armored undercover sedan and a Horse for tactical backup. Majdi,* one of the more experienced Speakers, was driving; Chief Inspector Nasser sat next to him. Abu Ahmed, another one of the Speakers and a combat medic, sat in the

---

* A pseudonym—true identity withheld for security considerations.

back seat next to Berman. The operators heading to Jenin checked their gear one final time. They checked their weapons—M4s and Glock 17Cs—as well as their ammo pouches. There was one final radio check before the vehicles headed toward Jenin. The sun would set soon. The unit's intelligence and operations officers made their way toward the tent where the brigade commander was waiting.

The coffee inside the command post set up outside the city was stale; it tasted horrible. The laptops were open, and the tapping of computer keys was muted by the hissing squelch of radio transmissions. The Shin Bet liaison agents walked outside for a cigarette or two; they were nervous and excited and lit new cigarettes with the burning ends of others. Ya'mas officers followed closely behind the intelligence agents, looking for their lighters inside their cargo pockets. Armies may have moved on their stomachs, but the counter-terrorist specialists survived on awful coffee and nicotine.

Members of the extended Jaradat family were enjoying a quiet summer's night in the courtyard of their rented home in the city's easternmost neighborhood. Saleh Jaradat was at the center of the family gathering, even though he knew that he was the target of a massive Israeli dragnet; the thirty-four-year-old was old enough and experienced enough to know that family homes were always on the Israeli radar. But being on the run, even with the popular support of sympathizers and safe houses, had taken its toll on the PIJ commander. He had been on the run for a long time, too long, and he missed his family. It had been many weeks since he had seen his pregnant wife, Ismath, and their two-year-old son who lived in this family enclave. Spending a few hours with them, he assessed, was worth the risk of the Israelis catching up with him. The Jaradats were, after all, preparing for a family event—a wedding. Saleh's cousin Fadi, twenty-four, was only three days from being married. Fadi, like Saleh, was also a PIJ operative. He wasn't at the top of the Jerusalem Brigade hierarchy, but he was a street-level commander, and worthy enough to be high on the Shin Bet's most-wanted list.

The date for Fadi's wedding had been pushed up because his father, Taisir, had been in and out of cancer treatments in hospitals inside Israel proper, as well as in Amman, for a long time and it was thought that by moving up the wedding, his spirits and health would improve—even if only temporarily. Jaradat weddings were huge events, especially those with the PIJ's blessing. The invitations were sent, the wedding dress paid for and altered, and the food purchased.

Saleh and Fadi sat on a long red sofa that had been brought to the courtyard so that the family could enjoy the brief eastern breezes and escape from the stifling heat inside the house. The mood was jovial, almost relaxed. Fadi's twenty-nine-year-old sister, Hanadi, sat with them. Hanadi was the oldest of nine children and was seen as an ambitious, modern, yet religious woman; many described her as stubborn.[9] She had graduated from Jerash University in Amman, Jordan, and was working on her legal apprenticeship in a Jenin law firm. She was slim and attractive but, nearing her thirtieth birthday, still single. Hanadi had been engaged eight years earlier, to a distant family member who was also a PIJ member and had been killed in a shoot-out with the IDF. Spinsters, especially professionals working outside the home, were looked upon with suspicion in the family's traditional religious circles. Hanadi acted like a deputy matriarch, looking after her eight siblings and helping her father with his medical care. She was particularly close to her younger brother Fadi.

Saleh and Fadi joked as they sat comfortably on the red sofa; both men drank cup after cup of strong Bedouin coffee laced with cardamom. Hanadi listened intently to the conversation and their war stories. Saleh wasn't at ease, though. Every noise made him jump. The ghosts from the *qawat al-hasa* were everywhere.[10] Saleh removed his calling-card nickel-plated 9mm semiautomatic pistol from the small of his back and placed the weapon on his right leg. Fadi gestured to his sister that he was thirsty. Hanadi happily ran into the house to prepare another pot of coffee. No one heard the drone flying overhead.

The two Israeli vehicles moved slowly into Jenin. After more entries into the town than he could remember, Majdi had become an expert at driving like one of the city's motorists: honk; brake; gas; brake; honk; and then honk again. Part of the unit's ability to enter and exit Palestinian towns and villages depended on their skills at acclimating their speech and their behavior to the local flavor. *Not* driving like a Palestinian would be a telltale giveaway. The vehicles followed a predetermined path moving off the main road toward side streets and then to where they could stage and deploy around the house according to the unit's tactical doctrine. Berman hoped that the intelligence was right.

At the Brigade CP outside of town, Ya'mas commander Levy and the operations officer Micah listened with subdued pride as high-ranking officers complimented the commander about how effortlessly his men were pushing their way into Jenin. The live feed, transmitted from the drone flying overhead, showed the two vehicles flowing into the city center without hesitation or trepidation. The colonels and other officers watching the feed were impressed by the way the Ya'mas units always acted as if they assumed ownership of the territories they operated in. The IDF officers felt confidence in the quick, almost machinelike radio bursts Berman and his men relayed back to command. The operators were very confident under pressure—perhaps too confident.

As the vehicles neared the targeted house, Nasser carefully removed his sidearm from his holster and placed the weapon into his firm and ready grip. The operators felt slightly more at ease away from the frenetic pace of Jenin's main avenues. There was no traffic ahead. Berman whispered into his microphone that the team was getting close. He ordered his men to get ready.

It only took a few minutes for Hanadi to boil the coffee. There was always something cooking on the stovetops, and finding an available burner could be a challenge. Hanadi prepared the cups and the sugar and brought out the pitcher on a metal tray. She resumed her spot on the sofa near her brother and poured the coffee. The first vehicle pulled up gently in front of the Jaradat home, grinding slowly on the poorly paved road. Hanadi thought that the men inside the car were friends of Fadi. The vehicle had green-and-white Palestinian license plates.

Nasser raised his head slowly and turned slightly toward the people on the couch. Abu Ahmed recognized Saleh right away. He had spent the better part of a month memorizing every facet of Saleh's face—his pale complexion and his ultra-straight jet-black hair parted to the side—and now he was a few feet away. Nasser noticed the pistol on Saleh's leg.

Saleh did not flinch when the Ya'mas contingent arrived. He simply stared at the vehicles in a frozen moment of shock, one of begrudging and fatal acceptance. Saleh glanced at Nasser and then at his pistol. He tried to reach for the gun on his leg. In a matter of seconds, a month's manhunt culminated in two shots to Saleh's shoulder and neck. Saleh's upper torso slithered down off the couch; his body went limp and he collapsed on the floor in a growing pool of blood. Fadi leaped off the couch the moment the shooting began. He tried to make a run for it and barricade himself inside the house; the intelligence on Fadi was that he never moved around without a weapon at the ready. Operators had jumped out of the Horse and were swarming all around the house. Abu Ahmed yelled for everyone to stand still and raise their hands in the air, but Fadi continued his move toward the house. Abu Ahmed took aim and shot him. "We were drinking coffee and then we saw a white car with Arab license plates drive up slowly and stop next to the house," Hanadi recalled in an interview with the Jordanian newspaper *al-Arab al-Yum*. "I thought that they were friends of Fadi. Suddenly two men got out of the car and started shooting at Saleh. I saw Saleh lying on the ground. Then suddenly another car pulled up and people started shooting from it, too."[11] Hanadi also stated that "Fadi was still breathing. Saleh lay motionless. I saw that he had been hit in the head. Three of the soldiers spoke fluent Arabic. One of them asked me, 'Where is Fadi's weapon?' I said, 'I don't know. He doesn't even have a weapon.' I saw my brother lying there. '*Allah akbar aleikum*, he'll die.'"[12]

The objective of the raid was to apprehend Saleh Jaradat—not kill him. The PIJ commander had, in his head, the keys to identify layer after layer of field commanders, networks, cells, and operatives. But the operators did not pit themselves against armed individuals for the sake of possible intelligence. Even though armed fugitives who were identified as being a clear and present threat were legitimate battlefield targets, Ya'mas combat medics worked feverishly to save the lives of the two wounded men. Abu Ahmed, who was one of the team's most experienced trauma-trained paramedics, attempted to stabilize Saleh. But Hanadi was hysterical. She jumped over her brother and was crying and screaming. "The sister was making it impossible for the medics to work," Nasser recalled, "grabbing everyone and pulling them off and getting in the way of the efforts to save her brother's life."[13]

The Speakers could barely contain her movements and her screams. "*Ichras!*" Nasser ordered. "Shut up!" She didn't stop, though; her screams grew louder. Hanadi's commotion threatened the operational security of the Ya'mas mission. The fighters were completely outnumbered in the PIJ neighborhood. The sounds of gunfire and the initial cries of the women were an alarm in the neighborhood that forces from the *qawat al-hasa* were operating nearby. Berman's arrest team expected gunfire to erupt at any moment, and from any and every corner. Nasser looked at Hanadi one more time and pleaded with her to be quiet. Her flailing became more exaggerated. So he hit her. "I slapped her so that she would be quiet. She was putting everyone at risk."[14]

Saleh Jaradat was declared dead at the scene. Fadi still had a slim chance. The decision was made to load Fadi's body into the entry car and to evacuate him to Israel, where he could receive emergency care; an IDF trauma team stood at the ready outside Jenin. The operators loaded Fadi into one of the cars and worked on him as the vehicles departed the targeted area. He would be declared dead a few minutes later.

The mission was over. One of the Shin Bet's most wanted men had been removed from the fugitive list—the terrorist enterprise of a man with buckets of blood on his hands had been terminated. The Ya'mas operators heading out of Jenin were pleased with the results of the operation. They hoped that this was the last they'd be hearing of the Jaradat clan for a while. Mostly they hoped to have a few hours of sleep and the chance to go home and see their wives and kids. They were all exhausted.

The funerals for Saleh and Fadi Jaradat were media events—all *shaheed* burials were public outpourings of rage and cries for revenge. Of course the PIJ always made sure that the media was invited to these displays. Cameramen, especially from the Western outlets, were always afforded a bird's-eye view of the funeral procession at a point safe from the gunmen who fired volleys of rifle fire into the sky. The PIJ also made sure that the bereaved families were available for interviews. Hanadi, an eyewitness to the Ya'mas operation, provided compelling fodder for the Arab media. She was also a person of great interest to the PIJ military arm.

Although it adhered to the strictest codes of Islam—especially in its definition of a woman's role in society—the PIJ did not express any religious or
philosophical objections to using females in the execution of suicide bombing
attacks. The use of female suicide bombers was both tactically and psycho-
logically effective: As a precision tactic, they were stealth-like and far more
likely to penetrate a target than a male since they aroused a lower profile of
suspicion; as a psychological force, the use of women expressed a sense of
desperation meant to embarrass the Israelis in the court of world opinion.
Even Hamas refused to send women into Israel's cities. Sheikh Ahmed Yassin,
the founder of Hamas and its spiritual leader, renounced the use of women as
suicide bombers on the grounds of modesty.[15] The PIJ, urged on by its political
leadership in Damascus and its Hezbollah sponsors, preferred pragmatism
to honor and cited a tradition, dating back to the Prophet Muhammad, that
justified a wife joining the Jihad, even without her husband's permission, to
reclaim conquered Muslim lands.[16]

But the PIJ had used women before. A week following Anas Jaradat's
arrest, Saleh Jaradat had ordered one of his most trusted lieutenants, Kamal
Tubasi, to activate a female operative for an attack in Afula, an Israeli city of
forty thousand inhabitants in the Jezreel Valley located eight miles east of
Jenin. The apprehension of Jaradat had to be avenged, Saleh ordered, and
a bold and powerful statement had to be broadcast to the rank and file that
Israeli actions would be met with death and suffering. Tubasi was a unique
character in the terrorist hierarchy of Jenin. An equal-opportunity operator,
he held a high military rank in several of the Palestinian factions.

Tubasi located a nineteen-year-old university student named Hiba
Draghma, from the West Bank village of Tubas. Draghma had been engaged
to a PIJ operative, but when he was apprehended by Israeli special forces en
route to carrying out a suicide bombing, the collective family disgrace fell
upon the young woman's shoulders; blowing herself up would be considered an act of vengeance and honor. PIJ commanders dressed Draghma in a
tight-fitting blouse and a pair of suggestively tighter-fitting jeans. She wore
makeup and her body was sprayed with perfume. She also carried close to
seven kilograms of TATP and nails inside a black pocketbook. On May 19,
2003, she was driven to the Gates of the Valley shopping mall in the center of Afula. An intrepid security guard posted to the mall's main entrance

suspected something about Draghma's appearance and the weight of her bag. Fearful that she would be apprehended like her fiancé, before he could become a martyr, Draghma blew herself up at the security checkpoint. Three people were killed in the blast—including two security guards, both new immigrants to Israel from the former Soviet Union. Forty-eight shoppers were wounded in the attack.

The Afula attack was deemed as a PIJ failure—Draghma, by the blood-soaked standards set in the intifada, had not killed enough Israelis. Draghma had also proved to be a poor femme fatale for the PIJ. She was considered pitiful and gullible. Draghma had no narrative that would hold the interest in the Western media and no backstory inside the community to use as a recruitment tool for more women eager to become suicide bombers. Hanadi Jaradat was different. The PIJ believed that she could be a star.

Hanadi Jaradat had always been a deeply religious woman, but the incident on the porch of her family's rented home propelled her deeper into the Quran and the mosque. The headhunters, those recruiting new *shaheeds*, were busiest around the funerals of those killed by Israeli forces—this was the time that a heart full of anger could be turned into a human missile driven by vengeance. A female operative from the PIJ, a recruiter, traveled to see Hanadi during the family's forty days of mourning. Hanadi was an easy target for the manipulation; many other suicide bombers had been recruited in such a way.[17] She was, in many ways, an outcast. The fact that she had once been engaged to be married, perhaps sexually active, had cast aspersions on her honor. She was in no frame of mind to resist the pitch and was easy prey for the PIJ sharks.[18]

In the early morning hours of Saturday, October 4, 2003, before the fall clouds could part to reveal a warm and heartening sunshine, Hanadi Jaradat received a suicide belt from her cousin Sami Suleiman Jaradat, the commander of the PIJ's military wing in the village of Silat al-Harithiya; Jaradat had received the equipment, and the instructions for the operation, from Amjad Ahmed Abeidi, the thirty-five-year-old PIJ commander in the northern West Bank. The belt was simple in design and potent in payload; it consisted of four kilograms of high explosive surrounded by several more kilograms of screws and nails. Hanadi and Abeidi had met in a safe house.

A smuggler was hired to transport Hanadi into Israel. He was a forty-eight-year-old Israeli-Arab from Umm el-Fahm named Jamal Mahajna, who was reliable when it came to helping Palestinians cross into Israel illegally; not only did he help them cross, but he drove them in an air-conditioned van. Sami Jaradat didn't think that Hanadi would have any problems getting into Israel. She had been given a Jordanian passport and her English was fluent. If challenged by an Israeli policeman, her cover story was that of a Jordanian tourist. It was considered a rock-solid cover story.

Hanadi Jaradat took a local commuter bus from Jenin to Barta, a village divided in two by the invisible frontier separating Israel from the Palestinian Authority. She crossed from the eastern part of town to the western half, inside Israeli proper, and hooked up with her driver. She took a seat in the front of the blue Volkswagen Transporter van. The driver watched as Hanadi changed out of her traditional clothes, agalabiya and the hijab, into Western clothes that had been prepared for her ahead of time. Peering into the mirror, Hanadi applied red lipstick and brushed her hair.

Sami Jaradat had given Hanadi strict tradecraft instructions. She was to travel south, then north to Haifa, in order to see if she was being followed and to evade any police checkpoints around the Arab villages. Mahajna drove to Hadera, a city in between Netanya and Haifa, and to the Hillel Yaffe Hospital on the outskirts of the city; Hanadi told her driver that she was searching for her hospitalized father and that she wanted to see if he had been admitted as a patient there. Hanadi said that she was hungry and she suggested that the two eat. Traffic was light on the coastal highway to Haifa. The Mediterranean glistened under the bright October sun. It was already after 1 p.m. Anyway, Hanadi promised to pay for the meal.

The Arab–Israeli conflict didn't exist inside the Maxim Restaurant. Nestled along Haganah Avenue at the southern approach to Haifa along the Carmel Beach, the Maxim Restaurant was jointly owned by Arab and Jewish proprietors. Haifa was a multiethnic city that prided itself on tolerance, and the restaurant embodied that spirit of coexistence. The Maxim Restaurant was a landmark in Haifa—diners came from all over Mount Carmel to savor generous portions of grilled meats and Middle Eastern salads. The Maccabi Haifa soccer team considered Maxim a safe haven, a hangout.

The restaurant was particularly crowded this particular Saturday afternoon. Yom Kippur eve was a little more than twenty-four hours away, and it was customary for Israelis—many of whom were on holiday because of the high holy days—to enjoy eating out in the days between the Jewish New Year and the solemn fasting of the Day of Atonement. Waiters carried heavy steel trays with plates of meat skewers still smoking from the open-flame grills, and freshly baked loaves of pita bread were rushed to the tables of hungry patrons. Terrorists had blown up restaurants and cafés before, and an armed security guard was supposed to be on duty, but the man manning the front door was a waiter drafted to be a sentinel for a few hours. Hanadi and her driver were never challenged when they walked into the restaurant. There was no searching of Hanadi's bag and no magnetometer swept across her torso. There was only a brief wait for a table.

The restaurant was noisy—Maxim always was. Children were everywhere, and some of the toddlers managed to wander away from their parents to munch on French fries smothered in ketchup as they sliced a path in between the crowded tables. Hanadi and Mahajna ordered plates of chicken kebabs along with several portions of salads; both ordered soft drinks. Jamal Mahajna ate like a man being treated to a free meal. Hanadi Jaradat barely touched her plate. Instead, witnesses would later say, she was detached. She smiled off into the distance and stared at the other diners with a satisfied grin. Hanadi told her driver that she would cover the tab and asked him to get the car ready. He grabbed a toothpick from the register and walked out the door to his van.

Hanadi didn't stand up as the waiters cleared her table. She simply smiled and detonated the carefully crafted antipersonnel explosive device she wore on her body. The detonation eviscerated the interior of the restaurant with a violent flash. The blast blew out windows and sent shards of glass flying everywhere. Shrapnel sliced through any flesh and bone in its path—the flesh and bone of pensioners and grandparents, and the flesh and bone of mothers and their children. It was 2:18 on a sun-scorched Saturday afternoon.

The Israel National Police had received word that a possible attack, one to be perpetrated by a female suicide bomber in Haifa, was imminent. Law enforcement units were busy setting roadblocks and implementing security protocols when news of the explosion came over the emergency frequencies.[19]

Rescue workers who rushed to the scene were appalled by the carnage. The bodies of children sat on their chairs, their heads sliced off cleanly by the sharpened metal fragments racing through the open spaces. Blood and burned flesh were everywhere. Twenty-one people were killed in the bombing, including five members of the Almog family and five members of the Zer-Aviv family. The oldest victim was seventy-one. The youngest fatality was one year old. Fifty-eight people were critically wounded.

Jamal Mahajna was arrested twelve hours after the bombing at his home in Umm el-Fahm. He had tried to burn any evidence that Hanadi had left behind in his car. As Mahajna was being interviewed by Shin Bet agents eager to unravel the network behind the bombing, the PIJ headquarters in Damascus, Syria, released a press release claiming credit for the carnage. The operation, the communiqué said, was carried out by the "Bride of Haifa."[20]

On the morning of October 5, a column of tanks and APCs churned its way toward Silat al-Harithiya. The armored thrust moved slowly. The vehicles—ferrying infantrymen, special operations elements, and combat engineers—ground a path behind the slow-moving Caterpillar D9 bulldozer, slowly and cautiously pushing up narrow roads and around hairpin turns. Helicopter gunships flew shotgun overhead. The residents of Silat al-Harithiya knew what was happening. The Jaradat family was allowed to remove their possessions before their home was razed.

The Ya'mas operators never took the work personally. When the men prepared for a mission—one with a month's worth of lead time or one where they coordinated the tactics en route to the target—their sole focus was on the operation: the intelligence, the risk, the tactics, and the escape plan. Who the terrorist was, who he had killed, and which organization he belonged to mattered little on the surface. The bombing in Haifa was different, though. Some of the men who had participated in the Jaradat raid sat quietly the morning after the suicide bombing at the Maxim Restaurant. Some knew that they would be back in the Jenin area shortly, hunting down those responsible for the deaths of the twenty-one women, men, and children that

Haifa afternoon. There was a network behind each act of terror—recruiters, intelligence-gatherers, operational commanders, facilitators, and, of course, bomb-building engineers—and the network would need to be neutralized. The operations and intelligence officers in the unit worked the phones that morning after Maxim, calling their counterparts in the Shin Bet and offering their services. Others, especially Nasser, wondered about something else. "Imagine all the lives that could have been saved," he thought to himself with frustrated hindsight, "had I just shot and killed her."[21]

The cycle of violence was not over. The Ya'mas would return to Jenin—to hunt those responsible for the most recent carnage and to hunt those who were planning and who would execute the future bloodshed.

CHAPTER NINE

Highest Value Targets

On a December afternoon in the winter of 1994, two scruffy-looking men sat next to each other in the front cabin of a Toyota pickup truck that was parked on the muddy shoulders of a narrow West Bank road. The bone-numbing drizzle that had followed the Toyota all day as it crisscrossed from village to village intensified under stormy skies, and a downpour began. Water entered the cab and the cold northern winds made it hard to stay warm, but the two men inside refused to roll up the windows. The men, Ya'mas operators in the nascent unit, had spent about ten hours in the truck driving all around the central West Bank and were prepared to spend the next ten hours watching and waiting. Neither looked at his wristwatch to check the time. Instead, the men, whose eyes teared from the cold, stared at the Shin Bet wanted sheet featuring photos of the man they hunted. The tattered photocopy was taped to the glove compartment and showed the suspect in a student ID photo, with a mustache and wearing gold wire-frame glasses. Another photo showed a more martial pose; the suspect hadn't shaved in a week and sat defiantly with a red-and-white keffiyeh worn around his neck. He was rumored to have moved in and out of Israeli checkpoints masquerading as a young woman and as an old man. He was considered armed and extremely dangerous. His name was Yehiya Ayyash.

Yehiya Ayyash, one of the founders of the Hamas military wing in the West Bank, was not just a terrorist commander. He was what was known in the field as *al-Muhandis*, Arabic for "The Engineer." An *al-Muhandis* was, at the time, a rare combination of field lieutenant and brilliant technician who could assemble potent explosive devices from store-bought materials. Ayyash had earned an electrical engineering bachelor of science degree from the West

Bank's Birzeit University, and had wanted to advance his studies and travel to Jordan to attend graduate school, but the Shin Bet refused to issue him with a travel permit. Embittered, he joined Hamas.[1]

Military-grade explosives were a rare commodity in the West Bank and Gaza before the arrival of Arafat and his U.S.-financed security services. Terrorist groups relied on small quantities of smuggled material or residues from IDF training fields. But Ayyash provided a low-cost option that could be mass-produced: TATP. TATP, the acronym for Triacetone Triperoxide, was a witch's brew of hydrogen peroxide and acetone that produced a powerful punch for pennies on the dollar. TATP was unstable, though; it was known as the Mother of Satan by senior Hamas commanders. The first device that Ayyash tried to dispatch into Israel was a massive van-bomb, fitted with five twelve-kilogram gasoline tanks attached to TATP detonators and destined for Tel Aviv, that was seized by Israeli police following a high-speed pursuit in a suburban neighborhood. When police bomb technicians attempted to disarm the device, the vehicle exploded in a massive fireball. An Israeli Police EOD supervisor on the scene said that it was one of the most powerful devices he had ever seen, and if it had made it through to a crowded Tel Aviv street, it would have killed hundreds.[2]

The man-portable devices that Ayyash cobbled together from the Mother of Satan became true killing machines when nails, screws, and other hardware were added to the explosive package. Often, the shrapnel was soaked in rat poison, an anticoagulant, to make sure that those hit by the chunks of metal would bleed out or suffer horrific infections. Ayyash's bombs were used to blow up buses in Afula, Hadera, and Tel Aviv. Ayyash introduced suicide bombings to Israel's cities. In 1994 alone, Ayyash's bloody campaign had left thirty-three dead and more than two hundred wounded; the bombing of the No. 5 bus on Tel Aviv's main boulevard on October 19, 1994, killed twenty-one and wounded nearly one hundred. Prime Minister Rabin, in cabinet meetings, referred to Ayyash as *Ha'Mehandes*, "The Engineer." The Ya'mas operators, masquerading as Palestinian laborers that December afternoon, had hunted Ayyash for nearly a year. Their orders were to shoot first and ask questions later. Each man in the truck hoped to have the chance to kill the Engineer with the 9mm Mini-Uzi submachine gun inside his jacket.

Every Israeli soldier serving in the West Bank had a photo of Ayyash, as did every soldier serving near Gaza. The Shin Bet and the undercover units had Ayyash's home and family under tight surveillance; every time a member of his family went to the market or visited a neighbor, an Israeli drone monitored his or her movements from high in the sky. Israeli special operations units from every branch of the service launched raids aimed at flushing out anyone who might have a thread of a clue as to where Ayyash could be. There were rumors he had fled to Lebanon, Syria, Jordan, and Egypt. Some believed that he had escaped through Sinai to Libya. Other Hamas terrorists had done it before. Until the Shin Bet succeeded in secreting a Motorola cell phone to their target, ingeniously fitted with one hundred grams of RDX high explosives, and subsequently ripping apart Ayyash's face one rainy day in January 1996 as he spoke on the phone with his father, Ayyash had been the most wanted terrorist in Israeli history.

Ayyash's ghostlike status was built by a slick Hamas propaganda machine and by Israel's inability to find him. Ayyash's truly insidious value was how he turned teenage boys into combustible cruise missiles for pennies. Ayyash's low-cost, high-yield form of warfare had redefined the Arab–Israeli battlefield. A forty-two-ton Soviet-era T-72 Main Battle Tank in Syrian Army service posed less of a threat to the State of Israel than ten dollars' worth of hardware store-bought components and a nineteen-year-old boy yearning for rock star status as a martyr in paradise. Ayyash had seemingly equalized Israel's qualitative and quantitative advantage of technology and First World military power.

Before his death, Ayyash had taught a small army of disciples, both in the West Bank and in Gaza, the art of manufacturing discount-store suicide devices. By the time the second intifada erupted in 2000, there were several dozen, if not hundreds, of highly valued Engineers working on behalf of the Palestinian terrorist factions. Mazen Salameh was one of the most ambitious and lethal *al-Muhandis* fighting Israel.

Mazen Yusef Salameh was not the stereotypical Islamic warrior who had been reared quoting suras from the Quran and following in the footsteps of his father and, perhaps, brothers who might have been killed or incarcerated by the Israelis. The thirty-year-old was half-Bedouin, with distinctively dark skin and jet-black hair with thick sheep-like curls. His face was flat and round. Shin Bet investigators looking at his photos thought his to be one of the most distinctive and unforgettable faces that they had ever come across.

Salameh hailed from a small north-central West Bank village. A farm boy born in abject poverty, Salameh began his terrorist career with the *Al-Jabha al-Dimuqratiya Li-Tahrir Filastin*, the Democratic Front for the Liberation of Palestine, or DFLP.* The DFLP was a radical Marxist-Leninist group founded by Nayif Hawatmeh in Damascus in 1969. The group's ideology was radical—and absolutely secular—pan-Arabic Communism; Hawatmeh, a.k.a. Abu a-Nuf, was a Jordanian-born Greek Orthodox Christian who had broken ranks with Dr. George Habash's PFLP for not being radical enough in thriving toward a vision of a secular anticolonial and Marxist Middle East. The DFLP was a relatively obscure group, though they were responsible for one of the most heinous crimes in the history of Israel's terrorist wars when, on May 15, 1974, three DFLP gunmen seized a school in the northern Israeli town of Ma'alot and with it more than one hundred hostages—most of them children. When Sayeret Mat'kal launched a rescue bid, the terrorists turned their weapons on their hostages instead of the assaulting Israeli commandos. Thirty-one hostages, including twenty-five children, were killed that day; seventy more were wounded.

The DFLP rode the exaltation of that event for years, and small cells of operatives made their presence known inside the refugee camps and universities of the West Bank and Gaza Strip. By 2000, though, the DFLP had been rendered to fringe irrelevance by the likes of Hamas and the al-Aqsa Martyrs Brigade. Salameh was far more the pragmatic professional than he was dedicated to any fading form of pan-Arab political ideology. Known as the DFLP's top—perhaps only—Engineer in the West Bank, Salameh was

---

* By the time the al-Aqsa intifada erupted in the fall of 2000, many of the "Popular Fronts" for the liberation of Palestine had been relegated to insignificance by the emergence of the Palestinian Authority and resistance groups like Hamas and the PIJ. Ideologically driven groups were cash poor and lacking a popular base inside the territories to compete with the religiously motivated armies promising paradise and delivering bloodshed. Even Ahmed Jibril's Popular Front for the Liberation of Palestine—General Command (PFLP-GC), a proxy of the Syrian regime, could muster few significant attacks to rival the carnage perpetrated by Hamas, the PIJ, and Arafat's covert forces.

courted by Hamas and the al-Aqsa recruiters, though the PIJ—with its Iranian money—paid more. Salameh became one of the PIJ's most capable bomb-builders in the West Bank. He shuttled between laboratories in Nablus and Tulkarm under heavy guard.

There was an entire terrorist order of battle built around the Engineers. There were Quartermasters who were responsible for gathering the materials needed to build a suicide vest. Financiers, the banking end of the underground army, had to provide budgets and funds for the Quartermasters. The Guardians were responsible for protecting the Engineer, his devices, and ultimately, the martyr-to-be who would volunteer to blow himself up inside Israel.[3] The Moral Guidance crews were responsible for videotaping the bomber's living will and taking the glamour shots of him—or her—holding the Quran, and an AK-47, that would later be turned into billboards, posters, T-shirts, and coffee cups. The Travel Agents would be responsible for coordinating the suicide bomber's transportation from the West Bank into Israel and then toward the target. All were interconnected through cell commanders and coordinators. Their instructions were received via throwaway SIM cards and in clandestine meetings at the mosque. But everyone revolved around the Engineer.

Salameh's expertise was designing and producing small devices that could easily be concealed inside a small bag or a jacket, but could yield powerful explosive payloads. Targets were getting harder to hit inside Israel—Israel's security services were becoming more successful in the day-in-and-day-out proactive patrols and interception operations in and around Israel's population centers—and the devices had to be inconspicuously smuggled. Armed guards stood at the entrance of rail stations and restaurants. Drivers scrutinized those who boarded their buses more carefully.

Salameh's devices were used in several lethal suicide bombings. Salameh was also a master recruiter. He was a confident speaker who made a young man feel at ease that the decision to become a martyr was a noble one. According to the intelligence, Salameh had a stable of a dozen suicide bombers that he could summon for missions inside Israel. One of his eager charges was Jamil Ranem, a twenty-year-old from the village of Deir el-Ghusuma, a few miles north of Tulkarm. A suicide vest was displayed on a bed, draped over white linen. Ranem was handed an AK-47 and a set of black fatigues.[4]

The photographer had set up the lights. The video camera was already on the tripod. Ranem was issued his headband.

Netanya's London Cafe was always crowded at noon—especially on an unseasonal winter's day when the sunshine was pure summer. Location was everything in the competitive world of seaside eateries, and the London Cafe had a prime location. Located a few paces from the beach, on Herzl Street, at the corner of Independence Square, the London Cafe was a spacious restaurant where French pensioners could enjoy a cup of coffee and a slice of strudel while reading the weekly copy of *L'Express*, and where businessmen could order soup and a burger as part of the lunch special while discussing who owed who money. An aqua-blue awning covered the storefront entrance, carved inside the ground floor of a four-story concrete-covered block of flats; dozens of rectangular blue tables and wicker chairs were spread out into the street. Young waitresses, many who had just completed their two years of mandatory military service, rushed from table to table taking orders and bringing out large trays of food. It was Sunday, March 30, 2003, and it was the beginning of the workweek. The girls working the floor found it hard to cope with the bustling lunch crowd that bright sunny afternoon.

Jamil Ranem was dressed to look like an Israeli—fashionable jeans and a jacket. He was fair-skinned and his hair was styled in a modern cut. A car with Israeli plates, driven by an Israeli-Arab from one of the villages inside the Green Line, had ferried him to Netanya and dropped him off a few blocks from his target. An armed security guard was supposed to be positioned on a studio chair just in front of the London Cafe to profile diners and make sure that anyone who looked like he or she didn't belong didn't get in; the guard checked handbags and even patted down suspicious individuals. But the post was empty. Gil Kuperman, a conscript soldier who was nearby, saw Ranem walking toward the main entrance. Intuitively, Kuperman leaped forward to jump in front of the Palestinian and order him to move away. Confused, perhaps daunted, Ranem took a few steps back and then flipped the toggle switch that ignited his explosive charge. The blast ripped across the eatery. Tables were overturned and glass shards tore through the flesh of the patrons enjoying an outdoor meal. A thick puff of black smoke quickly evaporated into the Mediterranean sun to reveal scores of wounded. A redolence of charred flesh filled the air.

Miraculously, no one was killed in the blast other than the bomber; Ranem's severed head was thrown by the force of the explosion across busy Herzl Street. Forty Israelis were critically wounded in the explosion, which came just over a year after the March 27, 2002, Passover Massacre that happened just a few blocks away. Israeli first responders, looking at the destruction, could not believe that the bomber had been the only fatality. Gil Kuperman, who had stood closest to the bomber, was hurt the worst. Crime scene investigators and Shin Bet agents rushed to the blast scene. Heavily armed Border Guard policemen forged a tactical perimeter and looked into the crowd to try and spot a possible second bomber.

In Tulkarm, inside the kitchen of the Ranem home, the women cooked with the synchronized precision of a German auto factory: Some women hovered over the rice and other stews simmering on a low heat, while others sliced and diced tomatoes, cucumbers, and parsley for the salad. The men readied the picnic table outside with bottles of Pepsi and 7UP and bowls of roasted sunflower and pumpkin seeds. The very best Kanafeh, fine shreds of pastry noodles and honey-sweetened cheese that are covered with pistachio nuts and dyed orange, was delivered from a bakery in Nablus. The PIJ was sparing no expense for the spread. It was important for the Islamic Jihad to show the Ranem family, and the families of other men and women who might be suitable candidates for suicide operations, that money would be no object when celebrating the martyr's sacrifice.

Mazen Salameh had been around enough to know that the Shin Bet would ultimately connect the dots and link his handiwork to the Netanya bombing. But Salameh didn't run. He felt safe inside his small fiefdom, deep inside the spiderweb of treacherous alleys in the Tulkarm refugee camp—a location that even Israel's top-flight command forces feared to enter.

There had been a time when the Shin Bet knew every inch of Tulkarm. Israel's counterintelligence and counterterrorist spies had assets positioned through the city; Shin Bet sources were involved in every trade, and they were located at every turn. The granular Israeli insight diminished after Oslo, only to reemerge—slowly—following Defensive Shield. Rebuilding intelligence networks was labor-intensive. The task required patience, resources, and the ability to manipulate human weakness and spread cash around toward a definitive and dedicated result. The intelligence usually came in one way or another. Shin Bet means and methods were incredibly effective. The case officers often placed themselves at great risk, meeting in secret locations with men and women they hoped they could trust. They fought in between the lines of right and wrong, on a battlefield that really had no rules. They often risked it all—surviving on wits, nicotine, and bellyfuls of stomach acid—to obtain a morsel of data that could be used somehow to bring a terrorist to justice. It took the data compiled from more than forty Shin Bet interviews of captured suspects to determine the highly compartmentalized matrix of cells and secrets that located the whereabouts of Muhaned Taher and his deputy Imad Droaza in June 2002, following a three-year manhunt.[5] Taher, dubbed "the Engineer No. 4," was considered the top Hamas bomb-builder in the West Bank, responsible for 121 Israelis killed and nearly 400 wounded. Naval commandos from Flotilla 13 killed Taher and Droaza in Nablus on June 30, 2002; less than two weeks earlier, one of Taher's bombs had killed nineteen people and wounded seventy on board a bus in Jerusalem.

The Tulkarm refugee camp, situated in the eastern section of the city, was the second largest such United Nations–administered site in the West Bank. Located close to the *muqata*, or municipal seat, and Tulkarm Prison, the camp was established in 1950 on land that the United Nations Relief Works Agency, UNRWA, leased from the Jordanian government. The camp sat on a plot of land no larger than one-tenth of a square mile and was home to a "registered" eighteen thousand inhabitants; most of the original camp dwellers fled the 1948 fighting and came from in and around the Haifa area. The camp came under the Palestinian Authority's rule in 1995, though Arafat's security forces made a point to stay clear of the camp's narrow alleys and its interconnected non-permanent structures that quickly became all-too-permanent realities. Tulkarm natives looked down on the residents of the camp. The life of a refugee was always filled with indignity.

The refugee camps throughout the West Bank were fertile recruiting grounds for Hamas and the PIJ. Belonging to one group or another meant status; the AK-47 assault rifle or the Carl Gustav submachine gun that membership entailed also provided security to one's family. Weapons, of course, were everywhere, as were explosives and IEDs. Indeed, each neighborhood, sometimes each block or even each building, owed an allegiance to this group or that. If a score had to be settled, an entire part of the camp could be engulfed in gunfire. The IDF had paid a dear price for operating inside the refugee camps during Defensive Shield. In anticipation of future Israeli operations inside the camps, residents pre-positioned boulders, soda bottles filled with gasoline, and even hand grenades on building rooftops so that the neighborhoods could be prepared for any incursion. Salameh felt incredibly safe inside the multiple layers of defense that existed for him inside such heavily armed squalor. Israeli operations inside the camps, Salameh knew, could be costly for the raiders. On August 8, 2003, Staff Sergeant Roi Oren, an NCO with the Flotilla 13 naval commando unit, was killed during an arrest operation of a wanted Hamas Engineer in the Aksar refugee camp east of Nablus.[6]

Days after the London Cafe bombing, the Shin Bet had a rough idea as to where Salameh was hiding. But the days soon turned into weeks and the weeks soon became months. As the summer passed, Salameh became emboldened. He hid in plain sight, almost daring the Shin Bet to come and get him. He wasn't the only fugitive in the Tulkarm refugee camp to believe he was outside Israel's grasp.

Colonel Tamir Hayman, commander of the Ephraim Brigade in the area, requested that each and every one of the IDF and Border Guard special operations units submit a plan detailing how they would go about capturing—or killing—Mazen Salameh. "Everyone said that the operation was too dangerous: the middle of a refugee camp, an armed terrorist, narrow alleys and streets, without a clean path in and without any chance of rescue," Colonel Hayman reflected. "I was told that it couldn't be done. The Ya'mas were the only unit that said that the mission was, indeed, possible."[7] The unit officers were probably the only ones crazy enough to want the mission.

Salameh was so confident that he was outside of Israel's reach that he routinely held court with his comrades just outside of a store deep inside the alleyways of the refugee camp. The store was on a narrow street of shops that was always crowded with shoppers. Many of the shops had awnings, some nothing more than corrugated tin roofs held together by rope and ingenuity, protecting pedestrians from the unforgiving sun but also shielding Salameh from the prying eyes of IAF drones. The street was so narrow that most commercial vehicles, especially those that could ferry a tactical backup force, were too wide to fit. The street was so constricting and the sidewalk so high, one vehicle in front or to the rear of the Israelis could block them in without any chance of pushing their way out. Berman and his officers' entire operation—one of enormously high risk and high stakes—would be built around those brief moments of the day when Salameh felt most secure and most confident to relax and chat with his closest comrades. The operation would commence the moment the Shin Bet source definitively placed Salameh in front of the store. That's when and where the Ya'mas raiding force would engage him.

There were many inside the IDF hierarchy, especially those responsible for approving the Ya'mas plan, who thought the raid inside the refugee camp was a suicide mission—risky politically and one that would result in dead Israeli policemen. Just the thought of the obstacles that lay before the Ya'mas operators, Colonel Hayman later confessed, "gave me an ulcer."[8] But Berman and his team leaders were confident that they could develop the means to enter the refugee camp unnoticed and with a large enough presence that they could handle any tactical resistance.

The unit used some discretionary funds to purchase a decrepit pickup truck that was just narrow enough to fit inside the restricting streets and alleys of the camp, yet large enough that four heavily armed operators could hide in the back, under a thick cover, shielded from view. Rigging the vehicle with the proper concealment methods required enormous imagination and some innovative design. Surprise was crucial. The operators knew that they would have a window of under ninety seconds from the time they emerged from their Horse to the moment the alarm was sounded inside the camp that Israeli commandos were inside the wire. Each dress rehearsal was timed with a stopwatch to make sure that the operators could meet this rigid timeline. The training went from dry runs to "wet" live-fire displays. Wooden cutouts were used on a training field to simulate women and children passing by; two targets, one for Salameh and one for the bodyguard who was always at his side, were marked by balloons. Salameh did not adhere to a specific daily schedule. If he woke up early, he met with his men before noon; if it had been a late night, he would confer with his charges well into the afternoon. Sometimes, Salameh would sit in front of the store for only a few minutes, and other times the gatherings would last much longer. Berman and his men were under the assumption that the moment word came down from the Shin Bet confirming Salameh's location, they would have only a few minutes in which to strike at their target—and that Berman's undercover team would have to be in Tulkarm, poised to strike, the moment the green light was received. That meant lingering about in Tulkarm, near the camp, for an extended period of time. The mission became more susceptible to disaster every minute that the operators found themselves inside Palestinian territory.

The Speakers would have to perfect a cover story just in case they were challenged by a Palestinian policeman, or confronted by Tanzim thugs looking for cash. The process of defining the infinite number of *Mikrim u'Tguvot*, the religiously adhered-to process of examining all conceivable "occurrences and reactions" of a particular mission, became a full-time endeavor for Berman and his men. Every member of the assault force, from the Speaker behind the wheel to the squadron commander, had to have an immediate and logical response. "The questions we asked were troubling. What will you do if you find yourselves under fire in a sea of innocent civilians? What will you do if you get a flat tire? What will you do if one of the men gets separated chasing Salameh as he tries to flee inside the labyrinth of the camp?" Chief Inspector Nasser recalled. "This was not the type of operation where anything could be left to chance, and still there was bound to be something that we missed that could happen."[9] Every answer given opened up ten new questions. It was an exhaustive process.

The likelihood of getting shot became an overriding concern—more so than on previous missions. The reality of an operation inside the camp would make it impossible to evacuate a casualty by helicopter; it would take considerable effort for a large-size IDF rescue force ambulance to cut a path through the gauntlet of Palestinians once a *qawat al-hasa* operation went bad. Once inside Tulkarm, the operators knew, they were on their own. Many of those slated to participate in the operation didn't know if they were confident professionals or simply crazy, brave-hearted fools.

Throughout the summer months, the Ya'mas pre-positioned itself near Tulkarm on half a dozen occasions. They were all false alarms. The impetus to get Salameh increased tenfold as the New Year holiday neared, because the Shin Bet learned that Salameh and his cell were preparing a series of suicide bombings, some involving vehicles laden with explosives, against Israeli cities.[10] Then, on the morning of October 2, the Ya'mas received the call that it had waited for. The operation was a go.

Much of the unit rushed to the forward command post just outside Tulkarm where Colonel Hayman was waiting. Several companies of mechanized infantrymen, all dressed in their battle rattle, were ready to respond to any critical rescue inside Tulkarm. The Subaru tender had been gassed and any incriminating details linking the vehicle to the Ya'mas removed; Berman was prepared for them to ditch the jalopy and fight their way out of the camp on foot. Sergeant First Class Ghassan,* the Speaker who would also drive the force into the camp, fired up the engine just to make sure. Two Horses, filled with operators, would be pre-positioned near the targeted area. The Horses could respond, in case of emergency, within a couple of minutes. Apache helicopter gunships were already flying a circuitous pattern over Netanya just in case. Also hovering high in the sky was an IAF Beechcraft Super King Air reconnaissance and intelligence-gathering twin-prop aircraft.[11] The aircraft was critical in coordinating different elements on the ground with an eye-in-the-sky perspective.

Chief Inspector Nasser and Sergeant First Class Ghassan sat up front. Yaakov Berman, the squadron commander, sat with the rest of the tactical force in the back of the impromptu undercover vehicle.

The call had conveniently come in early in the morning, and the hope was that there wouldn't be too many civilians milling about the storefront where Salameh was reported to be sitting. But traffic in Tulkarm was heavy. The driver pushed the Subaru deeper into the city, concerned that the gridlock would prevent them from reaching their target in time. The Shin Bet

---

* A pseudonym—true identity withheld for security considerations.

informant had just contacted his case officer to tell him that Salameh was at the location. Colonel Hayman, along with Ya'mas commander Levy, watched the events unfolding nervously.

Ghassan carefully negotiated the crowded alley, honking his horn to push the pedestrians out of the way. The streets had no names, but he had memorized the route in the weeks of preparation leading to the operation. The Subaru moved slowly up a narrow alley strewn with litter and spoiled produce. A small shop selling bootleg CDs blasted the latest hits from Damascus and Beirut on two giant speakers that caused much of the area to vibrate. Women, some wearing black *niqab* veils, haggled with the vegetable hawkers over the price and quality of the tomatoes. Ghassan ground the steering wheel to the right. "Ten seconds out," Nasser whispered into the microphone hidden in his sleeve.

The Subaru drove past the storefront, inching forward. Salameh was nowhere to be found. Nasser scanned the crowds and couldn't see the distinctive round face and unmistakable black curly locks. "Target's not here," Nasser whispered, the disappointment and surprise accented in his brief transmission. Neither Hayman nor Levy had any chance to call the operators back. Berman got on the frequency and burst through with an interruption. "We are going around again."

Ghassan and Nasser scanned the alleys and streets as they moved about slowly through the camp, trying to look for Salameh as they also desperately tried to maintain cover. They knew what to say and what not to say, with a well-rehearsed Tulkarm accent and with Tulkarm slang, if they needed to demand that the car in front of them blocking their path move out of their way. Their vehicle had already been inside the camp for too long, though. Several of the IDF officers watching the operation unfold were ready to reiterate their initial belief that the operation was a bad idea. The officers watching the Subaru twist and turn in and out of alleys congested with humanity were convinced that the task force of tanks and mechanized infantrymen would be needed to pull the undercover policemen out of the camp. Colonel Hayman had grown up inside the Armored Corps, rising up through the ranks in Israel's noted 7th Armored Brigade. He knew exactly how prolonged and bloody a tank foray into the Tulkarm would be. But the Ya'mas officers told their IDF counterparts to remain calm. "Other counterterrorist teams operating deep inside a Palestinian area could only function if the intelligence was ninety, perhaps ninety-five percent, correct," Superintendent (Ret.) Gil Kleiman, a former Ya'mas commander, explained. "They had to deploy on certainty. But the unit [Ya'mas] was capable of operating deep into hostile environments with the intelligence being only forty percent accurate. The ability to go with the information and plan and alter plans on the move was what made the unit so very effective."[12]

The Subaru twisted its course around the block with three sharp right turns. The locals were very wary of out-of-place vehicles, and eyes began to focus on the white pickup truck. Ghassan drove slowly, rounding the same shops and suspicious people on an open alley's worth of pavement. A figure had emerged some fifty meters away. He had dark skin, a round face, and dark curly hair. He was unmistakable from that far away. Ghassan took his foot off the gas, gliding the Subaru into position just in front of the store. Salameh was sitting in front next to a bodyguard.

Nasser opened the door and lowered his head at the sidewalk while raising his eyes to maintain a piercing stare toward Salameh. Salameh looked at Nasser and he knew. Any question that the vehicle belonged to the dreaded *qawat al-hasa* was answered the moment Berman emerged from the rear with his M4 in hand. Salameh rushed to remove his pistol, a 9mm semiautomatic, from the small of his back. Nasser fired several times from virtually point-blank range. Berman engaged the bodyguard who tried to flee, and the gunman was cut down by a burst of automatic fire. Mazen Salameh had been killed.

Seconds after Salameh's lifeless body slumped to the ground, Berman and his men came under immediate fire. Small arms fire soon emanated from the nearby alleyways; Molotov cocktails and boulders were thrown at the Subaru from nearby windows and rooftops. Those who could ran. Women and children scampered away to escape the area. Young men, though, grabbed their weapons and ran toward the gunfire, eager to engage the Israeli commandos.

Ghassan drove out of the chaos as fast as he could, but the streets were soon blocked by the oncoming wave of heavily armed men. Berman, sitting in the back of the Subaru, braced for battle. But Nasser opened his window and yelled, "*Jesh! Jesh!*" The fear in Nasser's eyes convinced many that he was a Palestinian fugitive desperately fleeing for his life; his Arabic was, after all, impeccable. The crowd opened up to let the Subaru through. Some of the younger boys, eager to participate in the chaos, actually guided the Israelis out of the camp through the back alleys and side streets. By the time the angry crowd in the refugee camp figured out what they had done, Ghassan had negotiated the maze and was heading back to Israeli lines.

Several thousand feet above the West Bank, the young lieutenant copiloting the Super King Air—known as the *Tzufit*, or Sunbird, in Hebrew—asked the pilot if he knew who the crazy guys were who were operating so deep behind enemy lines. "That's the Border Guard undercover unit," the veteran airman commented. "They are a unit you don't hear much about and they are the most serious unit operating in the territories."[13]

The raid in the Tulkarm refugee camp defined the absolute value of undercover units in the hunt for the field commanders of the intifada. The operation in Tulkarm unnerved many terrorist commanders throughout the area. Many went deeper into hiding, departing the crowded sanctuaries in the city and moving to the outskirts, where they hid in caves and in fields. Other high-value targets, the Shin Bet had learned, stopped meeting with subordinates altogether. Day-to-day functions became harder to coordinate. Operations against Israel became harder to execute. "They saw us in the shadows, in the markets, and even inside their mosques and town squares," a senior Israeli counterterrorist commander commented. "They saw us even when we weren't even there. We refused to take our foot off the pedal for a moment. We weren't about to let them breathe freely once again."[14]

Ya'mas operations throughout the area intensified. The Ya'mas returned to the Tulkarm refugee camp four weeks later.

Like Mazen Salameh, Ibrahim Aref Ibrahim a-N'anish's name populated many most-wanted lists. The twenty-eight-year-old commander of Fatah's al-Aqsa Martyrs Brigade in Tulkarm, a-N'anish was responsible for masterminding several suicide bombers into Israel, as well as ordering mortar and machine-gun attacks against Israeli civilians. A-N'anish likened himself to a modern-day Rambo of sorts. He always moved about with an M16 assault rifle slung over his shoulder, and he crisscrossed the refugee camp, from safe house to safe house, always wearing his U.S.-surplus woodland-pattern camouflage fatigues. The Shin Bet had tried to lure a-N'anish out of the camp before, but the Fatah commander was smart enough to resist any proposed meetings outside the refugee camp front gate. Ya'mas forays into the city yielded little operational intelligence on a-N'anish's whereabouts.

But as Ramadan arrived at the end of October 2003, the Shin Bet learned that a-N'anish fancied himself as the camp's security director. At night, as the inhabitants of the camp feasted following the daylong fast, a-N'anish would sit on a bench at the main gate with his M16 at the ready. The intelligence presented the Ya'mas with both an opportunity and a challenge. The fact that the target revealed his location on a nightly basis enabled the Ya'mas teams to formulate an operation plan that the squadron commander, the unit commander, and the IDF brigade and divisional commanders would approve. Team commanders, like Chief Inspector Nasser, could fine-tune both the tactics that would be employed and the tools to carry out the mission. But Ramadan created operational obstacles. At night there wouldn't be a soul on the streets. Everyone would be at home, or in communal feast tents feasting. It would be impossible for the Ya'mas to deploy several vehicles along with a Horse or two for tactical backup. Palestinian lookouts could rationalize one vehicle moving toward the camp, but a small convoy would spark immediate suspicion and gunfire. The foray would require a small footprint and a band of brave men who would be exposed to enormous risk.

On the night of October 28, 2003, approximately forty IDF and Ya'mas officers gathered at a field command post on the outskirts of Tulkarm to scan the radio frequencies and gaze into a poster-size monitor transmitting the black-and-white infrared footage from a drone launched over the camp. Nasser and First Sergeant Suleiman,* a Bedouin and a highly experienced Speaker known as the best driver in the unit, checked their clothing to make sure the masquerade was convincing. Two other operators were already sitting in the back seat; M4s were at their feet. The Ramadan fast had ended, and the alleys and narrow streets of the city—and the camp—had emptied of all

---

* A pseudonym—true identity concealed for security considerations.

human traffic. Horses would follow Chief Inspector Nasser into Tulkarm and then break off until and unless needed.

At the Command Post, word was received that a-N'anish had assumed his spot at the camp gate to start a night shift of guard duty. He ate a sandwich of grilled meats and salad stuffed into a pita. His M16 was at his side.

The streets of Tulkarm were deserted. Nasser had never seen the streets of the bustling city so empty. The drive to the camp took minutes. There weren't even Palestinian policemen on patrol. Everyone was eating. Nasser knew that the sight of the sedan driving toward the camp would pull on a-N'anish's fight-or-flight triggers, and the plan was for the vehicle to drive by the camp gate and engage the targeted militant after they had driven past him and then made a U-turn. The belief was that a-N'anish might believe that the vehicle had made a wrong turn, perhaps heading to the Iftar breaking-of-the-fast meal, and was returning back into the city. That, at least, was the plan.

The men in the sedan watched intently as they neared the refugee camp entrance. The sedan traveled at a slow but routine pace as it headed east, never moving faster than twenty-five miles per hour. If the masquerade warranted, he could drive at a snail's pace with the innocence of caution. Suleiman didn't even turn his head slightly to look over at a-N'anish. That would have given away the mission. A-N'anish had already stood up to clutch his M16 as the white sedan pushed closer. The other men inside the car glanced quickly at the main gate, and they noticed another armed individual standing next to a-N'anish, hidden from view by an awning.

Suleiman drove east toward the main camp entrance and then, as planned, slowly turned north. The sedan continued some two hundred meters along a narrowly paved avenue, and then Suleiman turned the steering wheel left, before shifting into reverse and then turning left again. The operators readied their weapons.

The two Palestinians at the entrance to the refugee camp felt something odd about the white sedan meandering slowly during the Iftar. A-N'anish threw his sandwich to the ground. When the Ya'mas operators were a hundred yards away, he unleashed a magazine-emptying burst of accurate fire. Bullets penetrated the hood and smashed the windshield; the rearview mirror exploded after taking several direct hits. But Suleiman did not pause or panic. He continued forward. "At one point, a-N'anish realized what was happening and who was coming for him, and he ran. So did his partner," Nasser recalled. "Three of us raced out of the car and followed the two men into the camp. We realized that we only had a short time—very short time—before people would leave their food and come out into the streets shooting."[15]

Two operators chased a-N'anish and his partner inside the camp, trying hard to close ranks before the suspects disappeared and before the Ya'mas officers found themselves drawn in too deep for comfort. In the Command Post, the assembled colonels and majors watched the events unfold. They feared the worst.

Thirty seconds into the pursuit, Ibrahim Aref Ibrahim a-N'anish decided to stop running. He swung around and took aim at the Israelis closing in on him. Nasser dropped to a knee and fired several shots, hitting a-N'anish dead center in the chest and abdomen. The al-Aqsa commander fell to the pavement, and dropped his coveted M16. His partner attempted to pick up the weapon and engage the Ya'mas operators, but he was also cut down by a hail of gunfire.

The Ya'mas tandem grabbed the M16 and rushed along with Nasser back outside the camp gates, where Suleiman and another operator were waiting by the vehicle. The sedan was not armored. The four-door car had sustained multiple hits from a-N'anish's M16, but the engine still worked. If the operators were lucky, they would be able to escape as quietly as they had come in.

It had been a good stretch for the Ya'mas. They had arrested and killed scores of terrorists, and much of the terrorist command structure inside Tulkarm had been neutralized. They had stopped countless suicide bombings. Brigadier General Moshe Kaplinsky, the commanding officer of the IDF's Central Command, awarded the unit a citation for their extraordinary operations in the fight against terror. But 2003 also marked the tenth year of suicide bombing attacks against Israel's towns and cities. There had been 250 suicide bombings in this bloody ten-year stretch.*

---

* Of the first 250 bombings, according to the article *"Ha'Mitabed Ha-250,"* by *Yediot Aharonot's* internationally recognized correspondent Roni Shaked, Hamas was responsible for 135 of the bombings; the PIJ was responsible for 70; Fatah and either the Tanzim or the al-Aqsa Brigade was responsible for 39; 3 suicide bombings were at the hands of the DFLP; and 3 were perpetrated by the PFLP.

By denying the Palestinian terrorist field commanders permanent sanctuary inside the West Bank, by continuously being on the offensive operating
in locations that the terrorists believed Israel's *qawat al-hasa* would never dare
enter, Israel's counterterrorist units in the West Bank had defeated the true
objectives of the al-Aqsa intifada.[16] The undercover campaign had unnerved
the terrorist leadership and it had depleted their ranks. But the reckoning of
victory, the *tahdiyya*, or lull,17 that was needed was still far off in the distance.

Members of the Pal'mach's Arab Platoon pose in indigenous outfits in pre-Independence Palestine in a photo believed to have been taken at the Mishmar Ha'Emek training facility in 1942. (PAL'MACH MUSEUM)

LEFT Uri Bar-Lev, the first commander of Duvdevan, the IDF's undercover counterterrorist unit for the West Bank, briefs then–defense minister Yitzhak Rabin at the height of the first intifada. (URI BAR-LEV)

BELOW LEFT The unit emblem of Meir Dagan's Sayeret Rimon—Israel's first tactical undercover unit. (SAMUEL M. KATZ)

BELOW RIGHT Superintendent Eli Avram, the first commander of the West Bank Ya'mas unit. He was killed in Jenin while leading an arrest operation in August 1992. (ANAT AVRAM)

A Jerusalem Ya'mas operator aims his service weapon while masquerading as a Palestinian woman. (SAMUEL M. KATZ)

Palestinians riot in the Old City of Jerusalem during the opening salvo of the al-Aqsa intifada. (AVI OHAYON / ISRAEL GOVERNMENT PRESS OFFICE)

August 9, 2001, Jerusalem. First responders deployed to the bombed-out shell of the Sbarro pizzeria on the corner of Jaffa Road and King George Street after a Hamas suicide bomber blew it up. (AVI OHAYON / ISRAEL GOVERNMENT PRESS OFFICE)

LEFT: Kobi Shabtai (left), the Ya'mas Gaza unit commander in the 1990s, drills his men before an arrest operation. (SHIMON/YA'MAS GAZA)

BELOW: A Ya'mas Gaza operator dressed as a woman aims his Mini-Uzi 9mm submachine gun at the shooting range during training. (SAMUEL M. KATZ)

A West Bank Ya'mas team runs through a "snatch and grab" exercise before embarking on a mission. (INP BORDER GUARD / WEST BANK YA'MAS)

Superintendent Patrick Pereg, the West Bank Ya'mas operations officer (center, face not pixilated), killed in action in Hebron on April 4, 2002, and seen here during a unit exercise. (ISRAEL NATIONAL POLICE BORDER GUARD SPOKESMAN'S OFFICE)

Operators from the Jerusalem Ya'mas race into an alley to apprehend a terror suspect. (ZIV KOREN)

Members of the Jerusalem Ya'mas break cover to make an arrest. (ZIV KOREN)

Body camera image showing two terror suspects the moment they learn that they are arrested in an undercover operation near Jenin. (ISRAEL NATIONAL POLICE BORDER GUARD SPOKESMAN'S OFFICE)

West Bank Ya'mas commander Uzi Levy *(far left)* and squadron commander Yaakov Berman *(facing camera)* pin the rank of Inspector to Sa'ar Shine. (SA'AR SHINE)

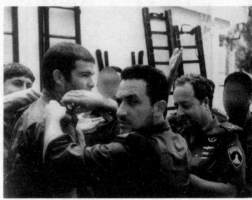

A Ya'mas operator covers an alleyway during an arrest operation in one of the northern villages of the West Bank. (ISRAEL NATIONAL POLICE BORDER GUARD SPOKESMAN'S OFFICE)

IDF Chief of Staff Lieutenant General Moshe Ya'alon presents Yaakov Berman with the "military's" second-highest medal for bravery. (YAAKOV BERMAN)

ABOVE: A Ya'mas operator covers the assault team during a raid near the Jabalya refugee camp in Gaza, May 2004. (SAMUEL M. KATZ)

RIGHT: The Ya'mas Gaza emblem. (SAMUEL M. KATZ)

ימ״ס עזה

In January 2019, Border Guard commander Kobi Shabtai (*standing, second from left*) poses with Prime Minister Netanyahu and Ya'ma'm operators at the unit's home base. When he was appointed Israel National Police commissioner, Shabtai continued to prepare the force's elite units for any terrorist eventuality. (KOBI GIDEON / ISRAEL GOVERNMENT PRESS OFFICE)

ABOVE: An Israeli soldier walks amid the ruins of homes in Kfar Aza, following the brutal battle to liberate the kibbutz from barricaded Hamas terrorists. (KOBI GIDEON / ISRAEL GOVERNMENT PRESS OFFICE)

LEFT: A Bring Her Home poster, seen in downtown Tel Aviv in June 2024, demanding that Hamas release Eden Yerushalmi, a twenty-four-year-old bartender kidnapped to Gaza from the Nova music festival. Israeli forces discovered Yerushalmi's body in a terror tunnel near Rafah on August 31, 2024. She had been executed when Israeli troops neared. (SAMUEL M. KATZ)

CHAPTER TEN

Jenin

Perhaps, as the cliché went, opposites did attract. In the case of Chief Inspector Yaakov Berman and Inspector Sa'ar Shine, opposites were also at each other's throat. The clash of wills—or an exchange of fists—was inevitable between the two stubborn-minded men who were entrenched in their opinions and ways of getting things done. That both men never rolled up their sleeves in an old-fashioned "let's settle this" way was both a miracle and a statement of how the two of them, an officer and his subordinate, grudgingly respected the hell out of each other during a time when respect was earned in the field.

Sa'ar Shine's arrival in the unit was a case of circumstance rather than choice. He had been sitting on a beach in Goa, India, when the intifada erupted, and enjoying some of the well-deserved personal self-exploration that many Israelis in their early twenties embark on following several years of difficult military service. Shine was a kibbutznik, a native son of a socialist collective in the northern tip of the country. Kibbutzniks, the slang for those from a kibbutz, were, even in egalitarian Israel, something of a national elite. The very fibers of Israel's pioneer narrative, of making the desert bloom and draining the swamps, was born on the kibbutz social collectives. The kibbutzim were farmer warriors known to have provided the backbone to Israel's military legends and its battlefield exploits. Virtually all military-age kibbutzniks served in combat units; most of these men served as commandos in special operations units and as fighter pilots in the Israeli Air Force. Sa'ar had followed this tradition to the letter. He served in an elite antitank reconnaissance unit from the famed 1st Golani Infantry Brigade. After his three years of service—much of it spent fighting Hezbollah in Lebanon—Sa'ar remained inside the bandit country north of Israel's border. He was an Israeli government security agent who protected the generals, politicians, and spies assigned to interface with the United Nations peacekeepers.

Five years of living inside the Hezbollah crosshairs was enough for Sa'ar. He collected the small sum of money that the IDF paid discharged soldiers and headed for Goa. Blue-eyed, handsome, and the owner of a very cutting sense of humor, he experienced the hippie-like freedom that Goa offered as a paradise of unimaginable splendor. The parties, the free love, and the freedom were such a welcome change from the years of humping antitank missiles to ambushes against Hezbollah suicide squads. But a month into the wild life, the al-Aqsa intifada erupted. Sa'ar simply couldn't remain on a beach in paradise while his country was embroiled in war. He caught one of the first flights he could find back to Israel so that he could do something—that something was to volunteer for the Ya'ma'm.

The Ya'ma'm, a unit so secretively selective that it accepted less than 1 percent of those vying for a spot in the force, was nearly impossible to get into. Sa'ar made it through the first phase of the selection process, where several thousand hopefuls became several hundred, but he washed out after that. He still wanted to fight the war on terror, though. Patriotism and a sense of mission had pulled him off the beaches of Goa; he still wanted to make a difference. He volunteered to serve as an NCO in the Ya'mas. After an intense counterterrorist and undercover warfare course, he found himself assigned to Yaakov Berman's team in the unit.

Serving inside the Ya'mas was a jarring case of culture shock to Sa'ar, who had been used to a very different human makeup in the IDF. Much of the Hebrew spoken in the unit was heavily accented. There were Russian accents, and they competed with other dialects from the far outreaches of the former Soviet Union. There was Arabic spoken, of course, and there was the street slang that was pervasive in the Border Guard that would not be tolerated in the IDF—especially in an elite Sayeret, or reconnaissance unit, such as the commando squad Sa'ar had grown up in. The Tower of Babel of accents, religions, and cultural quirks was wrapped neatly together by Berman. The team commander was an officer in the true Soviet model—unforgiving, disciplined, and very rigid in his day-to-day perspective and in his long-term outlook. Everything about Berman was about his way. Those who deviated from the unbendable line quickly found themselves off the team and, in all likelihood, out of the unit.

To say that Berman and Sa'ar locked horns would be an understatement of grand measure. But the two slowly—very slowly—developed admiration for each other. Over time, mutual respect eventually overpowered obvious sentiments of mutual hostility. As much as Sa'ar was driven insane by Berman's rigidness, in the field Berman displayed leadership qualities under fire that IDF officers could never have competed with. Berman, Russian accent and all, was just as audaciously arrogant in Arab costume as he was in full tactical kit. There was method to his madness. And, as much as Berman felt that Sa'ar's attitude undermined his command, he also realized that the kibbutz native was fearless and one of the hardest working tactical specialists that he had ever come across. Mutual disdain turned into an unbreakable friendship.

Berman had made Sa'ar the team sergeant, the man responsible for navigating the raiding party to its target. The sergeants had to memorize every small dirt road, smuggler's path, main thoroughfare, and route that the unit could traverse during the course of an operation. Before GPS, this required studying IDF maps and memorizing each coordinate: both in its IDF code designation, as well as its local Palestinian names. Team sergeant was a position of enormous personal responsibility. Sa'ar would often collapse in his bunk with his face immersed in maps, prior to a mission. But Sa'ar was much more than someone who could direct a force from Point A to Point B. His courage was beyond cliché. He was one of the most audacious and downright fearless men to be found once the bullets flew. Sa'ar's heroism at Itamar in June 2002 was one such example of his mettle under fire. He would soon earn the distinction of becoming one of the most decorated soldiers or policemen in Israel's history.

Berman and Sa'ar ultimately buried their differences in a long and very animated conversation followed by a warm embrace and a warrior's handshake. Both men never looked back. Sa'ar became, in essence, Berman's deputy team commander. When the squadrons were created as the unit grew during the intifada, Sa'ar was sent to officers' school so that he could return to the unit in a position of command. There were few operations that Berman led where Sa'ar wasn't beside him as the mission's deputy commander. In Nablus, in Tulkarm, in Qalqilya, and in all the villages and caves in between, the two men proved to be a lethal terrorist-hunting tandem. In just the beginning of 2004, Berman and his squadron were responsible for the termination of thirty-five high-value Palestinian terrorist targets; they were responsible for the apprehension of hundreds more.

Jenin was where both Berman and Sa'ar would do some of their best work.

"Nablus," a veteran Shin Bet agent once reflected, "was the brain of the West Bank. Nablus was where the terrorist masterminds hailed from. It was where the most horrible of attacks were planned. Jenin, on the other hand," the agent explained, "was the muscle. Jenin was where the killers came from. Jenin was where the men who killed on the orders of others called home."[1]

Jenin, after all, was where thirteen IDF reservists were killed in an ambush on April 9, 2002. The soldiers, many with children of their own, were lured into an alleyway by a young teenager begging for medical assistance for his mother; the area, known as the Bathtub, was an enclosure of tall buildings overlooking an alleyway. The Bathtub was fortified with Palestinian gunmen and booby-trapped explosives; the teenage boy turned out to be a suicide bomber. Rescue teams rushed into the gauntlet to try to save the lives of the reservists killed in the primary and secondary blasts, only to fall as casualties themselves. The battle inside the Bathtub raged for hours, and teams of Palestinians picked up the limbs and torsos of the Israeli dead in order to barter them off at a later date. Ultimately, a force of naval commandos assaulted the Bathtub, dislodged the Palestinian force, and recovered all the seized remains. It was one of the single bloodiest days for Israeli forces since the 1982 Lebanon War.

Some of the bloodiest engagements of the intifada were fought in Jenin. Every one of the IDF tip-of-the-spear units would fight there; a good number would be killed and wounded in action. The Ya'mas spent much of the intifada inside the small and treacherous city. "We had been to Jenin so many times, on so many different occasions, in such different capacities," Sa'ar Shine admitted, "that we knew the landscape better than anyone else."[2] Inspector Nasser remembered, "We became so familiar with the streets, with the cafés, the markets, and the places where the locals go to smoke and have coffee that we referred to these landmarks by their Palestinian names and not the coordinates on an IDF map."[3]

The familiarity created operational demands from the IDF. Units like Flotilla 13 and other elite commando forces began requesting that Ya'mas teams ferry them in and out of the city, and the unit always accommodated them. The Ya'mas operators hated these assignments. On one occasion, when delivering a force of naval commandos to a target, Yaakov Berman remembered that the undercover force was met by a wall of thunderous Palestinian fire. "The terrorists opened fire on us with FN MAG light machine guns," Berman said. "The fire was impassable. Where else but Jenin would the terrorists use such heavy firepower?"[4]

Escorting other forces to an objective deep behind enemy lines also ran the risk of blue-on-blue friendly fire engagements. There were too many moving parts, often, too many things that could go wrong. In one of the operations, Sa'ar Shine remembered guiding his Horse out of Jenin when all of a sudden the turret of a Merkava Main Battle Tank (MBT) swung around and the 120mm main armament gun acquired the Ya'mas vehicle. "Tell the gunner not to shoot," Sa'ar yelled over the frequency. "Tell him to turn the cannon away from me." But as the Ya'mas vehicles departed Jenin, a Golani Brigade Achzarit, an indigenously produced armored personnel carrier (APC) made out of recycled Soviet tank chassis that the IDF had captured in the Arab–Israeli wars, rolled with a rush into the open space in the center of a junction. Blocking the Ya'mas convoy, the Achzarit commander acquired the Border Guard vehicles with a remote-controlled multi-barrel 7.62mm minigun that was aimed dead center for Sa'ar's windshield. One false move, one scared nineteen-year-old soldier seeing an unrecognizable face wearing a kefiyeh through the windshield of a vehicle sporting Palestinian plates, and a half dozen or so of Israel's top-tier operators would have been chewed apart in a destructive burst of fire.

The Ya'mas preferred to carry out their own operations, their own way, with the support entrenched in the standard operational procedures. Many of these operations were defined by daring and remarkable results. On March 9, 2004, a Ya'mas force ventured to the eastern section of Jenin to arrest a terror suspect. As the undercover units maneuvered through the city, they suddenly saw a different suspect, driving around in a stolen Toyota pickup truck along with four other heavily armed Fatah gunmen. The driver of the undercover van stared at the wanted fugitive—the fugitive stared back. A high-speed car chase ensued inside the battle-scarred landscape of the city, both vehicles exchanging gunfire in a scene more reminiscent of a Hollywood action movie than a West Bank city. The Palestinians crashed their vehicle, and in the firefight that followed all five Fatah operatives were killed.[5] The Ya'mas operators uncovered AK-47s, M16s, and explosives in the cargo hold of the Toyota. The Shin Bet would later learn that the five were en route to perpetrate an active shooter attack against an Israeli town.

As the intifada dragged on into its fourth bloody year, and as the perimeter wall began to take shape and fulfill its designed mission of keeping the suicide bombers from entering into Israeli territory, the conflict pushed north—past Tulkarm and the towns that straddled the triangle, and up into Wadi Ara, toward the treacherous confines of Jenin; internal Fatah documents revealed communiqués between Arafat and Tanzim leader Barghouti in which it was stated that the "innovative and unbeatable" Palestinian fighters of Jenin who joined forces would never cease their operations against Israel, resulting in Jenin always being "the suicide bomber capital of the world."[6] Much of Jenin was dominated by the PIJ, controlled by the organization's leadership in Damascus, and lavishly financed by the Revolutionary Guard in Iran. The PIJ's rigid organizational structure—and all of that Iranian cash—helped to turn Jenin into a city where the various Palestinian factions closed ranks and worked as one. The Palestinians pooled their resources—and talent—in Jenin. Twenty-nine-year-old Kamal Abdullah Tubasi was the man who made the alliance work.

In another world, far from the West Bank, Tubasi could have been a corporate climber destined for upper management stardom. Confident and capable, he was energetic enough to have his hands in virtually every terror project emanating out of Jenin, and he was forward-thinking enough to work with the stubborn personalities and easily bruised egos inside the rival groups, to pull off catastrophic attacks inside Israel. Tubasi had learned his networking skills as an agent of the Palestinian security services. Much of his training was reportedly CIA-supported. When the intifada began, though, some of the more opportunistic characters sporting extensive counterintelligence CVs became well-paid executives in the terror start-ups that the main groups initiated throughout the West Bank, Jerusalem, and Gaza. Tubasi sold his services to the highest bidders, the Tanzim, and then contracted services out to Hamas, the Martyrs Brigade, and, of course, the PIJ, where the Iranian rials flowed through Syrian banks and then into West Bank pockets.

Tubasi had been responsible for the May 19, 2003, shopping mall suicide bombing in Afula. He had masterminded the attempted suicide car bombing of the Azrieli skyscrapers in Tel Aviv later that year—an attack that was thwarted by luck when Israeli police intercepted the three thousand pounds of explosives wired inside a van en route to its target during a routine traffic stop. Tubasi's name had long topped Shin Bet wanted lists, but he rarely ventured outside the well-protected perimeter of Jenin's refugee camp. Tubasi also surrounded himself with bodyguards and routinely sought shelter in the homes of innocent civilians; to deter any Israeli moves in the dark hours of the night, Tubasi's bodyguards routinely wired these homes with explosives. Tubasi never moved about without his AK-47 assault rifle close at hand.

If the Shin Bet's operational branch could have definitely pinpointed Tubasi's whereabouts at any one moment in time, then the capture-or-kill mission would have been assigned to the Ya'ma'm. The Special Police Unit was, after all, Israel's tactical oncologist that targeted the most dangerous of threats, but only when the intelligence was absolute and the threat imminent. The Special Police Unit didn't pursue threats—they neutralized them. The mission to locate, identify, and deal with Tubasi was assigned to Yaakov Berman's Ya'mas squadron.

Like many of the other coffee-stained files on Berman's desk that were littered with cigarette ash, Tubasi was a mug shot, a Shin Bet case number, and a dossier full of notes: some typewritten, neatly word processed in an eleven-point Aharoni font, and others scribbled by hand. The notes consisted of incidental bits of information—some important (known aliases, known associates, known mobile phone numbers, names of associates and family members) and some trivial (favorite soccer team, preferred cigarette brand, and favorite woman at the local brothel). These details constituted small threads in the multidimensional quilt that the Shin Bet, sometimes with Ya'mas help, would create on a target. Sometimes these dossiers took weeks, months, or longer to develop. And sometimes there was great urgency in terminating the career of a terror suspect as quickly as humanly possible.

The Shin Bet had learned that Tubasi was coordinating a multi-group, multi-target suicide bombing attack somewhere in northern Israel set to coincide with Israel's Independence Day on April 27, 2004. The Shin Bet pressed hard to identify the exact nature of the attack, the names of the perpetrators, those predetermined for martyrdom, and the intended targets, but Tubasi had been a prized pupil in the American-funded counterintelligence classes that were provided to the secret policemen in Arafat's PA. Tubasi's cells were known for being highly compartmentalized and very lethal. All that was known about the attack was that it would be a joint venture of the PIJ, Fatah, and Hamas. Tubasi was the operation's mastermind.

The PIJ was the prime contractor of the Independence Day operation—the PIJ paid in cash. Operations that were initiated from Tehran or Damascus were always lavishly funded and were attractive to cell commanders from the other groups who were eager to prove their worth without the out-of-pocket headaches. Tubasi relished the role of field marshal and financier. It was a position of great power and, for a young man who had yet to reach his thirtieth birthday, a position of unrivaled opportunity. The money that the terrorist groups handled was vast, and many operatives profited greatly from the misery. The outside money, and lack of eyes-on-the-books oversight from the paymasters in Damascus and Tehran, budgeted for "martyrdom operations." Some PIJ operations in Jenin, for example, were budgeted at approximately $31,000, according to materials confiscated by Israeli intelligence when the bomb-building materials, and other logistic tools needed to carry out a strike, never reached $1,000. The money earmarked for the families of the martyrs, the true selling point for many of those who would ultimately strap on a bomb and attempt to blow themselves up in Israel, began at $125,000 (sums were dependent on the shock value and success—or failure—of an attack).[7] Those who administered these funds became the most powerful—and the most corrupt—element of the Palestinian terrorist infrastructure.

But the Iranians demanded dividends from their investments. The Syrians, who administered the Iranian terror portfolios, demanded updates from their franchises in the territories. The back-and-forth between Tehran, Damascus, and the West Bank was done via coded cellular phone traffic and the internet.[8] And the chatter always left an electronic trail that Shin Bet signals experts could intercept. Less than seventy-two hours before Israelis were about to celebrate the nation's fifty-sixth birthday, when tens of thousands of Israeli families would flood national parks to barbecue and enjoy the holiday, Yaakov Berman received a call from someone he had become very close to, a senior Shin Bet case agent, who wanted to sit down for a meeting. The Kamal Tubasi file had risen to the top of the pile. The clock was ticking.

On the morning of April 24, 2004, the Shin Bet case agent phoned Berman. "We just learned that Tubasi was in the Jenin refugee camp," the agent explained. "We don't know how long he'll be there or who he's with, but we need to get him now." In reality, a Shin Bet source' had indicated that Tubasi was in the company of *one* of his female acquaintances, and this made the intelligence both urgent and fleeting. If the woman was single, then Tubasi could spend all day there. If the woman was married, then the rendezvous would have to be a quick one; in such a case, it was also more likely that Tubasi was being looked after by a bodyguard, just in case the woman's husband came home early and threatened to interrupt the act.

In a perfect world, under ideal circumstances, the Ya'mas and the Shin Bet would have weeks to plan an operation around specific intelligence, a specific location, and a specific time of day. Planning for the operation could involve weeks of preparation, including the building of a model on which the operators could train. The planning could be as extensive as to pre-position snipers along rooftops to provide close support for the undercover operatives raiding the safe house. But the al-Aqsa intifada was far from being a perfect world—it was a messy, ugly, and bloody war of nerves. Israel's conditions for victory were predicated on its ability to respond immediately and decisively to breaking intelligence that afforded an opportunity. And the ability of the Ya'mas to react to a Shin Bet case officer's telephone call was key to winning the war against the suicide bombers. The ability of the Ya'mas to turn raw intelligence into an immediate raid was crucial in Israel's ability to end the catastrophic carnage on the country's streets. When word came in of Tubasi's location, the Ya'mas was able to do much of its pre-operational planning and preparations on the fly. The cell phone became the most important

---

* The nature of that source, whether it was HUMINT, SIGINT, or ELINT, remains classified.

communication and coordination tool in the unit's arsenal. SMS messages replaced a call on the radio. Unit operators—as well as the unit's command staff—could be summoned quickly and reliably to a rendezvous point for the pre-mission briefing in a forward staging area.

Colonel Oren Abman, the Jenin Brigade commander, had to approve the Ya'mas plan, and coordinate the necessary IAF and ground forces assets. Abman had grown up inside the 1st Golani Infantry Brigade and its elite Egoz counter-guerrilla commando force. He spent years hunting Hezbollah squads in southern Lebanon and he understood the complexity of acting on immediate intelligence. Abman had hunted many top Hezbollah commanders whose instincts were razor-sharp, whetted by the Iranian Revolutionary Guard; these men feared every twig snap and every shadow blur, and they never let their guard down—not even for a second. Tubasi was such a man. And engagements with such men always ended in gunfire.

Abman also understood the dangerous landscape of Jenin when the undercover operatives were at work. In many such engagements, when gunfire erupted, the terrorists under fire were reinforced by legions of fighters who came to the gun battle by taxi and brought with them loads of ammunition and weapons. Any operation inside the city could turn into "Mogadishu," a term that virtually all Ya'mas operators would refer to when describing the reality of being attacked by overwhelming firepower in a hostile city. Abman was worried about the operation turning into a Mogadishu. All that mattered to Berman was that Tubasi was where the Shin Bet said he would be. The raiding force would take care of the rest.

First Sergeant Abu Ahmed was the Speaker responsible for driving the raiding party to its target. Abu Ahmed, considered one of the most courageous and capable operators in the unit, was also considered one of the coolest under fire. Nothing daunted him. Months earlier, in the Palestinian town of Salfit, located southeast of the sprawling Jewish city of Ariel, Abu Ahmed had participated in an operation that could have gone disastrously wrong. The Ya'mas was after Badr Yassin, a Tanzim executioner who murdered Palestinians accused of collaborating with Israeli intelligence. There was no trial, of course, and no appeal. Yassin tortured many of those who were suspected of working with the Shin Bet before tying them to a tree and shooting them. One of Yassin's haunts was the Strawberry Cafe, a popular place for sweets and small cups of rocket-fuel coffee, and that's where the Ya'mas hoped to get him. The café was popular with married couples, as well as single women, and as a result several members of the Ya'mas arrest team drove to the target dressed as Palestinian women.[9] The female masquerade was incredibly effective and surprisingly disarming. "You'd be surprised how beautiful some of our Russian operators were when they shaved and put on mascara and lipstick," Nasser, the mission commander, explained.[10] "Even the most suspicious and paranoid terrorist who was wanted for years felt safer when such beauties were around him."* But when the lead Ya'mas vehicle approached the main entrance to the coffeehouse, Yassin suspected something was amiss. He ran deep into Salfit's narrow and mile-long Kasbah, hoping to lose the Israelis inside the deep crevice of shops and twisting alleys. But Nasser and First Sergeant Abu Ahmed followed their target deep inside, out of reach of backup units and out of sight from the UAV flying overhead. Although Yassin attempted to warn residents of the Kasbah that he was being chased by the *Mustaraboon* (one of the colloquial names for the Ya'mas units), the two operators closed ranks to get to within pistol range. Yassin turned to shoot, but Nasser and Abu Ahmed both dropped to their knees and fired. Yassin's body was left behind on the cold stone floor outside a clothing shop. Abu Ahmed's actions deep inside Salfit's Kasbah earned the veteran operator one of the four medals of courage he would receive during the course of the intifada, making him one of the most decorated soldiers and policemen in Israeli military history.

Everyone in the unit felt safe when Abu Ahmed drove him into battle—especially when they would be sitting in the back of the Horse.

It was uncharacteristically cool in Jenin that Saturday morning. It was usually warmer in April. Some of the IDF officers in the CP blew into their cupped hands in the attempt to stay warm, though it was also a gesture to relieve the

---

* In one of the IDF's most audacious James Bond operations, Operation Spring of Youth, Sayeret Mat'kal commander and future Israeli chief of staff and prime minister Ehud Barak—along with several of the most iconic figures in Israeli military history—donned blond wigs, impressively large stuffed bras, and miniskirts in a Mossad raid to terminate the three acting heads of Black September in Beirut on April 9, 1973.

tension. Saturday was the start of the workweek in Jenin, and the streets of the city were packed with vehicles and pedestrians. The Horse drove slowly through the city streets, past Yehiya Ayyash Square, as the Israeli task force pushed closer toward the refugee camp. Colonel Abman stood stone-like, his M4 assault rifle slung across his chest, staring at the flat-screen monitor broadcasting the images from the IAF drone. The communications liaison officers both from the Ya'mas and from the IDF brigade worked the phones and the secure and encrypted radio frequencies in the attempt to coordinate events on the ground with the intelligence from the air. Senior Shin Bet agents stood in the center of the high-ranking officers, talking to their sources and their subordinates.

The UAV flying over Jenin, at an altitude remotely controlled by a nineteen-year-old female soldier, relayed a troubling reality back to the Command Post. Dozens of armed men were seen walking around the camp—the IAF intelligence specialists who translated the fuzzy drone images for the combat commanders could easily discern AK-47s and RPK light machine guns carried by the blurry figures walking around.

The Jenin refugee camp had not recovered from Operation Defensive Shield—many doubted it ever would. Large swaths of the camp, which sat on a square less than a third of a square mile in size, lay in ruins; hundreds of buildings had been destroyed in the vicious close-quarter ten-day battle in 2002. Many of the camp's buildings were crumpled, knocked off their pillar perches by gunfire and the almighty D9s. Power lines were still down. The Palestinians were masters at re-rigging the wiring of the camp, and wires that connected to other wires that connected to a light pole that might be working hung across the sunny sky. The camp residents were less resourceful when it came to water and sewage. Old women and young children struggled with jerry cans and pails of water from working wells. The flow of raw sewage, sometimes gushing after a spring rain, filled the potholes in the streets left behind by the fighting. The stench at places was simply overwhelming.

Abu Ahmed displayed great skill and finesse negotiating this maze and misery. He had to appear unaffected by the sights around him so that he could blend in seamlessly and without suspicion. The apartment building where Tubasi carried out his intimate encounters was a three-story box of concrete slab perched on four slim pillars. A narrow staircase without rails led to the first apartment on the second floor. Stray dogs licked water from a puddle near the building entrance. A large black water tower on the roof blocked the intermittent sunshine that peeked through the clouds. Loud music emanated from one of the top apartments; the clattering of pots and pans being banged together was loudly heard from a kitchen window. Abu Ahmed slowed the van down to a crawl as he swung the white vehicle into position, enabling the men in the rear to deploy quickly. "Ten seconds out," he whispered.

But as Abu Ahmed stepped slightly on the brake to slow down, Tubasi walked down the front stairs with his bodyguard. Tubasi wore an IDF surplus green satin nylon officer's jacket with a faux fur collar and a pair of blue jeans. He walked straight toward a yellow Volkswagen Jetta taxicab that had pulled up in front the apartment building. In order to evade the undercover units, and the drones overhead, the terrorist chieftains preferred to travel by taxi, in the hope that the Israelis would be wary of firing into a vehicle that could possibly be ferrying civilians; the taxis were driven by armed members of Fatah or the PIJ, and weapons and explosives were often stored in the vehicles. Tubasi kept his eye on the white van parked twenty meters away, and on Abu Ahmed, who was moving forward followed by several other Speakers in disguise. Berman followed close behind.

Abu Ahmed closed his distance to the cab and quickly removed his sidearm. Tubasi saw Abu Ahmed from the corner of his eye. Both men began to fire at the same time. Berman and the others took aim and began to fire at Tubasi, who found cover behind the Jetta taxi. Pistol, submachine gun, and M4 carbine fire was exchanged at precariously close range. The driver of the taxi, thirty-year-old Fatah operative Said Haradan, was killed in the opening burst of fire, and Berman was certain that the Fatah commander had also been hit. Berman tried to outflank Tubasi and race toward the trunk. He swung around the vehicle in order to make sure that Tubasi was dead, but instead the Fatah commander was sitting crouched behind the engine block, lying in wait with his AK-47 at the ready. The two men—the hunter and the hunted—looked into each other's eyes for a brief moment of frozen time, and then they began to fire in the Jenin version of a Mexican standoff. It was like a movie, Berman would recall, but it was all too real.[11] Berman fired first, and remembered hitting Tubasi several times, but the Palestinian fought back. He fought hard, Berman would later say in grudging respect. Tubasi's final burst of fire, before he succumbed to his wounds, managed to hit Berman in the M4's thirty-round magazine worn on his chest. The force of getting shot punched the weapon out of his clutches.

Fragments from Tubasi's rounds sliced into Berman's chest, throat, and cheek. Sa'ar Shine immediately grabbed his commander by the jacket collar and dragged him to safety. Abu Ahmed, both a Speaker and a combat medic, rendered emergency first aid. Berman was not an easy patient. He continued to bark orders even though blood quickly filled his airways. "Stop tending to me and get on with the mission," he screamed as blood spewed from his mouth. "The wounds aren't important."[12] Shine couldn't believe it. "Be quiet," he yelled at his former nemesis and now close friend. Even getting shot in the throat, Sa'ar thought, couldn't get him to be quiet.

The gunfire was a wake-up call to gunmen inside the camp. Everyone with an AK-47 at hand rushed to the developing battle. Abman's fears had materialized. Jenin had turned into Mogadishu. The entire Ya'mas raiding force found itself under thunderous fire and from all angles. Snipers fired from rooftop perches and gunmen volleyed magazine-emptying bursts of AK-47 fire from behind alley walls. Shine assumed command of the task force and coordinated the operators to return fire. An armored IDF ambulance rushed into the fray to remove Berman, though he fought the notion of being evacuated and continued to direct his men and position them in a perimeter in order to hold off the Palestinian fire. As the ambulance rushed off under heavily armed escort, back to Israeli lines, Sa'ar Shine walked through the gunfire smiling. Finally, he thought to himself, there would be peace and quiet amid the chaos.

Sa'ar Shine and his small team, reinforced by additional Ya'mas elements and IDF reinforcements, fought a pitched battle inside the refugee camp. An additional Fatah operative was killed in the firefight; scores more were wounded.

Tubasi's death was a crippling blow to his secretive and highly effective terror network, but his network—and, more importantly, his suicide bombers—were still in play. As the battle raged in the Jenin refugee camp, yards from where Tubasi's body lay on a dirty patch of a road that was now covered with spent shell casings and garbage thrown about by a strong afternoon wind, the Shin Bet received word on the location of the bombers who were being readied for their Independence Day attacks. Shine was ordered to disengage from the fight and bring his force to Qabatiya, a town of nearly twenty thousand inhabitants, six kilometers south of Jenin. Shine and his officers assembled the raw intelligence and the assault planning on the fly, coordinating details with cell phones and radios; operators wrote down key bits of information on the trouser legs of their combat fatigues. Less than an hour after Kamal Tubasi was killed, Sa'ar Shine's undercover raiding force stormed a safe house near the city's Salah a-Din Mosque. One of the bombers resisted the call to surrender and was killed. His partner was seriously wounded as he attempted to resist and was apprehended. The arrest led to additional members of the cell being rounded up in raids that continued throughout the next day.

The unit made it back to base shortly before midnight. It had been a long day.

Seventy-two hours after the shoot-out in Jenin, tens of thousands of Israelis flooded the country's parks, beaches, and forests, to celebrate Independence Day. Israelis barbecued record kilograms of beef, lamb, chicken, and turkey in what was a national tradition of festivities fueled by the grilling meats and overeating. Security was tight, but the holiday came and went without bloodshed.

Chief Inspector Yaakov Berman recovered from his wounds. A few hours after surgery, as he lay in his hospital bed, next to his wife, who was seven months pregnant, Border Guard commander Major General David Tzur and Ya'mas commander Uzi Levy made a surprise visit. Berman was in line to be promoted at the end of the year to the rank of superintendent, the Israel National Police equivalent to major, but Tzur presented the Ya'mas squadron commander with his new rank six months ahead of schedule. Tzur had commanded the Ya'ma'm during the bloody years of close-quarter warfare in the first intifada. He had commanded the operation that rescued the body of the first Ya'mas commander from the terrorist safe house in Jenin twelve years earlier; Tzur had also been decorated for leading a Ya'ma'm force against a heavily armed terror cell in 1990. He understood how very important it was for the officers of counterterrorist units to be equipped with the natural Kevlar threads of human initiative and courage.*

As work on the security barrier continued, and the special operations effort in the northern West Bank intensified, Israeli counterterrorist efforts in and around Jenin yielded greater dividends. On July 13, 2004, the Ya'mas killed Nueman Takhina, the commander of the al-Quds Brigade, in Jenin. Ya'mas units pursued the PIJ commander in a lengthy car chase before he crashed his vehicle into a fence and was then killed when he opened fire on the Israeli operators. Takhina's death came days after the Ya'mas had arrested Khaled Jaradat, the PIJ overall commander in the Jenin area, who served as the direct link between Tehran, Damascus, and the organization in the northern West Bank. The Ya'mas also arrested Fawzi Sa'adi, the PIJ financier who distributed Iranian money through Syrian banks throughout the Middle East, into the hands of PIJ operatives in the West Bank and even the Gaza Strip.[13]

The undercover unit war in the West Bank had been relentless and bloody, but it was also highly effective. In 2002, the bloodiest year of the intifada, 240 Israelis had been killed by suicide bombers and other terrorist attacks. In 2003, following a ramping up of Shin Bet access to the towns and cities and an escalation of undercover unit operations, the number of Israelis killed by suicide bombers decreased—105 were killed that year. In 2004, perhaps the most successful year of the Ya'mas campaign, 69 Israeli civilians were killed.

The Ya'mas brand of preventative—and punitive—deterrence was working.

---

* In an unprecedented ceremony a year later, IDF chief of staff Lieutenant General Moshe Ya'alon presented Superintendent Yaakov Berman with the Itur Ha'Oz Medal of Courage, the Israeli military's second highest award for valor, comparable to the U.S. Army's Distinguished Service Cross and the British Army's Military Cross. Berman was the first policeman to ever receive the coveted award, previously issued to only 232 Israeli soldiers for deeds of gallantry at great risk of life in combat.

CHAPTER ELEVEN

The Night Before Jerusalem

Veteran Israeli counterterrorist hands hated chasing the young terror chieftains. The young men in their twenties were psychopathically violent and volatile. Their behavior was rash and impulsive, and they were less susceptible to having their whereabouts compromised by wives, children, or other family responsibilities. Many of the young terrorists were children during the first intifada; their primary school education was one of street fighting and suicide bombings. Their education consisted of street justice and Israeli counterterrorist efforts—preventative and retaliatory. These young children grew up in a desensitized abyss of covert cruelty, and when they matured, they frightened the Israeli security forces that hunted them, as well as the senior Palestinian leaders who funded them and directed their actions.

Ibrahim Muhamed Mahmud Hashash was one of these young prodigies. The twenty-three-year-old Nablus native began his terrorist career in the service of the PIJ. Hashash didn't fit the Webster's dictionary definition of pious religious holy warrior: He rarely set foot inside a mosque, but the PIJ's fanaticism and endless bundles of Iranian cash sparked his imagination. Hashash's ascent up the ladder of command was swift, and he had a role in both the recruitment of operatives and the execution of attacks. But Hashash was considered too bloodthirsty even for the PIJ. He was booted from the group when he recruited a child to carry out a suicide bombing. Hashash wasn't unemployed for long. He was offered a command-level position inside Fatah's Tanzim. His small band of Tanzim thugs, known for butchering suspected collaborators with hatchets, terrorized much of Nablus. The Iranians saw promise in Hashash and invested in his network even though he was no longer inside the PIJ framework; the Iranians urged Hashash to carry on and expand his campaign with suicide bombings.[1]

Hashash possessed the DNA of a hunted man: razor-sharp instincts and the ability to smell those who pursued him even when they were nowhere close. Hashash never trusted a soul—not even those in his compartmentalized cell. But with his Iranian benefactors demanding results, Hashash was forced to expand his inner circle in the planning of a major suicide bombing operation. And that's what the Shin Bet was waiting for.

The Shin Bet case agents assigned the Hashash portfolio had hoped to lure the wily terrorist lieutenant out of his Nablus safety zone—the back alleys of the Kasbah and the inside passageways of the Balata refugee camp—so that he could be captured more easily. Nablus was a nerve center of terrorist planning, and the Shin Bet was eager to hear details of the growing Iranian intelligence and counterintelligence presence in the city that was still fueling the intifada, five years into the conflict. But it appeared as if all sources connected to Hashash had dried up. There was no mobile phone chatter that could be used to launch a complex ELINT and SIGINT trail. There was no HUMINT emanating from Nablus even indicating that Hashash was still alive. Shin Bet investigators and A'man specialists had no launchpad from which to begin a matrix of contacts, connections, and pressure points that would help them connect the dots. All that was known was that he was holed up somewhere inside the less than one-tenth of a square mile that was the Balata refugee camp, protected by the nearly twenty-five thousand inhabitants, some there since the camp was founded in 1950. The Palestinian Authority never really took ownership of Balata, even with their American-supplied weapons and training. The camps were all the human depots of Hamas and the PIJ. Any attempt by the Israelis to retake the camp, the Palestinians always pledged, would be paid for in the blood of a great many Jewish soldiers. The 1st Golani Infantry Brigade overcame street-to-street, house-to-house, and room-to-room fighting during Operation Defensive Shield. The Shin Bet never ventured to guess how many weapons were inside Balata, but a veteran Israeli intelligence officer once dared to suggest that if a division of Israeli tanks pushed into the camp, they would find themselves outgunned.

But in April 2005, Ibrahim Hashash materialized. He was planning a significant suicide bombing against Jerusalem and his operation required subcontractors and communications. Ambitious undertakings also required risk.

The Shin Bet knew that Hashash wasn't the type of terrorist lieutenant to be caught in bed with his girlfriend, and that it would take a complex lure to reel him out of Balata. The Shin Bet case officers were ambitious. They were confident that they had the resources and the tradecraft needed to locate Hashash. Chief Inspector Nasser was responsible for the apprehension.

It took weeks for the Shin Bet spymasters to assemble their trap. It took a little over a week for the manipulation of events to come together into an operational reality. Chief Inspector Nasser and his team were ready the moment the green light was flashed.

One road, the 5705, led into Nablus. The thoroughfare split the city up and down its center; Balata was off a turn to the west. A Shin Bet asset, acting as a liaison, was to connect Hashash with a covert contact who had ties outside the West Bank in connection to the upcoming operation being planned. The Shin Bet plan was to lure Hashash from Balata, to a location outside the main camp entrance, where Nasser and his team of undercover operatives would be waiting. The mission was considered high risk. The date of the snatch was set for April 14, 2005. Thursday, it was hoped, was a good day to bring Hashash to justice. Traffic around the mosque was expected to be light.

There were multiple moving parts to the Hashash operation, multiple chances for Murphy's Law to rear its ugly head and turn snatch into fiasco. Inspector Nasser had excelled in such high-risk ventures before, but the fact that the Shin Bet asset could be luring the force into an ambush was a grave concern; Shin Bet assets had lured them into ambushes before. On January 3, 1993, Haim Nahmani, a twenty-six-year-old Shin Bet case agent responsible for the al-Aida refugee camp near Bethlehem, was killed in a Jerusalem apartment by Mahmud Abu Srur, the Hamas double agent he ran.[2]

Nasser's Ya'mas arrest team would have to be fluid and flexible. Hashash, fearing an Israeli plot, could send his meet on a wild goose chase that would require the Ya'mas Horse and tactical backup to go from one end of Nablus to the other. In order to eliminate the confusion that such unscripted movement could entail—especially for the Nablus Brigade commander watching the events unfold in the Command Post at the unit's headquarters nearby—Nasser decided to place an identifying marker, a green towel, in the rear of the lead undercover vehicle. But the Shin Bet asset reported that Hashash was suspicious, especially of a particular white sedan with a green blanket that was driving near the entrance to the refugee camp. The intelligence, relayed by the Shin Bet case officer driving with them, daunted Inspector Nasser. He realized that Hashash had spotters in the field searching for Israeli commandos. Perhaps, he thought, Hashash had also positioned snipers on nearby rooftops. The afternoon sun began to wane. Nasser monitored the radio traffic through the transparent plastic earbud wedged tightly into his ear.

For the next two hours, Hashash ran the Shin Bet and the Ya'mas arrest team through a ringer of tasks and fake meets. The Israelis satisfied each challenge. First Sergeant Suleiman, who had been in the thick of many a hostile engagement with Inspector Nasser before in Tulkarm, Qalqilya, and Jenin, negotiated the Nablus traffic with a local's flair, even managing the crowded gridlock on Abu Baker al-Sadeik Street. The Ya'mas vehicles pushed in and around the crowded market, and around the side streets that buttressed al-Najah University, leading to Omar Ben al-Khatab Avenue. Some used to joke that had Suleiman been born under different circumstances, he could have been a test driver for Ferrari.

Shortly before 1600 hours, the Shin Bet asset signaled via an SMS message that Hashash was ready to meet. The rendezvous would be at a location near the entrance to the city, a few hundred meters from Balata.

Hashash identified himself to the Shin Bet asset so that the Iranian liaison agent could recognize him. He told them that he would be waiting in front of a building on the southwest side of the street. Suleiman drove close to the meeting point and identified Hashash standing where he had said he would be, dressed in the clothes he had said he'd be wearing. Nasser radioed the Command Post. The Shin Bet agents monitoring the events from the lead Ya'mas vehicle and from the brigade CP braced themselves.

Hashash's wily catlike instincts were razor-sharp that Thursday afternoon. As Suleiman and Nasser exited their vehicles, the twenty-three-year-old Palestinian removed a 9mm semiautomatic pistol from a clip in the small of his back. He fired wildly at the men approaching him. Realizing the risk of the operation as severe, Nasser had made sure that his men wore body armor. Just days earlier, the Ya'mas had been issued with a new type of body armor that was three times as bullet-resistant and three times lighter than the previously issued kit. One of Hashash's bullets punched Suleiman in the chest, but the round didn't pierce the protective measures. Suleiman fell to the ground, knocked off his feet, but he took aim with his Mini-Uzi 9mm submachine gun. Inspector Nasser and the other undercover operatives that emerged from the vehicle took aim, as well. The firefight was over in a brief explosive fusillade. Hashash's bullet-riddled body lay lifeless on a Nablus sidewalk. Ya'mas medics applied emergency aid to the Tanzim commander, and then placed him in the back of a Horse, where he was to be rushed to an aid station for lifesaving surgery. But Hashash died en route to the hospital.

The Shin Bet had really wanted the chance to question Hashash about Iranian intelligence activities in the area. Iranian money and spies, with aid from Hezbollah, attempted to fan the flames of an intifada whose fires had already been blazing for nearly six years and had cost Israel more than one thousand lives.

Ibrahim Hashash had been in the final stages of coordinating a catastrophic suicide attack aimed at the heart of downtown Jerusalem, the Israeli capital. The Tanzin operation was imminent—certainly no more than a day or two from being launched. The target could have been a bus full of commuters or a café packed with young men and women trying as best as possible to shake off the pressures of life inside the crosshairs of the intifada. Once Hashash was removed—compromised by a Shin Bet machine that grew more efficient with each day—his cell collapsed. People who might have been killed a night away were allowed to continue with the rest of their lives because of endless hours of intelligence work encased in risk and intrigue that culminated in a brief exchange of gunfire on a litter-strewn patch of West Bank pavement.

The efforts of the Judea and Samaria Ya'mas unit, together with the activities of other counterterrorist units and the construction of the separation barrier all along the Green Line, had dramatically decreased the ability of the terrorist groups to infiltrate suicide bombers into Israel's cities. The greater metropolitan areas along Israel's coastal plain were becoming much harder to hit. But Jerusalem, a ground zero of religious passion claimed by the world's three great monotheistic religions, remained a tempting target for bloodshed. Jerusalem was the symbolic trip wire that always had the potential to turn the intifada into a religious war that could spread far beyond the regional battlefield.

BOOK TWO

JERUSALEM

CHAPTER TWELVE

The City of Peace

Jerusalem was not a city that never slept—that was Tel Aviv's tagline. When compared to the frenetic-paced pulse of Tel Aviv, the capital of Israel was a sleepy town of pious souls, political meandering, and sacred ancient sites shared and contested by Judaism, Christianity, and Islam. The Israeli capital wasn't a great city for nightlife—most of the restaurants and cafés closed earlier in Jerusalem than they did elsewhere; the city boasted few night-clubs. At night, even in the summer when the winds coming off the Judean Hills lowered the temperature to a shivering chill, the city's streets slowed down to a self-imposed slumber long before midnight. Residents bragged to their more cosmopolitan neighbors in Tel Aviv that although they didn't have the trendy eateries and the hipper than hip bars and discos, they also didn't need their air conditioners at night. Jerusalem residents slept with their windows open during the summer, soothed by peaceful eastern winds and crisp, clean air. The muster began long before the first rays of dawn emerged over the hills in the east. The winds that August morning were not so peaceful. Jerusalem was under a Code Dagger alert—a suicide bomber was en route to the city.

The police and security service pagers began to buzz shortly after 4:00 a.m. The phone calls followed shortly thereafter. Some officers, the senior com-manders of the specialized units that worked the greater Jerusalem District, were still at their desks when the alert came in; they had forgotten to go home amid the daily grind of twenty-hour shifts. The alert required an all-hands effort—all leaves, no matter how overdue and how desperately needed, were immediately and in some cases retroactively canceled. Personnel were awak-ened at home and ordered back to work immediately.

Thousands of men and women worked tirelessly around the clock to stop one faceless individual from entering a city; Israel spared no expense or effort in the hope of preventing a terrorist attack. The entire Jerusalem Ya'mas force constituted several dozen of those thousands of men and women. A large percentage of the unit was already at headquarters, reviewing the raw intelligence, or in the armory checking their weapons for the long day ahead. Those who had gone home for a night with their families were awakened by their pagers and ordered back to base. Before the morning's 5:59 a.m. sunrise, all of the unmarked vehicles in the unit's motor pool had been gassed up and prepared for war. The various bands of men—some in plain clothes, some in masquerade, and others in full tactical kit—headed out to various points throughout the city.

The objective of the Code Dagger alert was to close off an entire city and choke off points of entry for a bomber heading toward the main and ancillary limits. Police checkpoints—some established and recognized barriers and others thrown together in a moment's notice utilizing portable barriers and tire-deflating hollow steel spikes—were designed to slow all incoming traffic to an absolute crawl. Police tactical units, including specialists from the Ya'mas and other SWAT-like specialized units that operated in the Israeli capital, were deployed to search each vehicle, each van, and especially each bus that attempted to squeeze through the ever-tightening vise. Israeli motorists were never known for their calm and accommodating driving habits, and they hated being caught inside one of the maddening avenues of gridlock. But they hated the alternative more.

Code Dagger was a tactical exercise of arbitrary hit-or-miss luck—the hunting of a needle in a haystack of honking horns and exhaust fumes. Most decisively, though, Code Dagger was designed to buy time for police so that the sketchy and sometimes absolutely incomplete intelligence could coalesce into a name, a face, an ID number, and the name and make of the car ferrying the bomber toward his target. The traffic snarls could buy an hour or two. Perhaps just enough time to prevent the suicide bomber from getting inside the city limits. But Code Daggers were wildly unpredictable. Sometimes an alert was sounded on a Monday morning at dawn only to be followed by nothing. Other times, hours—even days—would pass between the sounding of the alert and a bomber blowing up somewhere else entirely. Spokesmen told foreign reporters that the effort against the suicide bombers was a war of nerves. In reality it was a war of absolute stress and endless frustration.

Master Sergeant Alex* was a veteran of the war of nerves. Born in the former Soviet Union, Alex had cut his undercover unit teeth serving as an operator and then team NCO in the Ya'mas Gaza unit, and then as a junior officer. He had laterally transferred to the Jerusalem unit, after years in the Strip, in order to be closer to home, and wound up as one of the go-to veterans in the Jerusalem force during one of the bloodiest periods in the city's history. Alex had been through more Code Daggers than he cared to remember, but this morning's alert was different. It seemed absolute. Some of Alex's fellow operators, equipping the patrol vehicles with M4s and Mini-Uzi submachine guns, shared a kick-to-the-gut sense of foreboding as they made sure that the radios were in working order. There was no time for coffee or the first cigarette of the day that August morning. The vehicles rushed toward the Arab parts of the city to the east, north, and south. The Ya'mas operators didn't know who or what they were looking for. It didn't matter, though.

The bomber was already inside the city.

The Code Dagger alert continued all morning and afternoon. The harsh August sun was wearing down the physical alertness of the police officers patrolling in full tactical kit. The Kevlar vests and ballistic helmets were heavy; sweat rolled down everyone's back and blindingly into exhausted eyes. The checkpoints, roadblocks, and choke points were placed on all the entrances to the city: To the west, where Highway 1 brought Tel Aviv to the capital, the police presence was heavy; to the south, along Route 60 and the Hebron Road leading from Bethlehem, the tactical effort was more pronounced; and, to the east, along the neighborhood borders of Silwan and Abu Tor, near where the tourist buses unloaded Jewish tourists making their pilgrimage to the Western Wall in the Old City, the police and Border Guard presence was omnipresent.

On King George Street, in the heart of downtown Jerusalem, the beat cops and patrol cars had been deployed elsewhere. No one noticed the man and

---

* A pseudonym—true identity withheld for security considerations.

woman walking down King George Street toward the intersection with the Jaffa Road, moving at a relaxed stroll as they passed a sea of pedestrians on the crowded thoroughfare. The woman, Ahlam Tamimi, was a twenty-year-old journalism student at Birzeit University. She had olive skin, partly scarred by acne, and was slender. Tamimi had been to Jerusalem a hundred times before this visit and knew the city well; because she hailed from Ramallah, in the Palestinian Authority, it was not uncommon for her to travel to East Jerusalem and then cross the invisible barriers into the Jewish half of the city. She was dressed as if she belonged in a cosmopolitan city—even one with such ancient modesties as Jerusalem. She wore a tight-fitting dress that accentuated her curves, and her dark brownish-black hair was combed straight and stylish. She wasn't wearing the hijab that she usually wore at home. If anyone had bothered to speak to Ms. Tamimi, they would have discovered that she spoke fluent English with only the slightest hint of an Arab accent.

She walked together with a young man with a pale though slightly deceptive olive complexion. Only a few hours earlier the man had been photographed with a full beard and wearing a button-down beige blouse, the pattern of which was concealed by an ammunition vest loaded with thirty-round magazines for the M16 assault rifle he cradled with his right hand, but now he was clean shaven. In the photos—several hundred were taken—the man held a Quran with his left hand and he wore a green Hamas headband wrapped tightly around his forehead. The pose he struck in his photographs was one of resolve that seemed weakened by a sense of distraught resignation. The young man walked with his female companion wearing a T-shirt, jeans, and a hat. He carried a guitar case strapped to his back and, with the eagerness of his step, looked like a young tourist exploring the city with his girlfriend.

The young man, Izzedine al-Masri, hailed from Silat al-Harithiya, the village near Jenin in the northern chunk of the West Bank that had proven to be fertile recruiting ground for Hamas and the Islamic Jihad. Tamimi had been the first woman recruited into the ranks of the Hamas military wing—her determination to participate in attacks against Israel very much impressed Abdullah Barghouti, the Hamas military commander for Ramallah and Jerusalem and one of the most capable engineers in the organization's order of battle, and one of its most insidiously diabolical military commanders (a cousin to Fatah commander Marwan Barghouti). He was considered so dangerous that even a year into the intifada he topped both the Shin Bet and Palestinian Preventative Security Service most-wanted lists. Tamimi was one of Barghouti's most capable operatives. Her first mission had been to place a bomb hidden in a beer can inside a Jerusalem supermarket. The bomb exploded, but resulted in little damage and few casualties. She was eager to make amends for her earlier folly and to prove to her commander that women did have a place inside the all-male club that was Hamas.

Tamimi first met al-Masri before the dawn of the intended attack at a Ramallah safe house; he had already been prepped and photographed. Tamimi was to serve as his guide—his laser range finder—who would direct the young West Bank native to his target. She carried a Jordanian passport, and if she was stopped by police, it was hoped that her command of English and her feminine features would convince a beat cop that she was a tourist from the Hashemite Kingdom visiting the holy city. The two took a three-mile taxi ride from Ramallah to the Qalandiya Junction on the northwestern outskirts of Jerusalem and just outside the small, though ever-simmering Qalandiya refugee camp. Their cab was bottlenecked inside the traffic nightmare of the first efforts of the Code Dagger that had developed at the A-Ram checkpoint, so they paid a few shekels extra to the driver and exited the vehicle around a bend hidden from the police and IDF forces at the blockaded entrance to Jerusalem. The cluster of villages was known to be a Hamas bastion. Seven years earlier, Hamas had taken Nachshon Waxman, an Israeli soldier kidnapped while hitchhiking in October 1994, to a safe house in Bir Naballah, a village right near the junction; Waxman was executed by his captors as Israeli commandos from Sayeret Mat'kal stormed the fortified house to attempt the rescue.

Tamimi and al-Masri disappeared effortlessly into the rough of the rocky hills and sympathetic villages that dotted the entrance to Jerusalem. Before the security fence was constructed, the frontier had been porous and rife for infiltration. The two took a cab to East Jerusalem[1] and then walked without worry down the Jaffa Road.

The Jaffa Road was a principal artery in the City of David. The two walked past shoppers, young and old, and mothers buying ice cream for their children. Old men, trailing shopping carts, counted coins in the palms of their hands, hoping to have enough to board one of the many red-and-white Egged bus lines that went up and down the street intersecting to points all over the city. Female soldiers, teenagers barely out of high school, window-shopped with friends as they wondered how many army paychecks it would take to buy that dress in the window.

Tamimi brought al-Masri to the corner of King George Street and the Jaffa Road. Tamimi spoke to her male companion in English even though al-Masri didn't understand a word of it; he struggled with the weight of a heavy guitar case. A Sbarro pizzeria was on the southeast corner of the junction, adorned with the green, white, and red colors of the Italian flag. Days earlier, Tamimi had scoured the city's busiest streets looking for locations with high volume pedestrian traffic and porous security, and located what she thought was a perfect target. The Sbarro was kosher and, as a result, packed with a lunch crowd of observant Jews. Tamimi selected the location in particular because the eatery was usually crowded with families, including small children.[2]

Al-Masri continued toward the pizzeria. Tamimi turned around and walked east back down the Jaffa Road. She boarded a bus that would let her off near the Damascus Gate,[3] enabling her to disappear into the Old City and the Arab neighborhoods on the eastern fringes.

It was almost 1400 hours on Thursday, August 9, 2001.

Ahlam Tamimi could have very well walked by the Ya'mas van with Alex inside it when al-Masri blew himself up. Alex and his team were less than half-a-mile away from the Sbarro when they heard the loud explosion muffled to a dull thud by distance. The men didn't have to wait for the first calls over the radio of a *pigu'a*, an attack, before their insides were twisted every which way. But the calls came, and their pagers vibrated without stop. The first sirens were heard seconds later. The operators in the white van quickly broke their disguise and removed blue baseball caps from their back pockets and placed them on their heads; the hats, with the word "POLICE" embossed in reflective white print in Hebrew and English, were to identify the heavily armed plainclothes men as security personnel inside the perimeter of death and destruction they were rushing to. It had been nearly five years since the last suicide bombing in the Israeli capital. All of them had been horrific, with catastrophic loss of life.

Alex and his van full of undercover operators didn't have far to travel in order to reach the bloody scene. Alex remembered the carnage and the cries of the wounded, and the unforgettable stench of rust, the smell of blood in the sun, as he and his fellow operators attempted to help but felt so overwhelmed and helpless by the sheer horror before them.[4] The bloody mess on the corner of Jaffa Road and King George Street was horrific and punch-to-the-gut wrenching. Time stood still in an anguished snapshot of eviscerated bodies; and then everything seemed to drag, moving in a tortured still-framed sense of slow motion, until the shock was interrupted by the screams of the wounded, the wailing of ambulance sirens, and the endless chatter emanating from police radios. Police officers in the Jerusalem District were the world's foremost experts in handling the sickeningly destructive crime scenes. The emergency services in the city had learned, through bitter experience, to coordinate the actions of the fire brigade, paramedics, and hospital triage centers. The Israeli media was also well versed in the drill. The moment the television networks and radio stations issued bulletins confirming the blast, the telephone numbers of the hospitals where the dead and wounded had been rushed to were broadcast so that concerned loved ones would know where to call.

The Ya'mas squads on the Dagger Alert that horrible summer afternoon rushed to the bombed-out remains of the Sbarro pizzeria as fast as they could from points throughout the city. Their mission, in such after-the-fact realities, was to help and deploy a tactical shield around the kill zone to look for and eliminate secondary bombers: On July 30, 1997, a Hamas suicide bombing tandem had blown themselves up inside Jerusalem's Mahane Yehuda Market, only blocks away from the Sbarro kill zone, killing sixteen and wounding 178; and, on September 4, 1997, three Hamas suicide bombers had blown themselves up in the succession of several seconds on the Ben Yehuda Street promenade—two hundred meters away from Sbarro—killing four and wounding scores more. The Ya'mas operators who arrived at the Sbarro scene looked for anyone trying to break through the inner police perimeter, or who was suspiciously videotaping the events; the terrorist groups routinely broadcast footage of their handiwork on websites or published quickie CDs that could be mass-produced in secret West Bank workshops and distributed inside mosques and schools. But there was little for the Ya'mas responders to do other than help with the crime scene and with the wounded. Abdullah Barghouti had placed nearly ten kilograms of high explosives inside the guitar case that al-Masri carried on his back; the explosive payload was wrapped inside a cocoon of nails, screws, bolts, and ball bearings.

Fifteen people were killed in the blast; 130 were critically wounded. The oldest victim of the bombing was Jerusalem resident Freda Mendelsohn, sixty-two years old. The youngest victim was Hemda Schijveschuurder. She was barely two. Hemda's parents, Mordechai and Tzira Schijveschuurder, both children of Dutch Holocaust survivors, were killed, along with two of her siblings—Raya and Lilly; two other daughters, Leah and Chaya, were critically injured in the blast. The August 9, 2001, Hamas suicide bombing of the Sbarro restaurant killed thirteen Israelis, a Brazilian national, and an American woman, Shoshana Judy Greenbaum, from Passaic, New Jersey, who was five months pregnant.

Crime scene investigators, bomb squad EOD technicians, and Shin Bet agents examined the grisly shell of the restaurant in shocked disbelief. Blood and tissue were caked against the white walls that were decorated with red and green diamond tiles. The top portion of al-Masri's body had been sliced in half by the blast, and his upper torso had been thrust into one of the pizza oven vents above the rafters.[*] It took hours to clean up the shards of broken glass that were blown hundreds of feet from the restaurant. Crews of Orthodox Jewish volunteers, wearing white coveralls and bright yellow safety vests, went on their hands and knees to locate slivers of human remains for proper Jewish burial.

By the time the sun set on the shaken City of Peace, the entire Ya'mas unit had been deployed. The unit was in Silwan, Beit Hanina, A-Tur, Shuafat, Kfar A'qab, Jebel Mukaber, and the many neighborhoods and villages of Arab East Jerusalem, all administrated by Jordan before the Six Day War, that fed into

---

[*] The issue of the state of al-Masri's body sparked great controversy after Jack Kelley, a reporter for *U.S. News & World Report,* fabricated a report that an Israeli police officer noticed the bomber's head lying in the street and spit on it and kicked it. The report caused great uproar and controversy. It was, though, later learned that not only had Kelley concocted this tale, but he had a long history of making up events and sources that he included in his reportage.

the PA's Area A fortresses of Ramallah and Hebron. Virtually every man in the unit had spent time at the Sbarro crime scene earlier, and the horror of what they witnessed was evident in their focused stares and their impatient demeanors. The small talk so common inside the closed doors of an unmarked van was replaced by silence. There was nothing to say that could have diluted the sights and smells of hours before. All the men wanted to do was to follow Shin Bet leads and see what, if any, response was required in the sections of the city that must have been used as transit points into Jerusalem by the bomber and his helpers. The unit's day had already pushed the twelve-hour mark—twenty-four for some—and there was little chance that anyone would be heading home for the next seventy-two hours. Those whose wives were used to the ordeal didn't even expect a phone call.

The Ya'mas was inside the twisting streets of Arab East Jerusalem for much of the night following Sbarro, working with the Shin Bet and with military intelligence as a mobile apprehension force. The unit would be in East Jerusalem and a good swath of the West Bank every day and night for the next five years. The war for Jerusalem was well under way.

CHAPTER THIRTEEN

The Temple Mount

On June 7, 1967, Colonel Mordechai "Motta" Gur, the commander of the 55th Paratroop Brigade, led his reservists through the narrow and ancient alleyways of the Old City of Jerusalem under heavy Jordanian fire. Since the 1949 armistice ending the 1948 War of Israeli Independence, Jerusalem had been a divided city: The Arab Legion controlled the eastern half of the city and the West Bank, and the western half of Jerusalem had become the capital of the new Jewish State; some of the bloodiest fighting of the 1948 War of Israeli Independence was the push to connect an isolated Jerusalem with the rest of the fledgling country. When the 1967 War broke out, the Israeli strategic objective was to neutralize the threat that the combined Arab military powers of Egypt, Jordan, and Syria presented to the Jewish State and its indefensible borders. The reunification of Jerusalem had been a strategic necessity of enormous spiritual and nationalist importance. The fight wasn't easy. The Jordanian defense of Jerusalem was heroic; the British-trained legion made the IDF and Motta Gur's reservists pay a dear price for every inch of the city the Israelis conquered. But in the Old City, the paratroopers pushed cautiously. Every stone had some historic or religious significance. Finally, when the Jordanian defense in the city collapsed, the paratroopers reached the Wailing Wall, the holiest site in Judaism. Positioned atop where the Second Temple once stood, where the gold-covered Dome of the Rock Mosque now projected its majestic peak as the landmark of the city, Colonel Gur grabbed his radioman and contacted headquarters. "*Har ha'bayit be'ya-deinu!*" "The Temple Mount is in our hands!"

Thirty-three years later, on Thursday, September 28, 2000, when Likud chief Ariel Sharon made his visit to the Temple Mount, the number of

Israeli security men—Shin Bet, police, and Border Guard—far outnumbered the hundreds of news reporters from around the world who chron-
icled the event. Men from the Jerusalem Ya'mas unit were out in force that
sunny autumn day. Some were in uniform, in full tactical kit, searching for
possible armed threats to the ensemble of Israeli politicians and security
men. Others, dressed as Palestinians, had infiltrated the Temple Mount
area to identify the ringleaders of what was escalating into a full-scale riot
over Sharon's visit. By the time Sharon had been inserted into his Volvo,
surrounded by police motorcycles and security vehicles, the Ya'mas operators on the Temple Mount were in the fight of their lives. The crowds of
protesters had swelled into a full-scale riot. Rocks were hurled at Israeli
police units, who were quickly overwhelmed by the barrage of stones and
Molotov cocktails. Tires were set ablaze and Palestinian flags were waved
in a challenging defiance. The Ya'mas operators, who moved about in small
squads to try to identify the ringleaders so that they could be apprehended,
were outnumbered and seriously overwhelmed. There was little chance of
them removing the balaclava masks over their faces and quickly putting on
their blue cloth baseball caps in order to conceal their identities. There were
simply too many people around. The situation had disintegrated beyond
clear control. Riot police, some bleeding when their protective helmets
were shattered by the incoming stones, retreated to safer lines before firing
tear gas. Black, acrid smoke filled the striking blue skies from tires that had
been set alight. A pall of darkness soon covered the brilliant gold shine of
the Dome of the Rock Mosque.

Police officers were overwhelmed by the initial ignition of the rage and
violence. Police radios buzzed with requests for backup. The situation reports
coming in over the frequencies were bleak. One came in with foreboding
candor: "The Temple Mount isn't in our hands."[1]

The fires burned until darkness, illuminating the Temple Mount and the
adjacent al-Aqsa Mosque in an eerie orange glow. The intifada had begun
inside the heart of one of the world's most sensitive trip wires: Jerusalem.

Jerusalem wasn't just any city. Jerusalem was the true starting point—and
some say end of days—for the world's three monotheistic religions, the place

where elements of three varying faiths and cultures were forced to coexist until circumstances dictated otherwise. In the Old City, in fact, Muslims, Christians, Jews, and Armenians lived for centuries inside 0.35 square miles of walled-in combustion; each of these groups had sects and branches that were often at one another's throat. Jerusalem was the capital of the State of Israel, but it was also a city claimed by Palestinian nationalistic aspirations, and it was unquestionably a symbol of Muslim religious identity (as it was of Christian religious identity, as well). Everything that happened in the city had the potential to erupt into a conflict. It was a ground zero for the fissures of the Arab–Israeli dispute and wars that could spread far beyond.

Jerusalem was definitely one of the world's most difficult precincts to police. The scriptures serve as an in-depth police log of the troubles that the city's many rulers had in maintaining law and order there. The Assyrians, the Babylonians, the Persians, and the Macedonians discovered that Jerusalem was one tough beat. The Romans and the Ottoman Turks could conquer vast stretches of the world as they knew it, but keeping the peace in the City of Peace required endless struggle. The British fared no better. Neither did the Jordanians. Policemen, regardless of uniform or language, found it virtually impossible to keep the lid on the perpetual simmering of hatred and mistrust. Jerusalem police officers had to be diplomats as well as cops walking a beat; a shot fired in anger—justified or otherwise—could very well set the entire area ablaze.

The Israeli government formally annexed parts of the eastern section—the Arab section—of the city in 1980. But the unified Jerusalem was still a divided city. For the most part, the city's population of 750,000 lived, worked, and shopped in separate neighborhoods and sections of town. There were, however, few barriers—if any—that separated the two halves of the city, and that created a security nightmare when the intifada erupted.

According to Shin Bet analysis, there were some 250,000 Palestinians from the confines of greater East Jerusalem who, following annexation, possessed blue Israeli identity cards identical to those carried by all other citizens; 150,000 of these people lived directly in East Jerusalem and the remainder populated the areas surrounding the city. East Jerusalem became a favorite crossing point for the smuggling of terrorists inside Israel proper. Hamas, in particular, recognized the virtue of recruiting East Jerusalem residents as "mules" and logistics specialists in the execution of suicide strikes—these ID card–holding residents of Israel had a working knowledge of Hebrew, possessed legitimate identification and vehicle registration documentation, and they could legally rent flats in safe houses or even businesses to help organize and coordinate attacks. Once a suicide bomber made it into the city limits, an East Jerusalem resident could help the terrorist reach anywhere in Israel.

The East Jerusalem Palestinians were also key elements in the Hamas intelligence-gathering apparatus that assembled eyes-on-target surveillance of potential targets. These local operatives worked in the kitchens and cafeterias of popular eateries throughout the city and knew when the location would be crowded with diners. These spies in the field monitored bus schedules and the times when police cars drove by on patrol.

The Jerusalem Police District was one of the largest geographically in the country. The district covered a sizable swath of territory in south central Israel, reaching to the hills just east of Ben-Gurion International Airport, and to the areas in and around Ramallah and Bethlehem in what would become the Palestinian Authority. Nestled inside the district were Jewish settlements, Palestinian villages, and three of the world's holiest sites—the al-Aqsa Mosque, the Western Wall, and the Church of the Nativity. Jerusalem cops—patrolmen on the beat, detectives, and Border Guards assigned to the command—were experts at the day-to-day challenges of this most volatile beat. These policemen and -women possessed the cultural nuances and unflinching resolve to handle a population that included everyday Israelis of all backgrounds and temperaments, tourists from the four corners of the world, religious leaders from every faith, and Palestinians. Many of the professional policemen with the city's Border Guard contingent had a working knowledge of Arabic.

A decade earlier, the first intifada had reconfigured the disposition of forces inside Jerusalem. Rioting exploded throughout the Old City and in East Jerusalem, and the patrol forces and specialized units, such as the Ya'ma'm, had had to deploy to the Israeli capital—especially to the Temple Mount. Friday prayers at the Dome of the Rock and the al-Aqsa Mosque were especially problematic, as were Muslim holidays and general strikes called by the Palestinian leadership. On October 8, 1990, in response to a call to arms by Muslim clerics, Palestinian youths atop the parapets of the Temple Mount began to hurl rocks at Israeli worshippers praying at the Western Wall in the courtyard down below. Israeli police and Border Guard units stormed the Palestinian mobs, and what ensued was some of the bloodiest hand-to-hand and close-quarter knuckle-scraping combat seen yet in the city. Some twenty Palestinians were killed in the fighting; dozens of Israeli police officers were seriously wounded.

In the closing days of the first intifada, as the violence waned, Palestinian gangs resorted to vandalism and arson in their fight against Israel. Cars were set ablaze throughout the city, and the consequent property damage resulted in millions of shekels in damage; the tourism trade to the city was being severely hit, as well, when rental cars became a favorite target. The Shin Bet tried to locate the ringleaders of these small and independent vandal cells, but their efforts were unsuccessful. Even Prime Minister Shamir demanded that arsonists be apprehended and dealt with. The Israeli police commissioner at the time was Yaakov Turner, a former IAF fighter pilot. He contacted Duvdevan founder Uri Bar-Lev for help. Bar-Lev had continued his post-Duvdevan career and had risen to the rank of lieutenant colonel. Never one to balk at a challenge, Bar-Lev agreed to a lateral move over to the National Police and forming a new intelligence-based unit that could use espionage-like tradecraft in the war against the vandals and, ultimately, more violent and dangerous terrorist cells.

Bar-Lev named his new force Unit 33, but it became known simply as the Gidonim—Hebrew for "the Gideons"—after the mythical biblical destroyer who wielded so lethal a sword.[2] Bar-Lev tapped into the very talent pool he had assembled in Duvdevan for this new unit. Some had gone on to become officers, even team leaders, in some of the IDF's premier special operations units; others, some of the characters with uniquely outside-the-box personalities who found the confining realities of the military too restraining, had found ad hoc intelligence work here and there. Basic Arabic was one of the skill sets that Bar-Lev looked for in the cadre that would form Unit 33—the unit figured to be most operational in East Jerusalem—but not the only one. Men who spoke other languages and who could masquerade as other nationalities were also sought—Jerusalem was an international city, after all. Bar-Lev handpicked each and every one of the recruits to this new and somewhat undefined force. He looked for men who could drive like car thieves and pick locks better than the best burglars out there. The new unit was to be built around the type of men who could devise arrogantly inspired deception operations to gather intelligence on terrorists and hardcore criminals in operations inside Jerusalem, and then have the tactical wherewithal and capabilities to exact high-risk arrests against heavily armed suspects. It was an odd assemblage of talent and throwaways. Many of the men who would ultimately excel in the unit—operators who would not only rise up in the ranks to serve as senior officers but also those decorated for valor under fire—were those whom the IDF had basically given up on.

Unit 33 eventually caught many of the arsonists and, most important, their ringleaders. Masquerading as local East Jerusalem residents, tourists, and local merchants, the undercover operatives were able to videotape the perpetrators, locate where they lived, find out who gave the instructions and materials for setting the fires, and make arrests that ran all along the PLO's command structure in Jerusalem. The unit, almost immediately, was responsible for a sharp decrease in terrorist-related activity in and around the Israel capital. Yet the entire landscape of Palestinian terrorism was about to change. Unit 33 became operational a few months before Hamas terrorists kidnapped and murdered an Israeli Border Guard sergeant amid the backdrop of secret backdoor negotiations between the PLO and the State of Israel in Norway. A quiet though lethal lull had covered Jerusalem following the first intifada. The tranquility of that time would soon be looked upon with a cynical degree of sentimentality.

Few inside Israel boasted the special operations CV that Alek Ron could assemble. He had served in the paratroopers, Ehud Barak's Sayeret Mat'kal, and then in the Shin Bet as an air marshal on El Al. As a reservist in Sayeret Mat'kal, Ron had fought on the Golan Heights during the 1973 war. On July 3, 1976, he was part of the Sayeret Mat'kal task force that flew to Entebbe, Uganda, to rescue 103 Israeli and Jewish hostages held by a combined force of Palestinian and German terrorists and complicit Ugandan soldiers.

After Entebbe, Ron returned to active duty to create Shaldag—Hebrew for "Kingfisher"—a top-secret Israel Air Force commando unit whose mission was long-range operations. In 1987, Ron transferred over to the Border Guard and was given command of the Ya'ma'm. As Ya'ma'm commander, Ron personally led a 1988 hostage-rescue assault against a bus in southern Israel that had been seized by Palestinian terrorists. By the time he left the Ya'ma'm in early 1992, Ron had led Israel's counterterrorist unit through four years of intifada violence. The Border Guard—and, indeed, the National Police—saw great potential in Ron and he was named the Border Guard's Jerusalem commander.

One of Ron's first orders of business for Jerusalem was to create an undercover unit. The unit was formed shortly after the Oslo Accords were finalized. Mention of the unit was considered taboo. The existence of an undercover Arabist unit operating inside Israel's capital city was considered too controversial for public disclosure amid the delicate political atmosphere that followed the historic handshake between Arafat and Rabin on the White House lawn.

The man who replaced Alek Ron in Jerusalem, Brigadier General (Assistant Commissioner) Yitzhak "Jack" Dadon, had created the undercover unit in Judea and Samaria, and he ran with the idea of a Jerusalem Ya'mas and invested as much of the meager resources at his disposal in the new force as he could. The founding nucleus of the unit consisted of highly motivated men who met a demanding checklist of very specific criteria: language skills, tactical predisposition, and the ability to operate in small teams in disguise deep inside a hostile environment. Newcomers to the unit were sent to friendly Arab villages near the city limits for some intensive cultural immersion.[3] The Jerusalem undercover unit attracted men who had grown up inside the city's confines. These operators were intimately familiar with the city's contours and frequency; they knew every escape route and dead end, and they knew about the crime-controlled low-income housing sections, as well as where the city's notorious drug dealers, flesh merchants, gun runners, and information peddlers were located. There was an irrefutable connection between criminal activities and terrorist endeavors, and one of the primary missions of the Jerusalem unit was to operate invisibly inside the Arab neighborhoods of East Jerusalem that the regular police patrol units were hesitant to enter and clearly incapable of entering undetected. "The Palestinian neighborhoods near the Old City and around Jerusalem were no-go zones for detectives or plainclothes people," Superintendent Gil Kleiman, a retired major case detective, explained. "Everyone warned everyone else if the slightest thing looked out of place. It was incredibly difficult for the intelligence services to penetrate these houses, streets, and apartment complexes that were thick as thieves with watchful eyes. The intelligence services had a hard time operating here, as well. These areas were part of Israel but they really weren't. They were autonomous bastions, and as a result the terrorist groups flourished in this security service vacuum. Everyone who worked the city knew that there would be trouble coming from there."[4]

And precisely because these areas were part of Israel—the outer peripheries of the Israeli capital—the work of the newly formed Ya'mas unit became so precariously challenging. These suburbs, even the adjacent villages, were not considered the West Bank, even though they truly were areas seized by Jordan in the 1967 War. Still, the IDF did not handle terrorist targets inside Abu Tor or one of the other Palestinian suburbs in the capital in the same way that it handled a target in Jenin or in Gaza. Counterterrorism in Jerusalem required finesse and great delicacy. In Judea and Samaria, the disguise of a Ya'mas team was an essential element of reaching an objective, a veteran Ya'mas operator reflected, but in Jerusalem, the deceit and the disguise were essential in carrying out the operation.[5]

It was, however, impossible to separate the Palestinian terrorist infrastructure in East Jerusalem from the West Bank as a whole. And, as a result, the Jerusalem Ya'mas unit would intersect and compete with the operational domains of both Duvdevan and the Judea and Samaria Ya'mas. Jerusalem was a religious and commercial hub that connected the West Bank towns of Ramallah, Bethlehem, and Hebron, as well as the United Nations–administered but Hamas- and Fatah-run refugee camps that dotted the transportation routes along these critical arteries (Shu'fat, located north of Jerusalem, and Kalandia, situated eleven kilometers north of Jerusalem, on the main road to Ramallah).

Jerusalem's Ya'mas began at a paradoxically hopeful—yet violent—time in the history of Israel's war on terror. The optimism of the Oslo Accords was tangible to many inside Israel. At last, so many thought, the cycle of perpetual violence had come to an end, not through a last and bloody war, but through a diplomatic decision reached through negotiations and good faith. Peace seemed contagious. Later that year Jordan's King Hussein was scheduled to enter into a formal peace treaty with the Jewish State. Few thought that either Syria or Lebanon would enter into negotiations with Israel, but would the Gulf Arabs soon follow suit? Israelis openly spoke of a new Middle East—one in which they would finally be accepted.

But optimism in the Middle East is traditionally trounced upon by fanatics. On February 25, 1994, Baruch Goldstein, an American-born physician and religious extremist living in the right-wing settlement of Kiryat Arba, donned his reservist army uniform, grabbed his service-issue Galil assault rifle, and walked into the Cave of the Patriarchs, a large rectangular structure, built beneath a Saladin-era mosque in the old city of Hebron, that, according to tradition, was the burial spot of Abraham, Isaac, Jacob, Sarah, Rebecca, and Leah. The site, holy to both Jews and Muslims, consisted of both a synagogue and a mosque. Because he was in uniform, Goldstein wasn't challenged as he entered the ultrasensitive complex; soldiers, after all, were everywhere. But Goldstein cocked his assault rifle, took aim, and began methodically firing at the men and boys who were praying on the plush red and golden carpets of the mosque floor during Friday morning services. Bullets shattered the chandeliers hanging overhead; bullet holes and brain matter littered the dark lime-green walls of the ancient house of worship. The medical doctor sworn to save life killed 29 men and boys and wounded an additional 125 people before he was rushed and bludgeoned to death.

Israel condemned the massacre and arrested scores of religious fanatics who had expressed violent opposition to the Oslo Accords, but Hamas had the casus belli to start its jihad. On April 6, 1994, precisely forty days following the end of the Hamas-declared Muslim period of mourning for Goldstein's victims, the first of the Yahiya Ayyash–built suicide bombs was detonated in northern Israel. Hamas and PIJ suicide bombers would strike on six separate occasions in 1994 and 1995—killing forty-six civilians and wounding nearly three hundred—before the bloodshed reached Jerusalem. At precisely 7:45 a.m. on the morning of August 21, 1995, a Hamas suicide bomber blew himself up on the No. 26 bus traveling from Kiryat Yovel to Mount Scopus as it crossed the bustling Eshkol Boulevard. Many on board the bus, many of the several dozen wounded, were police officers traveling to Israel National Police headquarters in Sheikh Jarakh, in the northeastern part of the city. Four people were killed in the blast. One of the dead was a pretty twenty-six-year-old teacher named Rivka Cohen, who was on her way to volunteer at the infertility clinic at Jerusalem's famed Hadassah Hospital. One witness described the blast to the *New York Times*: "I saw dead people—one without a head, some on the ground. Two girls came toward me totally naked, covered with blood with no hair. I washed their faces. One asked me, 'Am I going to die?'"[6]

More, of course, would die. There would be four more suicide bombings before the outbreak of the al-Aqsa intifada in 2000.

Daily, Ya'mas squads—sometimes two- and four-man contingents—would be pre-positioned at strategic junctions in Jerusalem near where it was believed suicide bombers might strike. The Ya'mas presence was always in plain clothes. The operators wanted to blend in to the hustle and bustle of the Israeli capital, completely invisible and unimposing, and be at the right place at the right time to be able to pull out that one needle in the haystack and pounce on the suicide bomber before he could strike. The operators could disguise themselves as Palestinian laborers, and they even masqueraded as tourists and as Orthodox Jews. Being an undercover unit in Jerusalem didn't necessarily mean masquerading solely as Palestinians. Operators in the unit spoke French, English, Yiddish, and a Tower of Babel of other languages that was representative of the mosaic of faces, languages, dialects, and complexions that were seen on the city's streets—east and west—every day.

Stopping the terrorists before they could strike meant being at the right place at the right time, and that required planning, pre-positional intelligence, and a fair helping of propitious luck. On October 9, 1994, the unit encountered one such moment.

Nahalat Shiv'a was the third Jewish neighborhood built outside the Old City in 1860. Over time, as Jerusalem grew, Nahalat Shiv'a became a fashionable promenade where the city's young couples could enjoy a glass of wine and a nice gourmet meal inside one of the many sidewalk cafés and hole-in-the-wall bars that dotted the area. It was close to midnight. The glasses still clacked as waitresses rounded up empty beer mugs for yet another round of drinks and the young enjoyed the carefree splendor of being young. No one heard the car pull up fifty meters away on one of the few side streets that allowed vehicular traffic. No one saw the two young men remove AK-47s and Soviet-produced hand grenades from their knapsacks. The shooting started without warning.

A Ya'mas contingent was training nearby on room-clearing techniques, in an office building long after the last workers had left, when they heard the magazine-emptying bursts of AK fire followed by the explosive thuds of grenades. They radioed their position in to headquarters and then raced to the kill zone. Some inserted thirty-round magazines into their M4s as they ran toward the sounds of gunfire; others took their vehicles to block off any escape routes. Two gunmen, dressed as Christian clergy, had simply opened fire on diners and anyone else walking around. Shattered glass and blood were everywhere. Victims crawled toward the oncoming Ya'mas rescuers, begging for help. The terrorists managed to empty several thirty-round magazines at anyone within range before Ya'mas operators cut them down in a flurry of fire. Two people were killed in the attack—a dozen more were wounded.

The Ya'mas response to the dining promenade attack was fortunate— stakeouts, or deterrence deployments as they were known, were incredibly frustrating for the unit. It was impossible to gauge when their presence would actually halt a planned suicide bombing, or if they were watching and waiting for nothing. On the morning of February 25, 1996, forty days following the Shin Bet's assassination of Yehiya Ayyash, one team was positioned at the old central bus station, near the entrance to the city from the Tel Aviv highway, watching and waiting. It was cold that morning: February rains and February winds had turned the holy city into a frigid, unwelcoming gray; a steady, bone-numbing light rain fell. Danny,* a relative newcomer to the unit, flipped through the city's emergency frequencies searching for something—anything. He tapped the microphone of his walkie-talkie to see if the intelligence officer

---

* A pseudonym—true identity withheld for security considerations.

back at base had heard anything, but there was nothing to report on the Ya'mas frequency. The only noise heard inside the unmarked sedan belonged to the windshield wipers pushing left and right in a grinding cadence of their own. The blast came suddenly and unexpectedly. The sound of the explosion popped the eardrums of the two Ya'mas operators sitting inside the car. The unforgettable screams of women would remain with them forever.

Two hundred meters up the road, a Hamas suicide bomber had detonated ten kilograms of homemade explosives cocooned by nails and screws on board the No. 18 bus that was crowded with people traveling to work and kids who were off to school. The carnage was absolutely catastrophic: Twenty-six men, women, and children were killed that wet Sunday morning; more than one hundred were wounded. There was little for the Ya'mas operators to do after the fact, other than deploy to prevent a second strike, watch the Bomb Squad specialists sift through the mangled corpses in search of secondary devices, and look at the Orthodox volunteers on their knees picking up the smallest shards of human tissue so that they could receive a proper Jewish burial.

Exactly one week later, on March 3, a Hamas suicide bomber blew himself up on a No. 18 bus at the same location as a week before; 19 were killed in this bombing, and an additional 125 wounded.

On July 30, 1997, a Hamas Mutt-and-Jeff double-tap team, two bombers who would strategically blow themselves up moments apart, so that innocent victims as well as first responders could be killed, took the lives of 19 shoppers in the bustling Mahane Yehuda Market, and wounded 178 others. The editor of a Jordanian weekly magazine praised the two bombers: "The two holy martyrs illuminated the night in Jerusalem and gave meaning to Arab heroism."[7]

On the afternoon of September 4, 1997, Hamas perpetrated a triple-tap suicide bombing in the city's teeming Ben-Yehuda Street shopping promenade. Five were killed in the first ever three-pronged suicide bombing attack launched by Hamas. More than two hundred more were seriously wounded in the precisely coordinated attack.

The capital city of the State of Israel was a battlefield.

When the fires of the al-Aqsa intifada were lit, the Israeli (and American) political belief maintained—and the intelligence assessment supported—the notion that it was not in Arafat's political interest to set Jerusalem ablaze. Shin Bet director Ami Ayalon maintained regular contact with Jibril Rajoub, Arafat's security chief for the West Bank, to talk of coordinated preventative efforts to extinguish any fires before they could get out of hand.[8] But the politicians—and the spies—were wrong.

Reportedly, Palestinian chatter—the cellular phone traffic between Arafat's Ramallah headquarters, the *Muqata*, and his security chiefs in the West Bank and Gaza—intensified a day or two before Sharon's well-telegraphed visit to the Temple Mount. Two days after the event, as the rioting permeated throughout the West Bank and Jerusalem, Arafat, reportedly angry that the war had yet to begin, scolded his security chiefs, demanding that the disturbances commence.[9]

The violence in the streets was substantial, and it appeared to be spiraling out of control—especially on the Temple Mount near the Dome of the Rock and the al-Aqsa mosques. The Shin Bet received assurances from Jibril Rajoub, and from others inside Arafat's circle of power, that the rioting violence would dissipate. It didn't. Israeli authorities tried to work with the Jerusalem Islamic *Waqf*, the trust controlling Islamic landmarks and institutions in the Old City, to issue religious directives to end the rioting, but the religious leaders only inflamed the already combustible cauldron of rage. Tires were set alight throughout East Jerusalem and at strategic junctions connecting Jewish areas. Palestinian youths, led by Tanzim and Fatah ringleaders, used the parapets of the Old City as cover when throwing stones and Molotov cocktails at Israeli police units attempting to quell the disturbances. To many observers, the fighting resembled ancient times—even the Crusades—when armies stood at the gates of Jerusalem.

Prime Minister Ehud Barak was furious about the televised coverage of the Palestinians pelting Israeli security forces and, in the process, cremating any hope of the Camp David dream from ever materializing. At just after dawn on the morning of October 6, 2000, there was a sense of a looming showdown. Thousands of young men flocked to the Old City for morning prayers. Their heads were already covered in kefiyehs and many

carried jugs of petrol and bags of rocks with them. Some in the crowd carried Palestinian flags that they had intended to fly over the ultra-sensitive
location; others carried Hamas flags, and others carried the black banners
of jihad. Barak ordered the security services in. The orders were handed
down the chain of command to the Israeli police commissioner, who then
handed them to the Jerusalem district commander, who handed them to
the Border Guard chief for Jerusalem, who ultimately passed them on to
Superintendent Yossi Aberfeld, the Jerusalem Ya'mas commander. Yossi was
given ten minutes to get a plan together and for his men to restore order
inside the Old City.[10]

Yossi was a short and thin officer with light ginger hair. He looked more
like a university freshman than a counterterrorist unit commander, but his
appearance was absolutely deceiving. Yossi ran faster, climbed higher, and
shot straighter than men who looked more the part. He was a no-nonsense
commander and highly skilled operator who was used to assessing tactical challenges on the run and implementing responses efficiently. His calm
demeanor under pressure, on dark and dangerous nights when operating
against Hamas cells barricaded inside terrorist safe houses, had come to
define how the unit went about its business. The hope, therefore, was that the
battle for the Old City would be slick, quick, and without any incident that
would become an explosive issue in the international media. But Jerusalem
commanders knew that the battle for such symbolic real estate was going to
turn medieval—the fight was going to be waged with knuckles, fists, batons,
and boot heels.

The first order of business involved the Speakers. Yossi ordered his Arabic
speakers into the Old City to spearhead the operation. Dressed as local East
Jerusalemites, the Speakers hid their plastic-coiled radio headsets inside
their ears and then covered them with the kefiyeh headdresses they wore
as scarves; many of the young men who had been in position were already
covering their faces to shield their identities from prying eyes, as well as to
protect them from the canisters of tear gas that the Israeli police were bound
to launch in their direction. The Speakers crossed into the Old City and positioned themselves near the ringleaders who were assembling the crowds and
coordinating the disturbances. The Speakers did not wear body armor of any
kind. In fact, their only identifying bit of kit was a black balaclava, thin and in

need of a wash, with the protuberant word "POLICE" written in English and Hebrew on white reflective tape; when it was time to reveal themselves as the police, they'd remove the caps from their pockets and quickly put them on their heads. If their cover was blown before the takeover began, few doubted that the men would be beaten to death.

From a forward command post, Yossi monitored the Speakers as they secreted themselves into the ancient walled city. This wasn't the West Bank, where a battalion of paratroopers was awaiting the code word to extract the undercover operators should all hell break loose. The Speakers were on their own until the signal for the rest of the force—some in uniform but most in disguise—was issued. Several Ya'mas sniper teams, covering the events from the Jewish Quarter, could provide eyes-on-target intelligence to the commanders about when to go in. But from several hundred meters away, it was nearly impossible for the snipers to see the lone Speakers amid such a vast and fast-moving crowd. The billowing smoke from the burning tires soon obliterated much of the landscape.

Yossi had positioned his assault force strategically throughout the old stone streets that led into a mazelike labyrinth of ancient alley ways and dead ends. The plan was to hit the rioters with speed and sheer surprise.

Yossi gave the order to move in at just before 0800. Some areas were sealed by heavy cast-iron gates and padlocks, certainly dating back to the Ottoman Empire; locals manning these makeshift barricades tried to make sure that no one broke through. Adi and Yusef,* two of the veteran Speakers in the unit, walked key positions along ancient walls and in narrow alleys that hadn't changed much in centuries, and pushed their way inside the Old City and the confines of the non-Jewish quarters. The two tossed diversionary grenades into a main courtyard.[11] The blinding flash of light and the eardrum-splitting blast were a signal for Ya'mas squad leaders positioned just outside the choke point to toss smoke grenades into the crowds and then rush in. The Palestinians at first confronted the advancing undercover contingents who flowed into their ranks, but the Speakers had pinpointed

---

* Pseudonyms—true identities withheld for security considerations.

and apprehended several of the men choreographing the violence. Savage hand-to-hand fighting ensued. Ya'mas members were careful to only produce their sidearms when actually putting the cuffs on a suspect—the hope was that a gun shoved into a suspect's back would prevail over any thoughts of resisting arrest. News that the dreaded *Mistaraboon* were inside the Old City spread fear and foreboding among the crowd. The young men ran east. Hundreds of men, some with clubs and petrol bombs in their hands, raced toward the Lion's Gate. And that's where hundreds of Israeli policemen were waiting for them. So many police vehicles were needed to ferry the apprehended to the main police station at the Russian Compound that it took hours just to park the trucks.

The entire Old City, including the ultra-sensitive Temple Mount, was back in Israeli hands. It was something of a historic moment, the men thought. Yossi went on the radio and repeated the legendary words that Colonel Gur had uttered thirty-three years earlier when overlooking a vista of the Old City. Yossi gave his code name over the Border Guard frequency and said, "The Temple Mount is in our hands."[12]

Yossi's men returned to base bloodied and bruised. Clothes had been torn in the dozens of individual melees that broke out in the chaos; radios were damaged in the scuffles. The Palestinians fought a tough fight, and it was reflected in the men sitting inside the recreation room, chain-smoking cigarettes and placing ice packs over nasty bumps. The commander of the Border Guards in Jerusalem, a Druze officer named Ataf Dagesh, called Yossi to commend him and his men on their courage. Yossi had seen to it that elements within the assault force videotaped the takeover bid. He wanted to record the operation for training purposes, but more important he wanted to have in-house evidence that his men had performed their duties without the use of excessive or lethal force.[13]

The operations in the Old City gave the violence—and ultimately this undeclared war—its name: the al-Aqsa intifada. Ya'mas veterans hoped that they had seen the worst of it and that the Palestinian violence would dissipate as quickly as it began. Optimism, even for experienced men, was still a low-wattage beacon of hope. But on November 2, 2000, a bomb-laden car exploded near the main entrance of the Mahane Yehuda Market in the city—two people were killed and a dozen wounded in the attack. The PIJ claimed responsibility for the bombing and warned that there would be much more bloodshed ahead. The Ya'mas was not going to get off the hook that easy, to be able to end the fighting on the Jerusalem front with just fists and batons.

CHAPTER FOURTEEN

Proactive Deterrence

The Shin Bet agents working the phones at the Jerusalem field office knew that they weren't going to get any sleep that night. Nobody was. It had already been a day full of *Hatraot*, or alerts, throughout the country. In the north, along the border with Lebanon, there were indications that Hezbollah was planning to attack an IDF patrol as it moved along the security fence. In Western Galilee, the Shin Bet received indications that a suicide bomber from the northern West Bank, probably Jenin, was being transported to one of the northern cities for a midday attack. And then the most serious alert permeated across the mobile phone networks. The pagers that linked just about every policeman, counterterrorist specialist, and Shin Bet agent did not stop buzzing: A three-man Hamas shooter team was going to target Jerusalem later that evening. It was Thursday night, August 30, 2001, nearly a year into the al-Aqsa intifada, and three weeks after the city's sense of security had been shattered by the suicide bombing at the Sbarro pizzeria in the center of town that killed fifteen people and wounded more than one hundred.

The Shin Bet alert came late in the day. It was dinnertime: The summer sun had already begun to the set. Thursday was a night out for Jerusalem, and the city's major arteries were already clogged with cars from the surrounding suburbs trying to find parking spots inside packed-to-capacity malls and outside the best restaurants and drinking haunts. Police units throughout the city were ordered to work double shifts; the midnight tour had already been paged and ordered to muster before sunset. Roadblocks and check-points were established along all roads leading into Jerusalem from the West Bank and the Palestinian areas to the east. Even the main road leading into the Israeli capital from Tel Aviv was locked down, and heavily armed police units searched every incoming vehicle, looking for something—and someone—suspicious.

The attack, the real-time intelligence indicated, was imminent. The Hamas gunmen had already left Ramallah. They had been dropped off at one of the invisible crossing points separating the Third World and the First and waiting for the means and methods by which they would cross into the confines of Jerusalem.

The Shin Bet assessed that the terrorists would use Beit Hanina—a neighborhood that was in the no-man's-land of both the greater Jerusalem and greater Ramallah confines, only eight kilometers north of Jerusalem's city center—as a springboard into Israel. Beit Hanina had been a popular staging area for Hamas in the past, and it was a turnstile for illegal day laborers, car thieves, and terrorists to simply walk to a bus stop or to the northernmost Jewish suburbs. Once the terrorists were inside Beit Hanina, and once they had access to a driver and a vehicle with the proper Israeli registration, they could reach any corner of the Israeli capital without fuss. A Border Guard special operations unit in Jerusalem called Matilan (the Hebrew acronym for "ambush, observation, interception, and combat") that excelled in long-range observation and camouflage was deployed to the hills where greater Ramallah connected to Jerusalem's northern suburbs. If the terrorists were to cross over hills or gullies that smugglers used, the Matilan specialists would blend themselves into the landscape and observe the targets and engage them. But that was a measure of last resort. The Shin Bet wanted the gunmen alive—and talking. Ya'mas teams were already racing toward Beit Hanina as night cast its darkness over Jerusalem.

Beit Hanina was like any congested neighborhood in Jerusalem's Arab periphery: Multistory apartment blocks towered over narrow hilly streets where residents battled one another for parking spots; stores with bright neon lights illuminated the main roads, such as Taha Hussein Street. But Beit Hanina was also at war. It had become a battleground—a no-man's-land of sorts—used by Arafat, Hamas, and some of the older popular fronts, as the entrenched front line in the multidirectional assault on Jerusalem. The Ya'mas teams were very familiar with Beit Hanina—they had been there countless times before arresting terror suspects and facilitators who helped execute plans hatched in Ramallah and Damascus. Beit Hanina could be hardcore, and when the word went out that three Hamas gunmen were on the loose, the Ya'mas proceeded straight to the Nusseiba section of town—known as the Hamas stronghold.

The Speakers drove cautiously up and down the twisting and narrow streets, maneuvering parallel patterns all along Iskandar al-Khuri Street and the thoroughfares it intersected. They looked for anyone suspicious, but they were wary of being conspicuous themselves. Spotters, teenagers with cell phones, watched over the neighborhood at the behest of local terrorist commanders hunted by Israeli forces. At 2130, one of the Speakers noticed two men lurking in and out of the shadows. The Shin Bet intelligence listed three members of the shooting team, but the two young men looked suspicious enough; one of the men carried a black canvas tactical bag. The moment the Ya'mas team stopped the vehicle and emerged slowly, the two ran. Warning shots were fired into the air. One of the two men was apprehended immediately; the other ran a few blocks and barricaded himself inside a large building housing the Palestinian Engineering Union. The Ya'ma'm was summoned—out of concern that armed men would shoot it out with the police—and a standoff ensued.[1] It would be just before dawn when the men inside the engineering union surrendered and were taken in for questioning. A third suspect was located inside the trunk of a vehicle attempting to flee the area.

Ya'mas operators found two Heckler & Koch MP5A3 9mm submachine guns inside the black canvas bag, and enough ammunition to kill dozens of people.[2] Exotic weapons like the MP5s, rare in Hamas circles, were handed only to the most capable shooting teams. The Ya'mas had helped avert a tragedy in Jerusalem. But it was just another day at work for the unit at a time in the city's history of extraordinary threat and violence.

Just days after the Hamas arrests in Beit Hanina, twenty people were injured when a suicide bomber detonated a knapsack full of explosives and shrapnel on bustling Hanevi'im Street in central Jerusalem. The terrorist had been disguised as an Orthodox Jew.

When the intifada erupted in the West Bank, and even in Gaza, the impact of the rioting and violence was felt by a small segment of the Israeli population—the settlers and the army and police units that tried to keep the disturbances contained until cooler heads prevailed. Jerusalem, however, was Israel's second largest city and its capital. The city, although divided into the "Jewish" west and the "Arab" east, was in reality a united stew where each side was integrally in contact with the other, even while the buses and cafés blew up. Jerusalem was an important target for Palestinian terror groups to focus on because the city had such powerful religious significance, and it was the seat of Israeli political power, but it was also an easy location in which to strike.

The Shin Bet estimated that it thwarted over 90 percent of the attacks planned against Israel, but still the terrorist onslaught against Jerusalem was relentless. Between 2000 and 2003 alone, there were twenty-three suicide bombings perpetrated against the city, resulting in 160 dead and close to 1,000 seriously wounded. Normal daily life for Jerusalem's 650,000-plus residents was one of fear and angst. There were landmarks of sorrow everywhere—candles on a street corner to commemorate the dead from a bus obliterated in a suicide bombing; walls punctured by the shrapnel of a suicide vest. People walking to the market or standing in line at the post office lost a heartbeat when a car backfired. The wailing siren of an ambulance, even one responding to a heart attack or an elderly lady who had taken a fall, caused anyone within reach of a cell phone to call loved ones just to make sure that they were all right. Daily life continued, though. Israelis are a stubborn lot.

Every law enforcement officer in the Jerusalem District—the "blue police," or the regular patrolmen and -women named so for their blue tunics and trousers, and those in the green police, the Border Guard units stationed in and around the city—dedicated their efforts to counterterrorism duties. Israeli policemen did not earn overtime pay. Days stretched into weeks; alerts lasted well beyond anyone's ability to remain alert. Patrolmen and detectives still investigated burglaries, traffic hit-and-runs, and incidents of domestic abuse, but terrorism was the primary focus of all law enforcement entities in the city.[3]

The Jerusalem Ya'mas had, in better days, been both a counterterrorist and a crime-suppression unit. The unit had been built—with equipment and human talent—to be a capable force uniquely designed for operations inside the intricate and often maddening Jerusalem landscape. In quieter times, it was common for the unit to begin its week working a terrorist cell in East Jerusalem on behalf of the Shin Bet, and end the tour in Katamon, one of the rough-and-tumble neighborhoods of the capital, investigating a narcotics ring. Unlike Unit 33, which excelled in technical capabilities such as eavesdropping and lock-picking, the men of the Ya'mas were street cops who could blend into any situation, in any disguise, able to talk their way in or out of trouble, in virtually any language. "If the mission called for us to stake out a suspect from inside a garbage Dumpster, then we did," said Inspector Mike,* an officer with a beguiling and innocent smile that concealed his many years of conventional combat and undercover operations, the pedigree of being a long-timer with the Jerusalem Ya'mas and, previously, a veteran of IDF special operations. "If it called for us to dress up as an Arab laborer, or a rabbi, or a tourist, we did that, too. The ability to be flexible and adapt was critical to who we are and what we can do. If this mission calls for us to be silent, then we have to be silent. People recruited into this unit were deemed Ya'mas material because they had the patience and wherewithal to become invisible within their surroundings if necessary. Sometimes people called us alley cats," he added. "We were silent and if we didn't want you to, you would never know where we were until we made it a point to let you know we were there."[4]

The men of the Jerusalem Ya'mas unit were significantly older than their counterparts in Gaza and even the West Bank and, as a result, more mature in their overall approach to undercover work. Most of the men were in their late twenties or mid-thirties; others were pushing beyond the forty-years-of-age envelope. The unit was made up almost exclusively of professional policemen. There were very few conscripts in the force, and there were times during the intifada when the unit didn't have a single man completing his mandatory military service on its roster; in the West Bank and Gaza units, conscripts

---

* A pseudonym—true identity withheld for security considerations.

constituted 30 percent of the operational complement. The men working undercover in Jerusalem were experienced and precise.

There was a profound sense of duty and mission inside the ranks of the Jerusalem Ya'mas unit that transcended patriotism and even religion. Many of the operators—NCOs and officers alike—were Jerusalem natives and Jerusalem residents. Their wives worked on streets that were targeted by active shooter squads, and their children rode bus lines that were targeted by suicide bombers. Every time that the pager each man wore on his hip vibrated with the news flash of an attack, the undercover policeman felt a numbing punch-to-the-stomach sense of foreboding. If his wife and children weren't dead or wounded in the after-blast residue of the crime scene, then it was the wife and children of a friend, or a neighbor. It was flippant, cliché perhaps, to say that the men of this unit were venturing deep behind hostile lines in order to protect their homes, but these men were. This phenomenon was remarkable for a First World nation fighting an asymmetrical conflict specifically targeting its own civilian population.

The Jerusalem Ya'mas was the smallest of the three Border Guard undercover units in terms of the number of men it fielded. But size didn't matter. The unit was one of the busiest in all of Israel. During the apex of violence, from 2001 to 2004, the unit averaged an astounding six hundred missions a year—a remarkable mission log for a force that never came close to fielding a hundred men.

The Jerusalem theater of operations was the most condensed of the three combat regions during the intifada—for the most part, the unit deployed in and around Jerusalem, the neighboring cities of Bethlehem and Ramallah (and its surrounding periphery), and the transit and population centers that fed into the Israeli capital, such as Hebron and Yatta. The terrain was urban and crowded. The landscape was exclusively hostile, but the rules of engagement inside the Jerusalem District differed from locations directly inside the Palestinian Authority. The IDF did not back up operations in the neighborhoods of Silwan and At-Tur, locations inside Jerusalem proper that boasted some of the most hardcore terrorist cells encountered in the intifada; D9s were not used in Pressure Cookers mobilized a few miles from the Knesset and the prime minister's residence. Inside Jerusalem proper, tactical backup consisted of law enforcement personnel—Border Guard and other—and the Ya'mas handled most of its operations alone. The unit fielded operators who could put ten 9mm rounds into the same hole on the range, and the unit boasted breachers (men who could pick any lock, drive a sledgehammer across any doorframe, and blow a gate off its hinge), drivers, and snipers that were on par with the men who fought in Jenin and Jebalya. But there was a specialized finesse to operations inside East Jerusalem—the unit fought inside the trenches of a congested battlefield that required tactics of absolute guile, deception, and disguise.

A healthy competition existed between the Ya'mas and Unit 33; since the Ya'mas also operated in the Area A West Bank cities closest to the Israeli capital, the Ya'mas also competed with Duvdevan and some of the other IDF units for work. Major General Yoram Halevy, who commanded the West Bank Ya'mas unit as well as the Ya'ma'm, explained it best: "There is great coordination between the units. There is a coordinator in the division [IDF] that is expert in handing out the assignments. There are periods when there is no time to breathe [and there is work for everyone] and there are periods when people argue over an operation."[5] East Jerusalem was a hub of terrorist activity, though. There was enough work for everyone.

The residents of East Jerusalem were uncanny in their ability to detect someone—or something—out of place. The mere suspicion of an undercover unit operating on a raid, or during a stakeout, and the calls of "qawat al-hasa" would resonate throughout the congested landscape. These precincts were always considered to be somewhat lawless. During good times, city assessors, tax collectors, and water inspectors rarely dared enter into the neighborhoods that were controlled by lawlessness and violence; usually, they traveled under armed guard. During the intifada, attempts by police units or Border Guard patrols to establish law and order were almost invariably met with a barrage of rocks and firebombs. The inhabitants were always on guard for something. Small children playing soccer in the street and women in the market had an uncanny skill for sensing men—and vehicles—that were out of place. One SMS message sent from a mobile phone, one call-out in a courtyard, and an entire neighborhood could be mobilized for war and fortified. Even for the Ya'mas, operations inside these outer reaches of the city limits were always "enter at your own risk."

For the undercover unit, one error, one moment of compromise, and a force's exit from a neighborhood would be impeded by rocks, Molotov cocktails, and gunfire. One operation stood out especially in the memory of unit operators, in particular Shai,* a philosophical officer who had served in IDF special operations before returning from security work overseas to join the Ya'mas. Jovial by nature, Shai, who looked more like a college professor than a tactical specialist, remembered an arrest operation inside a crowded café in an East Jerusalem refugee camp. Ya'mas Speakers, along with their non-Speaker counterparts, sat inside the establishment, ordered coffee and some food, and waited for the targeted individual to show up. The Speakers were able to blend in effortlessly inside the crowded eatery, assuming tables at strategic locations throughout; the non-Speakers, dressed as East Jerusalem locals having a coffee after a long day at work, blended in as well, though they were careful not to engage anyone in conversation. Waiters dressed in white shirts and black vests brought tray after tray of coffee and tea to the tables; the sounds of Hayat FM radio resonated against the white tiles stained yellow by nicotine. When the suspect appeared, the Ya'mas men put down their cups and made their move. Within seconds, the bewildered suspect was dragged outside, a gun jammed into his back, and ushered into one of the awaiting undercover vehicles: a classic undercover operation.

But this was East Jerusalem. The moment the suspect was inside the Ya'mas transport, less than thirty seconds after being hustled out of the café, the undercover force was bombarded by rocks and sporadic gunfire. Garbage, bottles, and Molotov cocktails were tossed from the windows overhead. Discarded kitchen appliances, as well as sacks of cement and boulders, had been pre-positioned on rooftops to be used as catapulted missiles against Israeli security forces. "It was remarkable," Shai commented. "One minute we are whisking the suspect away and then moments later a stove has crushed the roof of our armored vehicle. We suddenly found ourselves under attack from all sides. Our vehicles were suddenly blocked from all directions and we had to fight a pitched battle just to get out."[6] Armored tow trucks had to rescue the vehicles damaged in the conflagration.

Some in the East Jerusalem periphery played a decisively active role in the intifada. Ahmed Sa'adeh, twenty-one years old, from the At-Tur

---

* A pseudonym—true identity withheld for security considerations.

neighborhood, one kilometer east of the Old City, near the Mount of Olives, was recruited into the ranks of Hamas in 2001. Residents of At-Tur were full- fledged residents of the State of Israel, and Sa'adeh had all the benefits of an Israeli identity card, including state benefits, but he joined a cell in Bethlehem and underwent firearms training with handguns and M16 assault rifles. Sa'adeh served as an intelligence spotter, loitering around Checkpoint 300, a roadblock in south Jerusalem, to see how he could smuggle armed terrorists into the Israeli capital. Every tip, every morsel of intel that he provided, earned him a $100 bill.[7]

On November 14, 2002, Sa'adeh received explicit instructions from his Hamas commanders: gather operational intelligence on the No. 20 bus line that crossed the working class Kiryat Menachem neighborhood in the southwest part of the city, very close to the no-man's-land separating Jerusalem from Bethlehem. Sa'adeh checked bus schedules, monitored which stops were the most crowded, and helped his Hamas handlers assemble a lethal operational blueprint for the bomber—Na'el Abu Hilail, a twenty-three-year-old from the small hamlet of al-Khader in the shadow of Bethlehem. Sa'adeh even transported Abu Hilail from his staging area near Bethlehem into the heart of the Israeli capital. At 7:00 a.m. on the morning of November 21, 2002, Abu Hilail boarded the green-and-white bus at a stop on Mexico Street. The bus was full of women taking their children to school and workers heading to nearby offices; the bomber had to struggle to get on the crowded vehicle, pushing up against the small children carrying their schoolbooks in backpacks as he went through the motions to pay his fare. Abu Hilail's bomb consisted of five kilograms of powerful explosives cocooned by loads of lethal shrapnel. The blast was so powerful that it partially ripped the roof off the bus. Eleven people were killed in the explosion, including four children; one of the victims, Ilan Perlman, was eight years old and being taken to school by his grandmother Kira, who was also killed. Fifty people were critically wounded.[8]

Israeli counterterrorist units, including the Ya'mas, raided al-Khader once the bomber's identity was revealed. They would raid At-Tur months later once Sa'adeh's identity was revealed in a Shin Bet investigation and his arrest ordered. In a complex operation, involving the Ya'mas and other special operations assets, including Unit 33, Sa'adeh was apprehended. Israeli authorities kept word of his arrest secret for several months so that the Shin Bet could assemble a multidimensional matrix of the Hamas operation in Bethlehem, to include names, faces, addresses, and terror attacks that each man was linked to. The Jerusalem special operations units took care of the apprehensions.

Hamas invested enormous resources in bolstering its Jerusalem front. The operation was handled by the Hamas political and military command in Syria, and was financed with generous doses of Iranian cash. The funds were directed toward the Jerusalem cells through charitable accounts that laundered the cash under the cover of various religious social service and educational institutions but funded Usras, or Youth Cells, that recruited Israeli identity card–holding teenagers and young men for military operations against targets in Jerusalem.

One of the most lethal Hamas terror cells based in East Jerusalem came from Silwan, a neighborhood of close to fifty thousand inhabitants southeast of the walls of the Old City. The cell, known as the Gang of Death,[9] was responsible for the death of thirty-five Israelis and some of the most horrific attacks of the intifada, including the bombing of the Moment Café and the bombing of the Frank Sinatra Student Center in the Hebrew University of Jerusalem on Mount Scopus; nine were killed in the latter attack, and more than one hundred wounded. The Ya'mas and Unit 33 had been hunting the cell for months and had operated inside East Jerusalem and Palestinian cities in Area A during their pursuit of the operatives; Muhmad Arwan, a Ramallah native, was the cell coordinator for Hamas, and the link between the command in Syria and the bomb-making engineers in the Palestinian Authority who built the devices that the cells used in attacks throughout Jerusalem and the greater Tel Aviv area. The cell had been planning a mega-attack, the suicide bombing of a crowded nightclub, when units raided their homes in a multipronged assault on August 17, 2002. Several of those arrested (five members of the cell plus ten assistants and facilitators in East Jerusalem) were seized after midnight as they were en route to carrying out a suicide bombing somewhere in central Jerusalem. Prime Minister Sharon praised the arrests as one of the most meaningful operations since the outbreak of violence between the Palestinians and Israelis.[10]

Dynamic arrest operations, centered around the concept of hit-and-run,[11] was what the undercover units excelled at, but the Jerusalem Ya'mas also patrolled stretches of the city and its outer reaches to search for anything that looked suspicious and anyone who appeared out of place. The plainclothes patrols were conducted in the ultra-Orthodox neighborhoods of the city where secular Israelis rarely traveled, and they were carried out inside the Palestinian areas in the hope of intercepting a bomber before he or she could be transported toward the city center. The work was tedious, tiresome, and, to many in the unit, depressing. "During the tough months when we suffered attack after attack, we would drive along the main streets of the city and see that stores were empty and that the streets looked like a ghost town," Shai recalled. "Restaurants and stores went out of business. People were afraid to walk around town."[12] On numerous occasions, the unit managed to intercept a suicide bomber before he or she could strike. On June 8, 2002, a teenage Palestinian girl was arrested in Bir Naballah, a Palestinian village north of the city, hours before she planned to travel to the center of Jerusalem to blow herself up.

When an alert came in of a possible suicide bomber poised to attack Jerusalem, the unit patrolled for hours, sometimes from dawn until further notice, in the attempt to intercept a faceless ghost heading everywhere and anywhere. Often, this work culminated in failure. The faint thud of an explosion, harried radio traffic on the police frequencies, and the wail of emergency sirens signaled that they had been unsuccessful in locating a bomber before he or she could strike. Not all patrols ended in failure.

On Friday night, April 23, 2004, a Ya'mas squad arrested a three-man Palestinian active shooter cell that had been the center of a monthlong Shin Bet manhunt. The Palestinians had shot and killed George Huri, an Israeli-Arab university student from a prominent family, and had wounded another student weeks later. There was no pattern to the attacks, and there was no chatter that compromised the shooters' identities. Shin Bet case officers turned to the Ya'mas for help, and thirty minutes into a patrol inside the French Hill area in the northern outreach of the city, the plainclothes officers noticed three men in a red sedan who appeared out of place, driving slowly near an elderly gentleman walking his dog. A regular Border Patrol unit was summoned and the vehicle pulled over. Inside the car, the Border Guard officers found the murder weapon, a Czech-made CZ 9mm pistol, and a camcorder that had been used to record both of the earlier shootings.

In July 2004, the Shin Bet released statistics claiming that it had prevented eighty-three suicide attacks since the start of the year.[13] It was said that the Shin Bet—assisted by the tip of the spear of Israel's counterterrorist forces—had managed to undermine, deter, and destroy some 90 percent of the suicide bombing attacks that had been planned by the terrorist groups. The Israeli effort was ongoing, and it relied on a relentless approach and the occasional slivers of luck. Many of the attacks that never took place had been earmarked for Jerusalem.

The Ya'mas found that its brand of tactical interdiction and proactive deterrence was yielding dividends. The patrols in the heart of the Israeli capital became less frequent. The unit found itself proactively deterring terrorist plots outside of Jerusalem's city limits—inside the cities of Area A.

CHAPTER FIFTEEN

A Ticking Bomb in Hebron

The day following the Sbarro pizzeria bombing, eateries on King George Street opened for business. Shop owners swept the shards of broken glass from in front of their businesses and greeted throngs of patrons who, out of spiteful resolve—a truly unique Israeli phenomenon known as *Davka*—refused to let the suicide bombers interfere with the fabric of daily life. Eating out was an Israeli passion, and there was no way that Israelis would allow Hamas, or any of the other groups, to claim a victory of any kind. Yet targeting eateries remained a strategic objective for the terror factions. Tourists frequented the pizza parlors and falafel stands; the city's movers and shakers, the who's who of life in the city, dined at the city's trendy cafés and most-talked-about restaurants.

The German Colony was one of Jerusalem's most upscale neighborhoods, and the Café Caffit was its gastronomical and social hangout. One of the true "in" spots in Jerusalem, a city that was known more for spiritual landmarks than culinary finds, Café Caffit was iconic in the capital for lavish salads and salmon burgers, and its sweet potato pancakes summoned the hungry morning-meal faithful from across the city. The neighborhood was a bastion of Anglo-Saxon expats, so as much English was heard behind the café's gray gates as Hebrew. Patrons could pick the outdoor area of wooden chairs positioned around spacious tables for a meal or a coffee, or they could sit inside and look at the passing traffic crisscrossing Emek Refa'im Street through the walls of glass that surrounded the eatery. Café Caffit was always packed to capacity. The breakfast and lunch traffic often resulted in a long line of patrons waiting outside for a table. Those who waited for only a few minutes were considered lucky.

On the afternoon of March 7, 2002, the patrons fortunate enough for a table inside Café Caffit were lucky for a different reason. A young man, with a distinctive Middle Eastern appearance, had managed to slink past the security guard posted outside the establishment and to locate a table in the outdoor courtyard next to one of the main glass windows. He was nervous and agitated. A steady film of sweat covered his forehead even though the temperature was cool and crisp. The Caffit's owner, Gabi Altaratz, walked over to the young man to see if he was all right and to take his order; Altaratz had been the first restaurant owner to hire a full-time security guard to stand outside the Caffit's entrance. "Can I get you anything?" he asked as he handed the young man a menu. "Just water," the man, in his mid-twenties, answered, as if bothered by the intrusion.[1] Altaratz noticed a large backpack by the man's legs and immediately summoned one of his waiters, twenty-three-year-old Shlomi Harel, who had recently completed his compulsory military service in an elite combat unit. Harel walked to the table and, in IDF Arabic, asked the man for his ID card. The man, an East Jerusalem resident, produced a blue Teudat Zehut, or identity card, indicating that he was an Israeli resident. He smiled. Harel noticed the bag and a wire protruding from it that ran inside his jacket and then came out through the man's right sleeve, where it was connected to what appeared to be a detonating device. Harel immediately manhandled the Palestinian and shoved him outside the restaurant while removing the wire from its connections. The young waiter, at the right place at the right time, used his commando-taught Krav Maga skills to subdue the foiled bomber until police units and the bomb squad could arrive. The device that the police robot neutralized consisted of more than ten kilograms of high explosives and shrapnel. Fifty people had been sitting inside the restaurant that cool winter afternoon. Superintendent Gil Kleiman, a veteran police bomb disposal officer and foreign press spokesman, assessed that everyone inside the eatery would have been killed by the yield of the powerful explosive device.

The failed suicide bombing in Café Caffit was an embarrassment for Hamas. The humiliation was short-lived. Forty-eight hours later, Fuad al-Hourani, a twenty-year-old from the al-Arroub refugee camp, located fifteen kilometers south of Bethlehem, blew himself up in the Moment Café, located just down the road from Prime Minister Sharon's official residence. Eleven people were killed in the attack; more than fifty were wounded.

Immediately after the Moment Café bombing, the restaurants around Jerusalem began to post armed guards, in the best case recently discharged soldiers, at the entrances to their establishments. The young guards—and even the older men who gravitated to the relatively mundane and low-paying job—were meant to be a deterrent rather than a solution. Restaurant owners simply wanted the suicide bombers to go elsewhere.

Yet Hamas never abandoned its desire to hit major Jerusalem eateries; the obliteration of the who's who of Jerusalem society, as they sipped cups of coffee and munched on sandwiches, was a top-priority objective for the organization's military arm. At 2320 on the night of September 9, 2003, a Hamas suicide bomber made a failed attempt to enter a pizzeria—up the road from the Café Caffit—when a security guard pushed him away. The bomber, undaunted by the alarm, ran inside the nearby Café Hillel, where he wrestled with the security guard and managed to push seven meters inside the crowded restaurant before detonating his lethal payload. Seven people were killed in the blast. Fifty more were wounded.

Hamas still had plans for Café Caffit.

Israel's policy of targeted killings had a profound effect on the strands that connected the Hamas leadership in the West Bank and Gaza. The Shin Bet—post–Operation Defense Shield—had successfully reaffirmed its espionage mastery of the Palestinian landscape and developed an extensive and irremovable reach inside the most secretive of Palestinian organizations. The intelligence that the Shin Bet provided the IDF commands was pinpoint accurate. The accuracy—and intimacy—of the information enabled Israel's special operations units to decimate the senior and mid-level ranks of the terrorist organizations with catch-or-kill raids deep inside Palestinian territory. Another significant factor obstructing the terrorists from striking at more targets inside Israel was the separation barrier. The formidable fence had more or less been completed around East Jerusalem, and it had become a near-hermetic impediment to smuggling suicide bombers into Israel. Hamas was in dire need of a victory.

Imad Qawasmeh, one of the most active Hamas military commanders in Hebron, was selected by the organization's commanders outside the West Bank to be the architect of a grandiose Jerusalem operation. Qawasmeh hailed from one of the dominant clans of the Hamas infrastructure in Hebron, and Imad was considered a prodigal son endowed with excessive cunning. The Jerusalem operation was a top Hamas priority, and Qawasmeh was ordered to select the top men at his disposal to carry out the bombing. Qawasmeh selected Allah Kapisha, another favorite son of Hamas, from a clan that dominated the Hamas ranks inside Hebron, to be the operational commander. Although he was all of thirty-one, Kapisha—like many of his contemporaries—had spent a good part of his adult life fighting Israel; a fair percentage of his personal war had been waged from behind the walls of an Israeli prison.

Qawasmeh and Kapisha handled the money and the logistics. They enlisted the support of Ibrahim Mohammad Ahmed Halbiye, a Hamas operative living in Abu Dis, a small suburb in East Jerusalem that was officially part of Area B; Halbiye, in turn, recruited Wasim Salim Mustafa Jelad, a resident of Isawiya, an Arab neighborhood near Hadassah Hospital, who possessed an Israeli ID card. Halbiye would be responsible for acquiring the car with Israeli license plates that would transport the bomber to the target, while Jelad would drive the bomber toward his target from a yet-to-be-completed section of the separation barrier where smugglers and day laborers crossed into Israel without problem.

Three other low-level Hamas operatives, all residents of East Jerusalem and all of whom possessed valid Israeli identification papers and driver's licenses, would reconnoiter the neighborhoods of the capital and selectively observe which restaurants were most crowded, which were the most vulnerable, and which were constructed with huge panes of glass that could create thousands of lethal shrapnel-like shards. There were endless target possibilities. It was summer, and despite the bloodshed of the intifada, tourism brought tens of thousands of visitors to Jerusalem, and the eateries were open to the wee hours of the morning to accommodate the crowds. The intelligence crew scoured the city's hot spots for days, and returned to Hebron with a unanimously selected target: the Café Caffit. Malik Salem Matzbah Nasser A-Din was chosen to be the bomber.

Malik wasn't just any myopically witted recruit that had been pulled out of a mosque for the opportunity to encounter the paradise pleasures of seventy-two virgins. Malik was old for a suicide bomber—forty-one—and that provided operational flexibility: Israeli security forces profiling suspicious young men and women would be less wary of a man in his early forties. But Malik was more than just the right age. The Hebron native had been a semi-pro soccer player who had been something of a local superstar among athletes and sports fans. Qawasmeh fathomed the enormous propaganda windfall that would be generated in the promotion of this sports star turned martyr. The young kids throughout the West Bank who wore counterfeit Real Madrid and Manchester United jerseys would flock to Hamas recruiters to volunteer for the chance to follow in Malik's footsteps. Photos of Malik were already at the printer in preparation of his martyrdom: His face, bearded and narrow, revealing a receding hairline and a nose that had taken its fair share of elbows on the soccer pitch, looked like it belonged to someone no-nonsense and physical. The posters had already been designed.

It was exceptionally hot early on the morning of Sunday, July 11, 2004, when Allah Kapisha finished loading the delivery van for his family's biscuit company in Hebron. A hundred or so cookie tins were packed inside the white van that was to deliver sweets and dried yeast crackers with sesame seeds to food shops and restaurants throughout the southern West Bank. One tin, hidden deep inside the cargo hold, concealed an explosive vest with nearly ten kilograms of TATP and shrapnel, along with a 9mm semiautomatic pistol. The van snaked its way out of early morning Hebron traffic to take the circuitous nineteen-mile route, avoiding IDF checkpoints, toward Abu Dis.

Malik was driven from his sister's house in the heart of Hebron to Abu Dis hours later—the chauffeur, a member of the military wing's internal security force, was stone-faced and silent during the journey. Inside the Abu Dis safe house, Malik read his living will as Hamas operatives videotaped him, and he was given detailed instructions on the operation he was about to embark on. Malik was handed the 9mm semiautomatic pistol and asked if he knew how to use it. There was a guard in front of the café; Malik was told to shoot him in the head and then proceed inside. There was still time for a last meal and afternoon prayers before darkness.

As the sun migrated west, over the Jerusalem hills toward the coastal plains and the Mediterranean, Ibrahim Halbiye used the concealing cover of the purple dusk to bring Malik to a gap in the security barrier where he could cross into Jerusalem proper without being seen by the Israeli watchtowers. The terrain on the Abu Dis side of the fence was strewn with rubble, and Malik found it hard to maintain steady footing as he carried the extra weight around his midsection, camouflaging his athletic frame inside a shirt that was three sizes too big for him. Jelad was waiting across the fence, smoking a cigarette inside the car that would ferry Malik to his target. Nighttime traffic was dense. More than a dozen buses crisscrossed Emek Refa'im Street, and the number of cars trying to find parking for the restaurants, cafés, falafel stands, and bakeries that filled the area turned the summer night into a gridlocked nightmare. Jelad drove past the Café Caffit and brought his car to a stop at the Oranim Junction, approximately a thousand meters down the road. There were no parting words exchanged between driver and bomber. Malik slammed the door shut, and Jelad drove quickly back to his home in Isawiya. The car would be brought to a chop shop and destroyed so that all forensic evidence could be obliterated.

Malik Salem Matzbah Nasser A-Din began his lonely walk up the street toward where people laughed out loud and young couples embraced in the cool night's breeze. Malik was used to being on the soccer pitch with fans screaming his name as he maneuvered up the field with his teammates, passing the ball in displays of fancy footwork. He had no team to support him now as he walked toward his target all alone. He suddenly walked at a sullen pace.

Malik made it up to the Café Caffit's entrance. People brushed by him as they jostled for a place in the line to get in. Malik looked at the security guard manning his small table at the front gate, and he glanced around at the dizzying traffic pushing up and down the street. He took one step toward his target and then hurriedly turned back. Malik walked quickly and nervously in search of concealing darkness. He walked into an alley separating two buildings and hurried toward a row of Dumpsters and a wall of discarded pallets. Malik quickly opened his shirt and removed the explosive vest he carried. He wiped the sweat off his brow and walked back to Emek Refa'im Street. Young men and women embraced in the cool summer breeze sweeping in from the Judean Hills that July Jerusalem night. The couples kissed and laughed as they stood in line to eat.

With no money or ID on him at all, the man who was to have been celebrated as a martyr walked silently, hands in pockets, toward the same gap in the security fence where he had crossed a short time earlier. Once safely in Abu Dis, he made his way to a cab stand, where he negotiated the rate with a driver, telling him that someone in Hebron would have to pay him.

Malik Salem Matzbah Nasser A-Din spent the rest of the night in the mosque, searching for the spiritual strength that had abandoned him.

Both Qawasmeh and Kapisha had gone to separate mosques to watch the breaking news of the Café Caffit bombing on al-Jazeera and Israeli television. They waited for several hours, but the evening news programs spoke nothing of mass carnage on a Jerusalem street corner. Perhaps, they thought, the Israelis had kept word of the bombing secret so that the Shin Bet could intercept cell phone communications of the conspirators for the post-event series of raids and arrests. The two men stayed awake all night. They didn't even think to look for Malik.

Hamas commanders in Damascus had also expected to watch live breaking news of a blast in Jerusalem. The organization's political arm in Gaza had already prepared a lengthy statement to be released to the international press. There was, however, nothing. In the panic of failure, commanders in Damascus and Gaza began dispatching urgent calls to their lieutenants in Hebron. The Shin Bet was suddenly alerted to the increased frenzy of back-and-forth chatter. It didn't take long to connect the electronic intercepts to Qawasmeh and his group.

On the morning of July 12, 2004, Qawasmeh realized that Malik had returned home to Hebron. The cell commanders had to talk to Malik and discuss the details of what had happened and, more important, what *hadn't* happened. They spoke on the phone. Malik was repentant, but adamant. He told his handlers that he needed a few additional days on this earth before returning to Jerusalem to carry out his mission. His vest and pistol were safely hidden, he thought, and he could confidently get into Jerusalem without too much fuss or bother. He swore that he would carry out his mission shortly.

But forty-eight hours after the aborted plot, Qawasmeh's cell had already been shattered. Kapisha, Halbiye, and Jelad had all been arrested by Unit 33 in separate raids throughout East Jerusalem and the Hebron Hills, and the three were already talking to the Shin Bet.[2] The arrests were carried out with the utmost speed, guile, and effectiveness; as one former member of the unit and a Ya'mas commander would reflect on their capabilities, "The unit used such trickery and such cunning that suspects didn't realize that they had been arrested until they were sitting inside the police station."[3]

The raids were all carried out under a tremendous veil of secrecy. Virtually no one knew that the operatives were connected to one another or that they were even in Israeli custody; the Shin Bet arrested the three under administrative detention protocols where no one—including a defense attorney—was notified that the Palestinians had been seized by Israeli security forces. It was not uncommon for Hamas operatives, perhaps on the run from the Shin Bet, to disappear and leave no word where they were going. The Shin Bet used this compartmentalized mindset to their advantage. They needed to make sure that Malik had no idea that his inner circle was somewhere in a windowless room, smoking Time cigarettes and giving up details of the failed operation. But Malik was, as per the Shin Bet definition, a ticking bomb. He could cross into Jerusalem the next morning or in a month, but in order to regain his honor—and preserve the benefits due a martyr—he would most definitely blow himself up. The clock was, indeed, ticking—especially since Qawasmeh could call on hundreds—if not more—of clan members in the Hebron area for support and shelter, and had evaded the Israeli dragnet.

The apprehension of Malik Salem Matzbah Nasser A-Din *before* he could blow himself up on a bus, inside a café, or on a crowded Jerusalem street corner became a mission of Israeli national urgency.

Representatives from a half a dozen Israeli special operations units camped out inside the operations center of the heavily protected confines of the Hebron Brigade compound outside the city—all competing for work. These units, the creme de la creme of the IDF's tip of the spear—the naval commandos, IAF special ops teams, reconnaissance paratrooper units, and Golani's Egoz counterinsurgency specialists—all interfaced with the local Shin Bet case agents and the brigade command staff, looking for work. There was no shortage of work, of course; every day, the list of terrorist suspects provided these units with more work than they could handle. But the junior commando officers wanted missions of substance—operations that would be a feather in the cap of their commanding officers and headline worthy. This was an operation, though, that required enormous cunning, a fluid presence, and the ability to move in and out of enemy-controlled areas invisibly. The operation also had threads that one way or another would lead back to East Jerusalem.

Hebron was really Duvdevan's jurisdiction. But the Shin Bet wanted Malik taken alive at almost any cost. "Duvdevan," a veteran of the unit—and the Shin Bet—said, "punctured and lacerated the terrain while infiltrating the Palestinian areas. The Border Guard units," he added, "invaded its pores and injected themselves inside the local population's nerve endings in a way that they didn't realize that they were there until it was way too late."[4] The Shin Bet desperately wanted Malik inside one of its interrogation rooms. Malik could add complexion and defining detail on so many others involved in the operation, from the lowest ranks all the way to the top. There was a hope that Malik would be able to identify the men who drove him to the Abu Dis safe house to hand him his explosive vest and pistol; gathered intelligence on the target inside the confines of Jerusalem; the men who recruited him for the operation inside the mosque; promised his family financial support after the execution of his martyrdom operation; coordinated the network of facilitators inside the Hamas underworld in Hebron; sold the pistol he was given; built the bomb he was carrying; and, who were the lieutenants, captains, and commanders of the Hebron infrastructure inside the city. The Shin Bet desperately wanted to know if Malik could lead them to the liaison officers, the men who communicated with contacts in Lebanon and Syria, in the hope that an entire and vast network could be forever compromised.

The Shin Bet case agent assigned to locating Malik knew the Jerusalem Ya'mas intelligence officer's mobile phone number by heart. "I have a suspect in Hebron that we need to bring in right away," the case agent said. "Is this something the unit is interested in?"[5] The question, of course, was superfluous. Within an hour of receiving the call, Superintendent Hayim,* the Jerusalem Ya'mas commander, had mobilized much of the unit. The call came in the morning. The unit was in the Hebron Brigade's briefing room reviewing aerial photographs of Hebron before lunch was served in the mess hall. The *Ishur Tochniot*, the approval of operational plans for Malik's apprehension, were prepared on the fly and presented to the brigade commander before lunch. Usually the gathering, known by its Hebrew acronym of *Ka'pak*, or Command Group, would take place at a predisposed time and place and include a room full of colonels, majors, and captains. "The brigade commander would be there, as would the Shin Bet case agent, as would our commanding officer and our intelligence officer," Master Sergeant Yoni,[†] a veteran Jerusalem Ya'mas NCO, explained. "The brigade intelligence officer would also be at the Command Group, as would the IAF liaison officer, brigade medical officer, and just about every unit or command represented in an operation. There was exhaustive preparation involved so that the unit hoping to have its plans approved could cobble together a slick presentation for the colonel who would have to give his blessing. The brigade commander would usually say yes to twenty elements of a plan, but nix ten other details. The process took time."[6]

There was no time to spare with Malik, though. Jerusalem's Ya'mas was—on paper, at least—under the control of the Jerusalem Police District and not the IDF. The district was usually quite liberal as to where the Ya'mas worked, especially if the target was a terrorist intent on attacking Jerusalem. The Command Group also operated without bother or too much fuss in Malik's case. An hour or so later—before the day's hearty midday meal of

---

* A pseudonym—true identity concealed for security considerations.

† A pseudonym—true identity concealed for security considerations.

schnitzel and mashed potatoes could be properly digested—elements of the unit were already in Hebron reconnoitering the terrain. By sundown on the evening of July 13, virtually the entire Jerusalem Ya'mas unit was operational deep inside of Hebron looking for one man. Only one man remained behind at the Ya'mas home base in the capital: the unit's cook.

Colonel Motti Baruch, the Hebron Brigade commander, gave the order that checkpoints around Hebron were to be reinforced to make sure that Malik didn't leave the city. The plan was to find the forty-one-year-old inside Hebron and deal with him there. The Shin Bet knew that Malik Salem Matzbah Nasser A-Din was a bachelor. He didn't own or rent his own home. There were four possibilities where the Shin Bet could locate him: his parents' home, the houses of his two married sisters inside the city, and a store inside the *suq*, or market, of Hebron where he sometimes worked and in the back room of which the owners sometimes let him sleep. Hayim, the unit commander, split the unit into two forces: One task force covered the homes of the two sisters, and another covered the marketplace and the parents' house. A Command Post was established inside the brigade's base to cover the intelligence, aerial, and logistics side of the operation—senior IDF, Shin Bet, and Border Guard officers monitored the drone feeds and the chatter. Sleeping bags and military cots were brought in to accommodate the top brass who were starting an operation that in reality was built on luck and courage—the officers involved had no idea if Malik would be located in an hour or in a week. There was no training model to prepare on. The Ya'mas search force would have to learn how to get from Point A to Point B in a discreet manner and to deal, in rough sketches, with whatever they could glean from the aerial photography about the layout of the four possible locations where the Shin Bet believed Malik could be found. Each house was different, each street was different. Each possible location, in Hamas-controlled neighborhoods protected by the Palestinian police forces, presented the team leaders with challenging—and daunting—concerns. Did Malik have a bodyguard? Were his hideouts booby-trapped? How many armed gunmen lingered around each location?

A rescue force of paratroopers—a complete battalion—was at the ready around the clock to rush into the city to rescue any Ya'mas contingent that found itself in danger.

The rest of the equation was simply an exercise of patience-exhausting tedium and dynamic, fluid flexibility. The two task forces had to remain in costume—and, for those who would be in the undercover vehicle, in full tactical kit—next to their vehicles from dawn until dusk. The operators didn't eat much or drink much; a fear, of course, was to have to rush to the toilet just as the Shin Bet received definitive word of Malik's immediate whereabouts. The operators would have to spend the entire day in deep concentration, almost like an adrenaline-fueled trance, in which they would focus on their specific assignments. The longer the day dragged on with no word of Malik, the more pinpoint—albeit anxious—the mental preparations became.

The flip side of the coin was that Malik was not in any of the locations that the Shin Bet had designated as likely. Perhaps Malik was inside a café protected by a phalanx of Izzedine al-Qassam triggermen? Perhaps he had decided to spend his last moments on earth in the company of a woman? Or was he deep in prayer inside a mosque?

The moment, though, that one of the Shin Bet resources could confirm Malik's location, the Ya'mas contingent had to be ready to race out of the brigade base and know where to go. "Hebron was a huge city," one of the operators remembered, "and if we received word that he was on the corner of X and Y, we had to know how to get there quickly, how to avoid Palestinian roadblocks, and how to position ourselves invisibly."

Intelligence indications provided a daily window of 0800 to 2000 hours for Malik to "appear." After 2000 hours, if there were no reports of his whereabouts, the Ya'mas task force—as well as the Command Post and the rescue force—would fold their tents, disassemble their gear, and leave, to return the next morning at the crack of dawn.

Shutting down the operation for the night was incredibly time-consuming. When the task force was told to stand down at 2000 hours, it took ninety minutes to remove the battle rattle, place the weapons back in their cases, do ammo and grenade checks, and make sure that all the radios were in working order. It was another hour or so back to Jerusalem, and then another hour or so for the unit to shower and eat. If the men were lucky, there were no late night developments that required work and it was lights-out and a last cigarette at 0100. Wake-up was at 0430. There was breakfast—hearty portions of *shakshuka*, an Israeli staple of eggs cooked in a spicy tomato sauce—and a review of the overnight intelligence. The drive to Hebron took an hour—sometimes longer in the maddening Jerusalem traffic—and the unit was back at the brigade by 0700. There were last-minute details to finalize with the brigade command staff, rudimentary preparations of costume and tactical kit, and then at 0800 the Ya'mas force declared itself operationally ready.

This routine continued for three long and tedious days. The operators were used to it—it was part of the job. There were assignments when the Ya'mas operators were ordered to stop whatever they were doing and to rush to an East Jerusalem or Ramallah neighborhood because there were eyes and ears on a suspect and he had to be apprehended right then and there, and there were times when they waited for weeks—months—for pinpoint intelligence of a suspect's whereabouts. The operators waited near their vehicles. The summer heat was unbearable, and the men who were not in disguise endured twelve-hour days of dehydrating perspiration. The men smoked as they waited, but the day dragged on and there was nothing. The Shin Bet case agent worked his phones and maintained a constant relay with headquarters, but there was nothing. No news; no inkling that any word was imminent. The sun began to set over the Judean Hills, and the operators hydrated themselves from the endless supply of bottled water. The men checked their watches, and they looked at their pagers and mobile phones for anything to disrupt the boredom and to alleviate the stress. They watched the sun go down, and they observed as the sunny skies suddenly turned into an amber gray.

The operators took the hunt for Malik—like the hunt for any one of the terrorists they pursued—very personally. They were hot, hungry, and tired beyond words. They missed their homes, and most, out of superstition, tried not to phone home during the days of wait. Yet the men were reticent about calling it a day when the clock struck 2000 hours. "Let's stay here another twenty minutes," they would say to the team leaders and to Hayim, the unit commander. What difference was another thirty minutes here or there going to make? Nobody wanted to go home until Malik was in custody and the plot to blow up a restaurant in Jerusalem completely unraveled.

The sun began to set on the Hebron Brigade HQ at the onset of evening on Thursday, July 15. Thursday night was when Israel's young went out and partied before the Sabbath and the operators in disguise and in full tactical kit knew that the streets of Jerusalem would be packed with young men and women out for a meal or simple stroll. Yet there was still no word on Malik. Shai checked his Casio G-Shock. He had been on the wrong side of luck several times before, searching for a suicide bomber during a Dagger Alert only to respond after the heart-stopping explosion and see the human collateral damage torn and thrown about like bloody scraps on a butcher shop floor. It would be 2000 hours in a few minutes. Shai, like everyone in the unit, had absolutely no intention of breaking down the operation just yet.

The sun had sunk behind the hills deep to the west of the Hebron Brigade headquarters complex. It was already 2015. Only thirty minutes of peripheral summer daylight remained, and the men were despondently resigned to the fact that the day had come to an end. Last drags were drawn on one of the too many cigarettes smoked that day, and some of the operators stretched before removing the M4 assault rifles that were slung over their shoulders. Some of the operators worried that Malik had slipped back into Jerusalem. They checked their pagers to make sure there were no urgent alerts from the police reporting of an attack.

The doors of the unit's vehicles were open and the equipment ready to be thrown inside when Hayim came running out of Colonel Baruch's office, sprinting across the compound with an Olympian's speed. "He's at his sister's house. He's at his sister's house. Move out now!" The task force assigned to the homes of his two sisters immediately fastened their body armor and entered the back of the undercover vehicles. The Speakers and squad commanders checked their disguises one last time in the mirror and rushed to sit comfortably inside in their predetermined spots. On a perfect day, with no checkpoints, the home of Malik's sister was a fifteen-minute drive from the Hebron Brigade. The drivers were determined to make it there in less than ten. The undercover vehicles set out. The arrest of Malik Salem Matzbah Nasser A-Din was designed to be a smooth operation—what was known in Hebrew as *Halak*. Malik didn't know that his original cell had been apprehended, and he didn't know that the Israelis had invested enormous resources to bring him in alive. The arrest plan was simple—grab him before he could realize what was happening. Surprise was essential. The unit wanted to be in and out of Hebron before anyone was the wiser.

Hebron was vibrant that Thursday night—there were always last-minute shoppers out and about on the eve of the Muslim *sabt.* Traffic was difficult to negotiate once the checkpoints were overcome and the obstacle course of double- and triple-parked cars was negotiated. Shoppers bought stacks of pita bread from neighborhood bakeries; the bread, piping hot, was carried in membrane-like blue plastic bags that miraculously carried enormous loads without breaking. Shopkeepers had already turned on their lights. Livery cabdrivers, after a long shift of bringing day laborers home, assembled outside shawarma stands for a quick dinner on the go. Drivers honked their horns to get through the chaos. The sounds of Lebanese sirens belting out tunes on car radios competed with the fiery sermons of Hamas clerics who handed out their CDs for free in the market. No one heard the muffled buzz of the drone flying overhead.

Malik's younger sister lived in a three-story house on one of the main streets of Hebron, in the center of town. The Ya'mas task force divided the house into four quadrants so that elements of the raiding force could report their locations and minimize the risk of a friendly fire incident. Each Ya'mas element grabbed a corner, so that the operators would have a 180-degree vantage point to watch one another's backs.

The undercover vehicles pushed forward into the darkening streets. The operators in disguise flexed their fingers slightly, ready to open their doors and then race out of the vehicles in a flash. One minute out, one of the Speakers heard Hayim utter from the Command Post. The clear plastic radio earbud was pressed deep inside his ear. The operation commander, one of the unit's junior officers, whispered for his men to get ready. Inside the undercover vehicle, the operators in tactical kit clutched their M4s; their hands were sweaty from the heat and from the adrenaline surging through their systems. The two undercover vehicles glided to a complete stop a couple of meters from the targeted building. Those wearing Palestinian disguises removed thin black balaclavas from their pockets and used them to cover their faces; a white reflective tape bearing the word "POLICE" in

English covered the sides of the concealing mask. The operators moved into position, seizing the four corners of the house. The backup force, made up of the second Ya'mas element, which was supposed to target the market and the parents' home, stood by at the ready. Back at the Hebron Brigade, the entire choreography of the assault was watched in real time on a large-screen monitor.

Malik was on the back porch of the house, an open space with a white marble tile floor. His entire family was present, including his sisters and parents. According to the Israeli rules of engagement, Malik was considered a ticking bomb—someone that could be shot on sight. But the Israeli military and security forces lived by a creed—in fact, it was one of the pillars of Israel's operational doctrine—called *Tohar Ha'Neshek*, or Purity of Arms, that dictated the moral restraints that needed to be applied in the use of deadly force. Malik was holding a baby, one of his nephews, when the Ya'mas arrest team arrived. The operators had to act decisively and instinctively to protect the mission and to maintain the ethical guidelines that would later be scrutinized, so they fired warning shots into the ground in the hope that Malik would realize that he was targeted for arrest and surrender without struggle. Malik looked around and suddenly resigned himself to his inevitable fate. He saw the masked men in the darkness taking aim, and he threw the infant on the floor and rushed inside the house.[7]

The hopes for anything *Halak* evaporated into the darkness that Hebron night. There was no more element of surprise. There were hostages now, human shields, and the sounds of gunfire had alarmed a hornet's nest of curiosity and concern in a city that could summon thousands of Hamas fighters and Palestinian policemen with the flash of a text message. A handful of Ya'mas operators were now alone and exposed. The men trained their ACOG sights on nearby windows, wary of snipers. They remained calm even though they were horrifically outnumbered inside darkened confines in a city on the edge of eruption. The Ya'mas operators surrounded the house and waited for backup. The seconds dragged on slowly as the men checked their watches. The arrest operation had turned into a Pressure Cooker.

There was nothing quiet about Pressure Cookers—they were loud and over-whelmingly large. Fifteen minutes after the warning shots were fired for Malik to come in peacefully, what appeared to be the entire Israeli military arrived in Hebron. The remaining Ya'mas elements came first. Colonel Baruch arrived along with Superintendent Hayim, as did virtually all of the senior officers that had been watching events unfold live at the Command Post. A large con-tingent of Shin Bet commanders also rushed to the area. The paratroopers, who were supposed to provide backup in case the arrest team found itself under fire, established a wide and secure perimeter around the entire area. The Pressure Cooker became a closed military zone. Dozens of assault rifles and squad support machine guns were now trained on the house where Malik was barricaded inside and, in essence, using his family as human shields.

Several hundred men, women, and children filled the streets to see what the fuss was about. Some of those who had gathered cursed the Israeli forces. Some brought snacks. It was like going to the movies for many of them, one of the Ya'mas NCOs reflected. But the Israeli paratroopers manning the perimeter were young and nervous. How many AK-47s were there in the crowd, or taking aim from nearby rooftops? the soldiers wondered. The senior officers at the scene knew that it was imperative to end the Malik barricade as quickly as possible. The potential for the Pressure Cooker denigrating into bloodshed and an international political incident was very real in the thick summer night air.

The fear was that Malik would blow himself up and kill himself and his family. "Let all the women and children go," one of the Speakers demanded over a megaphone. The Arabic was perfect and authoritative. The message was repeated over and over again. It took twenty minutes before the front door cracked open slightly. Red and green laser beams focused on the individuals emerging from behind the darkness. A Ya'mas Speaker cautiously moved forward to direct Malik's parents, his sisters, and their children outside so that they could be searched and removed to a safer area. The family members were asked how many men were inside, as well as how many weapons and what type. There were strict protocols to preserve the family honor. The Shin Bet agent in charge spoke only to Malik's father; all questions for the women were directed through the family patriarch. Was the house wired with explosives?

the father was asked. Was Malik wearing an explosive vest? And then there was gunfire.

Malik emerged for a second at a second-story window and emptied a dozen shots from his semiautomatic pistol at the Ya'mas operators below. The Israelis responded with gunfire of their own, though the Ya'mas still hoped to take Malik in alive. But the Israeli intelligence and counterterrorist officers, huddled behind their armored jeeps, sensed how this night would end. Colonel Baruch had already summoned the D9.

The Shin Bet officer asked Malik's father if he would mind going back inside the house to plead with his son to surrender. There was a pantomime of respect and honor that had to be adhered to, and it was important to enable the family patriarch to play a central role in Malik's surrender. The father agreed, and as one of the Speakers attended to the loudspeaker informing Malik that his father was entering the location alone and that he shouldn't shoot, Malik's father walked inside his daughter's home with a resigned expression of fear.

The meeting between father and son, inside the darkened caverns of the spacious building, lasted for nearly twenty minutes. It was already past midnight. Legions of Israeli counterterrorist specialists and IDF paratroopers waited anxiously while father and son talked. The crowds outside the perimeter grew larger and the tension level rose dramatically with each minute that passed. Palestinian police units in Hebron retreated to their headquarters and refused to return to the streets. Hamas gunmen were nowhere to be found. Ya'mas officers taking aim on the house knew that the center of Hebron was a terrible location for a Pressure Cooker.

Malik's father walked out of the house with his hands in the air as he left his son. He had bad news for the assembled Israeli officers: Malik refused to surrender. The Shin Bet asked Malik's father to go back into the house again and again. Each time the old man emerged with his hands in the air, the answer from his son was the same. After he emerged from the house the third and final time, the father told the Shin Bet agents not to worry, though—his son promised that he wouldn't allow the army to destroy his sister's house. Ya'mas operators knew what that meant. Hayim ordered his men to be extra sharp, extra alert, for any attempt by Malik to rush outside and blow himself up. The D9 was ordered in.

A Ya'mas officer climbed atop the high tracks of the D9 to sit next to the bulldozer's driver inside his protective cocoon of ballistic steel and transparent armor. The unit was still surrounding the building, and it was imperative that their safety be considered when the D9 slowly raised its steel blade and began to destroy the structure. The treads of the D9 chewed up the Hebron pavement as it pushed forward; Ya'mas operators trained their weapons on the windows and the front door. The D9 tapped the building slightly, causing some of the bricks to shift. When Malik emerged out of the darkness, he crouched into the firing position of a man who had had firearms training. He fired wildly, trying to advance as he shot, and take out at least one Ya'mas operator before he, too, was killed.[8] More than a dozen Ya'mas operators returned fire. Malik was killed by the fusillade of fire. What was left of him lay strewn about the street.

Malik's parents screamed off in the distance. The radio chatter on the Israeli frequencies intensified. A military ambulance was rushed into the secure corridor to remove Malik's remains.

The Ya'mas operators were ordered into the sister's house to search for terrorists who might be hiding inside closets or in secret storage areas; they also searched for any explosive devices or firearms, as well as any intelligence material that could be of use. Floor by floor, hallway by hallway, room by room, and closet by closest, the Ya'mas force searched every inch of the home. The men took no chances. Locked closets were riddled with automatic weapons fire just in case one of Malik's comrades was hiding out in a secret crawl space, hoping for one final encounter with Israeli forces.

The Ya'mas operators emerged from the building without an explosive vest and without any other telltale links connecting Malik to the larger cell. Most of the men could have assessed how the events would unfold that night. Hamas terrorists almost never surrendered.

It was almost dawn by the time the men departed Hebron. The sun was rising over the Jordan River.

There wasn't enough coffee in the Hebron Brigade mess hall to flush out the exhaustion from the bones of the men who had worked the Malik arrest operation. The clinical description would have explained that they had been awake for over twenty-four hours, but in reality the men had managed little more than twelve hours of sleep in five days. There was still a lot of work to do before the unit could call it a day. There were last-minute sign-offs and arrangements to be made with the brigade staff and the Shin Bet contingent who worked the region. There was equipment to account for, pack up, and return to the cargo holds of their vehicles. For some, there was breakfast.

The drive back to Jerusalem brought the convoy straight into rush-hour traffic. Fridays were bad traffic days in the Israeli capital—the Muslim *sabt* was under way and preparations for the Jewish Sabbath were in full swing. Several dozen very tired men returned to their home base shortly before 1:00 a.m. They unloaded their gear, safeguarded their weapons, and washed their faces with cold water. The unit cook brewed several pots of coffee; knowing how the Druze and Bedouin drank theirs, cardamom was added to the strong, black, mud-like brew to give it that extra boost and turn it into rocket fuel. Then the entire group assembled in the briefing room. Everyone had to be there—no exceptions.

There was a postmortem performed after every Israeli military or police operation—regardless of size and scope, success or failure. The process was even more involved and complex for the special operations and counterterrorist components. Each and every man that participated in an operation was required to review his performance, explain his moments of brilliance and his absentminded mistakes. The debriefing sessions were honest and open and not for those with thin skins and fragile egos. The purpose of these gatherings was to fine-tune an already very fine-tuned machine so that it ran smoother, more effectively, and safer the next dark night in Hebron, or wherever else the unit might find itself. The discussions lasted for hours. Each debriefing always began with succinct recountings of movements and positioning, and continued hours later into discussions of tactics and innovation. Many of the ingredients of what outside observers call Israel's magical way of executing special operations originated in these frank and fair post-mission analysis discussions.

By the time the unit had reviewed every angle and every element of the Malik operation, there was still work to do. The intelligence officer and his NCO attended to the material that had assembled on their desks during the week; the weapons officer checked the ammunition supplies and made sure that the unit's armory was ready for next week's operation and perhaps the weekend's call-out. The team whose turn it was to be the district's special response force showered while everyone was still around, and then suited up to be ready to react to any tactical situation at a moment's notice.

Many of the men headed home at the height of the midday sun, when a brilliant glow of light basked the stone streets of Jerusalem with warmth. Some of the operators lived inside the city, less than a few miles from base, but they hadn't been home in a week. Others, living near Tel Aviv, or to the north, prepared for the long drive home. If they were lucky, the stores would still be open so that they could buy a bouquet of flowers for the Sabbath table, or a toy for their children—there were lots of school plays, soccer games, and meals that had been missed that week and the countless weeks beforehand.

The operators filed out of the unit's headquarters and went their separate ways, confident that taking out Malik had ultimately saved lives. As they drove away, to points all around, and looked out their windshields to see people going about their business and living average and seemingly uninterrupted lives, they wondered how many of these lives had been spared by a hesitant suicide bomber and the relentless work of the Shin Bet in tracking him—and his colleagues—down. But nothing was ever that cut-and-dry in the murky world of Israeli counterterrorism. Because Malik had opted for martyrdom rather than a prison cell, the Shin Bet never got the chance to talk to him and try to piece together the links in the terror chain that would lead to Imad Qawasmeh and perhaps those who were above him in the Hamas hierarchy. The fact that Qawasmeh was now in hiding—deep hiding—troubled the men as they headed home.

At 1450 hours on the afternoon of August 31, 2004, the No. 6 bus crossing Rager Boulevard in the heart of Beersheba erupted into a fiery ball of death and destruction. The blast shattered windows hundreds of feet away, and shrapnel from the bus—and the bomb—peppered city hall, a short distance away. Beersheba, Israel's population center of the south, in the Negev Desert, had been spared the catastrophic bloodshed endured by Israel's other cities. But Beersheba was only twenty-six miles southwest of Hebron. The security barrier—and the efforts of units like the Ya'mas—so limited the ability of the

Hamas Hebron command to infiltrate suicide bombers into Jerusalem that new targets had to be found. Beersheba—a relaxed, close-knit town that was known for its Bedouin markets and renowned university—was a target of practical convenience for Hamas planners.

Two minutes later, as police and emergency medical crews rushed to the remains of the smoldering bus, the No. 12 bus, approximately one hundred meters away, erupted in a blinding explosive flash followed by a deafening eardrum-popping thud.

The city's intersecting downtown boulevards of sandstone high-rises and rows of plush palm trees were engulfed in clouds of thick, acrid black smoke. Beersheba had never seen anything like this before. Burned bodies had been flung against the windows and at the entrance to the bus, the head of the firefighting services said, bodies burned in the bus, and people were trapped inside and on the ground, crying for help.[9] Those who could be saved were rushed to the city's Soroka Hospital, which boasted—thanks to receiving a steady stream of combat casualties from Gaza—one of the most experienced trauma centers in Israel. Orthodox volunteers from Zaka crawled on their hands and knees for hours, trying to gather up all the flesh and bone fragments from the kill zones around each destroyed bus. The force of both blasts was so powerful that it was nearly impossible for Israeli forensic experts to identify which limb fragment belonged to which victim. Sixteen people were killed in the twin bombing; more than 150 were seriously wounded. The youngest victim was a toddler, a three-and-a-half-year-old boy, who was sitting on his mother's lap.

The two bombers were identified as twenty-two-year-old Nassem Jabari and twenty-six-year-old Ahmad Qawasmeh, both of Hebron. The two were seen posing, in martial stances, in front of posters of slain Hamas founder Sheikh Ahmed Yassin, in a videotaped living will released to the Reuters office in Ramallah, and in photographs and posters that were disseminated throughout the West Bank just hours after the bombing.

The Jerusalem Ya'mas—along with other IDF special operations units—would be in Hebron to prepare the homes of the two bombers for demolition and to hunt down the man who'd masterminded the Beersheba bombings—the same Imad Qawasmeh who had recruited and dispatched Malik Salem Matzbah Nasser A-Din to the Café Caffit six weeks earlier.[10]

When the intelligence was analyzed and his name attached to the carnage, Shin Bet case agents and Jerusalem Ya'mas operators felt as if they had been kicked in the gut. They wondered how the fate of the victims in Beersheba would have been altered if only they could have captured Malik alive.

Imad Qawasmeh, unlike Malik, was unwilling to die in a blaze of glory. On the morning of October 13, 2004, a Ya'ma'm and IDF task force apprehended Qawasmeh as he tried to hide inside the family home in the heart of Hebron. A Shin Bet tip had proved to be spot-on, and Israeli forces had little difficulty pulling the Hamas commander out of a hiding spot and placing him in handcuffs. Wearing nothing but a pair of much-weathered white underwear, the chubby thirty-one-year-old terrorist chieftain was blindfolded and led outside of his home by a team of heavily armed operators as crowds looked on.[11]

He did not resist arrest.

CHAPTER SIXTEEN

Anywhere We Want
by Any Means We Choose

The industry of terror required a full-time labor force. There were worker bees—men and women whose names and faces all began to look alike and sound alike to the Shin Bet and Military Intelligence investigators. These were the people who smuggled bullets in bags, hid weapons in their homes, and brought food to the men hiding in the safe houses. There were the contractors, as well. Women hired to walk arm in arm with a suicide bomber on his way to a target, and men with Israeli identification cards who provided taxi service to the suicide bombers on their way to martyrdom. The suicide bombers—those who actually blew themselves up and those who ended up as guests of the Israeli security services because of cold feet or technical malfunction—were the salesmen of the intifada. These bombers, nameless nobodies who were promised their commissions in paradise, were insignificant in life and glorified after death. But the names and faces of the men who recruited them, armed them, and dispatched them on their way—the mid-level managers of the terror corporations—were engraved inside the eyelids of the Shin Bet case agents who hunted them; the agents saw these men in their sleep and spent endless hours following leads and cultivating sources that would lead to their deaths or arrests. But these mid-level transients were just expendable executives. The true masterminds of destruction—the CEOs, COOs, and CFOs of the corporate web of terror who were compensated generously by their board of directors in Beirut, Damascus, or Tehran—truly controlled the conflict, though none would ever think it worthy to become martyrs themselves. Their names and faces mattered. Khalil Mahsin was one such man.

By appearances alone, Mahsin was an unremarkable man. His hair and beard were salt-and-pepper, and the paunch he carried was typical for a man in his fifties. Mahsin could easily have been mistaken for a merchant, a teacher, or another one of those invisible middle-aged men who never warrant a second look. He was married with children; he owned a home in the city of Yatta. But Mahsin was the head of the PIJ in Hebron. He had, at his fingertips, access to hundreds of thousands of dollars, or dinars, straight from Hezbollah and Iranian Revolutionary Guard bank accounts, drawn on Syrian banks, and funneled to the West Bank electronically or through smuggled bundles of cash. Mahsin could dispatch one messenger out into the night and summon several hundred men with AK-47s ready to do battle with Israeli forces. Mahsin ran a terrorist franchise that was strong and vibrant, for powers and interests that were far away.

Mahsin had maintained a spot atop the Shin Bet's list of top terror chieftains still on the run for nearly a decade. The name *Harakat al-Jihad al-Islami fi Filastin*, or Palestine Islamic Jihad, first entered the Shin Bet lexicon in August 1987, when militants using the name of the organization took credit for the assassination of the IDF Military Police commander in Gaza. Over the years the PIJ would take credit for lethal attacks on Israeli buses and even the machine gun massacre of Israeli tourists as they traveled on a sightseeing bus in the Sinai Desert on February 4, 1990.[1] The organization thrived as a secretive and highly compartmentalized entity—both when Israel controlled the Gaza Strip and the West Bank and after, when the Palestinian Authority was created. Both Hamas and the PIJ enjoyed strong links to the Palestinian Diaspora in the United States—especially in the realm of fundraising. The head of the PIJ, Dr. Ramadan Abdullah Shalah, was born in the Shejai'ya District of Gaza in 1958 and had been a professor at the University of South Florida at Tampa before departing for Damascus in 1995 to run the terrorist group; his predecessor, Dr. Fathi Shiqaqi, was gunned down on October 26, 1995, in front of the Diplomat Hotel in Sliema, Malta, by a hit team composed of—according to published accounts—two Mossad gunmen. The PIJ always played second fiddle to Hamas, and Shiqaqi was assassinated shortly after the PIJ—following in the footsteps of Hamas—perpetrated suicide bombings against Israeli civilians. The PIJ's first suicide bombing was also one of its most lethal. On the morning of January 22, 1995, a Palestinian suicide bomber blew himself up at a bus stop and road side stand in Beit Lid Junction, approximately a mile east of Netanya. The area was crowded with unsuspecting soldiers returning to their bases in the West Bank after the weekend, and the destruction of the blast killed and wounded scores of them. Several minutes later a second bomber, also disguised as an Israeli soldier, blew himself up in the same location, killing many of those who had been wounded in the first blast, as well as passersby and first responders who had rushed to the scene. The attack, which killed nineteen and wounded more than one hundred, was the first "double tap" suicide bombing ever perpetrated against Israel. Reportedly, a third bomb—for a third bomber—had been left behind at the scene to be used later when Israeli dignitaries visited the crime scene.

The Shin Bet hunted the PIJ's West Bank leadership after the blast, and Mahsin had been on the run ever since. Hebron, though, was not an easy town for PIJ aspirations. The PIJ was strongest in the northern tiers of Samaria, where the West Bank brushed up against the roadways leading to Galilee and Israel's northern frontier with Lebanon. Hebron was without question a Hamas stronghold. Both the PIJ and Hamas, when necessity dictated, cooperated—after all, the Middle East had for centuries been run on the fuel that the enemy of my enemy is my friend. Yet both the PIJ and Hamas competed for Iranian money and Hezbollah favor. Hamas had been a truly populist-centric force inside Hebron, with political threads that mirrored Hezbollah's rise in Lebanon as a fringe and minority terrorist group to major power brokers inside the Lebanese government. The PIJ refused to participate in the parlor games of Palestinian Authority politics: They were a military resistance group, a proxy army of Iran, and at night their fighters emerged from their hiding holes to embark on military training and live-fire exercises.

The PIJ branch in Hebron had professed its military proficiency in promotional videos that were shared online, and in posters plastered throughout the Kasbah at night. The PIJ also fought the Israelis head-on when possible—yet almost always on their own terms.

On Friday night, November 15, 2002, the last of the Jewish worshippers had just concluded prayers at the Tomb of the Patriarchs in Hebron and walked home to the settlement of Kiryat Arba a kilometer away. The worshippers always walked with an IDF and Border Guard escort, especially for the last stretch of pathway known as the Worshipper's Route, almost a kilometer in length, which connected Hebron with Kiryat Arba. The Worshipper's Way, as the roadway was known, was narrow and treacherous. In some areas it was shielded on both sides by Palestinian homes that commanded the high ground overlooking the sensitive roadway. Other parts of the path splintered off into a maze of darkened alleyways covered by stone walls; some areas of the roadway were tree-lined. The soldiers and Border Guards walked the settlers back to the southern gate of Kiryat Arba, where heavily armed local security guards let them in. The settlers wished the soldiers a good Shabbat and then headed home, where the festive Friday night meals were waiting for them.

The Palestinians of Hebron were also enjoying their Friday night dinner. The smell of lamb stews cooking cut through cold Judean Hill winter winds. The soldiers—four infantrymen from the IDF's Nahal Brigade, supported by an up-armored Border Guard jeep—heard pots and pans banging together in nearby kitchens as they slowly walked back toward their fortified observation post—weapons at the ready—weighed down by their body armor, load-bearing equipment, and heavy winter parkas. It was 1930 when the shooting began.[2]

Three PIJ terrorists—one positioned near the Kiryat Arba gate and two others lying in wait along the path, concealed by concrete walls and the tree line—opened fire at the Israeli soldiers from what appeared to be point-blank range; each terrorist carried an M16 assault rifle and was equipped with eight thirty-round magazines.[3] Two of the infantrymen were killed instantly in the opening burst of fire; a third, a combat medic, was cut down as he rushed to assist a wounded soldier. The terrorist assault was so intense that the transparent armor in the Border Guard jeep buckled and shattered in the spall of the murderous fire. All four policemen inside the vehicle were killed.

Colonel Dror Weinberg, the Hebron Brigade commander, happened to be the duty officer for the entire region that night. The moment that the first reports of an attack buzzed through the emergency frequency, the former Sayeret Mat'kal team leader grabbed his tactical kit and responded to the kill zone. The belief was that the terrorists had broken off contact with the patrol and disappeared into the darkness, but when Weinberg arrived along with his cadre of staff officers to assess the situation, they were met by a murderous volley of fire. Colonel Weinberg was shot in the chest and stomach; he died moments later. Weinberg's junior officers engaged the terrorists in a pitched battle, and they were joined by residents from Kiryat Arba. The settlers managed to isolate and kill one of the Palestinians, but they soon found themselves in a lethal cross fire. Three members of the Kiryat Arba security team were shot and killed in the exchange of gunfire.

When Weinberg was killed, Superintendent Samih Sweidan, the operations officer for the Border Guard company stationed in Hebron, assumed command of a rapidly deteriorating situation. The thirty-one-year-old Bedouin from the village of Arab al-Aramshe, which sat in the rough hills that straddled the treacherous border with Lebanon, had spent a good part of his military career with the paratroopers fighting Hezbollah in villages like his own. An exemplary officer, he transferred to the Border Guard and excelled in what was considered the volatile Hebron post. Sweidan was in the unit mess hall that Friday night talking about his two young children when the radio frequency broke in with the frantic sounds of men in battle. Superintendent Sweidan grabbed his gear and raced toward the firefight, maneuvering tight turns in the ancient city at speeds that defied the laws of gravity. The two surviving PIJ terrorists were lying in wait. In a brief exchange of gunfire, Superintendent Sweidan was killed moments after arriving.

Reinforcements continued to stream into the area. The battle for Worshipper's Way continued for several hours inside the dark Hebron cold. Additional units arrived for the battle. Duvdevan arrived. The Ya'ma'm was mobilized.

One of the gunmen was killed near the Border Guard jeep peppered with bullets in the first moments of the attack; the second terrorist was cornered and killed on a roof over one of the nearby alleys. Twelve Israeli soldiers, Border Guard policemen, and civilian security personnel were killed that night and another fourteen wounded. It was the deadliest shooting attack against Israeli forces of the entire intifada.

The Shin Bet vowed to crush the PIJ in Hebron following the battle for Worshipper's Way. But Khalil Mahsin commanded such a highly effective terrorist force inside the city and the villages that surrounded Hebron that the Israelis found it difficult to penetrate. On Friday night, December 27, 2002, two PIJ terrorists wearing IDF uniforms and carrying assault rifles and knapsacks loaded with antipersonnel grenades infiltrated the Orthodox settlement of Otniel, located in the southern Hebron Hills west of Yatta, a city of fifty thousand residents a few miles south of Hebron. They cut a path through the thick rows of barbed-wire concertina and proceeded toward the communal dining hall where more than one hundred seminary students had assembled for the Friday night dinner. The terrorists opened fire as they burst through the kitchen entrance, but an alert student locked the sliding doors leading to the dining hall. Four of the students were killed in the attack, and dozens more were wounded. Responding IDF units, including Bedouin trackers to pursue one of the gunmen who fled, killed both terrorists.[4]

Khalil Mahsin was already one of the most wanted men in Judea by the time the press release from Damascus claimed responsibility for the attack in Otniel. Soon, the Shin Bet intensified its efforts to locate the elusive terrorist chieftain, but the agency was overwhelmed by its workload. There were hundreds of major terror suspects in each city; there were thousands of men, low-level operatives, whom the Shin Bet needed to talk to in order to develop leads that would result in a capture or a kill. Sometimes the man hours invested into locating one man revealed nothing but futility and frustration. A Shin Bet case agent could not maintain his sanity—or be any good at his job—if he wasn't made up of three parts stubbornness and four parts resolve. Patience was also a key component in any Shin Bet agent's DNA. In early May 2003, the Shin Bet laid its hands on Nur Jabar, Mahsin's military commander in Hebron; Jabar received seventeen life sentences for his role in the Worshipper's Way and Otniel attacks.[5] Soon, many of Mahsin's key lieutenants and deputies were dead or in Israeli custody.

Life on the run wasn't easy for a middle-aged man—especially one with a wife and children. Exhaustion and falling into the trap of routine were lethal for men on the run. Virtually every one of Israel's top-tier counterterrorist units raided homes, caves, hideouts, and cellars where they believed Mahsin was hiding. Mahsin's survival instincts—according to one of the men who hunted him—were razor-sharp. But even the most carefully shaped blade sometimes became dull and sluggish. The Shin Bet waited.

In January 2005, it was election time in the Palestinian Authority, a time when the ballot box and the AK-47 were of indistinguishable importance. It had been a few months since Arafat's death; Arafat, weakened to a trembling recluse inside the *Muqata* after Defensive Shield, succumbed to a rapid and mysterious ailment and died in a Paris hospital. Shin Bet agents working the Hebron area were busy monitoring the campaigning leading up to the election in the hope that some wanted Hamas commanders would emerge from their life on the run. And then the mundane turned into exhilaration.

The Shin Bet had learned that Mahsin was making regular trips home to be with his wife and children. Even men with a price on their head get complacent and sloppy. He began to shed some of the erratic trappings of a man on the run—bodyguards and sleeping in a different location every night. The visits were in the evening—family dinners and some intimate moments with his spouse. For nine years the Shin Bet had come close—but only close enough to find empty rooms and teakettles that were still warm. But this intelligence, it was believed, was spot on target.

It was January 12, 2005, when the Shin Bet case agent called the Ya'mas intelligence officer with a question, the answer to which was obvious. "Are you interested in this job?" the agent asked. The answer was always yes. As usual, the call came through well after midnight. The Jerusalem Ya'mas was in Hebron by dawn.

The planning of Mahsin's apprehension began after an early breakfast. Ya'mas intelligence and operations officers hovered over a long worktable to examine aerial photographs of the Yatta neighborhood where Mahsin lived and the many access routes that could lead them to and from the target. A cloud of cigarette smoke billowed to the lamp overhead. The intelligence officers commented that Palestinian security forces would be on high alert in Hebron and in its suburban satellite of Yatta, where Mahsin's wife and children lived in a modest home with a marble-tiled porch and a small garden; they warned that Palestinian elections were definitely chaotic and potentially violent. Ahmed Abbas, Arafat's successor as president of the Palestinian Authority, (also known by his nom de guerre of Abu Mazen), had his security services out in force to make sure that the opposition parties—including Hamas and the smaller Communist groups all funded through Syria—were deterred by the uniforms and weapons on the street.

That many guns on the street presented the Ya'mas with a worrisome reality: There would be more checkpoints than usual at key junctions and intersections, and that meant the odds that the undercover task force would be discovered by Palestinian security forces increased exponentially. Operationally, a target like Mahsin warranted a large force consisting of multiple elements of backup, but the more moving parts, Ya'mas commanders knew all too well, the more chances of there being a confrontation. On the street, with the need to summon tactical backup against an already on-alert Palestinian contingent, a confrontation could result in a large-scale battle. Politically, a shoot-out between Israeli counterterrorist forces and the Palestinian police so close to an election monitored by international groups would have ramifications in Jerusalem, Ramallah, and Washington, D.C. Ya'mas commanders—and the Shin Bet—all agreed to go after Khalil Mahsin with a small footprint: two undercover vehicles, nothing more. The timing of when to strike was all in Mahsin's hands, of course. The moment the Shin Bet learned—somehow from their means or sources—that Mahsin was home, the Ya'mas force would race out. No one knew exactly how long his visits were. Ya'mas officers hoped that they would receive the green light in the afternoon—before darkness fell—when Mahsin would take a break from his hearty midday meal. Hebron Brigade commander Colonel Motti Baruch approved of the plan. A Command Post was assembled quickly to coordinate the raid and possible rescue elements.

Outside of the Command Post, the operators checked their gear before the drive to Yatta. They fastened their load-bearing vests snugly around body armor corsets that they hoped would protect their midsections from automatic weapons fire and shrapnel. They checked their sidearms and M4s one final time, and tightened the straps that fastened their ballistic helmets to their heads. Hebron was in the throes of a frosty winter, and the tactical gloves the operators wore were needed more for warmth than for grip. The operators piled into the back of the two undercover vehicles and shut the cargo holds to conceal themselves. One of the Speakers, a Druze from northern Israel, checked his disguise in the side mirror of the vehicle one last time. He took a final drag on his cigarette and entered the vehicle. He took a deep breath to allow the adrenaline to dilute the fear before starting the truck.

Colonel Baruch had ordered that a drone be launched over the city. A corporal from IDF Intelligence Corps logged into the operational software with her password and began to type. The nineteen-year-old coughed in an exaggerated gesture to let everyone know her disapproval of the cigarette smoke and then gathered her dark, long curls with an elastic bow. She typed the date. January 13, 2005. She checked her wristwatch to log the time.

Khalil Mahsin had just finished lunch when the Ya'mas operators crossed the Israeli checkpoint and headed toward the Palestinian outpost that controlled access in and out of Yatta. The two vehicles, innocuous to the pedestrians on Route 3226 as nothing more than commercial vehicles, moved slowly through the city's traffic. The Speakers and the unit's operations cadre had preplanned a route that was deemed safe and quick, but the two vehicles suddenly came across something that no one had expected or planned for. Nearly eight hundred men, perhaps a thousand, moved quickly through the center of Yatta carrying Hamas signs and the photos of Hamas political candidates. They chanted Hamas slogans and they waved their fists—and their AK-47s—defiantly into the darkening skies of a winter's sunset. Once the swarm of men, many wearing the green headband of the jihad, came across the thoroughfare, the two vehicles were trapped. The drone operator, sitting back at brigade HQ, ordered the men out of there at once, but his instructions were too late and impossible to execute. The Ya'mas operators were trapped.

The demonstration was both joyous and angry—the mood was like that at an English soccer match. Some of the demonstrators banged on the vehicles to create a cadence for their rhyming chants; the men inside dared not breathe or heaven forbid cough and compromise the ruse. The fear and claustrophobia inside the darkened undercover vehicle was maddening. One slip of a rifle, one uncontrolled cough or sneeze, and an armored brigade wouldn't have pulled the men out alive. The Speakers were forced to put on an Academy Award–winning performance of deceit and calm. Some of the demonstrators stuck their heads inside the cab of the undercover vehicle and looked around. If anything had been out of place—a radio wire protruding from somewhere it shouldn't have been, or one concealed weapon that wasn't so concealed, and a dozen men would have been bludgeoned and ripped apart that late afternoon. Nothing would have saved them.

For nearly forty minutes, the demonstration blocked the main roads near the city center and the smaller lanes spreading out to the rest of the city. When the mass of armed humanity dissipated into the darkening dusk, the Ya'mas task force received the order to stand down. "We've just received word that he's left the location," the strike commander heard over his radio. "Find a spot to park and wait for further instructions."[6] The men inside the two vehicles tried to breathe, but they couldn't even allow themselves to move a muscle. The drivers parked separately, at opposite ends of a side street, near a row of stores; much to their chagrin, the pedestrian traffic that moved about and around was nonstop. The men inside the vehicles sat like stone statues, and they waited. For two long hours they waited for word that Mahsin had returned home, but the code word to proceed never came. Finally, Brigade HQ ordered the contingent back to base. By the time the men inside the vehicles could exit them in safety, their legs were so numb that many of the operators needed assistance to get out.

The Ya'mas day had ended. The men ate a quick dinner and then returned their equipment to their vehicles. There was always tomorrow.

The Ya'mas raiding force had spent nearly four unsuccessful hours inside Yatta. Hundreds—if not more—had had the chance to see their vehicles, look at their license plates, and wonder what company these vehicles belonged to. It would be operationally reckless to use the same vehicles two days in a row. Day two in the hunt for Khalil Mahsin would require a more creative approach.

The Ya'mas plan called for one squad of operators, all dressed like Palestinian laborers, to drive to Mahsin's house in an inconspicuous livery van that commonly brought day workers to and from their menial tasks throughout the area. The men would be completely in disguise and carry their assault rifles, tactical coveralls, helmets, body armor, and load-bearing equipment in green canvas kit bags that were hidden from view; a stretcher and the team's medical gear were also ingeniously hidden from outside view. When the vehicle neared the targeted home, under cover of darkness, the operators would take their gear with them and dress on the fly. Two men would dress while the third watched their backs. When the two were finished, the third man would suit up. Being undercover in what could develop into a shoot-out risked a blue-on-blue incident. The last thing the command echelon needed was friendly fire casualties in the heart of Hebron.

A second vehicle, a nondescript sedan, would travel to the target along a different, more circuitous route driven by a Beauty and Beast tandem, where one man was allowed to remain close to his own appearance while the other had to be disguised to look decrepit. Majalli,* the Speaker, would drive and be dressed like a typical resident. Yoni would be the passenger masquerading as an old man. Two men in a car was always viewed as innocuous and commonplace. A third operator, Shai, would cower in the trunk—in full tactical kit—and emerge when the sedan parked to the rear of Mahsin's home, in the courtyard of an adjacent mosque. Shai would move forward toward the house that had already been secured by the operators in the passenger van.

At just after 2000 hours, the call came in to the Shin Bet liaison at the Command Post that Mahsin was home. The operators were already sitting in the van. Shai cleared the trunk of the sedan and laid down an old carpet in the back to make the rough ride more comfortable—and less noisy. He was handed his M4 and the trunk was closed. The drone was already over Yatta.

Bright, festive lights had been strewn across the main avenues of the city, drooping over both lanes of traffic that still bustled late in the chilly night's darkness. The Palestinian policemen had retreated to the warmth of the space heaters in their offices and the piping hot tea they drank indoors that was so thick with sugar the mixing spoon often stood tall in the glass. The Ya'mas

---

* A pseudonym—true identity withheld for security considerations.

vehicles pushed through Yatta without challenge or even a red light. The drone flew a pattern over Mahsin's home. He was reported to still be indoors. No one was seen leaving the house.

Shai arrived first—as planned. Yoni sat in the passenger seat and emerged from the sedan slowly, cautiously. He glanced around carefully to make sure there were no eyes on him and then headed to the trunk. He let Shai out of the back and then quickly dressed in his tactical gear. The Speaker departed, allowing Shai and Yoni to rush to the twelve-o'clock side of the house—the back porch.

The Ya'mas van pulled into a slow stop behind the mosque across the street so delicately that the brakes didn't even squeak. The operators emerged silently, though swiftly; each man held a satchel containing a separate piece of gear for the team. They raced from the drop-off point behind the mosque and split into three groups to secure each corner of the house. It was critical that they be absolutely stealth-like. Mahsin's instincts were still sharp, even after nine years on the run, and the operators knew that if they made even the slightest compromising sound the PIJ commander would run into the darkness and once again disappear and become a *Shabah*, a ghost. Hebron was a great place to hide in, after all; there were hundreds of caves, some interconnecting, in the hills around the city.

The vehicles left to head back to base so that the Speakers would not be compromised. The arrest team—both components—were now on their own.

Before the main force could get into position, though, the drone operator reported that the target had emerged from the three-o'clock position, the house's front door, to smoke a cigarette. The operators laughed—even if for only a silent second—that a man who handled a king's ransom of Iranian money and who had so much blood on his hands was not allowed to smoke in his house. But then the sound of gunfire ripped through the windy darkness. The operators from the main force stopped in their tracks for a second, unsure of what had happened. They immediately donned their balaclavas and moved into position—assembling their tactical kit once they were secure in the corners of the house. Shai then indicated that the gunfire was his. Mahsin was taking a drag on his cigarette when he sensed a threat in the darkness. Mahsin tried to flee, and that's when Shai shot him in the legs. Mahsin was not armed—if he had been, Shai would have killed him.

The moment Shai fired three 5.56mm rounds into Khalil Mahsin's legs, the covert operation became overt. Because the mission was considered so sensitive—because of Mahsin's high value and his penchant for escaping the long arm of the law—the rescue force had positioned its response units far from Yatta so as not to alert any Palestinian intelligence spotters that "something" was afoot. It was now, in the ten minutes or so that the Ya'mas operators were alone securing Mahsin, that they were most vulnerable.

Although badly wounded, Mahsin tried to escape. He crawled along the cold marble entranceway, smearing blood in his efforts to move away from the Israeli operators. "Fuck your mothers, you sons of whores," he yelled in flawless Hebrew. The operators were impressed, though unmoved. They secured their prisoner and secured the perimeter. Mahsin's wife and extended family attempted to rush out into the courtyard and intervene, but they were held at bay. The operators were in no mood to be challenged, yet they were also careful to adhere to the key cultural protocols in dealing with Muslim women so as not to dishonor them—no physical contact and no verbal insults. Several of the Ya'mas operators explained to the family members that they had to search the house for explosives and weapons. The Arabic intimacy, as well as the cultural keys in dealing with women and homes, was essential in neutralizing a potentially explosive situation.

As the Ya'mas team deployed and secured their position, the operators were startled when the lights and sirens of a private ambulance from a nearby Islamic medical clinic punctured the darkness. "We're here to treat the patient," one of the medics said. The Ya'mas operators shook their heads in disbelief that the family would call for an ambulance. They quickly dispatched the crew in some very direct—and pointed—words in Arabic.

And then the gunfire erupted. Several volleys of AK-47 fire were fired at them from nearby alleys. Tracer rounds illuminated the black sky, and the sounds of the lead projectiles whizzing too close to everyone's head from long range was unnerving. Shai summoned the backup force, wondering where they were. They were minutes out.

When help came, it came in a massive show of force. The Ya'mas perimeter was widened to make room for the companies of paratroopers, all in full combat kit, that responded. Mahsin was evacuated in an IDF ambulance to a military hospital in Israel where he would be treated for his gunshot wounds.

The Ya'mas operators on scene were evacuated in an armored bus. The IDF left shortly thereafter. It would be an early night for the Ya'mas. After they unloaded their gear, returned to base, and debriefed, they turned in sometime before 4:00 a.m. the following morning. They would get a couple hours of sleep before returning to work in the Palestinian neighborhoods of East Jerusalem.

Khalil Mahsin had been wanted by the Shin Bet for nine long years. He had been a fugitive from the long arm of Israeli forces, and during that time of living in caves and never sleeping in the same bed twice, he had built a successful and lavishly funded terrorist infrastructure that was militarily proficient and highly compartmentalized. Mahsin's PIJ army in Hebron killed the highest-ranking IDF officer to die during the intifada, and it invested enormous resources to spread its operations north, toward the Israeli capital. Killing Mahsin would have been an easier task once his location was confirmed. An AH-64 Apache could have launched a Hellfire missile and obliterated him into shards of flesh once he walked out the front door to light his cigarette. But there could have been collateral damage of such a strike, and the intelligence he yielded was priceless when compared to the operational justification for—and satisfaction of—his death.

Mahsin's capture all but single-handedly dismantled the operational effectiveness of the PIJ in the Hebron area. The Mahsins of the intifada were ending up dead or in prison thanks to the impressive capabilities of Israeli intelligence and the resolve of men who did not hesitate to enter into the darkness of terrorist-controlled confines on a cold winter's night.

CHAPTER SEVENTEEN

O' Jerusalem

The reconnaissance sortie was routine. The pre-operational eyes-on-target look at a targeted neighborhood, a targeted street, and possibly, the men who were the focus of the arrest raid, was an integral element of many Yamas raids. So when the Shin Bet case officer provided the Ya'mas with the file of a suspected terrorist cell—one that was planning a catastrophic wave of suicide bombings inside Jerusalem—the men whose job it would be to formulate an actionable tactical takedown plan selected a suitable vehicle from the motor pool, proceeded to select their costumes from a large wardrobe inside the unit's armory, and headed in the direction of the Old City. Sometimes, an intelligence-gathering drive by the target didn't require more than two operators. Majalli drove. He had earned his stripes fighting the knuckle-scraping battles atop the Temple Mount when the intifada erupted. Yoni was his partner, one of the old hands in the force, the longest serving member of the unit. They were considered the true experts at the Beauty and Beast tandems. Majalli, as usual, was allowed to retain his olive good looks, while Yoni, as was custom, masqueraded as an old man in need of a bath and a Laundromat.

Both men, their sidearms hidden deep inside holsters concealed in their disguises, drove a carefully plotted route toward Ras al-Amud, a Palestinian neighborhood of twelve thousand souls southeast of the Old City and only a few steps outside the walls from the al-Aqsa mosque and the Temple Mount. Ras al-Amud was something of a dichotomy—it was a neighborhood that during peaceful times catered gleefully to the tens of thousands of tourists from around the world who flocked to the Western Wall, but there was always a violent underbelly to the area, a series of narrow streets and apartment blocks that boasted tangible signs of being a bastion of terrorist activity.

Routine Border Guard patrols there were targeted by rocks and bottles. The special operations units working the Jerusalem District—Unit 33, Matilan, and the Ya'mas—were frequent visitors. Hamas and the al-Aqsa Martyrs Brigade maintained a vibrant presence in the area. The Jerusalem cells had, traditionally, been among the most violent throughout the intifada.

Although Majalli and Yoni knew Ras al-Amud like the back of their hands, it was an operational necessity to compare the Shin Bet intelligence with what both men saw with their own eyes at street level. There was an endless slew of preplanning questions that could only be answered with a street-level view: Was the targeted area isolated or was it inundated with pedestrians? How narrow were the streets and where should the assault vehicles be positioned for the raid? What were the best locations for snipers? Because the targeted cell was planning a bombing campaign, even worst case–scenario questions, such as how accessible the area was to fire trucks, were essential in the pre-raid reconnaissance. As Majalli and Yoni maneuvered their beat-up undercover sedan into Ras al-Amud, carefully past a row of shops and a block of flats above it, they noticed discrepancies between what they could see with their own eyes and what was noted in the Shin Bet report. Even though it had carried out thousands of operations during the intifada, the unit had managed to survive the fighting without suffering any combat fatalities or serious injuries because of such meticulous preparation.

Days later, under a crimson sunset, a Ya'mas team ventured to Ras al-Amud armed with a battle plan devised around the reconnaissance. Snipers were positioned atop rooftop perches, and the Speakers carefully inserted the men in battle rattle into the congested area. The terrorists, captured without a shot being fired, had been planning to dispatch a suicide bomber against a popular café in the heart of town when it was packed with people. It was June 2005, nearly five years into the intifada, and the men captured in the Ya'mas operation had earned their stripes fighting the Israelis in the trenches of Jerusalem but had little to show for their efforts. Hamas and the other groups had failed them. Israel, at least in Jerusalem, had won the war. On the sunny afternoon of September 22, 2004, at just before 1600 hours, an eighteen-year-old Palestinian woman from Nablus walked up toward a hitchhiking post and bus stop in Jerusalem's northern French Hill neighborhood, on the main road that headed south toward the Dead Sea. The woman, a hijab covering her face and modest clothing draped over her small frame, struggled with a heavy bag as she walked to a group of Israeli soldiers and students waiting for a ride. The woman sparked the suspicion of two Border Guard policemen—Lance Corporal Menashe Komemi and Lance Corporal Mamoya Tahio—who were on patrol in the area looking out for suicide bombers. The two young conscripts moved to question the young Palestinian woman, and demanded to search her bag and her person. She refused. And as the two Border policemen moved to detain her, she pulled a toggle switch and detonated the five kilograms of densely packed explosives that her handlers in the Askar refugee camp in Nablus had prepared for her. The two conscripts were killed in the explosion. The blast was so powerful that it destroyed the bus shelter, propelling shards of glass and twisted bits of metal and bone hundreds of feet away. First responders rushing to the scene had experienced the corrosive stench of burned rubber and scorched flesh before.

Immediately after the blast, police units rushed toward the checkpoints that separated Jerusalem from the West Bank to prevent additional bombers from entering the city. But the bomber, claimed by the al-Aqsa Martyrs Brigade, had been the only human cruise missile sent into Israel that day. The French Hill bombing, the third suicide bombing at the northern tip of the city, was the last suicide bombing inside Jerusalem during the al-Aqsa intifada.

Jerusalem had been battered during the intifada like no other city in Israel. For five years, the Israeli capital had been subjected to dozens of attacks that resulted in nearly two hundred civilians killed, and scores more wounded. Jerusalem residents may have shrugged off those terrible years as par for the course: another layer of scar-tissue armor inside that stubborn Israeli psyche of whatever doesn't kill you makes you stronger. But there were few places inside the city where Jerusalem's citizens felt safe. The bombers struck in the leafy upscale neighborhoods, and they hit in the gritty working-class sections of town. There was a collective numbness to the carnage that could perhaps be explained by a municipally felt outbreak of post-traumatic stress disorder. Parents feared the worst every time their telephones rang. Many to this day still are haunted by the fear of being notified that a loved one boarded the wrong bus or decided to sit at the wrong café.

The men who spearheaded the counterterrorist efforts in Jerusalem, inside the ranks of the Ya'mas, lived through a horrific period of unending stress and ceaseless operations. There was nothing clean about the Ya'mas war—nothing push-button or remote. The arrest raids required that the operators enter people's homes and search rooms where small children slept in cribs next to closets where hand grenades and AK-47s were stored. There was nothing romantic about undercover warfare, just bloodshot eyes and a daily grind that ran on nicotine and nerves. The men may have used James Bond tactics of deception and disguise in their work, but theirs was no James Bond lifestyle. The Ya'mas war was one of great personal sacrifice. Unit personnel missed their children's soccer games and their wives' birthday celebrations. The children of close to one hundred men spent a good part of their childhoods asking their mothers, "*Eifo Aba?*" "Where's Dad?" Dad was nearby, a short drive away, but he was undercover in Silwan, gathering intelligence on a terrorist cell responsible for the murders of dozens of men, women, and children, or Dad was in the outskirts of Bethlehem shooting it out with Hamas gunmen.

To many in the unit—men who were still young enough to be thrilled by the work and too overworked to remember the details of every raid and every stakeout—the counterterrorist campaign in Jerusalem was a fight void of landmarks or turning points. There were no pivotal engagements on which the conflict hinged; the intifada didn't simply die; it petered out. The Ya'mas—like their counterparts elsewhere—fought a war of attrition against all of the Palestinian terrorist factions. Whoever was still left standing would ultimately be declared the winner.

The Ya'mas did not win this campaign on its own, of course. Jerusalem's policemen and policewomen waged a tireless campaign of alert deterrence. The controversial yet irrefutably effective separation barrier played an integral part in keeping terrorists out of the city. The Shin Bet were masters at infiltrating the ranks of all the terrorist factions, brilliant at the tradecraft of infiltrating the most compartmentalized of terrorist cells. The longer the intifada raged, the more entrenched the Shin Bet capabilities became. And with this intimate intelligence portal came special operations raids that apprehended men with murder on their minds.

Winston Churchill, when speaking of the brave Royal Air Force pilots who saved Great Britain during the blitzkrieg, said, "Never has so much been owed by so many to so few." The men of the Jerusalem Ya'mas fought the fight of their lives inside a trip wire of a battlefield that was the most contested patch of real estate on the planet. They fought this relentless campaign because there simply was no other option. There was no other choice. The men of the Ya'mas spearheaded a dedicated campaign to guarantee that Jerusalem survived the relentless terrorist blitz.

BOOK THREE

THE GAZA STRIP

CHAPTER EIGHTEEN

In the Footsteps of the Philistines

Imad Hassan Imbrahim Akel had fiery ambitions that were fueled by vengeance. Akel was born in Jebalya, a United Nations–administered refugee camp in the Gaza Strip, in July 1971. Born four years after the thunderous Arab defeat in the Six Day War, Akel was raised under Israeli rule in a religious home. He had dreamed of being a pharmacist, but he had also been drawn into the life of Islamic militancy as a member of the nefarious organization that would soon become known to the world as Hamas. At the age of eighteen, Akel became a street fighter. Like many of his comrades, he was arrested by Israeli security forces and spent eighteen months in prison. Because he was known to the Shin Bet as an active participant in a terrorist organization, the Shin Bet reportedly vetoed his request to study Islamic law in Amman. Trapped inside Gaza, Imad Akel would become the commander of the military arm of Hamas.

The Izzedine al-Qassam Brigade took its name from a fiery Islamic cleric from Jenin killed by British forces in 1935 and was created by Salah Shehada, one of the founders of the Hamas terror network, who organized teams of roaming hit squads that targeted Arafat loyalists and suspected collaborators with the Shin Bet. The intifada widened the scope of these activities to include attacks against Israeli civilians and soldiers. One of the first Izzedine al-Qassam Brigade campaigns was the kidnapping and murder of two IDF soldiers, Avi Sasportas and Ilan Saadon in 1989.* By 1991, the military foot soldiers of the Hamas had grown in size and scope into a full-fledged underground army that openly engaged Israeli forces in terrorist operations. Akel had impressed the Hamas leadership with his combat skills and organizational capabilities, and he was ordered to the West Bank to establish Izzedine al-Qassam cells in the major towns and villages. Akel specialized in the ambushes of Israeli military patrols in the West Bank and in Gaza, and he had been personally responsible for eleven murders, and the wounding of nearly fifty others. Hamas took notice. In May 1992, Akel was appointed commander of all Hamas forces in the West Bank and Gaza. The Shin Bet also took notice. Every Shin Bet case agent in the Strip memorized the haunted pale complexion, faint beard, and thick widow's peak of the young man they hunted.

For two years, Akel evaded the Israeli dragnet. He never slept in the same bed twice and moved about only at night, all the while commanding an underground army of hardcore terrorists who became more emboldened with each operation. The very best of Israel's special operations units hunted him, but no matter how many doors were kicked in and people rousted from their sleep, Akel was always a step ahead of the men with guns. Shin Bet case officers called him the man with nine lives.

Akel's luck came to an end on November 24, 1993, inside Sheja'iya, a congested battlefield that also doubled as a neighborhood in eastern Gaza City. Countless man hours of intensive intelligence work and pre-raid reconnaissance went into the operation to catch or kill Akel, but it all culminated in a few moments of dedicated firepower. The unit that removed Akel from the most-wanted list was Samson, one of the two Israeli undercover counterterrorist units operating in the Gaza Strip.

---

* The kidnappings were reportedly ordered by Hamas founder Sheikh Ahmed Yassin, who demanded that the bodies of the Israeli soldiers seized be kept secret so that the organization could use them as barter in negotiations with the Shin Bet over the release of imprisoned Hamas operatives. The graves of these soldiers were considered highly valued secrets: Sergeant Avi Sasportas was kidnapped and murdered on February 3, 1989, but his body was found several months later; Sergeant Ilan Saadon was kidnapped and murdered on May 3, 1989, though his remains were found on August 11, 1996.

The population of the Gaza Strip in 1948 consisted of 82,500 men, women, and children,[1] living inside a densely packed twenty-eight-mile-long, four-mile-wide wedge bordering the southwestern tip of the Israeli frontier and the northwestern shores of Sinai along the Mediterranean coast. After the establishment of the State of Israel, more than 160,000 Palestinian refugees flooded to the ancient Philistine stronghold where the Book of Judges details Samson's destruction of the Temple of Dagon. The refugees were quickly warehoused inside eight United Nations–administered shanty camps quickly buttressed around the Strip's three cities—Gaza City in the north, Khan Yunis in the center, and Rafah, which straddled the Egyptian frontier in the south. The camps soon became permanent, alongside an inescapable reality of poverty and hopelessness. The Egyptians occupied the Strip from 1949 to 1967, and they found it to be frustratingly contumacious and violent. Egyptian intelligence allowed the Gaza Strip to be used as a launching pad for Palestinian guerrilla, or fedayeen, attacks against Israeli agricultural towns and collectives; knowing that they could mobilize Palestinian misery into self-serving Egyptian interests by opportunistically keeping the Palestinians boiling with indignation,[2] the Egyptians, like many other Arab states, could deflect their own internal fissures by mobilizing the dream of vengeance against Israel. But Israeli retaliation to each fedayeen attack was swift and severe; the precarious misery of those living in the Strip became entangled in the unstoppable cycle of violence.

The fedayeen attacks, as well as increasing tensions with Egypt, cul-minated with the Sinai invasion on October 29, 1956, during which Israeli forces captured the Gaza Strip.[*] Eleven years later, the Israeli armor fist that punched through the Egyptian lines in the opening hours of the June 1967 Six Day War once again captured the Gaza Strip—this time in less than two days of fighting. In 1956, Israeli forces remained in the Gaza Strip for five months. Following the 1967 War, Israel's entanglement inside the volatile and perpetually explosive sliver of combustion has been ongoing.

---

[*] Israel's operation to capture the Sinai Desert and open its shipping through the Straits of Tiran into the Red Sea was carried out in coordination with *Opération Mousquetaire*, the Anglo-French plan to capture the Suez Canal during the Suez Crisis.

The first years of Israeli control of the Strip was tenuous and bloody. Palestinian terrorist groups, no longer controlled by Egyptian intelligence, attempted to reclaim ownership of the Gaza Strip through violence, but Israel's countermeasures were swift and decisive. Captain Meir Dagan's Sayeret Rimon undercover counterterrorist unit in the IDF Southern Command was a textbook case study in the use of undercover special operations forces in crushing a terrorist uprising. Dagan's men, deploying in small teams and in full disguise, made a point of operating everywhere in the Strip, including the treacherous and claustrophobic shantytowns of the refugee camps. Dagan wanted to send a message of *Davka*, or stubborn spite, to the Palestinian gunmen who thought that they could seek refuge inside the human maze of overcrowded neighborhoods that there wasn't an inch of the Strip that his men would be dissuaded or deterred from entering.

Sayeret Rimon's campaign—and a heavy military and Border Guard police presence—brought relative calm and moderate prosperity to the Strip—a tenuous, perhaps imagined, calm that lasted sixteen years. Gazans worked inside Israel, and the local economy improved by leaps and bounds from what it was when Egypt ruled the Strip; quality-of-life conditions, even for a population with one of the highest birth rates in the world, improved. But the calm on the surface masked the simmering fractures that betrayed the bedrock beneath.

To the more cosmopolitan Palestinians of the West Bank's major cities—and certainly to the Israelis—the Gaza Strip was a forgotten frontier of sand-strewn misery. The Gaza Strip was conservative and, many in the West Bank would say, provincially primitive. The Palestinian symbol of nationalism was the golden reflection of the Dome of the Rock mosque—not the dusty back roads of Khan Yunis. Israelis, especially those caught up in the messianic-driven euphoria of post-1967 reconnection to the landmarks of the Old Testament that could be found in the West Bank, did not share the same connection to the biblical sites in Gaza that proved, at least in their eyes, Jewish provenance of the land. Still, Israel established twenty-one settlements in the Gaza Strip, with most being located in Gush Katif, bordered on the southwest by Rafah and the Egyptian border, on the east by Khan Yunis, on the northeast by the Deir el-Balah refugee camp, and on the west

and northwest by the Mediterranean Sea. The settlements required military
protection, as did the two roads that served the communities and proved
to be their land links to the rest of Israel. Israeli soldiers and Border Guard
policemen who served tours of duty in the Strip worked a hazardous post that
few in Israel understood or cared to think of much. Gaza was distant, remote,
and dangerous. By the mid-1980s, there were close to six hundred thousand
people living in the Gaza Strip.

The seismic fissure came on December 8, 1987. A fatal traffic accident in
the Jebalya refugee camp, near the Erez Crossing, involving an Israeli driver,
brought Palestinians to the streets in the thousands. Violent demonstrations
followed. The rioting that ensued was unlike anything that had ever been seen
before in Gaza. It soon spread to East Jerusalem and the West Bank. The first
intifada had begun.

Unit 367, better known simply as Samson (*Shimshon* in Hebrew), was the
IDF undercover unit in Gaza. The unit was established in 1986 shortly after
Duvdevan's creation and was the project of Major General Yitzhak Mordechai,
commander of the IDE's Southern Command. Born in the Kurdistan area of
Iraq, Mordechai was a granite block of a man who earned one of Israel's highest decorations for valor as a paratroop battalion commander during the savage battle for the Chinese Farm in Sinai against Egyptian commandos during
the 1973 Yom Kippur War. Mordechai had risen up the IDF ladder of command, earning his stripes and his scars on dark nights inside enemy domains,
in command of small forces of elite fighting men who drastically altered the
balance of power on any battlefield. Mordechai built Samson around a cadre
of like-minded unconventional military thinkers—adventurous officers,
all former reconnaissance paratroopers or commandos, who were keen to
write history as it was fought, as well as volunteers who had special human
traits that were usually sought after in spies and scoundrels. The unit's first
commander, Major Ilan,* had just completed a stint at the IDF officer's school,

---

* Due to sensitive postings that have followed, Major Ilan's full identity has still not been released.

serving as a battalion commander in the prestigious factory of Israel's future leaders, when he was offered the chance to return to combat duty in the most unconventional of settings. Major Ilan was a paratroop officer and had never led men inside the covert world of shadow warfare. He accepted the daunting challenge but first conferred with commanders of the Ya'ma'm and Israel's intelligence community. He also listened intently to the advice of Colonel Moshe Ya'alon, the commander of Sayeret Mat'kal (and future IDF chief of staff and defense minister) on the use of small teams and MOUT—military operations in urban terrain.[3]

Major Ilan recruited men with impeccable combat service records, virtually all of them from the paratroop brigade, who were adventurous, forward thinkers who could thrive in a rogue setting in a very dangerous theater of operations. The unit recruited men from diverse backgrounds who spoke myriad languages. Fluency in Arabic was a plus when being considered for a slot in the small unit, but it wasn't a prerequisite. Extensive background checks were conducted on volunteers, as anyone who had had a family member killed in a terrorist attack was automatically precluded from serving in the unit; Samson wanted men who were threat-oriented and not fixated on vigilantism.[4]

There was no shortage of work in the Gaza Strip. Palestinian terrorist cells inside the Strip received their operational orders from PLO headquarters in Tunis, as well as from the various other fronts based in Syria and Iraq. Hamas and the nascent PIJ had for years both been viewed as challengers to Arafat and his rule, and they had been able to stockpile weapons with little interruption from the Shin Bet. The terrorists mustered an odd arsenal that ranged from medieval to Soviet-bloc: The weapons included everything from improvised hand-tooled axes and medieval flails, to Egyptian-made submachine guns left behind before 1967, to brand-spanking-new AK-47s and stolen IDF Uzis and M16s, all bought on a thriving black market of smuggled weapons. Explosives and grenades were smuggled into the porous confines of the Strip. Attacks against Israeli forces grew both in frequency and in intensity. A full-scale guerrilla war was under way—this front becoming increasingly fanatical and religious in nature.

The Samson unit was small by comparison to their West Bank counterpart, but the unit had more work than it could handle. Acting as the spearhead for Shin Bet and Military Intelligence information, the unit launched what amounted to an endless roster of arrest raids and proactive ambushes throughout the Strip; the unit captured or killed many of the most dangerous terrorists there, and their most capable commanders—such as Imad Hassan Imbrahim Akel, a man the British journalist Robert Fisk inimically called at the time "the Hamas's greatest martyr."[5] The man who led the operation was Captain Uri Azulay, an officer who left the cloak-and-dagger top-secret world of long-range reconnaissance operations with Sayeret Mat'kal to serve as a team leader in Samson. Azulay wanted to serve where he was needed, and he brought a level of top-tier professionalism to the small force of conscripts.[6]

The men that Azulay and the other Samson unit officers commanded operated on pure courage and adrenaline in the hundreds of operations that they mounted in very difficult terrain. "Our enemy is the armed terrorist, not the local citizens. The people of Gaza have a right to live; they live in difficult situations, but the only ones who are targeted are those who are armed and who refused to surrender," a team leader told his men before an operation. "I want you all to think of yourselves as wearing neckties, not uniforms, when you operate in the closed-confines of a home in search of a suspect or a family. If you have to break a wall to search for weapons or explosives, then do it, but always remember that the family that's there has to live there after we are gone."[7]

The median age in the unit was nineteen or twenty. The soldiers were young and enthusiastic, and Gaza was a highly complex and often difficult tactical terrain to navigate. During Samson's tenure there, four of its operators were killed in action.

Major General Matan Vilnai, the head of IDF Southern Command during the violent years of the intifada and an officer who had spent his entire career in the paratroopers and its elite reconnaissance formations, understood the enormous—perhaps impossible—burden that was placed on the shoulders of these commandos in Gaza. "To build a true undercover unit that can blend itself into the terrain requires years of training and is virtually impossible to do with conscripts. You need the resources and the time to turn such a unit into a professional [full-time] force. Under these conditions, the operators were compromised quickly. The costumes only worked for the initial contact.

Immediately, after the exchange of a few words, it would be obvious to the locals that they are face-to-face with a Jew and not someone born here [in Gaza]."[8]

Vilnai's words praised the courage and doggedness of the Samson operators who carried out hundreds of capture-or-kill operations against a fanatical and determined terrorist foe in the Gaza Strip, against insurmountable odds. But his comments were also a begrudging acceptance that undercover work was not a temporary profession. There was, after all, another undercover unit that worked in Southern Command for the Shin Bet and the Gaza Division.

In September 1989, a Border Guard undercover unit was established in the Gaza Strip. The unit, the first of the Ya'mas units in the Border Guard order of battle, was authorized by Chief Superintendent Husen Fares, a highly decorated Druze officer, who was the regional Border Guard commander and foresaw the value in a highly specialized Arabic-speaking counterterrorist force for the area. Fares had served in the region long enough to understand the pulse of the precinct: The Gaza Strip had been the beat for permanently stationed Border Guard companies since 1967—companies that consisted of Druze, Bedouin, Circassian, and Christian policemen who had made careers policing the treacherous precincts where the Philistines once ruled. These men not only spoke the language of the locals, understood their customs and their cultural sensitivities, but they also had a wealth of territorial familiarity with the area that a battalion of IDF conscripts could never acquire during their mandatory years of military service. These Border Guard policemen knew every Fatah sympathizer, every cleric, every law-abiding laborer trying to eke out an existence with construction jobs in Israel while living inside the sardine-like rows of cinder-block housing in the Nuseirat refugee camp, and they knew the prominent families who lived in more spacious surroundings, in the villas and penthouse flats of Gaza City. These men knew the lay of the land and they knew the currency of day-to-day existence. These men formed the original cadre of this new undercover force.

The new unit was small. Ya'mas Gaza consisted of only a handful of men, who used costumes they purchased in local markets to cobble together a wardrobe of disguises for use in the field; the unit's miniscule fleet of unmarked vehicles was commandeered from police motor pools, as well as vehicles that were confiscated. The unit was, in essence, two separate forces: One platoon, or team, was responsible for operations in the southern portion of the Strip, to include Khan Yunis, Rafah, and the refugee camps in the central areas (Deir el-Balah, Nuseirat, and Maghazi); a second platoon covered the northern sector to Gaza City, Beit Hanoun, and the treacherous streets of the Sheja'iya, as well as the Jebalya and Shati refugee camps. But the workload was so hectic, and the pursuit of terrorists crisscrossed so many neighborhoods, that the unit was consolidated in 1990.

One of the unit's first commanding officers was Yaakov "Kobi" Shabtai. A former paratrooper with an endearing smile and a soft-spoken confidence, he oversaw the counterterrorism landscape like a chess master viewing the board. He understood the complexities and explosiveness of the Gaza battlefield and how entrenched the terrorist underground there was. Shabtai also understood the dangers that were implicit with every Shin Bet file that came the unit's way.

Gaza was a world unto itself—a congested labyrinth of narrow alleyways and homes. There were very few street signs in the Strip; most homes were not numbered. The intelligence that the unit received was often sketchy and incomplete. Operators routinely had to surveil a location for days—or longer—just to make sure that the targeted individual lived inside the third house from the left, and not two doors down, where twenty people slept on the floor of a one-story space. Children were everywhere, on the street and in vacant lots, at all hours of the day and night. Laundry lines intermingled with electricity lines; Dumpsters filled to capacity spilled over into puddles of raw sewage. The incessant blaring of car horns and car radios was an inescapable soundtrack to life in the Strip; carts pulled by donkeys brought produce to market. Multistory dwellings hovered over shacks. Buildings and walls were all covered in the graffiti of one group or another; it appeared as if every other structure in the Strip was still under construction. At night, under the orange glow of street lamps, ambulance sirens wailed. There was always a burst of gunfire heard somewhere in the distance. There were always street battles of some kind, somewhere. When the Palestinians and Israelis weren't fighting each other, the Palestinians fought among themselves. There were always scores to settle. The bodies of collaborators—some who worked for the Shin Bet and others who were innocent but luckless—were usually found in the morning.

The men involved in the terror movements found sanctuary in the crowded chaos. So, too, did the men in the Islamic underground, who also could rely on the mosques and Islamic institutions to hide and safeguard their weapons and explosives. As the intifada turned into an asymmetrical conflict, a harbinger of worse to come, the battlefield became increasingly dangerous. Hamas and the PIJ, especially, began to display a suicidal fanaticism that had not been seen before in the conflict. Arrest raids were no longer foregone conclusions; Hamas fought back, determined to kill and eager to die. Israel's top-tier units found the battleground to be truly foreboding.

Shabtai realized this tactical complexion of the terrain and honed a force that could penetrate these obstacles safely, seamlessly, and effectively. The masquerade was critical in these Wild West years—the ability to reconnoiter terrorist-controlled streets and neighborhoods for intelligence-gathering and arrests. Shimon, a young NCO serving inside one of the Border Guard companies in Gaza, joined the Ya'mas in 1991 after a grueling selection process and lengthy interview with the unit command echelon. As a young conscript working the Strip, he wanted to be part of this unit, the name of which, "Ya'mas," had become legendary in terms of its James Bond–like covert capabilities. He was small-framed, and his cover was usually that of a woman—a woman in a *hijab* or in a full *abaya* black dress—or of a teen- ager. The ability to operate freely inside the Palestinian areas was a critical component of the unit's effectiveness. "We operated freely everywhere and anywhere in the Strip," Shimon recalled of those early days in his career. "We operated in markets, in neighborhoods, and everywhere else to identify suspects and to neutralize them. Sometimes there were battles, some serious ones; other times there were snatch operations and there were raids, lots of them, at night. This was the dynamic of life inside the unit, life inside Gaza. Our work was very precise, and designed to avoid hostile encounters. We arrived, grabbed our target out, and then left before anyone ever knew we were there."[9]

Some of the operations involved small bands of operators, supported by an on-call backup force. Some involved the entire unit. In one operation, the hunt for a Hamas suspect wanted in Zaitun, a section of Gaza City, for the murder of an Israeli soldier, a plainclothes Ya'mas section filtered into the crowded neighborhood without the locals noticing anything out of place as the men and women moved by in a taxicab with the proper license plates. Nearby, the remainder of the Ya'mas unit, in full tactical kit, had been flown in by IAF helicopter to provide backup and disrupt any Hamas attempts to resist. The entire raid, from boots off the landing skids of the chopper to the suspect in cuffs being whisked away in a Palestinian taxi, took less than five minutes.

Gaza wasn't for everyone, of course. Old hands likened the all-or-nothing rules to combat duty in Lebanon, where suicide bombers rammed cars into convoys, and cleverly camouflaged IEDs decimated lightly armored vehicles. The unit recruited men—conscripts and veteran policemen—who scored impressive results in their selection process and who made it through the grueling training course at the top of their class. But most important, the men who led the unit looked for people who could think on their feet and improvise. The unit looked for men who could find themselves alone and out-numbered and not panic. The Gaza Ya'mas required men with the cold-as-ice nerves of a spy and the cunning and patience of a hunter. Most important, the unit sought men who were fluid in their reaction to the unknown and who could survive the unpredictable reality of Gaza.

In the afternoon hours of September 13, 1993, Ya'mas grabbed chairs and hovered around a battered Philips color television to watch Prime Minister Yitzhak Rabin and Yasir Arafat meet together on the White House lawn. Some of the men sat with their hands folded across their chests and kept saying that they couldn't believe what they were seeing; some smoked silently, rendered speechless in utter disbelief. Some of them were already partially dressed in their Palestinian disguises, ready for the night's mission. There were men from every ethnic and religious group watching history unfold that day. Every political persuasion was represented, as well. There were hopes for peace and fears for the future in each breath the Ya'mas operators took that unforgettable moment. Every man knew the Gaza Strip—and their role in it—was about to change forever.

Politics were never discussed in the unit, it was the one taboo of life in the field, but there were genuine misgivings about the peace process. Even if Arafat could keep his legions in check and create an atmosphere that was conducive to peace, there was still Hamas and the PIJ to contend with. Ya'mas counterterrorist operations in Gaza intensified as the plans for Israel's withdrawal were set in motion.

On July 1, 1994, under a cloudless Mediterranean sky, Yasir Arafat and the twenty thousand security personnel that the Oslo provisions permitted to keep peace in the newly established Palestinian Authority made a triumphant return to Gaza City. Arafat's entourage snaked its way through Sinai, across Rafah terminal, and through a special festive trellis that had been built for the occasion. The Palestinian flag, outlawed during Israel's administration of the Strip, flew everywhere. Tens of thousands of people rallied along the motorcade's route to greet the moment of liberation; twice as many portraits of Arafat had been plastered along every light post, electricity pole, and wall in sight. Men in green and red berets and sage-green fatigues that had been starched and pressed for this special occasion cocooned the Palestinian leader. They carried AK-47s and brand-new pistols that U.S. aid, in support of the peace process, had paid for, in their shiny new leather holsters. The security personnel, old stalwarts from the trenches of southern Lebanon and Beirut, had followed Arafat into exile in Tunis; some had been garrisoned in prison-like barracks in Algeria and elsewhere, just waiting for the day of liberation. There were many in this ring of steel that boasted sinister CVs; some had served sentences inside Israeli prisons, while others had been incarcerated in other Arab states. The nucleus of Arafat's new army was trained in Cairo and in Amman to meet the task of security for the planted seeds of Palestinian statehood. Egyptian and Jordanian intelligence instructors had taught these men the tradecraft of state security; CIA and other American entities had tried to instill in them the need to use that tradecraft within a legal framework. Under the protocols of the Oslo Accords, tens of thousands of weapons were permitted into the Strip to bolster preexisting arsenals. The security forces manned an astounding forty-four security checkpoints along the twenty-mile path from the Egyptian border to Gaza City.[10]

The euphoria of liberation ended quickly, though. The men who fought in the intifada and whose families suffered in the trenches against Israeli forces were not those who reaped the rewards of Arafat's return. Corruption in Gaza, even by Middle Eastern standards, was infectiously rampant. The cronies who followed Arafat to Tunis and the other Arab capitals inherited the perks of governance: plum appointments and contracts that allowed them to partake in siphoning off the hundreds of millions of dollars flowing in from the United States, the United Nations, the European Union, and the Gulf Arabs. These men and their families, wearing Ralph Lauren and Rolex, honked the horns of their shiny brand-new German luxury sedans to nudge the locals out of their way. Arafat's intelligence and security services collected taxes for protection and dealt brutally with anyone deemed disloyal, who dared to voice discontent.

Compared to Arafat and his forces, Hamas and the PIJ were—at the time—seen as clean, incorruptible. Fatah, Arafat's own movement, had always been viewed as self-serving and opportunistic. The politicized form of militant Islam that emerged primarily in Gaza blossomed *because* of all that was wrong with the crony-laced world of Arafat's professional sycophants and extortionists. The PIJ, an offshoot of the Egyptian Muslim Brotherhood, was the first to embark on the armed struggle in the name of Islam.[11] Hamas would soon follow suit. Both Hamas and the PIJ harnessed religious rage with nationalistic aspirations. Both organizations, handsomely funded by donations from the Palestinian Diaspora in North America and Europe, as well as from the Islamic Republic of Iran, ran food programs for the hungry and medical clinics for the ill; they provided social services that the newly established Palestinian Authority was incapable of or unwilling to provide. Hamas and the PIJ had also, by the time Arafat arrived in Gaza City, already declared their own wars on Israel. The suicide bombings had already begun, and the Islamic groups were perceived as the vanguard of the continuing struggle against Israel. The ranks of both Islamic terror groups soon swelled with the disenchanted and disappointed who saw promise in the jihad, as well as security for their families.

The Israeli intelligence community knew that it still had to operate inside Gaza. One such strike came on January 5, 1996, when the Shin Bet assassinated Yehiya Ayyash, the infamous Hamas Engineer. Ayyash was hiding in Gaza and was killed when an explosive-laden cellular phone that had been given him by a Shin Bet asset exploded while he talked to his father. But Gaza was, for the most part, left alone. The IDF disbanded the Samson unit in early 1996. The conscripts in the unit, and some of the officers, were reassigned to Duvdevan or to the Golani Brigade's Egoz counter-guerrilla force that was in the throes of a lethal war against Hezbollah in southern Lebanon. The Gaza Ya'mas unit remained, however. Bolstered with resources as the front became ever more strategic and volatile, the unit became a full-fledged commando reconnaissance force covering the entire area.

In September 1996, the Palestinian Authority orchestrated riots throughout the territories. Israeli prime minister Benjamin Netanyahu ordered the opening of the Hasmonean Channel, an archaeological tunnel by the Western Wall. Clashes erupted throughout the West Bank; heavily armed Palestinian security forces joined the fight, rather than disperse the crowds. On September 27, Arafat gave the green light for his security forces to open fire. The combat was fiercest in southern Gaza, around the Gush Katif settlements and the Rafah crossing that connected Gaza, and the Sinai Desert, with the rest of the Arab world. Palestinian security forces engaged Israeli forces in open warfare and attempted, in several locations, to overrun the Israeli lines—especially Israeli forces garrisoned in and around the Termit (Hebrew for Thermal) fortification. Ya'mas snipers engaged the Palestinian forces at long range, while teams of Israeli operators fought pitched battles against an entrenched and well-equipped adversary; plumes of acrid black smoke billowed in the air from Palestinian police vehicles destroyed by Israeli fire. The most hard fought of the Ya'mas battles centered on securing and rescuing soldiers who had been killed or wounded in the voracious exchanges. Seventeen Israeli soldiers were killed in battle, including Colonel Nabi Mer'i, a Druze officer and the deputy commander of the Gaza Division. The fighting was fierce and underscored how damaged the fragile peace accords actually were.

Ya'mas veterans who had fought in Gaza for seven years straight returned to base in solemn resignation once the gunfire ended. As the men removed their gear, and tossed their fatigues stained with the blood of the dead and the wounded to the floor, these veterans of the Gaza beat realized just how explosive the area was and how dangerous it was going to be. Once the funerals were over and the postmortem of the fighting conducted, the unit hit the training grounds running. Veterans like Shimon, now an officer in the force, knew that the battle for the Gaza Strip was far from over.

The war in Gaza, in fact, had only just begun.

CHAPTER NINETEEN

War

It was a slice of paradise—paradise redux. Elei Sinai was a small picture-perfect community that was home to close to one hundred families, complete with beachfront access to the Mediterranean surf. Located at the northwestern-most tip of the Strip, Elei Sinai consisted of white one-family houses with red ceramic roofs; they looked like vacation villas in a seaside resort, but they were more middle-class suburban than lavish. Trees had been planted everywhere—in backyards and along the wide streets—to provide protective shade from the merciless sun. Elei Sinai was established in 1982 as a new home for families that had been displaced from the Yamit settlement in the Sinai Desert when Israel returned the peninsula to Egypt as part of the Camp David peace accords; Elei Sinai meant "Toward Sinai" in Hebrew, and it was so named to remind everyone—especially the politicians—of the residents' desire to return to Sinai. The community was close-knit and secular, the kind of place where everyone knew everyone else. It would have been perfect were it not for the fact that it was situated at the northwestern tip of the Gaza Strip, in the crosshairs of the terrorists.

Elei Sinai was one of the Israeli settlements allowed to remain in place inside the Gaza Strip by the Oslo Accords. Its residents knew—and stubbornly accepted—the fact that daily existence was rife with threat. But this was home, and they weren't moving. The settlement was, of course, fortified against infiltration. Elei Sinai was surrounded by security fences and walls, and dense rows of concertina. Entry in and out of the settlement was controlled by heavily armed security forces and the IDF; a heavy metal security gate, painted a maroon red, controlled road access in and out of the small neighborhood. Virtually all the residents of Elei Sinai were armed; weapons, from pistols to M16s, went with them wherever they went. But still there was a sense of calm and home. At night sometimes, when the helicopter gunships weren't overhead and the sounds of gunfire dissipated, one could actually hear the Mediterranean surf bounce against the pristine sandy shore.

The winter clock brought darkness early on the night of October 2, 2001. A full moon had begun to cast a brilliant lunar glow on the Mediterranean. The bright light helped to illuminate a path for the three figures navigating their way through the thick coils of razor wire, across the steep dunes, from Gaza City toward Elei Sinai. Two of the men wore camouflage fatigues and specially made rubber boots for traction on the slippery sand. Each of them carried an AK-47 and wore a combat vest with enough pouches to accommodate dozens of thirty-round magazines for his Soviet-made assault rifle; fragmentation hand grenades, smaller than baseballs, were crammed inside the cargo pockets of each man's loose-fitting utility belt. The two men had had their faces painted in a slick pattern of green and black, and a green silk-like bandana sporting a verse from the Quran and the symbol of Hamas had been draped around their heads. The third man was the operation commander. His job was to ensure that the two young men, already resigned to their fate as martyrs, carried out their assignment. The Palestinians positioned themselves at a point across the fence where it would be easiest to cross. They turned their heads southeast one final time. The lights from the high-rise apartment buildings in Beit Lehiya shined brightly in the evening's purple sky.

The terrorists had planned to attack the IDF vehicle that made its rounds along the security fence every few minutes. Once the soldiers were killed, the attack against the settlement would be uninterrupted. But the patrol never came. The two Palestinians waited; they were eager to earn the accolades they had been promised in death. The commander was anxious. Twenty minutes passed and still nothing. The wire cutters sliced through the first row of fence at 1730 hours. The commander walked back toward Gaza City.

Twenty miles south of Elei Sinai, Ya'mas Inspector Yaron,* one of the unit's two team commanders, was about to lead a mission at a location

---

* He can only be known by his first name for security considerations.

somewhere between Khan Yunis and Deir el-Balach, in the very center of the Gaza Strip. The mission had been days in planning, and the preparation—together with the Shin Bet intelligence that it was built around—constituted hundreds of man hours of tradecraft. The operation was going to be one of the first over-the-wall forays for Ze'ev,* a newcomer to the unit who had served as a policeman in one of the Border Guard companies that patrolled the Gaza Strip shortly after the Oslo Accords and Arafat's return. Although Ze'ev had gone on to join an elite detective squad fighting crime in central Israel, the events of September 2000 prompted him to return to the Strip and do his part to fight terror. He made some calls, found out when the next tryouts to the unit would be held, and prepared for the arduous selection process. On one sunny morning, Ze'ev found himself at the Border Guard anti-terrorist training center, along with hundreds of other men who had his same aspirations. Ze'ev persevered. He made it to the top of the acceptance cut and then excelled in the basic Ya'mas course. When it came time to be assigned to one of the three undercover units, Ze'ev demanded Gaza. A year had passed since his decision to become an active combatant in Israel's counterterrorist campaign. He returned to Gaza to settle into one of the Ya'mas teams and then had to go through a lengthy process of reacquainting himself with the terrain and learning the difference between the sanitized practice areas of training and the life-and-death reality of actual operations in the field. He now found himself suited up, heavy body armor across his chest, and serving as a spotter and designated marksman in Yaron's squad. There was a cool autumn breeze that night. But the men, prepared to go inside enemy territory, still perspired under the weight of their gear and the pall of fear each man tried to contain.

But before Yaron could embark on the operation, the unit commander, Superintendent Nissim, came running out of headquarters with word that a terrorist attack was under way in Elei Sinai. Yaron ordered his men into one van, and Nissim led a task force in another. Both vehicles raced toward the northwestern edge of Gaza, receiving the intelligence as they sped closer toward the battle. The route to the battle was circuitous, crisscrossing checkpoints, gates, and bypass roads. The operators adjusted their helmets and

* A pseudonym—true identity withheld for security considerations.

their balaclavas; they checked their pouches to make sure they had enough ammunition for a prolonged engagement. There were already reports of heavy gunfire and casualties.

The terrorist attack coincided with the eighteenth anniversary of the settlement's founding as well as the Jewish festival of Sukkot.* The entire area had been decorated for the holiday. Colorful lights were strewn across doorways and bushes. Liran Harpaz, a nineteen-year-old home on leave from the army, and her boyfriend, twenty-year-old Assaf Yitzhaki, were sitting on a bench holding hands when the terrorists cut through the fence. The two never heard the terrorists slinking silently across the wire. Both were shot and killed at point-blank range. The attack had begun.

The terrorists moved swiftly across Elei Sinai, firing into the houses along the tree-lined avenue and hurling grenades. They shot at anyone and anything they saw. Parents raced outside to bring their children to safety, and some were shot and seriously wounded. Bullet holes riddled the white stucco walls of the pristinely kept homes; the grenades started several small fires that thickened the air with dense black smoke. The cries of women screaming were muffled only by the incessant gunfire. One of the victims was an infant, hit by AK fire.

Several IDF reservists stationed at the settlement, along with a force of infantrymen from a Giva'ati Brigade antitank company, chased the terrorists toward the north, firing at them on the move, hoping to pin them down and kill them. But the terrorists fought back and, in a series of brief firefights, managed to wound several of the charging soldiers, including the force's commander, Captain David Cohen, who was critically injured.[1]

The moment the word of the attack hit the IDF communications networks, roads were closed and a state of maximum alert was declared throughout the Strip. At one of the roadblocks, along a northbound lane of traffic in the middle of the Strip, a young conscript raised his arms and stopped the two Ya'mas vans. Covered in his battle rattle and conspicuously frightened, the young soldier told Yaron that the roads were closed because of an attack.

---

* Sukkot is a seven-day holiday, also known as the Feast of Tabernacles, that commemorates the temporary huts used by the Israelites in the desert conditions and how God protected them in the wilderness.

Yaron smiled at the hapless corporal. There was time for protocol, Yaron thought, but never when active shooters were on the loose. He waved off the corporal and led the procession through side roads and shortcuts to cut the travel time down by half. The Ya'mas response team vans pulled up to the main gate of Elei Sinai roughly thirty minutes after the terrorists fired their first shots.

At the main gate the Ya'mas force encountered what looked like a ghost town. "Where is the incident?" Yaron asked a member of the settlement's security force, a man in his forties wearing shorts and sandals, who looked absolutely bewildered. The man could barely produce a sentence. He just pointed toward a series of homes to the north about a mile away. Elei Sinai was covered by darkness and an eerie silence interrupted by the odd shots off in the distance. Elei Sinai's residents were already hunkered down inside their homes, inside their shelters. They had shut off their lights, as per procedure, to make it harder for the terrorists to find them. Yaron and his men grabbed their gear and deployed in the darkness. They humped over the dunes on foot, moving forward as trained, to search the area for any threats.

The forward Command Post for the incident consisted of an old four-wheeled troop carrier known in the IDF vernacular as a Nun-Nun, and several men hunkered down inside overlooking a row of houses. Gaza Northern Brigade commander Colonel Hamada Janem, a veteran Druze officer, was relieved to see Superintendent Nissim and Yaron, and he briefly explained the situation and the mission: The Ya'mas was to take a sector of the settlement and attempt to engage the enemy as quickly as possible—to kill them before they would have a chance to kill anybody else.

As the force of a dozen or so men moved across backyards and neatly manicured lawns, stepping on children's bikes and knocking down barbecue grills in the process, Yaron and Ze'ev moved together as a tandem. The two operators noticed blood trails littered with what looked like hundreds of spent 7.62mm round casings. Ze'ev wondered just how many terrorists were involved. The Ya'mas was closing in, however. The bursts of gunfire were getting louder.

There were inaccurate reports as to how many gunmen were in the settlement and what type of firepower they possessed. The Ya'mas force searched homes and gardens, and finally Yaron and Ze'ev assumed position overlooking a home where it was determined the terrorists must be hiding. The Ya'mas force moved toward the house in tactical formation. They were joined by a few officers from the Israel National Police hostage-negotiation team who had made it from their base in central Israel to Gaza. The force moved in, determined to pluck any hostages to safety, but the home was empty. There was a period of quiet before one of the operators noticed movement next to a large plastic shed that was next to the house. The terrorists, one who had been wounded, attempted to hide behind the shed and engage Israeli forces that were now flooding into the area. Yaron and Ze'ev, moving forward in a tight and textbook formation, opened fire on the two Hamas gunmen, killing them both.

By the time the shooting stopped, the Ya'ma'm had arrived on scene, as had Major General Doron Almog, the head of Southern Command. Forward units from the IDF's best commando forces had rushed to Elei Sinai, as had the IDF chief of staff and the defense minister. Colonels were everywhere. Yaron had tried to tell the brass that the operation was over, but the units remained behind all night and well into the next morning in order to make sure that all the terrorists were accounted for. Explosive ordnance technicians from the Border Guard's Gaza bomb squad, the busiest such unit in the world, painstakingly examined the bodies of the two dead terrorists for suicide vests. A small yellow robot was used to detonate the dozens of hand grenades each man carried. Shin Bet agents checked the dead men's fingerprints and examined the weapons and gear they carried. Helicopter gunships circled the area. A drone flew overhead to provide the generals with a detailed and accurate overview of the area.

Two people had been killed in the attack; sixteen more were seriously wounded. IDF infantry units and armor cut a kilometer into Gaza proper, into Area A, to create a buffer zone for Israeli forces responding to Elei Sinai. Yaron and his force returned to base to debrief and prepare for the resumption of the interrupted mission from the previous night.

The rocks and bottles that were thrown on the first day of the al-Aqsa intifada
in the Gaza Strip were almost immediately replaced by bullets, bombs, and
RPGs. The ferocity of the choreographed violence was absolute and it was
daunting. A Gaza Strip in the throes of war presented the Israeli military with
a security nightmare of unimaginable implications. The jigsaw puzzles of
roadways and junctions that connected the isolated Israeli settlements were
all within reach of Palestinian heavy weapons. The security barriers that separated the Area A of the Palestinian Authority from the towns of agricultural
communities in southern Israel were precariously porous. The separation
of Area A and the Israeli settlements and towns—both inside and outside of
the Gaza Strip—was insanely close-quarter: Kibbutz Nahal Oz, located in
the northwestern part of the Negev desert, inside the pre-1967 boundaries of
the State of Israel, was just two kilometers from the heart of Gaza City; Kfar
Darom, a kibbutz that dated back to 1930 but had been abandoned during
the 1948 fighting, only to be reclaimed in 1970, was in a pocket carved *inside*
the Gaza Strip, only a kilometer from the Deir el-Balach refugee camp. Both
Hamas and the PIJ launched daily attacks against the Jewish settlements
and the Israeli defensive positions set up at strategic locations surrounding
the Strip, as well as the routes that serviced these lifelines. The attacks were
daily and deadly.

The Palestinian Authority was incapable of or unwilling to stem the violence; in most cases its forces perpetrated wave after wave of attacks against
Israeli civilian and military targets. On November 18, 2000, an IDF sergeant
was killed by a senior officer in Arafat's Preventative Security Service, after
he infiltrated into Israeli lines through a greenhouse in Kfar Darom. Two
days later, two Israelis were killed when an IED, planted along the roadside
leading from Kfar Darom, exploded alongside a bus carrying children from
their homes to their school in Gush Katif; nine were seriously wounded in
the attack, including five children.

The Palestinian Authority, along with Fatah's offshoots and factions,
were notoriously weak inside the fiery confines of the Strip. The Gaza Strip
belonged to Hamas and the PIJ, and ownership was documented at the barrel
of a gun. The years of Palestinian rule had transformed the Strip into one of
the largest arsenals on earth. It was impossible to estimate just how many

AK-47s, Drugenov sniper rifles, RPK light machine guns, RPG antitank rockets, and mortar tubes were inside the Gaza Strip; it was impossible to gauge just how many millions of rounds of ammunition were being stored inside locations that Hamas assessed were safe from Israeli military action (schools, mosques, hospitals, and people's homes); it was beyond the algorithms to even begin to ascertain how many tons of high explosives had made their way across the Egyptian frontier, from the smuggler's haven of Sinai into the Gaza Strip. The only absolute was that the ordnance was prepositioned for the fight against Israel.

The very top echelon of Hamas and PIJ terrorist leadership called the Gaza postal code home. These men lived in Gaza City, in Khan Yunis, and in Rafah, often in modest flats, wedged inside crowded neighborhoods protected by unsuspecting and innocent neighbors. Sheikh Ahmed Yassin, the quadriplegic Hamas founder, lived in Gaza's al-Shati refugee camp. Yassin had been incarcerated by the Israelis in 1989 for terrorist activity but was released from prison in October 1997 in exchange for Mossad agents captured in Amman, Jordan, after a failed assassination attempt of a Hamas political and military leader in the Jordanian capital. Arafat's security forces occasionally arrested Hamas operatives; sometimes, they even arrested high-ranking commanders. More often than not, the arrests were temporary. Hamas, in times of peace, was a convenient proxy force for the war against Israel.

Superintendent Nissim served as the Ya'mas commander when the intifada erupted in 2000. Nissim was a veteran of the covert world of Israel's counterterrorist efforts in the West Bank and beyond. A man who had seen his fair share of dangerous nights all alone behind enemy lines, Nissim commanded a veteran unit of men who possessed a career's worth of experience inside Gaza. In the years between the "September Troubles" of 1996 and the outbreak of the al-Aqsa intifada, the Gaza Ya'mas was a shadow force that many Israeli soldiers—and officers—in the division had never heard of, let alone seen. Some of the Ya'mas missions were to preemptively disrupt terror plots before they could be carried out, by neutralizing those involved. The Palestinian Authority was sworn to combat terrorism inside its own territory, and Arafat's security forces could not cry foul when Israel took decidedly unilateral steps to keep a quiet status quo. Such top-secret undertakings were usually the domain of the Israeli military's top-secret commando forces, but the Ya'mas showed such indefatigable creativity in carrying out these strikes, the unit possessed such back-of-the-hand intimate knowledge of the terrain, that they became the go-to force for the Shin Bet command responsible for the Gaza Strip.

There had been rumors of dismantling the Gaza undercover unit after Oslo.[2] Even though the unit was at the forefront of Shin Bet's covert efforts inside the Strip, bean counters in the Ministry of Defense were also looking to trim the budget one way or another, and a small unit, especially one in the Border Guard order of battle, seemed a good candidate for removal. Although part of the Border Guard organizational chart, the Ya'mas served the IDF at the brigade and divisional level, and the costs of maintaining such a unit (salaries, equipment, vehicles, weapons, and ammunition) were subsidized by the IDF. Some in the ministry, looking at ledgers and spreadsheets and not at the tactical intelligence, looked at the Gaza Ya'mas in the same way the IDF had been forced to look at Samson.

Before September 2000 and the eruption of the intifada, the Shin Bet and other facets of Israel's intelligence community relied on Mohammed Dahlan's Preventative Security apparatus in Gaza for up-to-date information on Hamas, the PIJ, and other non-Fatah underground movements that posed a threat to Israel and, by endangering the Oslo Accords, the Palestinian Authority, as well. Dahlan was a wily operative who'd learned Hebrew inside an Israeli prison and who had proved his cunning and ruthlessness during the intifada. Many called the Gaza Strip "Dahlanistan" because Mohammed Dahlan's men under arms were the true enforcers and the true rulers of the area (the West Bank, in turn, was often called "Rajoubistan" because Arafat's Preventative Security commander Jibril Rajoub ruthlessly wielded such enormous power and control there).[3] While the peace lasted, the Shin Bet and Mohammed Dahlan worked together, and for the most part law and order was maintained; Dahlan was also a favorite son of Langley (as was Rajoub)[4] and also met regularly with the CIA. Once the intifada erupted, however, all bets were off, as Dahlan became the man who raised and lowered the bloodshed at Arafat's whim. The Shin Bet's Gaza command, like their counterparts in the West Bank when the intifada broke out, no longer received inside information; their Palestinian partners were now their enemies. The Shin Bet in Gaza was on its own. The Ya'mas was one of the only forces that the intelligence specialists could call upon for long-range eyes-on-target intelligence work and more dangerous and highly secretive tactical assignments behind enemy lines.

The opening chapter for the intifada in Gaza was a massive display of choreographed rage—a contagion of violence that was directed by the security forces ostensibly dedicated to keeping the peace. The bombardment of rocks and Molotov cocktails was but the first wave. Gunfire was to follow.

The Ya'mas was at its headquarters, near Kissufim (equidistant from both Khan Yunis and Deir el-Balach), when the violence first erupted. Unit personnel grabbed their helmets and tactical vests and rushed to the fence along the frontier. A mass of thousands of people had assembled to throw rocks, bottles, and petrol bombs. Barricades were set up and tires set alight. Palestinian policemen, bedecked in their gray-and-blue camouflage attire, as well as plainclothes men from Preventative Security, soon joined the fray. The Palestinian forces entrusted to keep the peace hunkered down behind concrete barriers and their shiny white vans to unleash fusillades of automatic weapons fire into the Israeli positions. Pickup trucks soon arrived with more gunmen, men in American-supplied woodland camouflage fatigues; some carried RPGs and heavier machine guns. Explosions were heard in the distance.

The average age of the men inside the Gaza Ya'mas force was believed to be around thirty. There were a few conscripts in the unit, though most in the Ya'mas roster were career men who were raised inside the violence of the first intifada. The men were mature and calculating. Many were married; some were the fathers of young children. These veterans approached undercover work inside the Gaza Strip with a precise focus and a deft and careful hand. The job, the mission, was all important. But so, too, was coming home alive. There was nothing impetuous about how they went about preparing for a mission and executing a strike behind Palestinian lines. The operators had no illusions as to the gruesome fate that would befall them should they be captured. But the men in the Gaza Ya'mas force viewed themselves as highly skilled professional technicians. They were built from a special DNA composite that gave them the gumption and stubbornness—and perhaps stupidity—to venture inside one of the most dangerous places on the planet for mission after mission.

Superintendent Nissim's men suffered through a love-hate relationship with the area, but when Israel pulled out of Gaza in 1994, not one of the veterans believed that they would ever have to go back into Gaza, back into the refugee camps, to combat the Palestinian Authority as well as the other terrorist factions in absolute open warfare. No one believed that the unit would need to use tanks and armored personnel carriers. No one in the unit believed that they would ultimately need to know how to call in air strikes. But peering through their ACOG sights and returning fire across the barbed wire barriers, the men of the Gaza Ya'mas knew that there was no turning back. "This wasn't 1996 again," one of the operators said. "We understood that we were at war!"[5]

The Gaza Ya'mas unit operated in an entirely different universe than their counterparts in the West Bank and Jerusalem. In Gaza, the main challenge wasn't getting to the target unnoticed, it was getting out alive. "The arsenals that were assembled inside the Gaza Strip and inside the refugee camps were mind-boggling," Shimon recalled. "Everyone had assault rifles, everyone had grenades and explosives. RPGs and IEDs were everywhere. And when one of our teams was discovered while operating inside the confines of a camp or a crowded neighborhood, everyone came out with their weapons and their fingers on the trigger. Suddenly, you could find yourself alone, ten or twelve men, under attack by a thousand people closing in from all sides."[6] Unlike the backup forces that stood at the ready to respond to the West Bank and Jerusalem units when they ventured into Palestinian areas, the Gaza Ya'mas did not enter the Strip unless a sizable force of armor was ready to punch through the barriers that separated Palestinian and Israeli lines; each and every Ya'mas entry into the Strip was coordinated with IAF helicopter gunships that hovered nearby, ready to rain down missiles and cannon fire on forces that threatened the undercover unit. Conditions warranted that the Gaza Ya'mas serve the two brigades in the Gaza regional division as an on-call commando force—one with unrivaled topographical recognition capabilities and specialized language skill sets.

Even the smallest undercover operation in Gaza was considered extremely high-risk. More than one million inhabitants and three million AK-47s were on a trigger fuse expecting some sort of *qawat al-hasa* operation anytime and anyplace; each man in the Ya'mas knew that regardless of the IDF units that were on standby to pull them out of the fire, they always operated alone, outnumbered and outgunned. Every man embarking on a foray across the wire knew this. It was a daunting reality.

The colloquial Arabic spoken in the Gaza Strip was very different from that spoken in the West Bank. Known as *Gazawee*, the slang and the mannerisms of speech were very similar to the Arabic spoken in Egypt but distinctively different from the Arabic spoken in the West Bank or even in West Beirut. The Speakers studied the local speech, just like their counterparts in Judea and Samaria studied the locals' dialects of Jenin, Nablus, and Jerusalem, but the *Gazawee* dialect was not easy to mimic—especially since the vast majority of the Speakers hailed from the Druze villages of northern Israel, where the language was markedly different. But the Speakers were some of the longest-serving operators in Gaza; they had worked inside the camps and they had patrolled the avenues before Oslo. They knew the pantomime of the street talk and they could get by in a brief verbal exchange. Still, a slip of the tongue could be deadly.

One type of undercover operation that the unit carried out was code-named "Check Post." Several operators, led by the Speakers, would masquerade as local gunmen and look for specific suspects, or hope to intercept terrorists heading toward one of the settlements. The operations were incredibly dangerous. The Speakers could not wear body armor while on such assignments, in order to look authentic. The Speakers were older than many of the officers and operators. Almost all of them were married with families. Standing in pairs along a route somewhere in the Strip where terrorists were known to pass, they had to remove thoughts of their wives and children from their circuitry and focus solely on the frenetic reality of their surroundings: the vehicular traffic that passed by without letup; the distance separating them from the Horse with the backup force; the suspicious passersby who might just suspect an Israeli operation and call Hamas, or even the Palestinian police. IDF officers, who watched these operations from the safety of a nearby

Command Post, used to comment on the special brand of courage that the Speakers displayed.

"We accepted the danger and we all understood the risk," Shimon reflected. "I believe in a higher authority and I believe in fate, but as a commander, someone who led these operations, my biggest concern was always with the soldiers in the backup force that would have to rush to my aid in case we found ourselves in a difficult situation. And that's why we underwent exhaustive preparations before each and every mission. Because we didn't want to mess up and then bring others into the mix as a result. Whenever we needed emergency backup, the risk of an operation becoming a full-scale battle was real."[7] The Check Post operations were highly successful. Set up at random locations along routes that had been used in the past by terrorists moving toward their targets, the sting operations netted extraordinary eyes-on-target HUMINT. Dozens of wanted men were rounded up in these dragnet operations.

On January 3, 2002, naval commandos from Flotilla 13 intercepted the Tonga-registered MV *Karine A*, a freighter loaded with Iranian weapons, as it sailed in the Red Sea toward the Suez Canal. The ship, captained by a Fatah crew, carried a sizable cargo of weapons and ammunition that consisted of 122mm Katyusha rockets; 107mm rockets; 80mm mortar shells; 120mm mortar shells; Sagger wire-guided antitank missiles; antitank mines; thousands of AK-47 assault rifles; sniper rifles; and enough ammunition to arm brigades of infantrymen. The ship's hold also carried nearly three tons of high-grade military explosives. The *Karine A* had intended to dock covertly off the coast of El Arish, in Sinai on the Mediterranean coast, some twenty-eight miles south of Rafah, and deliver the payload to Palestinian forces inside the Strip.[8] The ammunition had been packaged in ingeniously designed tubes, each approximately eight feet long and two feet in diameter, that could be dumped in the surf off of the Sinai coast and then retrieved by divers; each canister was painted sea-green and attached to two smaller tubes connected by a valve for buoyancy. The entire load of weapons was meant to be retrieved by divers operating off of Palestinian fishing vessels.[9]

The weapons, worth $10 million, had been arranged through the auspices of Hezbollah as a measure to gain a foothold—with Hamas, the PIJ, and Arafat's Fatah—inside Gaza for operations against Israel.

The seizure of the *Karine A* was revealed on the same day that Yasir Arafat pledged his efforts for peace with U.S. Marine Corps General (Ret.) Anthony C. Zinni, U.S. president George Bush's special envoy to Israel and the Palestinian Authority.

There was no peace in the West Bank. The war for Gaza continued. The violence escalated at an alarming pace.

CHAPTER TWENTY

Mogadishu

The first word of the mission reached Ya'mas headquarters very early in the morning—before any of the officers had had time to sleep much, and before the first cup of high-octane rocket fuel coffee could hit their systems. Operations of this size and magnitude were usually in the works for weeks, if not longer, but this call to action was immediate. The officers, reviewing the orders, did not like anything on such short notice.

The Palestinian terrorist campaign was spiraling out of control. The seizure of the *Karine A* was a stark and conclusive statement that the Palestinians, enlisting sponsors with deep pockets and vast arsenals, had hoped to escalate the intifada into a full-blown Middle Eastern war. The long-range capabilities of the weapons seized—as well as Arafat's long-range strategic intentions—were game changers. The Israeli response would be symbolic and measured. The target circled in red on the map by the generals in Tel Aviv was the seven-story broadcast center in the Ali el-Montar section of Gaza City that had transmitted inciting propaganda to the entire area; the station, used as a media hub for all of the Palestinian factions, including Hezbollah, had been a propaganda tool in the recruitment of operatives and a strategic—and tactical—link with cells operating in the West Bank and East Jerusalem. The decision to destroy the facility was made in a midnight meeting at the highest levels. Ya'mas operations and intelligence officers were fine-tuning the details of the commando strike by breakfast.

The broadcast center had to be taken out by men on the ground. The IDF General Staff wanted to avoid unnecessary collateral damage at all costs—otherwise an IAFF-16 would simply have dropped a one-ton bomb on the building and returned to its hangar before the dust cloud of debris cleared.

Ali al-Montar was a heavily populated area in the eastern part of Gaza City and one of the few areas of the Strip with hills; the area's high ground, in fact, had made it a formidable Ottoman Turkish fortress meant to stop colonial forces during the First World War. To the southwest of Ali al-Montar was the Kami Crossing, a cargo terminal on the Israel–Gaza Strip frontier that was opened in 1994 to enable Palestinian merchants to export and import goods.

The plan called for a small force of Ya'mas operators to spearhead the takeover of the broadcast center and secure the location while combat engineers rigged the building with explosives. The building was known as a Fatah nerve center—heavily armed members of Arafat's security services, especially the notorious Force 17 Praetorian Guard, had fortified positions nearby. In the effort to keep civilian casualties down to a minimum and limit the collateral damage, the Israelis announced that they'd be coming and warnings were issued for the residents of Ali al-Montar to keep off the streets.

The staging area for the raid was a forward base used by the Giva'ati Infantry Brigade's Almond Battalion at Netzarim, near the Mediterranean coast deep into the Strip. Because of the heavy gunfire that the assault force was expected to encounter, the eighteen men participating in the raid were to cross the six miles of thick Gaza squalor inside the belly of three Merkava Main Battle Tanks; the cargo hold of the tank, where the forty-eight 120mm shells were stored, was emptied in order to make room for the twelve Ya'mas operators and the combat engineer demolitions experts. A backup force of Giva'ati infantrymen, and the raid's overall command echelon, would follow in armored personnel carriers.

Chief Inspector Shimon commanded the Ya'mas portion of the operation. This sort of conventional commando strike wasn't the Ya'mas specialty, but they knew the terrain and they knew the language. Their assignment was to clear the building of all noncombatants and secure the perimeter so that the combat engineers could work safely and quickly inside the building.

Shimon and Yaron selected their men and used the daylight hours to review the brigade intelligence files, aerial photographs, and route maps. Yaron, whose background was as a training officer, found an abandoned structure so that the men could practice room clearing. The day evaporated in the exhausting pre-raid preparations. The Ya'mas operators ate a small dinner and then reviewed the intelligence once again. They suited up shortly before

2200. The hope was that the force would be back for the debriefing before dawn, but hopes were usually dashed inside the unpredictable bullet trap of the Strip. The operators grabbed extra provisions. Pistol and M4 magazines that could no longer fit inside pouches were crammed inside trouser cargo pockets. It was closing in on midnight.

It was just after 2300 when Lieutenant Colonel Erez Katz, the Almond Battalion commander, addressed everyone participating in the assault in order to outline each and every aspect of the operation. His infantrymen were conscripts, as were the combat engineers; some were only a year out of high school and a few months out of basic training. The soldiers struggled to balance the weight of their body armor and equipment with the clashing forces of fear and adrenaline that raced through their veins. Many of the infantrymen were half the age of the Ya'mas veterans who stood nonchalantly next to them. The thumping cadence of a helicopter gunship was heard in the darkened skies to the north. A crisp winter's wind flowed in from the sea. The hatches of the armored vehicles were sealed and the engines fired up. The convoy crossed into Palestinian territory at 2330.

The tanks were claustrophobic, the air inside stifling. The fifteen-hundred-horsepower turbocharged engine created a disheartening vibration that those unaccustomed to armored warfare found unnerving. The Ya'mas operators preferred to enter Gaza silently, stealth-like on foot, or inside any vehicle that you could see out of. The men inside each tank sat silently for the slow journey, as the Merkava's heavy tracks ground a course for the sixty-five-ton behemoth across dirt roads and paved thoroughfares. The deeper the convoy pushed into Gaza City, the more frequent the ping of AK-47 rounds bouncing off the Merkava's top-secret composite armor.

The armored vehicles arrived on schedule but were met by a thunderous greeting of small arms and sniper fire. The rear latch doors of the Merkava tanks were lowered slowly. The twelve Ya'mas operators and the six combat engineers rushed out of the hulking vehicles and into the building to evade the rounds that whizzed dangerously close overhead. The Shin Bet had sent a warning to their Palestinian counterparts informing them of the raid, but the gesture meant to avoid an armed clash had only served as an invitation to those itching for a fight. Clearing seven stories of rooms, offices, closets, and corners should have been assigned to a sizable contingent of tactical operators, but the task was left to only a handful of men from the Ya'mas. Danger lurked everywhere inside the building; the search for explosives and booby traps was as extensive as the hunt for hidden gunmen. Shimon and Yaron, along with their squads, had to spread out and methodically search every corner of the building as they made their way up toward the roof. Technicians and broadcasters, defiantly preparing the next day's programming, had to be convinced to leave. The Ya'mas Arabic-language skills were essential in de-escalating a potentially explosive confrontation, as the broadcasters angrily left the building.

But there were Palestinian gunmen in the building who refused to leave. They barricaded themselves inside offices and reception areas, and fired at the encroaching Ya'mas forces. Fierce battles developed in stairwells and inside studios crammed with sound-attenuating foam and expensive electrical equipment. A Palestinian gunman standing by a window was killed when he opened fire on the Ya'mas, and his body was thrown to the street below. When Shimon made it to the roof, he radioed Lieutenant Colonel Katz that the building was secured and that the demolitions team could start their work. The Ya'mas room clearing had taken all of twenty minutes.

Shimon positioned his men on the rooftop. Snipers peered through the scopes of their rifles to scan the horizon. The night was murky and an orange haze glistened over the darkness. The Ya'mas contingent attempted to locate—and neutralize—the source of sporadic gunfire directed toward the broadcast center from the outer periphery. But then the call to war came from a nearby mosque, broadcast on speakers usually used to summon the faithful to prayer. The Israeli Army was nearby, a voice bellowed in a loud and resolute message that sliced through the night, and everyone with a weapon was urged to kill them.

Suddenly, the snipers noticed hundreds of figures scampering in the distance, closing range on the Israeli perimeter. Gunmen invaded nearby apartment blocks and began firing at will toward the seven-story structure, from the living rooms of families woken by the developing battle. Tracer rounds crisscrossed the darkness from everywhere, in a dazzling display of green light. Shimon ordered his snipers to engage.

The battle raged for over an hour. The Palestinian gunfire was incessant. So, too, was the Ya'mas response. The snipers and their designated marksmen were able to pick off the figures in the shadows taking aim with their AKs. Quite a few were killed in the exchange, but still they continued to come in the hundreds. Shimon checked with the battalion commander. The charges were in place. Nearly ninety minutes had passed since the rear doors of the tanks had been lowered to launch the strike, and now the building was ready for obliteration. The soldiers and Ya'mas operators were ordered out. Officers made sure that no man was left behind.

The Speakers used megaphones and the loudspeakers on the armored vehicles to implore residents to go nowhere near the building. The warnings were emphatic; the message that the building was rigged with explosives and that people were to stay far clear was repeated in impeccable Arabic over and over again. The operators called these endeavors "Discotheque": like DJs calling dancers to the floor, the Speakers called on local residents to stand back.

The Israeli raiders returned to their tanks and APCs to begin the slow-moving journey out of Ali al-Montar. Heavy bursts of machine-gun fire were launched at the Israeli armor; Palestinian snipers did their best to try and shoot at the tank commanders, in the hope of disabling one of the tanks, but the convoy pushed ahead toward Israeli lines. A radio signal detonated the carefully placed explosive charges, causing the seven-story structure to implode and collapse to its foundation. The mission had been a success. Seven Palestinian gunmen had been killed in the mini-battles that developed. There were no Israeli casualties.

Chief Inspector Yaron always made sure that new operators to the unit received a proper welcome when arriving at the Ya'mas home base near Kissufim Junction. He made sure that each new man's paperwork was in order, and he personally walked the new arrivals through the process of receiving their coveralls, web gear, weapons, and a bunk in their team's quarters. Yaron made sure that each man was fed and that he had time for a coffee. And then he popped a videocassette into a battered VCR so that the men could watch a movie. Every member of the Gaza Ya'mas force was treated to Yaron's personal theater of the 2001 film *Black Hawk Down*, directed by Ridley Scott and scripted by Ken Nolan.

There were lessons—operational and tactical—in the story of America's top-tier special operations forces and a raid that turned into a desperate battle for survival inside the heart of a city ripped apart by famine and guerrilla warfare. And Yaron appreciated just how effective a learning aid a Hollywood blockbuster could be. But rather than revel in the big picture, he was determined to show how improper planning and Murphy's Law could turn any operation into a deadly fiasco. "Never ever go out in the field without all your gear," Yaron used to tell the men following the film. "You never know when a three-hour operation will turn in a three-day ordeal." But there was another, more daunting, similarity between the events of *Black Hawk Down* and the Ya'mas campaign in the Gaza Strip. The Ya'mas found itself operating in every corner of the Gaza Strip, often seven kilometers deep inside Palestinian territory, all alone and surrounded by thousands of heavily armed men. Every day in Gaza had become Mogadishu.

The Ya'mas mission in Gaza was threefold: serve as a rapid response force to counter any terrorist attack against the Israeli settlements that dotted the northern, central, and southern tiers of the Strip; carry out special assignments for the command and for Israeli intelligence against hostile terrorist targets in Gaza, to include the capture or killing of high-value terrorist suspects; and spearhead operations meant to stop the flow of arms and explosives reaching the terrorist groups through the smuggling tunnels that popped up along the entire Egyptian frontier. Every Israeli operation inside Gaza resulted in a full-blown battle. Other elite units, including Israel's top-tier forces, soon began to seek assignments against targets there. The Shin Bet preferred, almost exclusively, to use the Ya'mas.

Every encounter turned into a battle, and every battle turned into a daylong military endeavor that was complex, high-risk, and involved tanks and helicopter gunships. On December 6, 2002, a raid into the Bureij refugee camp, a sprawling squalor of 33,000-plus inhabitants squeezed into one-fifth of a square mile, in the center of the Gaza Strip, turned into a daylong battle. The raid had been planned as a tweezers operation, but it turned into an all-hands conflagration when mosque loudspeakers urged all armed men to join the fight.[1] Ten Palestinians were killed in the fighting.

The following day, combat engineers worked under fire to neutralize a forty-five-kilogram IED that had been buried underneath a stretch of roadway that was patrolled near Khan Yunis. There was what appeared to be an inexhaustible supply of military-grade explosives entering the Gaza Strip. The devices, as well, were of an intricate sophistication that had not been seen since Hezbollah's use of powerful IEDs during the IDF's costly anti-guerrilla campaign in southern Lebanon; it was believed that Hezbollah bomb-builders, true masters at creating camouflaged improvised explosive devices, had been smuggled into the Gaza Strip through Egypt in order to help Hamas and the PIJ create their own highly sophisticated explosive workshops.[2] Ya'mas teams embarking on missions inside the Strip soon located IEDs planted in rubbish bins and even on the outer walls of family homes. On some missions, the unit ventured into the Strip together with explosive-sniffing dogs from the IDF's elite Oketz (Hebrew for "Sting") K9 unit. Dangerous work was becoming all the more treacherous.

The objective of all Ya'mas operations was to get in and out of an area without being noticed. Although the Gaza Strip was sealed off by barbed wire fencing, walls, sensors, and other barriers meant to stop all traffic in and out, with the exception of the controlled crossing points, the unit had a series of locations that only they knew about where they could enter the Strip concealed from prying eyes. Entries were all about stealth. Palestinian dogs barked at anything suspicious that moved in the night, so unit operators would immerse their coveralls and their load-bearing gear near garbage fires, in order for the garments to smell like burned trash and confuse and quiet the dogs. Speakers—and the unit veterans whose Arabic was passable—would sometimes enter the Strip in costume, walking point for the remainder of the raiding force that would walk quickly and silently behind them. Many operations required that the Ya'mas team deploy on foot, sometimes but not always followed by backup teams in vehicles. Often, a target could be as close as several hundred feet to a kilometer away from the point of entry, but other times unit personnel walked ten kilometers or even more toward their target. The classic use of the undercover unit Horse was not applicable to the Gaza battlefield. There was always a drone or an aircraft hovering overhead to monitor the unit's progress and to provide eyes-in-the-sky real-time intelligence. A force of tanks and APCs was always at the ready to respond to any trouble; a Cobra or Apache gunship hovered to react with missiles at a moment's notice. The mood in the CP, where the unit commander and his

IDF and Shin Bet counterparts looked at shadows on the screen, was always nail-bitingly tense.

The Gaza Strip, for all intents and purposes, was another country—another universe—from the West Bank and Jerusalem. "There were actual borders separating Gaza from Israel, true barriers and obstacles, and permanent crossing points," a veteran counterterrorist officer explained about operations in the Strip. "Gaza, to many in the defense establishment, was no different than Syria or Lebanon; it was enemy territory rife with risk. Once we were inside, we were in a foreign universe of absolute danger where we knew of the horrible fate that would befall us if any of us were captured. Even if killed, we knew that our corpses would be violated and then held as bargaining chips. But there was also great reward in Gaza. Gaza was where the terrorist leadership lived and operated openly."[3]

Dozens of top terrorist commanders were killed in the Gaza Strip by the Israeli military and intelligence services: On February 13, 2001, an IAF AH1-S Cobra helicopter gunship fired three missiles at a Hyundai driven by Masoud Hussein A'ayyad, a colonel in Arafat's Force 17 and a man identified by Israeli intelligence as behind efforts to establish Hezbollah cells in the Strip; and on July 23, 2002, an IAF F-16 dropped a one-ton bomb on the home of Salah Shehada, the commander of the Izzedine al-Qassam Brigade (the bomb killed Shehada, his wife and daughter, and twelve others, in addition to wounding 150 more and destroying much of the Gaza City block). There were other airborne targeted killings, as they were known in the Israeli vernacular—some run-of-the-mill, others game changing. The campaign in Gaza, though, could only be won by a relentless ground effort to unnerve the terrorist underground and place them in such a state of fear and disarray that their focus would be on day-to-day self-preservation rather than attacks against Israel. The role of the Ya'mas teams in Israel's campaign targeting the top Palestinian terrorist leadership remains classified.

The Ya'mas work schedule was one of absolute overload. The operational calendar encompassed ambushes, rotating deployments to the settlements, direct action work with the Shin Bet, and of course arrests. The week passed by quickly. There was little time to sleep, let alone think. Any free time was dedicated to training: shooting on the range, perfecting vehicle takedowns in squad-size ambushes, and unit-size exercises involving large-scale apprehension techniques. When they weren't leading the teams and squads in the field, Ya'mas officers and NCOs were always behind a desk putting the last details of plans together, or they were in a vehicle, rushing from one location to another. It was better, some thought, not to have any downtime, since it was usually spent fast asleep slumped over in a horrifically uncomfortable position.

Unit commanders attempted to allow their men to maintain something of a regular schedule that enabled those with wives and children to maintain the semblance of a normal existence. Weekend leaves were cherished. Wives were happy to see their husbands, and the men were deliriously grateful to see their small children. Leaves began on Friday, usually before noon, and the men were expected back at base bright and early Sunday morning to start the operational workweek. When the week's calendar was marked off with scheduled apprehension raids, the men were paged Saturday afternoon and ordered back to base. The arrest procedures involved an absolutely excruciating work schedule. Some of the arrest operations were multipronged and far-reaching and incredibly ambitious for a battlefield so treacherous. In one dragnet, in Khan Yunis, the Ya'mas spearheaded a four-tiered entry into the Strip to simultaneously take down four high-ranking Hamas commanders. The operation required that a large portion of the force enter Khan Yunis undercover, while another force, in full tactical attire, was supported by armor and mechanized infantry.

"We were a service provider," commented Vlad,* a no-nonsense product of the Soviet republics who had fought with the Ya'mas immediately in the undefined days following the Oslo Accords and then returned to the Ya'mas when the war broke out. "We were there to provide the Shin Bet with tactical answers to their needs. Each success we had, each ambush carried out in which terrorists were killed, and each arrest mission where we brought a high-value individual back for questioning, earned us more work; greater

---

* A pseudonym—true identity withheld for security considerations.

responsibility and greater expectations. Commanders, at the brigade and battalion level, and at much higher ranks, soon were on a first-name basis with many of us."[4]

Brigade and divisional commanders were always reticent about arrest operations in Gaza because they were so involved and so high threat. But as the conflict continued with no sign of abatement, the Ya'mas began to apprehend more and more high-value targets in an intensive schedule of deep-penetration forays.

In December 2002, one of the names that popped up repeatedly on the Shin Bet's radar was Yassin Ayda, a Hamas weapons officer and the architect of a long string of mortar and bomb attacks against Israeli settlements and Israeli forces in the area. Ayda was one of the top Hamas commanders in the southern portion of the Gaza Strip; the men he commanded attempted to hit the settlements of Gush Katif on what appeared to be a daily basis. The Gaza Division assembled a voluminous rap sheet of strikes—and attempted strikes—that had been perpetrated by Ayda's cells. He was in charge of dozens of operatives, the Shin Bet surmised, and he had links to other cell commanders throughout the Gaza Strip as well as to smugglers and operatives on the Egyptian side of the border that fed his cells with a healthy supply of weapons and ammunition. The Shin Bet wanted to place him inside an interrogation facility and find out everything he knew, and to get the names and numbers of everyone he knew. The mission was handed off to the Ya'mas.

Unlike many of the top-level terror suspects in the West Bank, Ayda did not sleep in a different bed every night and emerge from his hiding spot surrounded by a phalanx of armed guards. Ayda hid in plain sight, in his home with his wife and children, in the center of Khan Yunis, almost daring the Israelis to come and get him; the neighborhood where he lived was a small metropolis of buildings, crowded streets, sprawling avenues, shops and cafés, schools, mosques, and an intertwining network of alleyways that were maze-like and treacherous. There were 142,000 residents in Khan Yunis, all packed inside twenty-one square miles of poor urban planning and abandoned civil services. The city's residents possessed a reputation of being resilient and stubbornly defiant—first against the Ottoman Turks, then against the British, as well as against the Egyptians, and finally the Israelis.

The Palestinian Authority thought that it controlled Khan Yunis, but the city was unquestionably a Hamas bastion.[5]

The Ya'mas had been to Khan Yunis before, after all. Some of the veterans, such as Inspector Shimon, who had been serving in the Strip for fourteen years, had the name of each street, each alley, engraved inside their memory banks. Shimon knew the names of the prominent clans who lived there, he knew which streets were most exposed to sniper fire, and he knew the quickest ways in and the most direct lanes out. From locations alongside the intricate, crisscrossing, almost M. C. Escher–like labyrinth of entry points and access roadways—hidden and some less so—the unit didn't consider it a significant challenge to enter the confines of Khan Yunis covertly. But getting out of Khan Yunis safe and sound—with a high-value target like Ayda in tow—was not going to be easy: One trip wire pulled, one cat stepped on, one potted plant knocked to the ground, one misplaced cough, and the stealth-like entry would be compromised and the raiding force subjected to fire all around. There could be no Hunting Days like in the West Bank—no prolonged forays to target a ledger list full of suspects and see who popped up on the radar. In the Strip, each operation was finite and pinpoint. Each entry demanded precise intelligence and enormous resources set aside to back the force up and pull it out of harm's way. Each arrest operation was a full-blown military commitment.

The details of every Ya'mas foray inside Gaza required intensive preparation. The Speakers needed to rehearse their role in reaching the target first—some in disguise, and others in full tactical kit—to be followed by the remainder of the assault force that would cordon off the home and secure it. Additional units of Ya'mas operators would then flood the area and create a ring-tight perimeter so that the arrest team, along with the Shin Bet case agents, could make the identification and apprehension. The Shin Bet agents always came along. Sometimes they dressed as one of the Ya'mas operators; other times, to their choosing, they wore the casual shirt and blue jeans uniform that personified their gritty work.

The Speakers, along with the backup forces, would usually prepare for the operation on a mock-up of the targeted location. Sometimes, a building with the same layout could be found in one of the army bases or towns of southern Israel close to the Gaza Strip. Other times the unit would simply find some plywood—by hook or by crook—and build the mock-up on their own. Thousands of collective man hours went into determining the minutest details of each and every operation. Nothing would be left to chance. The exhausting question-and-answer session of *Mikrim ve'Tguvot* that Shimon would make the officers and NCOs go through was designed to make sure that every scenario, any contingency, and any bizarre possibility was considered well in advance. The arrest plans had to be approved at the brigade and then divisional levels. There were lots of moving pieces to effect one man's apprehension.

The Yassin Ayda raid was slated for just after midnight on December 10, 2002. The forecast called for stormy skies.

Winter was a good time for arrest operations. The cool winds that hit off the Mediterranean shore limited the number of people moving about late at night. Most families were huddled together under blankets in an attempt to stay warm; those lucky enough to have a space heater and functioning electricity to power it were able to avoid the chill with better success. A few taxicabs could be seen maneuvering through the empty streets at top speeds. The fares were few and far between. Impromptu roadblocks always sprang up. Gangs allied to Hamas, or the PIJ, always attempted to profess their territoriality with an armed showing. The mosques, though, ran a 24/7 operation. There were always gunmen near the mosques.

The Speakers and their tactical support moved silently in the Khan Yunis dark, darting in and out of the shadows. Dogs barked in the distance. The Speakers demonstrated remarkable poise as they walked forward, knowing that untold numbers of Hamas gunmen were all around, and only a few heavily armed men had their backs. The exact foot route had been predetermined days in advance. Aerial photographs had mapped out the path. Extensive intelligence files had choreographed every step that the operators would take toward Ayda's house. The Speakers moved gingerly under the winter sky and the orange glow from the few streetlights that worked. The cover story had been worked on at headquarters, together with Shin Bet coordinators; the Speakers had spent days practicing their Gaza slang and researching the latest and greatest inside the Strip, in case anyone popped out of the darkness to challenge them. As the Speakers walked forward, they searched for trip wires and IEDs. The first pincer of the tactical force moved closely behind. The men raised their weapons toward the windows and openings they encountered. Not everyone was asleep. The sounds of pots and pans clanking together could be heard coming from some of the homes. Some of the men heard the low-volume hum of ballads coming from a radio.

The targeted house was one of two three-story homes that made up a complex for an extended clan and were typical for the Strip. The clan, generations of the same family, lived in the homes that had been dormered in a jigsaw puzzle manner to accommodate a growing patriarchal family. The homes were situated on a side street, cornered on three sides by alleys. The building where Ayda was reportedly living was dark and isolated.

The raiding force moved silently in and out of the shadows and into position. One element covered their north, east, west, and southern points, securing the building. The Speakers, who had moved ahead of everyone else, lowered their balaclavas over their faces. The code word was transmitted for the rest of the arrest team to race on in.

The distance between the Israeli point of entry and Ayda's house was just a few kilometers. It took the entry team, in vans and military vehicles, only a few minutes to reach the targeted buildings. The procedure mandated that one force search the house, together with the Shin Bet case officer, while the other two secure the perimeter and hold off anyone who might attempt to interfere with the arrest operation. The ideal scenario for an entry team was to snatch the target while he was still asleep. There were operations when the Speakers made it to the house, the entry force entered the location, and the suspect was cuffed without anyone in the house knowing what was happening until it was too late; sometimes, the terror groups only learned that one of their own had been seized days after he had spent a fair amount of time talking to the Shin Bet. It was hoped, at least, that in Ayda's case he could be found quickly and whisked away with little fuss. But the first search yielded nothing. Family members living in apartments were brought outside and questioned while a bomb-sniffing dog from Oketz was brought in to search for booby traps and any caches of arms and explosives that could be on the premises. The entry team found nothing, though; their search was thorough, but apparently Ayda wasn't at home. The operators were under strict guidelines not to disrupt any element of the home as long as their lives were not in danger, though items such as floppy disks and papers were gathered for their intelligence value. But the target of the operation was nowhere to be found.

"He's not here," one of the Ya'mas officers told the Shin Bet case agent as the sounds of distant shots became more prevalent. "We've looked every-where."[6] The Shin Bet officer looked at his mobile phone and dismissed the Ya'mas findings. "He's here," the man in his thirties said, careful not to remove the balaclava that had become uncomfortable during the search. "Look again."[7] The force was ordered in again.

Outside, along the perimeter, the odd gunshot turned into a flurry of tracer rounds and automatic bursts. Some of the conscripts, new members to the unit who had yet to be truly tested under fire, needed one of the older hands to calm them down. Their trepidation was well founded. Soon all of Khan Yunis would be alerted, one of the operators thought. How long would the search go on? But then Lior,* the team leader responsible for the perimeter force, heard a noise coming from one of the rear doors. "*Tawaqaf Jesh*," Vlad yelled in Arabic laced with a distinctively Urals accent, as he identified himself as a soldier and ordered anyone out there to stop. The perimeter commander radioed the incident to the men directing the entry team, but they assured everyone that the house was empty. The perimeter team grew nervous. The operators raised their M4s all around, worried that they were being set up for an ambush. They scanned the house—and the doorways and windows—with their night-vision goggles but could see no movement. "We were focused on any place where the suspect could escape from," Vlad reflected. "If he tried to flee, we would have been right there on top of him."[8]

Lior was convinced that the unit had missed something, and once again he ordered the search of the premises. The entry team departed to the perime-ter and the perimeter team entered the house to search. The operators looked under beds and in closets. Cupboards in a kitchen were searched as the men used the flashlights attached to their M4s to illuminate every crevice and corner of the home. The team searched storage areas above closets and inside

---

* A pseudonym—true identity withheld for security considerations.

the cramped apartments, storerooms, and large interconnecting passageways that were built when the house was modified to accommodate the growing extended family. The only part of the house that hadn't been searched was the roof—protocols dictated that the search parties avoid rooftops for tactical considerations. But Ayda was high-value, and the noises heard outside indicated that he was nearby.

Several men positioned themselves in a single-line stick formation at the foot of a small staircase leading toward a landing by the roof. Lior, the team leader, was on point. He inched his way upward. The staircase was narrow; the marble tiles were slippery. Lior meticulously placed his feet, negotiating each step cautiously; one of the unit's veteran Speakers followed right behind him. As Lior neared the top of the stairs, he caught a fleeting glimpse of a shadow moving slowly in a corner behind a rooftop wall. He moved forward and quickly took aim. The face he saw resembled the Shin Bet wanted sheet mug shot of Ayda, but he didn't know if the suspect was armed or not, and that impacted what level of force could be used—it was within legal guidelines to shoot an unarmed suspect in the legs in order to immobilize him; the appearance of a firearm, or any other weapon, justified the use of lethal force.

Lior's procedural dilemma was solved when Ayda tossed a pipe bomb at the approaching Ya'mas stick. The device landed at the foot of the staircase, but failed to detonate. Lior took aim with his M4 and pulled on the trigger, but his assault rifle jammed. Lior reached for his secondary weapon, a 9mm pistol, but Ayda moved to swing his AK-47 at the approaching Ya'mas team. Before Lior could reach his sidearm, the operator standing directly behind him took aim and fired a dedicated burst at center mass. Ayda was thrown off his perch by the multiple hits to the chest and midsection, and he landed on the pavement of the alley below. The Shin Bet was right. Ayda had been at home all along.

The alleyway was strewn with litter and small puddles of rainwater from a previous day's storm. Ayda was still alive, still conscious, and he even tried to crawl away from the Ya'mas operators in the alley. He was quickly cuffed and searched. He was loaded onto one of the Ya'mas vehicles, with Ya'mas paramedics at his side.

Khan Yunis had already been awakened to a call to war. The sounds of shots fired awoke many inside the neighborhood, and many nearby, to the presence of Israeli forces. The mobile phone networks were abuzz with SMS messages and calls summoning armed men into the fray. The drone overhead transmitted images of dozens of men emerging into the dark Khan Yunis night; soon there would be hundreds of armed men moving toward Ayda's besieged house. Every operation became *Black Hawk Down*. Racing rounds, illuminated into a fierce glow, flew nearby, hitting the nearby buildings and causing plaster and concrete to fall to the street below. The Ya'mas force returned fire, selectively pinpointing hostile targets, careful to avoid hitting buildings or individuals who weren't armed. The radio frequencies were overloaded with transmissions and updates. Ground assets were on standby, as were IAF attack helicopters. Medical evacuation helicopters were on call, as well—if one of the Israelis was wounded, he would be airlifted to the trauma care unit at Soroka Medical Center in Beersheba, the largest hospital in southern Israel and one of the most experienced combat medical facilities in the world.

The Ya'mas force was virtually surrounded, albeit with access to a narrow escape path secured by IDF infantrymen. The undercover operators fought while positioned back-to-back, fighting threats all around, waiting for the order to withdraw.

The search of Ayda's secluded rooftop hiding spot revealed an impressive arsenal. Canvas satchels were shielded from overhead view by a corrugated metal awning. Ya'mas operators found AK-47s, pistols, suicide vests, hand grenades, explosives, wiring, and enough ammunition to equip a platoon. Seven sophisticated pipe bombs were also found atop the roof.[9] The raid commander did not want to leave the explosives behind, nor was he going to transport the volatile materials inside the cabin of one of the Ya'mas Horses, so he ordered his men to grab the firearms and bring them to the vehicles down below and summoned a D9 that was on standby as part of the rescue force. When dawn broke, there would be nothing left of the explosives or Ayda's hideout. Gunfire followed the convoy of vehicles all the way back to Israeli lines.

Circumstances prevented the Ya'mas from fulfilling the Shin Bet's demand that Ayda be captured and not killed; he died from his wounds at an Israeli aid station.

The Ya'mas would be back in Gaza again later that night—a different target and a different mission in the hunt for fugitives. But the Palestinians would be waiting. The Gaza Strip was quickly escalating into the Ground Zero of the intifada. Israeli counterterrorist efforts inside the West Bank and Jerusalem, together with the construction of the Separation Barrier, were strangling Palestinian efforts to set Israel ablaze.

CHAPTER TWENTY-ONE

The Unit Commander

The Nablus Kasbah was bustling that frosty December morning; shoppers moved about, concerned with completing their haggling at rival stalls and getting in out of the cold. The delectable smell of a dozen versions of flat bread, baked in the same way for centuries, competed with the sharp bite of hundreds of different spices, piled in ski slope–like mountains. Merchants sat outside their shops, chain-smoking Imperial cigarettes, while kittens, shivering in the cold, picked through scraps of discarded fat by a Dumpster near a butcher shop. The recent bone-numbing drizzle made the stone pavement treacherous and slippery, but people kept to themselves inside the narrow and ancient confines of the crowded Kasbah, home to some thirty thousand people,[1] and no one offered to help the woman, covered from head to toe in the *abaya*, struggling with the blanketed baby she cradled in her arms. She had come to the area in a red Mercedes sedan with local Palestinian license plates.[2]

The woman walked slowly, deliberately, looking at the shop windows and at her baby as she negotiated the decline and the steep steps. A man followed several paces behind her. He was old and walked with his back arched forward, finding it hard to carry a small bag that held the vegetables and herbs that he had purchased in the market. Two other men walked behind him. They walked cautiously, their eyes focused forward.

The woman made her way down the Yasmina stairs. Thirty-five meters long, four meters wide, the Yasmina stairs were the lifeblood of the old quarter. A few steps down the stairs, the woman paused for a second outside Kamal's, a small but popular barbershop and hangout carved into the stone walls. Loud music, the impassioned love song of a Syrian diva, blared on a pair of speakers that had been hung on the walls. The woman saw a man whose face she had studied for months. It was Imad Nasser. The woman tried to catch her breath, but her heart had swelled and was pounding a stiff fist that punched through her chest at 120 beats a minute. Nasser was leaning with his back against the wall sipping a small cup of pungent Arabic coffee from a small ceramic cup. One hand was poised behind his back. Another man whose face was familiar, Omar Arafat, was standing across from him. Several other men, faces unknown, were loitering about.

No one paid notice to the woman. Women were, after all, rarely considered and never noticed in public. She walked past Nasser and then swung around, producing an Israel Military Industries Mini-Uzi 9mm submachine gun from the blanket holding what was a doll of an infant child, but the weapon became tangled inside the cotton spread. Nasser was coiled. He removed a pistol from the small of his back and aimed at the woman's head. The woman contorted her body, bending her back toward the floor, and fired through the blanket. The old man, steps behind, grabbed the woman's head and fired as well. More than twenty bullets were fired into Nasser. He collapsed dead on the cold stone floor, in a puddle of his own blood.

Arafat was next. One of the two men who followed the old man shot and killed Arafat, Nasser's faithful bodyguard. A third man with a weapon, Hani Tayem, was shot and killed by the other man. The woman entered deeper into the shop to search for other armed men. The floor was wet, it had just been washed, and she slipped, falling square onto her back. Suddenly, a man jumped on her and attempted to seize the Mini-Uzi. The woman fought hard and then twisted the weapon so that the barrel pointed squarely into the man's chest. A squeeze of the trigger and the individual was flung back as if yanked by a rope. The burst had emptied the Mini-Uzi's thirty-round magazine. The woman got up and saw that Arafat had an Uzi magazine in his pocket. "Mind if I take this?" she asked politely, not quite fathoming that the bodyguard was dead.

Those who could, the armed men with a price on their heads, escaped off into the labyrinth of the Kasbah. Their time would come.

Operation Barbershop, December 1, 1989, was one of the most remarkable, complex, and highly successful Duvdevan operations of the first intifada—the operation took months of planning, had a dozen false alarms over time, and once the gunfire commenced, it took all of fifteen seconds for it to be over. The Kasbah was owned by the Black Panthers. Lookouts were everywhere. Anytime someone looked like he or she didn't belong, sentries would whistle a code; people who didn't belong could be abducted and killed. Imad Nasser, the target of the raid, was the head of Fatah's Black Panthers cell in Nablus, and a man personally responsible for the murders of fifteen people, most of whom were merely suspected of being collaborators with the Israeli security services. Duvdevan worked on Nasser's cell for months and had prepared several daring operations involving a handful of intrepid operators to take the cell out. Any operation inside the Kasbah was considered suicide, too dangerous to contemplate. Both chief of staff Lieutenant General Dan Shomron, the hero of Entebbe, and Prime Minister Yitzhak Shamir had to authorize the operation. Major General Uri Saguy, the head of Military Intelligence, laughed at the young sergeant responsible for planning the raid, who would masquerade as the woman. "You think you're in the movies?"[3]

The sergeant was, indeed, ballsy. He told the general that not only would the operation succeed, but that he would owe him an apology. The sergeant, the operator dressed as the woman with a child, was a twenty-one-year-old soldier known as Yehonatan.[*] Yehonatan began his military career in the IDF/navy's elite Flotilla 13 commando unit, before medical issues forced his transfer. He found a home in Uri Bar-Lev's fledgling Duvdevan force as an operations coordinator. Olive-skinned and gifted with an inherent knack for languages and Arabic in particular, Yehonatan pleaded with Bar-Lev to put him in the field as an undercover operative. Bar-Lev recognized Yehonatan's raw talent, and he cherished his exuberance and daring. Bar-Lev taught the enthusiastic sergeant how to rein in his enthusiasm and how to think outside the box while part of elaborate undercover missions.[4] Yehonatan quickly developed into one of the unit's most capable commandos. And General Saguy would, indeed, apologize to him.

Duvdevan was only the beginning for Yehonatan. He completed his military service and, as a result of his relationship with Uri Bar-Lev, was recruited to Unit 33 along with many others from Duvdevan. Unit 33 was a

---

[*] A pseudonym—true identity withheld for security considerations.

working laboratory for Yehonatan, a place where he honed many of his tactical and undercover skills in a difficult and politically charged environment. Following several intense years of operation inside Jerusalem, Yehonatan was promoted to the regular "blue" police, where he established an intelligence unit for major case work, in which he activated deep-cover agents in the field. His work, and an inherent knack for the covert world of intelligence work, earned him a spot in the Ya'ma'm, where he was tasked to create an intelligence squadron inside the counterterrorist and hostage rescue unit. His undercover experience, operating tactically amid a hostile population, was unprecedented.

In early 2003, Major General David Tzur, the Border Guard commanding officer, appointed Yehonatan the new commander of the Gaza Ya'mas unit. Yehonatan had been groomed to take over the West Bank Ya'mas unit, but at the last minute it was decided to send him to Gaza. He hadn't worked in the Strip for close to fifteen years.

By 2003 the Gaza theater of operations was embroiled in full-scale conflict. Palestinian attacks against Israeli forces and settlements had become almost daily occurrences; the small Border Guard bomb squad based in the Strip became, undoubtedly, the busiest EOD team in the world, rendering safe each day's bounty of confiscated ordnance and explosives planted near Israeli lines. Palestinian mortar teams wreaked untold havoc on Israeli settlements and on Israeli forces. The mortars, some of them relics from the Egyptian Army left behind in the Strip before 1967 and others that had been produced in fledgling weapon factories, were lethal and incredibly difficult to locate and destroy. Mortar teams sometimes used donkeys to carry the metal launching tubes, to hide them from the drones that constantly flew overhead. One mortar team, in particular, had evaded the Shin Bet for months. Operating near Khan Yunis, the team would launch one or two rounds and then usually disappear before IDF forces could respond. Yaron led a Ya'mas team into a citrus grove to try to surprise the mortar squad. The undercover squad remained in position, in improvised ghillie suits, invisible to all around—even the Palestinian farmers who came to tend their trees. Just as the order was about to be issued to end the operation, a small pickup truck pushed through the tall grass to a position in an open patch of the field. Before they could ready the tube for firing, a fusillade of fire erupted from the surrounding grounds. The mortar team never knew what hit them.

The Israeli response to the persistent Palestinian attacks was designed to retaliate and deter—to create an atmosphere of unrelenting force that would compel an end to the violence without precondition. But the war continued and escalated with each passing day.

The primary mission handed down to Yehonatan was for the Ya'mas to play an integral part in the IDF's effort to disrupt and destroy the arms-smuggling tunnels that served as a ballistic lifeline to the terrorist groups fighting Israel. Early on in the intifada, according to an interview with the television channel that Hamas had launched, Mahmoud al-Zahar, a cofounder of Hamas, along with a representative from Arafat's Preventative Security forces, held court with Izzedine al-Qassam Brigade commander Salah Shehada and informed him that he (a reference to Arafat) had no problem with Hamas carrying out operations against Israel.[5] Fatah and the Palestinian Authority established a shadowy—and deniable—entity called Omar al-Mukhtar to facilitate the transfer of weaponry, much of which was financed by the United States and other nations following the Oslo Peace Accords, although much of the firepower, such as RPGs, antitank rockets and grenades,[6] was never permitted under the peace understanding and the 1998 Wye River Memorandum that was designed to halt the flow of illegal weaponry into the Palestinian Authority. In order for the Palestinians to be able to maintain their combat operations against Israel, replenishment supplies of arms and ammunition had to flow into the Gaza Strip daily. That pipeline was found underground, beneath the fourteen-kilometer-long no-man's-land that separated Egyptian Sinai and Gaza, on a strip of ultra-strategic roadway known as the Philadelphi Corridor.

The Philadelphi Route, as it was known in IDF vernacular, had been established in 1979 as a buffer zone between the Egyptian frontier and the Gaza Strip, as well as a physical barrier designed to stem the flow of illegal arms from the smugglers in Sinai to the Palestinian groups in Rafah. Israel maintained control of the route as part of the 1995 Oslo Peace Accords, but relinquished control of most of the Strip to the newly formed Palestinian Authority. The roadway, wide enough to accommodate two lanes of traffic, stretched from the Mediterranean Sea, near the southernmost Gush Katif beachfront settlements, to the Keren Shalom crossing point that connected Egypt, Israel, and the Palestinian Authority.

The Philadelphi Route soon became one of the most heavily fortified—and contested—pieces of real estate inside the Palestinian–Israeli conflict. The IDF maintained constant security patrols of the route with armored vehicles and rapid deployment forces. Gigantic and heavily fortified observation posts, built upon mountain-size heaps of dirt that overlooked key sections of the roadway—especially near the city of Rafah, which had been virtually split in two by the Camp David Accords and Israel's return of Sinai to Egypt, and the adjacent Rafah refugee camp to the west of the city's boundaries. Rafah was a sprawling metropolis of congestion that packaged its seventy thousand inhabitants into a sardine can of a municipality. The United Nations–administered refugee camp set up to the west of the city was originally home to some forty thousand Palestinians, but by the time the intifada erupted the population had ballooned to nearly a hundred thousand people, including those living in a housing project called Tel el-Sultan.

When Rafah was split in two by the Egyptian–Israeli Peace Treaty, underground tunnels became a favored link connecting families, businesses, and terrorist organizations split by the fortified frontier. Initially, the tunnels were primitive. They were prone to cave-ins and discovery by Israeli forces; Arafat's security agencies, eager to earn a percentage from the contraband smuggled into the Strip, also made an effort to locate and control the tunnel traffic. The al-Aqsa intifada transformed the tunnels into an underground superhighway. The tunnels became more sophisticated and formidable, as well.

Building the tunnels was no small feat—in most cases, they had to be more than one thousand feet long and designed and dug by individuals with sound engineering fundamentals. The tunnels began in Gaza, in the basement of a home, a mosque, or a school; the location of preference was somewhere in the provenance of a family that the Shin Bet did not have on its radar. The tunnel had to be deep enough to avoid Israeli sensors placed near the border and to not undermine sewage or other underground lines as it spread toward the frontier. Telltale ventilation shafts had to be dug as well—a problem that would be later solved by diggers who wore self-contained breathing systems while underground. The deepest part of the tunnels were directly under the concrete walls that surrounded the most precarious portions of the Philadelphi Route, where the path was surrounded by both halves of Rafah—IDF engineers had placed steel plates deep underground to disrupt the ability to dig underground, but the Palestinians, undeterred, simply dug deeper. The tunnels would have to pass under the border security fence with Egypt and then several hundred more feet inside North Rafah on the Egyptian side, where an opening would be made in the basement of a home across the border. Egyptian Border Guards, uninterested in fighting the smugglers and usually earning a hefty percentage of what went in under their noses, did little to stop the enterprise. Luxurious goods, computers, electronics, black market pharmaceuticals, illicit narcotics, and the tools of war passed underground. The economies of both halves of Rafah depended on what flowed back and forth fifty feet below the topsoil.

As the battles intensified, Hamas and the PIJ depended on the tunnels for heavier weapons and more powerful explosives. Outside money—primarily through Iran and several endowments in the Gulf States—paid unimaginable premiums for every bullet, every grenade, and every kilo of Semtex and C4 that made it into Rafah. Weapons that were smuggled into Palestinian Authority–controlled areas had come from Egypt, Iraq, the Sudan, and Libya. They included Katyusha rockets, shoulder-fired antiaircraft missiles, antitank grenades and launchers, explosives, mortar shells, and AK-47s; the retail price for a Kalashnikov rifle in Gaza was $1,000, the same rate as it would cost to smuggle someone across the frontier.[7]

The smuggling operations became a twenty-four-hour-a-day, seven-day-a-week enterprise. A handful of tunnels soon sprouted dozens more; dozens turned into close to one hundred underground avenues. The tunnels also expanded in scale and ambition. Architectural designs were innovative. Concrete was siphoned off from Palestinian building and public works projects in order to line the walls and ceilings of tunnels with a durable infrastructure. Electrical lines even ran across many of the underground networks, as did telephone landlines. Some of the tunnels were high enough for men to stand upright in; others were wide enough to smuggle motorcycles and parts of SUVs.

The tunnels provided Bedouin arms smugglers inside Sinai with a starved market willing to pay top dollar for bullets and bombs. The tunnels

also provided Palestinian terrorist groups with a roundabout means of entering Israel that allowed them to evade the fenced-in confines of the traditional
borders. Known in Hebrew as the "Khet Route," because the terrorists could
follow a path that resembled the eighth letter in the Hebrew alphabet, it was
a route going down into Sinai, south toward the Gulf of Aqaba, and then
back up into Israel across the loosely fortified Egyptian border. The tunnels
became a tactical threat to Israel's day-to-day counterterrorist operations
inside Gaza and a strategic threat to the security of southern Israel. They
had to be stopped.

Early on, the Ya'mas dealt with the tunnel threat as part of its day-to-day
operational mission inside the Strip—if a Shin Bet case agent or coordinator
came up with information concerning a home under which a tunnel had been
operating, a Ya'mas team would usually go and examine it. These missions
were covert and designed to yield a small footprint. Some of the tunnels were
booby-trapped—rigged with explosives in order to deter inexperienced IDF
units from exposing the underground networks. Other tunnels were heavily
defended. Access points to the tunnels, and even the homes where they were
secretly dug, were wired with powerful IEDs.

In one operation, a Ya'mas team uncovered a small tunnel in the basement
of a home directly across the Philadelphi Route, with the Egyptian side clearly
within view. An operator thought that he heard a noise coming from inside
the darkened cavity dug deep in the earth below, and he decided to follow it
alone, determined not to let the digger get away. He tossed his helmet to the
ground, removed his flashlight and sidearm, and ventured underground.
He crawled on his knees when possible; in some areas he had to crawl on
his belly. He tried to guess how far he traveled underground, but there was
no way to gauge distance in the stifling darkness. The stench of urine, wood,
and concrete was suffocating in a tube that felt as if its air supply was being
drawn away minute by minute. When the operator finally found a small ray
of light emerging from the other side, he rushed in, as eager to breathe again
as he was to hopefully take care of the terrorist he thought had gotten away.
The operator shut off his flashlight, clutched his pistol, and raised his head at
the tunnel's exit, only to see Egyptian Border Guards only a few feet away. The
operator, who was only a cough away from creating an international incident,
having invaded Egyptian territory, feared that he would be taken prisoner

or worse. He took one last silent breath of fresh air before he resubmerged himself inside the tunnel, to hurriedly crawl back toward Palestinian Rafah as fast as humanly possible.

Neutralizing the tunnels became one of Chief Superintendent Yehonatan's primary missions, but the mission mandate underscored the unit's operational shortcomings, as well. The unit was not trained in the classic "Tunnel Rat" role; the unit's workload was so intensive, in fact, that it had little time to train at all. The unit's equipment was antiquated—operators ventured into active fields of fire with old rifles, old vests, and communications equipment that was ready for the trash bin. The unit did not have the proper ropes and other climbing gear required to enter tunnels that were ten meters deep, and they didn't have the rescue equipment to pull someone out in case of collapse. The unit had guts, a lot of motivation, and a great deal of good fortune that no one had been killed or wounded in the fighting. But one operation, shortly after Yehonatan's arrival, went poorly. The unit failed to bring in a terror suspect, and its standing at the divisional and brigade level was diminished. There were no excuses in the Gaza war. Failure was not tolerated.

It was not an auspicious beginning for Yehonatan's tenure of command and "it pushed the unit back somewhat," he would later admit. But throughout his career Yehonatan had learned to take adversity and turn it into opportunity.[8] He returned to the drawing board and accepted the fact that the unit could not operate safely—or successfully—unless structural and conceptual changes were made in its makeup, mission, and resources. Yehonatan and his staff drew up contingency reorganizational proposals to grow the unit in size and scope—the new Ya'mas. Yehonatan envisioned a larger unit, a more self-contained force that, like the Ya'ma'm, could handle most tactical assignments alone, without having to summon assistance from the IDF. Yehonatan also made sure that his men found the time to train. The little downtime that existed before Yehonatan's arrival would soon disappear altogether. Yehonatan, who, traffic permitting, could be home from the bowels of Khan Yunis to his living room couch in ninety minutes, rarely made it home at all. "We had wives and families waiting for us at home," team leader Yaron would comment. "Everyone wanted to be at home with their wives and their children. We wanted to have normal lives, visit friends and watch TV. In one way we didn't want to be in Gaza at all. In reality, we didn't want to be anywhere else. Our biggest concern in the unit wasn't that we would be killed or wounded. It was that we wouldn't be here [Gaza] when something major went down. No one wanted to hear about an operation the following day. We all wanted to be a part of it."[9]

There were plans to nearly double the size of the unit. Yehonatan lobbied the generals, both in the IDF and in the Border Guard, for increased funding so that the unit could acquire new equipment, new weapons, and new technologies. Yehonatan, a tall and solid figure with an endearing smile, was expert at promoting his men to the decision-makers and bean counters, alike. Yehonatan was the face of the Ya'mas Gaza—he was the unit's most vocal and impassioned ambassador, and he slowly but surely achieved many of his objectives. The incoming OC Southern Command, Major General Dan Harel, Yehonatan reflected, soon became a fan of the unit; the division commanders, as well, knew that the unit had a multidirectional operational outlook that rivaled—and often exceeded—the tip of the spear of IDF special operations units that also wanted in on the covert missions taking place inside the Strip.[10] The Ya'mas would no longer venture into harm's way without the backing and the tools it needed.

Yehonatan's plan was long-term, a process. Yehonatan's expanded framework involved the recruitment of top-flight personnel into the force, including from the very elite of the Israeli intelligence and special operations community, upon whose talents the unit could rewrite the counterterrorism doctrine for the Gaza front. And it was done on the fly while the unit went in day in and day out across the wire into Rafah. The tunnels, after all, were still being dug.

An essential element of all Israeli counterterrorism thinking was the notion of innovative *Davka*, that uniquely Hebrew term for stubborn and unflinching outside-the-box spite. The undercover counterterrorist units were formed to bring terror to the terrorists, and the protocol known as *Almanat Kash*, or Grass Widow, was created out of necessity as a means to operate indivisibly and undisturbed inside heavily populated hostile areas in order to prevent terrorist attacks against Israeli civilian and military targets; according to a paratroop officer credited with fine-tuning the protocol, it was "giving guerrilla to the guerrillas."[11]

Grass Widows were basically sniper operations—the use of multiple long-range snipers to selectively target armed individuals (weapons and explosives) that threatened Israeli forces operating in the area—primarily those engaged in the search for and destruction of smuggler tunnels. Snipers, traditionally, worked alone or in tandem and found vantage points suited to their own requirements and camouflaging opportunities. But in a landscape such as Gaza, two men operating alone was tantamount to suicide; risking two highly trained and very skilled professional sharpshooters was against all military logic. The Grass Widow protocol was simply a measure by which the snipers could focus all their energies on hostile targets and not be concerned with watching their backs. Yehonatan and his Ya'mas force didn't invent the Grass Widow tactic—but over time they would perfect it in some of the hardest fought engagements of the al-Aqsa intifada.

Yehonatan's first such operation, as unit commander, was a memorable one. The Ya'mas was responsible for leading mechanized soldiers from the Bedouin Reconnaissance Battalion, a force made up solely of Bedouin volunteers into the IDF, who served the Gaza Division's Southern Brigade along the border with Egypt and the ultra-strategic and sensitive Philadelphi Route, on an anti-tunnel operation. The Bedouins were fierce and stoic warriors in their own right; many of them were desert trackers who worked along the southern frontier, looking at footprints along the road near the border fence; the reconnaissance unit was one of the primary units that fought the Tunnel Wars opposite Rafah. Yehonatan was very comfortable working with the Bedouins because of his fluency in Arabic, but he had never led APCs into battle before. The Ya'mas mission that night in 2003 was to lead the Bedouin M113 APCs to a deployment point near the border in search of tunnels, while the unit's snipers set up positions a few kilometers away to protect the soldiers. Yehonatan had never worked with armored vehicles before, and he didn't like it. An RPG could come from anywhere and slice through the M113 without difficulty and kill everyone inside.

The landscape of Rafah was surreal, apocalyptic. Darkness punctuated by the flash of gunfire and bursts of flames from IEDs and explosive charges. Automatic bursts of machine-gun fire crackled in the distance. Palestinian sniper fire whizzed close by. Yehonatan looked at the Bedouins, and they were focused; this was routine for them. The new Ya'mas commander then looked at Shimon, his deputy, and Yaron, the trusted and experienced team leader. They were cool and composed. They had done this so many times before.

Virtually all of the entries into Gaza to carry out the Grass Widows operations were carried out under cover of darkness. At a predesignated location, the Ya'mas force disembarked from the APCs. Two teams led by Yehonatan scurried to seize control of one complex; a third team, led by one of the unit NCOs, crawled to avoid bursts of errant AK fire, to seize another building. Speakers and other operators in disguise helped cut a silent path into the sprawling southern neighborhoods of Rafah and the homes that had been preselected as observation posts. Some homes consisted of courtyards and walls and gates that shielded the structures from outside view, and the operators scaled the fences in order to open the iron gates so as not to alert anyone of their presence. Homes with courtyards and high and sturdy stone or metal fences were preferred—just in case one of the terrorist groups decided to send a suicide bomber into the building in a rigged vehicle.

The two Ya'mas forces quickly reached their objective and secured the homes. Grass Widows were very unpleasant operations. Innocent families had to be awoken from their slumber and assembled into a single room where they could be watched. The women were always frightened; the children always cowered behind someone. Speakers, or personnel who spoke Arabic, always tried to calm the situation down. The home was searched for weapons and tunnels, and one of the men, usually the family patriarch, was interviewed by one of the Speakers; the women were never searched, never touched, and always spoken to through a male member of the family. "Cultural sensitivities that we displayed were critical in preventing disrespect or undue difficulties," Yehonatan would reflect.[12]

The operators always brought extra provisions with them—extra food, extra water, and even plastic bags in which they would go to the bathroom if necessary. The operators were forbidden to touch the family's food or water; they were not allowed to accept sweets that the children sometimes offered to the men who stood guard over them. The families were always scared, though, knowing that Hamas or the al-Aqsa Martyrs Brigade would use all the firepower at their disposal to fight off the Israelis, destroying the house if necessary. Yet, as was once reflected to one of the Arabic-speaking operators by the patriarch of a clan, the family was relieved that the men in the house were Israelis and not Palestinian security. Families in Rafah had little access to banks and they kept all their valuables at home; Arafat's security men were prone to home invasions in search of ways to augment their miniscule salaries.

Yaron's use of the film *Black Hawk Down*, to instill the notion that more was always better than less, guaranteed that the Grass Widow teams always brought with them as many bullets, batteries, and bandages as they could carry, on every mission. An operation could take several hours or it could take several days. Once discovered, the Ya'mas team was on its own for as long as it took for help to arrive.

The snipers rushed to the top floor, negotiating the darkness carefully. The marksmen teams carried special hammers to punch out small holes in the walls to be used as firing ports. Furniture was moved to conceal the presence of Israeli forces inside a room and to make the long hours of sitting and waiting more comfortable. The ambush was all about patience, persistence, and perseverance. "Some of the best snipers in the unit were the newcomers to the unit from the former Soviet Union," Yehonatan reflected. "They had military experience in the Russian Army and we called them the 'Chechens.' They had the ability to lay still for hours, sometimes days, while waiting for a target. They never complained, they never moved. When they had the shot in their sights, they always hit their targets."[13]

Most of the snipers did not carry suppressed weapons. Instead, they developed a system where two or even ten shooters would count down from three and then fire synchronously at individual targets. Five or six Hamas gunmen some three hundred meters away would drop simultaneously and all anyone would hear was a single shot off to the distance.

Yehonatan maintained constant radio communications with the men in the other house. The operation proceeded as planned. But one of Yehonatan's men, a newcomer to the unit, accidentally activated his helmet mounted flashlight. That singular display of light, lasting no more than a few seconds, gave away the entire Ya'mas operation. "All of a sudden it felt as if tens of thousands of rounds were coming at us from all directions," Yehonatan remembered. "Hundreds of weapons opened up on us at once and we were pinned down unable to move. I thought to myself, FUCK, this is my first Grass Widow as unit commander and I am about to have wounded and killed in action."[14] Yehonatan radioed the brigade commander, attempting to summon a calm voice, to provide a situation report and request assistance. Colonel Pinchas "Pinky" Zuaretz, the Gaza southern brigade commander, was watching the events in Rafah unfold live at the forward CP. Yehonatan requested that the helicopter gunship be summoned to provide cover fire, but the Ya'mas force was too close to the advancing Palestinian gunmen and the risk of a blue-on-blue incident was very real. The Ya'mas force would have to wait until the Bedouin soldiers were finished destroying their tunnel and could come and remove the undercover teams.

The Ya'mas operators, even the usually calm Shimon, could not believe the intensity of the fire directed their way. The operators hugged the floor as the plaster around them was torn to shreds and evaporated into a thick and suffocating cloud of white. Thin shards of marble tile flew into the faces of the men hunkered down to avoid the incoming ordnance; faces were lacerated by the razor-sharp splinters, and goggles were scratched by the stone and ceramic version of shrapnel. The skies over Rafah resembled a special effects studio with the crisscrossing streaks of light that illuminated the thick, pea soup–like dark. Explosive devices exploded everywhere, as the Palestinians activated hidden IEDs in the attempt to flush out the Israeli raiders.

The moments between the incessant gunfire were used by Yehonatan and his men to move lower down toward a narrow staircase, toward safer ground. That's when the RPG barrage began. The cone-like warhead of the RPG, designed to penetrate 500mm (19.65 inches) of rolled homogeneous armor, punched gaping holes in the building's concrete walls and then detonated in fiery devastation. Some RPGs hit the building; others landed nearby. It was as if the Palestinians were still unsure of where the Israelis were located and were attempting to flush them out with a mad fusillade of every weapon at their disposal. The Ya'mas force suffered scrapes and bruises, but miraculously nothing else. The Palestinian family was unharmed.

As daylight neared, the first elements of the Bedouin battalion arrived to evacuate the Ya'mas; the APCs were supported by tanks and the ubiquitous D9s. Palestinian antitank teams attempted to hit the convoy with parting rounds of RPG. The dreaded *Mistaraboon* were hated; the Palestinian groups had given the Ya'mas the grudgingly respectful nickname of the *Ibn Sharmuta*, the "Sons of Whores." To the Palestinians in Rafah, the Ya'mas had become real bastards.

Although not a religious man, Yehonatan thanked the almighty upon the unit's return to base. Yet these "skirmishes" would soon become the routine. One or two of these missions were carried out each week.

The battles that ensued once a Grass Widow was compromised were absolutely ferocious. Hundreds of Palestinian gunmen, firing what appeared to be an endless supply of ammunition, launched thousands of rounds at the Israeli sniper positions, while quickly advancing in the hope of surrounding the building and storming it. It was impossible for the Ya'mas teams to prop themselves up and respond, so they would raise their weapons into the firing hole and launch bursts to try and pin down the advancing Palestinians. "The battles were difficult and virtually impossible to describe," Vlad commented. "You took fire from every side and every angle. We had to conceal ourselves as best we could, and we knew when we hit someone usually when we heard an ambulance arriving. Other times, though, an ambulance reached a battle zone with its lights and sirens blaring and waving the white flag, or the Red Crescent flag, and then half a dozen men with AK-47s and RPGs emerged. It was truly the Wild West. It was absolutely Mogadishu."[15]

Palestinian sniper teams situated themselves on rooftops to hunt the Ya'mas teams; RPK machine gun squads and roving bands of men with RPGs patrolled areas near where IDF tunnel teams operated. As the Grass Widow incursions became more prevalent, the Palestinian terror factions began booby-trapping large swaths of Rafah and the areas around the tunnels with Hezbollah-inspired lEDs—many of which were EFPs, or explosively formed penetrators, shape charges designed to penetrate armor with deformed metal slugs, usually consisting of molten steel or copper. Hezbollah had perfected the use of EFPs against Israeli armor and infantry forces in southern Lebanon, and they were now in vast supply in Gaza.

Hamas and the PIJ booby-trapped many homes along the tunnel front with lEDs, with little regard for the families who lived in them. Children played soccer in courtyards next to hidden bombs, some packing as much as a hundred kilograms of high explosives, wired to cell phones or other detonating systems. In some cases, the terrorists wired the homes with lEDs that were hung on walls, so that when they exploded they could decapitate the operators in the room.

During one Grass Widow, the Ya'mas team entered a house that had been ingeniously wired with explosives throughout the structure; the family had long since abandoned the three-story structure. An Oketz dog that the unit took with it on many of the Grass Widow operations sat near one location and refused to move. "We have a hit," Shimon reported to the Command Post, his voice steady, but pointed and concerned. "The house is booby-trapped." Shimon, although diminutive in stature, always cast a giant shadow of confidence and capability. But his tone in communicating with the CP was worrisome to the operators, especially the new ones. A further search of the house by the Oketz crew revealed additional lEDs. The force was sitting atop several hundred kilograms of explosives.

Shimon faced an immediate dilemma. If he ordered his force out of the location on foot and the terrorists were watching, they could find themselves in an ambush. If they stayed put, the location could disappear at any second. Shimon summoned an immediate extraction and sappers to neutralize the explosives. An Achzarit, an Israeli-made armored personnel carrier created from the chassis of a captured T-54/55 Soviet-made tank, backed into the house and crashed through the living room, where the soldiers were waiting. The Achzarit lowered its rear hatch so that the operators could get inside. The combat engineers neutralized the charges while the Ya'mas team, nearly twelve of them, squeezed inside the sardine can–like constraints of the APC's interior. Once the force had thrown in its gear and everyone was accounted for, the rear hatch was closed and the vehicle drove off, led by a D9 that plowed a path to disrupt and destroy any TEDs that might have been planted on the withdrawal route back to Israeli lines. A Rafael Overhead Weapons Station 7.62mm light machine gun, controlled from within the cabin, engaged Palestinian RPG teams that attempted to strike at the departing Ya'mas force. The operators sat anxiously, crammed together in the rear of the Achzarit's tight confines, as the pings of AK fire bounced off the APC's armor.

The controlled explosion of the booby-trapped house not only leveled the home, but the concussion was so strong that it virtually knocked down half the buildings on the block.

The Ya'mas Grass Widows were highly successful—the Bedouin battalion, along with other infantry and combat engineer forces, were able to dedicate their efforts to locating tunnels and destroying them while, off in the distance, Ya'mas snipers made sure that generous perimeters were free from any threats. The decision of who to engage was often dictated by the politics of the day and the Israeli military's code of *Tohar Ha'Neshek*, or Purity of Arms, that ruled how deadly force could be used. Mostly, in the heat of battle, the decision fell to the discretion of the commander and the team leaders.

Once a Ya'mas location was compromised and the team found itself under fire, the first protocol was always to determine exactly where the shots were coming from and who was shooting. "There was always the danger of friendly fire in such circumstances," an operator remembered. "We were firing at armed individuals moving in on an armed position. The terrorists were firing at us, and even though our position was identifiable to the commanders in the field—it was all part of the extensive pre-mission briefings—we frequently heard radio bursts from a tank commander, or the operator of a heavy machine gun, that he was about to engage a suspicious source of gunfire. That suspicious source was us! The soldiers could be heavy on the trigger, ready to engage, and we had to say it's us, don't shoot."[16]

As a rule, the unit did not engage Palestinian Authority security forces who were not involved in hostile actions against Israeli forces. The Ya'mas also didn't fire on unarmed individuals or anyone attempting to provide medical care to the wounded. "As a father it is heartbreaking to see a child cry, or to see people who are just trying to get on with their lives suffering, and I don't know of a single instance where we have shot someone who was innocent. But we have also encountered children, *children*, who have been involved in placing IEDs, and we have encountered terrorists who have used children, absolutely terrified children, as human shields when shooting at us."[17]

One operation illustrated well the dilemmas of the battlefield and the command decisions that faced the men of the Gaza Ya'mas unit.

The Ya'mas was summoned to set up a large-scale Grass Widow operation inside one of the refugee camps in central Gaza, near Deir el-Balach, in
order to support an armored operation against terrorist targets. The operation
involved virtually the entire unit, as the force was split into three elements,
assigned to take over three houses and create protective rings of fire around
where the armored units and infantry forces would be operating. The Ya'mas
had to enter the camp "quiet," on foot, traversing nearly four kilometers of
terrain inside Palestinian territory. The Speakers, some in disguise, led the
advance, followed by the teams moving forward in tight formation. Three
houses were selected and the Grass Widow sniper operations set in place.
Darkness still hovered over the camp. Yehonatan radioed to the brigade
commander that everything was in place. The drone hovered overhead. As
always, the D9s were never far behind. And an attack chopper was on immediate standby circling the skies nearby just in case.

As dawn broke, a surreal reality emerged. Hundreds of armed men, faces
covered with keffiyehs, AK-47s and RPGs in hand, emerged out of the morning fog en route to engage the IDF armored units working nearby. The snipers
stood at the ready, waiting for the targets to move closer. The radio transmissions buzzed with reports from the three Grass Widow buildings, as the
shooters called out targets. Yehonatan scanned the horizon. Suddenly, though,
the landscape filled with women and with children. Palestinian policemen
were seen manning posts, as well. Yehonatan looked around and radioed his
findings to the brigade commander. If the snipers fired, Yehonatan knew, the
Palestinians would shoot back and the civilians would get caught in the cross
fire. Many would die. The brigade commander was adamant that the sniper
fire commence. Yehonatan argued against it. "Had we started shooting, there
would have been a massacre there. It would have been pointless."[18]

Each arrest operation, each venture into a refugee camp, each discovery of a
smuggler's tunnel, and each Grass Widow earned the Ya'mas accolades and
notice. Soon, men inside the top IDF special operations units put in transfer
papers to serve with the Ya'mas force in Gaza. Teams from the very top IDF
units that lobbied for work inside the Strip came to Yehonatan and his men

in order to learn and to be guided as to the intricacies and mind-boggling danger of working inside Gaza. Others came to learn as well.

When the American-led war in Iraq commenced and turned into an asymmetrical counterinsurgency nightmare, representatives from several branches of the United States military, primarily its Special Forces arms, visited IDF and Border Guard units to unravel the secrets of the Grass Widow operations.[19] The Americans visited units in the West Bank, and Chief Superintendent Yehonatan entertained these men, some in camouflage fatigues with eagles on their epaulets. Others, wearing Under Armour polo shirts and khaki slacks, were more mysterious and represented secretive commands and units, intelligence and counterterrorist, that were better left unmentioned. The Americans came to watch and to be impressed. The senior officers realized that they had a problem in Baghdad, in Fallujah, and elsewhere in Iraq, and that learning about the Ya'mas experience in Gaza would be very useful.

The Americans looked physically fit and healthy. Their skin was a clean shade of sun-baked red, and their hair was meticulously close-cropped—all of the officers were straight out of central casting. The uniforms—and other articles of clothing—they wore were crisply pressed, as if they'd be undergoing inspection shortly. They looked like counterterrorist tourists, explorers into another universe. Some smoked Cuban cigars. They kept the stogies in neat plastic cases.

Yehonatan's men looked beat. The operators wore the wear and tear of incessant combat on their fatigues and inside the wrinkles on their faces. Their eyes were bloodshot and their fingers stained by gun grease and layers of nerve-soothing nicotine; at a training ground in southern Israel, it looked as if the Americans had slept more on their flight to Israel than the Ya'mas operators had slept in a week. The Ya'mas veterans didn't envy their American counterparts; in fact, they felt sorry for them. The undercover operators knew that they were inching along toward some sort of cessation of combat against a fanatical foe that relished death. They were at their apex. The Israelis, at least, understood their enemy. The Americans, on the other hand, were at the starting line of their bloody fight for the neighborhoods and cities, the hearts and minds, of an Arab world they did not comprehend at all.

The American visitors greeted the Israelis with enormous reverence and well-deserved awe. The Ya'mas officers put on an extensive dog-and-pony show. Yehonatan had seen his fair share of these high-level delegations during his tenure with Ya'ma'm and he knew what to do. PowerPoint presentations were prepared in the best English the training cadre could muster, and the reviews of the Grass Widow concept—Gaza-style—was explained and displayed to the American officers. The Ya'mas officers hoped that the Americans could glean something from the tactics, and from the experiences they shared, so the lives of soldiers serving so far from home could be saved in a battlefield similar to Gaza, against a common foe.

As the fight in Gaza entered its fourth year, the IDF hierarchy also appreciated just how essential the Ya'mas was to Israel's efforts in the Strip. The unit became vital, an essential layer of armor to the overall effort to crush the violence. Major General Dan Harel, the head of IDF Southern Command, and the division and brigade commanders did not conceive of an operation that didn't involve the Ya'mas. The generals also realized that the unit needed to be equipped accordingly. Chief Superintendent Yehonatan was allowed to submit a wish list of arms and tools needed, and many of his requests were honored. Soon Ya'mas snipers received new weapons—including the SR-25 7.62mm NATO and even .50-caliber rifles. The unit received new scopes, new night-vision systems, and new vehicles. Chief Superintendent Yehonatan's vision for the unit was taking hold.

CHAPTER TWENTY-TWO

A Bloody Separation

At just after midnight on May 11, 2004, the Giva'ati Brigade dispatched a small force of reconnaissance infantrymen and combat engineers into Zaitun, a dangerous patchwork of overcrowded streets and alleys at the western fringe of Beit Hanoun, near the Israeli frontier, to destroy a weapons shop that was producing Qassam rockets, which had been launched against civilian targets in southern Israel. The force, led by a D9 and supported by Merkava tanks, came under incessant machine-gun and RPG fire the moment it crossed into Palestinian territory; Israeli soldiers returned fire, launching .50-caliber machine-gun bursts from inside armored booths, complete with bullet- and blast-resistant glass, affixed atop their armored vehicles. Saguy Bashan, a reporter for Israel's Channel Two news, and a cameraman accompanied the young soldiers, most of them under the age of twenty, into battle. The men, their faces painted with black streaks of camouflage paint for the night's fight, seemed relaxed and at ease. They relayed their status calmly as the RPGs flew only a few feet off target.

The force reached their objective under the darkened night that had been interrupted by the flashes of gunfire. The combat engineers wired with explosives a machine shop and six heavy lathes that were used to manufacture indigenous Qassam rockets. As the black sky turned a soft shade of blue, hinting at the coming dawn, the building disappeared in a flash of fire and a plume of smoke and rubble. Lieutenant Colonel Ofer Vinter, the operation commander, gave the order to withdraw.

The convoy of dozers and armored personnel carriers pushed out of Zaitun as fast as it could, though the streets were now filled with people. Children threw rocks at the Israeli vehicles, and gunmen fired wildly. It was difficult for the young soldiers to maintain a singular column amid so many people. Some vehicles were cut off, out of sight to the other tanks and dozers in the column; others were diverted by the crowds. One M113 was knocked out of service by a powerful roadside IED. The vehicle was torn apart like a twisted soda can, but miraculously all of the soldiers inside were accounted for and unharmed. Seconds later, a second M113 disappeared inside a deadly plume of black smoke. A powerful IED, perhaps containing as much as one hundred kilograms of explosives, destroyed the armored vehicle and killed the six soldiers on board. All that was left of the APC was its discarded engine block.

The street soon flooded with people, some wearing the black headbands of the PIJ, who raced into the street to try to steal what was left of some of the mangled bodies. Women stomped on the lifeless mounds of bloodied and charred flesh in ghoulish displays. It was absolutely medieval.

Lieutenant Colonel Vinter ordered his infantrymen out of the vehicles and into several apartment buildings, where they seized the high ground. The battle for the bodies of the fallen soldiers would go on all day and be one of the most ferocious of the intifada. By nightfall the Giva'ati force had left Zaitun with the remains of the dead, sealed in plastic bags, carefully transported back to Israel for burial.

It had been a horrible day in Gaza. It had been a horrible and bloody year.

Chief Superintendent Yehonatan was hunkered down and under fire when the Giva'ati Brigade APC disintegrated twenty miles away in Zaitun. A small operation with another Giva'ati unit, searching for tunnels under the Philadelphi Corridor, had turned into a full-fledged battle, and Yehonatan coordinated a dozen moving parts of the developing firefight. Palestinian RPG teams were everywhere. Palestinian snipers and machine gun crews peppered the rooftops with sustained fire in the hope of hitting Ya'mas sniper teams, while IEDs, some planted by children forced at gunpoint to enter the no-man's-land, were laid across roadways and alongside buildings. The children turned every mission into a moral dilemma. "Once, one of our men saw a thirteen- or fourteen-year-old placing an IED near our position. He had the boy in his sights but didn't fire. It was his personal decision and he chose to let the kid run away and deal with the device later."[1]

The Giva'ati soldiers were children, too, Yehonatan thought. One of the operators, one of the veterans, went on the radio to ask if any of the names of the dead had been released. The Ya'mas had worked with every unit in the Giva'ati Brigade, in every corner of the Strip, and the operators wanted to know if anyone they knew was among the dead. It was doubtful that anyone would recognize a name. It was the faces of these young soldiers that would be remembered, faces at nighttime briefings, faces covered by green-and-black camouflage paint. The young soldiers did not wear name tags. They were simply called *Ahi* ("brother") when seen at the PX, at the dining hall, or in front of an apartment block in Rafah under fire.

When daylight emerged, the decision was made to pull out the task force. The operation commander contacted Yehonatan and told him to assemble his men—the armored vehicles would be waiting, at a junction known by a coded designation on a map, to pick up the undercover forces. No one was in the mood to sit inside an armored vehicle given what had happened in Zaitun. Bullets were better than bombs, the undercovers felt. Apprehensively, they entered the M113s and the modified tanks for the ride back to Israel. Bullets and RPGs followed their trail all the way back to Israeli lines.

The Ya'mas base, located near division headquarters, felt like a fortress under siege. Everyone—even the young soldiers guarding the entrance—appeared to be on a war footing. The percussion-like thuds of rotor blades beat a cadence off to the distance. Ambulances were everywhere. Television news crews parked at the side of the road, ready for the evening news. Yehonatan ordered his men to the briefing room where the post-mission analysis was held. The men were covered in a thin, almost silk-like caking of Rafah dust. Their throats were parched, but still they preferred nicotine and caffeine to water.

The briefing was detailed and pointed. The operation was analyzed, and each operator that engaged a threat had to explain the why, the where, and the what. The post-mission analysis always lasted longer than planned, even on dire days of loss like this and even when the men were starving and in desperate need of sleep. Before the assembly broke up, there was some discussion of a few missions that were being planned—an arrest in Khan Yunis, a raid in Jebalya—and tomorrow's assignment: to serve as a brigade emergency response force for a combat engineer tunnel-locating unit working the Philadelphi Route. The combat engineers, demolition specialists from a unit whose acronym spelled out *Yahalom*, or Diamond, in Hebrew, had done a lot of work with the Ya'mas along the Egyptian frontier. The soldiers were so young and, after serving in the Strip, so full of combat experience. The unit's commander, Captain Aviv Hakani, had become friends with many of the Ya'mas officers, especially Chief Inspector Yaron, who respected the courage and doggedness of the young officer from Ashdod, forty miles away. Yaron had led more Grass Widow operations than he could remember in support of these intrepid burrowers.[2]

When the briefing ended, Yehonatan dismissed his men and ordered them to eat; they didn't have to be told to take care of their gear and ready everything for tomorrow's muster. Yehonatan stepped outside, his eyes squinting from the harsh sun, and realized that he needed a few hours at home. This was the quiet before the inevitable eruption, and Yehonatan wanted a few hours at home. There were moments when only the embrace of a wife and the sweet smile of a child could erase the fear and blood of Gaza from one's peripheral memory. Yehonatan knew that the unit would be in good hands. Shimon, his deputy, was as good as they came. Yaron, the team leader, was one of the best officers in Israel's counterterrorist community. The sun was setting by the time Yehonatan finished his paperwork, his meetings with Shin Bet commanders, and a few meetings with various IDF officers and intelligence personnel. He hoped to make it home by dinner and to have the chance to read a bedtime story to his young child. There would still be no escaping Gaza. The names of the fallen would be released on the evening news.

The command of a Ya'mas unit—the command of any operational unit for that matter—carried with it unimaginable burdens of responsibility that few mortals could bear. The commander was responsible for making sure his men made it home alive and in one piece. This was the fabric of the commander's existence; it was a sacrosanct responsibility. Commanders made sure that every facet of a mission, even those daring behind-enemy-lines forays, were as safe as they could be; the planning, preparation, and execution were always done with bringing the boys home alive in mind. Unit commanders tangled with generals; they fought with quartermasters and with bean counters. Part of the job of keeping the men safe was to make sure that they had the best weapons and equipment possible. Unit commanders, and their direct subordinates, the team leaders and the intelligence and operations officers, worked around the clock to take care of all the small nuances of life inside a high-octane unit whose daily grind consisted of secret missions behind enemy lines. The commander and his staff worried about the food that the men ate, and the beds in which they slept; in the Gaza unit, when it was discovered that some operators, new immigrants from the former Soviet Union, were in financial hardship, the officers assembled cash to furnish their apartments and to make sure that their families were looked after. The commander and the officers were the last ones to go to bed and they were always up before anyone else.

It was impossible to escape the pressure of Gaza and the encumbrance of being in charge. When Yehonatan closed his eyes, he saw the images from the UAVs while inside a Command Post, watching his men take incoming RPGs. He couldn't wash the stench of poverty out of his senses, nor could he extinguish the fear of being mistaken for Palestinian snipers by trigger-happy and terrified-out-of-their-wits soldiers who only ten months earlier where still in high school. Being home could not expunge seconds dragging into hours as the force waited for extraction. In Gaza it was all about being pulled out to safety.

On the morning of May 12, Yehonatan had the chance to wake up in a comfortable bed and prepare breakfast for his wife and child. Instinctively, he checked his pager every few minutes. There were no urgent messages from Gaza. It was a brilliant spring day. May was certainly the most splendid month in Israel—cool enough for a light jacket at night and warm enough during the day that the sun could gently toast your face. Yehonatan was going to take the little one out of nursery school early for a few hours at the playground.

Ninety minutes away—give or take the always maddening Israeli traffic—Vlad was peering through the sights of his M4, awaiting the order to fire, before throwing some lead downrange on an impromptu training ground set up near the frontier next to Rafah. The unit was on call, a standby

emergency response force of sorts, for Captain Aviv Khakani's tunnel hunting unit, which was set to respond to intelligence that Hamas, borrowing
First World War tactics, was planning to burrow underneath the *Termit*
("Thermal") Fortification.[3] The *Termit* Fortification on the Philadelphi route
consisted of an armored observation post built atop the frame of a three-story
building buttressed by dirt, sandbags, steel, and mesh. *Termit* was a punching
bag. It had been hit before by suicide bombers and incessant RPG and mortar
fire—Israeli commentators called the fortification the most dangerous place
on the planet.[4]

Captain Khakani told Yaron and Vlad that he was just going to go inside
the suspected area to have a look and that he would summon the Ya'mas if
they were needed. The ad hoc range, a desert clearing with a natural sand
berm, was three kilometers from the staging area. Vlad and his fellow operators fired their pistols and M4s as the May sun showed hints of fading into
the Mediterranean.

At just after 1700, Captain Khakani and his crew of four sergeants set out
inside their M113 equipped with nearly a ton of explosives, robotics, rap-
pelling gear, and other underground sensors. The D9 plowed ahead. Khakani
and his men followed close behind. The operation was routine.

Vlad and his squad were cleaning up their brass from the desert floor
when the earth shook violently beneath them. The explosion was like nothing they had ever heard before. The operators wearing their radios raised the
volume and scanned the emergency frequencies; they looked at one another
in a state of damning resignation. Their fears were confirmed seconds later
when they heard an ominous radio burst from a bewildered soldier stationed
at the *Termit* observation post: "The APC just vanished!"[5]

It had been a blissful day, Yehonatan thought as he pushed the swing in a
playground that was a universe away from Gaza. And then his mobile phone
rang. The division operations officer called, his voice frayed by the stress,
demanding that Yehonatan return to Gaza immediately—there had been a
tragedy and the unit was needed for a vital operation. The burden of command gushed with the adrenaline that raced through Yehonatan's system.
Yehonatan pushed his daughter on the swings one last time and then tried,

as best as he could, to tell her that he had to leave immediately. He dropped to one knee and looked at her. His heart sank deep below his chest as he told her that he had to rush back to work. With his wife still at work, he scrambled to find a neighbor who could look after his little girl. Gaza had once again shattered normalcy.

The drive back to Gaza should have taken two hours, even with lights and sirens. Yehonatan made it back in half that time. He maneuvered his Border Guard take-home vehicle, a Toyota pickup, in and out of all obstacles on the highways heading south. Darkness neared as the traffic quickly changed from civilian to military once he entered the grasps of the Strip's outer roadways. Helicopters hovered overhead. Tank transporters were clogging up the lanes heading toward Rafah. Yehonatan looked back into his rearview mirror and saw a small convoy of ambulances, as well. It was still too early, he realized, for the parents of the dead to have been notified.

Imad,* the unit operations officer, updated Yehonatan throughout his Formula One scurry back to Gaza. Imad, a Druze officer who was known as one of the calmest men in the unit in a tight spot, cooly relayed updates to the unit commander. It was hard to hear the story on the phone. The tunnel-hunting M113 had taken a direct hit from an RPG fired by a PIJ team that had used a play area in between two buildings for cover. Even with Israeli upgrades to the original American design, the Soviet-era antitank rocket had little difficulty in penetrating the M113's aluminum armor cover, resulting in the one ton of military-grade high explosives detonating in a thunderous blast felt miles away. The vehicle evaporated into a mushroom cloud of dust and debris. Captain Khakani and his crew could not have survived the fiery fulmination.

Yehonatan ordered the entire unit, all hands, to assemble at headquarters and then deploy to the Southern Brigade. Everyone was to bring extra provisions, especially ammunition; the unit's tactical medics prepared for casualties.

Gaza's Southern Brigade commander was a veteran paratroop officer who had seen his share of combat as a young officer in southern Lebanon, but he

---

* A pseudonym—true identity withheld for security considerations.

was wearing the destruction of two APCs, less than forty-eight hours apart, on his face. The colonel took Yehonatan aside and told him that the Ya'mas was the only unit that had the skills and experience to operate on foot inside Rafah and that the unit was to enter the city near the site of the blast and sift through the sands to find fragments of flesh and bone from the fallen men. Armored units and helicopter gunships attempted to keep Palestinian gunmen from raiding the blast crater. Yehonatan readied officers and men. He was daunted, almost disturbed, by their lack of fear or personal concern. All of Rafah knew what was coming. The terrorist groups knew that the Israelis would make an effort to locate the remnants of those killed. The battle was going to be like nothing any of the operators had ever seen before, but yet the men were determined—anxious—to go in and get the job done; they didn't want to wait until daylight. They wanted in, now. Yehonatan worried that they had become too used to the combat, too used to the thrill, the danger, or even the fact that no one had been hurt, to feel fear anymore.[6]

Throughout the night, a small army readied to enter Rafah. Yehonatan handled his men. The Giva'ati commander made sure that his force, elements from the brigade's engineering battalion, were ready, as well; the engineers would handle the Grass Widow piece of the operation, taking over buildings that overlooked the area where the M113 had been destroyed so that Yehonatan's men could work unencumbered by Palestinian snipers and gunmen. Each and every Ya'mas operator was handed a plastic food bag that had been emptied so that the men could fill them with bones and shards of flesh. Yehonatan thought of his wife and child back at home, back in a different universe.

The force set out before dawn. The Ya'mas might have been *the* special operations unit in Gaza, but the D9 was king. The D9s, armored to withstand the most ambitious IED and repetitive RPG strikes, plowed a 4.5-meter-wide path on any surface, from dirt to asphalt; the behemoth's blade dug into the turf to disrupt and destroy any explosive booby traps. The Merkava tanks and the M113s with the engineers followed close behind. Yehonatan wouldn't let his men inside the M113. He had two of the more heavily armored Achzarit APCs at his disposal.

The Giva'ati combat engineers quickly took over the homes that over-looked the scene of the blast. The soldiers rustled up the families into a central room and then the snipers went to work. Even with such a show of force on such a sensitive mission, the Palestinians still held the numerical advantage. Hundreds of gunmen were determined to make the most of the Israelis at their most exposed and vulnerable. But the Israelis held the optics, and the precision fire was holding the line temporarily.

One by one, the Ya'mas operators emerged from the bellies of the two Achzarit APCs and dropped to their hands and knees. They saw the huge hole where the M113 had been destroyed, and they carefully sifted through the thin sand, looking for anything. "We were like mice crawling through a maze," Yaron would comment, "but we had to bring something back for the families to bury, even if it was a bone fragment."[7] The Palestinian fire, including RPGs and heavy machine guns fired at great range, intensified, it appeared, with each passing minute, but the operators did not stop what they were doing. "We knew Captain Khakani very well," Yehonatan stated. "We had worked with him on countless operations. We respected him and we cared for him. He was, in many ways, one of us. The gunfire could be dealt with, but picking up the pieces was something that we viewed as a holy mission."[8]

The search was grueling, time-consuming. The men, officers and new-comers alike, sank their hands deep into the dirt and then looked at the dusty remnants left in their hands, hoping to find something. The weight carried by each man, loads of ammunition worn under heavy body armor fastened tightly, was hard enough on a cool summer's night but constraining and dehydrating under the day's full sun. Sweat poured down under helmets and balaclavas, as eyes were burned by the salt of unstoppable perspiration. The pings of bullets hitting nearby wasn't as bothersome as the surreal feel of the assignment and the surroundings.

Ya'mas operators moved in and out of courtyards and buildings to peer around corners and provide covering fire for the men on the ground. The incoming fire was incessant. Yehonatan ordered the D9s to plow small berms, high enough to cover a man on his knees, along each stretch of street the men searched. The D9s also raised their blades and were placed in between streets, so that the Ya'mas search teams could race across without getting hit.

Slowly, the main pieces of the M113 were found near the blast site. The armored chassis had disintegrated with such force that the only bits remaining were no larger than a credit card. A few bits of bloody flesh were painstakingly handled and placed inside the plastic sacks. Bone splinters, small, that looked like they came from a small bird were also found. Yaron managed to locate the dog tags belonging to First Sergeant Lior Vishinsky;[9] Vishinsky's dad, Shlomo, was a popular theater and television actor.

There was no break from the grind, even though the men were hungry and dehydrated. The Palestinian sniper fire intensified.

The men on their knees, along with the operators who covered their crawl, focused solely on the carpet of sand before them. No one paid attention to the thumping of attack helicopters overhead and the engines of the heavy armor being fired up to move here or there. The classic undercover operation was small, a deft footprint; Gaza was somewhat larger. Here, the men were part of a full army.

As the afternoon threatened to turn into evening, an urgent call for help came over the Giva'ati frequency. An infantryman in one of the two Grass Widows had walked with an old woman near a terrace in order to help her get to the bathroom. The trip to the lavatory was intentional. The family knew that Palestinian snipers would be searching the open spaces. The soldier, showing inexperience in dealing with the intricacies of a Grass Widow, had taken a shot to the neck and was bleeding out. Another infantryman was also hit, and severely wounded. The young officer in charge was in an awful state; the threads of shell shock were heard in his brief and frantic transmissions, and the medical condition of the wounded was unclear. The unit's company commander, back at the CP, indicated that he was going in to get his men out.

Thunderous fire rained on their exposed position. The Palestinians had laid their trap.

Behind the walls, just out of sight of the Palestinian gunners, the Giva'ati rescue force entered the fight. The Giva'ati engineers were transported on Nag'machon armored personnel carriers. The Nag'machon, a typical Israeli by-product of surplus that could still be salvaged and new technologies that could be added on, was a hybrid of an armored fighting vehicle made from the chassis of the British-made Centurion Main Battle Tank; some of the vehicles were even fitted with add-on turrets, juxtaposed on top of the vehicle, for visibility and protection. Unlike the thin-skinned M113, the Nag'machon was equipped with reactive armor blocks that detonated upon impact to destroy the penetrating capabilities of an RPG, and they had thick cubes of transparent armor so that gunners inside could fire back at any threat; mesh armor, steel fencing, ringed the turret to stop RPGs and antitank missiles from hitting the vehicle. But the Nag'machon did not have a rear entry hatch. The moment the Giva'ati combat engineers made it to the location of the Grass Widow and the soldiers emerged, they were also hit by Palestinian sniper fire. It was what Yehonatan had feared all along. Now there were two Giva'ati soldiers killed in the operation, and several more were wounded. The situation deteriorated rapidly.

The two armored personnel carriers at Yehonatan's disposal, the Achzarits, had a rear ramp that could be lowered into the besieged house. Yehonatan switched over to divisional radio and requested that he be given command of the sector to oversee the rescue of the Giva'ati force. Permission was immediately granted. Yehonatan had never directed a full-scale operation with armor, artillery, mechanized forces, and heavy engineering equipment before. His specialty was small-unit penetration and top-secret strikes with a handful of men watching his back.

A mission to retrieve pieces of the dead had developed into a full-scale nightmare. The operation was now a mission to rescue those who still had a fighting chance. Two Achzarit APCs set out toward the Grass Widow. Yaron and Yehonatan were in the lead vehicle.

There were members of the Gaza Ya'mas unit who had been at war since the unit's first day in the field. They had seen a lot in fifteen years inside danger, and they had found themselves under permanent fire. Other members of the unit, some who had served in Lebanon during their army days, and who had served in Gaza at the height of al-Aqsa, had never encountered gunfire like the type encountered on this Wednesday afternoon. Hundreds of

Palestinian gunmen representing all of the terror factions had now focused on a complex of homes where Israeli soldiers were trapped. Some newcomers to the unit used to scoff at Yaron and his insistence that everyone sit down and watch the film *Black Hawk Down* from start to finish and take away something from the story of the U.S. Special Forces operation that was bogged down inside interminable violence. But this was the real deal, some would later comment; this was their moment surrounded on all sides by an endless stream of fire.

The Ya'mas mission to find body parts continued; nearly half the unit remained on their hands and knees under the hot sun. But Yehonatan directed other members of the unit toward positions to provide cover fire for the Ya'mas rescue force that Yaron was leading toward the beleaguered Giva'ati infantrymen. A small team of Ya'mas operators rushed to the besieged home on foot, to help stabilize the Grass Widow and to calm the men down. The Ya'mas paramedics carried small emergency room triage centers on their backs. Yaron and his small force rushed to their vehicles. They had approximately a thousand meters to traverse in order to reach the soldiers—a thousand meters of treacherous corners, blind spots, one-family homes, and open ground. There was no time to call in a D9 to clear out the safety strip. Yaron ordered the two hulking APCs to charge forward into the fire. Yehonatan feared that his men would be hit by hidden devices.

There were IEDs everywhere in Rafah, especially among the homes that straddled Philadelphi. Yaron felt what must have been thousands of 7.62mm rounds pinging off his lead vehicle; the massive explosions thundering outside were like mighty fists jabbing the sides. Yaron lifted one of the hatches to peer out for a second just to make sure that the vehicles were not straying off course. The aerial maps and photographs were clear and pinpoint, but the chaos and confusion was quite the opposite. "I know that I wasn't supposed to stick my head out and look outside," Yaron reflected, "but I just wanted to make sure that we got there."[10] Yaron informed the Giva'ati position that his APCs were two minutes out.

The two Achzarits positioned themselves so that they could back into the home. The clash of concrete and armored steel created a tumbling crash, as the rear ramps dropped into the living room and out of the line of fire. The dead and seriously wounded were evacuated in the Giva'ati APC. Ya'mas paramedics tended to the others who were hurt. The Giva'ati officers were surprised, relieved, by the composure of the Ya'mas rescuers. They were calm and they called out threats before identifying which targets they would engage.

The Achzarit had a crew of three and was designed to carry seven fully equipped soldiers in and out of battle. Together with the Ya'mas operators, each vehicle now had to cram twenty-five men inside its belly for the ride back to safety. Men were lying on top of one another, helmets battered into legs. Yaron attempted to calm the soldiers and reassure them that they were all right. It took less than an hour for the Israeli forces to return back to the safety of Israeli lines, but it seemed like it took days. Combat medics rushed the wounded to the heliport, where UH-60 Black Hawks, known as Owls in the IAF lexicon of nicknames, would fly them to Soroka Medical Center. Military rabbis attended to the dead, and the body slivers that the Ya'mas had collected.

There were still a few hours of daylight left. The Ya'mas returned to the blast zone for a few more hours of the painstaking work of searching for body fragments. The unit stayed on its knees and under fire for the next two days.

Hamas commanders took notice of the massive Israeli effort to retrieve the thread-like shards of their fallen's flesh. They witnessed the political risk taken by the military commanders to carry out so risky a mission just so that a nation could help the families of the dead cope with their loss. The Israelis' display, on their hands and knees amid the bullets and RPGs, impressed Hamas military commanders, especially the new heir apparent, Ahmed Jabari, who saw great virtue and great opportunity in this window of Israeli sense and sensibility. If the Israelis were to go to such efforts for dead soldiers, Jabari must have thought to himself, imagine what they would do, imagine what they would forfeit, for a live one. Hamas planners went to work.

Captain Khakani and his four men were laid to rest four days after their APC evaporated into a cloud of destruction along the Philadelphi Route. The funerals took place the day after 150,000 protesters gathered in Tel Aviv to demand that Israel withdraw—once and for all—from the Gaza Strip.

Less than forty-eight hours after the funerals, after the prayers for the dead, the IDF launched Operation Rainbow, a massive weeklong offensive against terrorist targets throughout the Gaza Strip; some three hundred homes along the smuggling route of Rafah were destroyed. It would be a last effort—for the status quo. Prime Minister Ariel Sharon, a man known to never buckle, realized that Israel's stance in Gaza was untenable. There were rumors of unilateral Israeli disengagement. In June 2004, the rumors became a statement of intent. Israel would unilaterally remove the settlements (all twenty-one of them), the settlers, and its military forces from the Gaza Strip by the fall of 2005. The intifada was waning. It was time for the killing to stop.

There would be parting shots, Chief Superintendent Yehonatan knew. The men of the Gaza Ya'mas had been at war for a long time. Until they were told otherwise, it was simply business as usual. Yehonatan and his men continued operating inside the Strip—the arrest operations, the targeted killings, and the deniable special operations on behalf of the highest levels of Israeli intelligence continued. Late at night on June 2, 2004, a Ya'mas team spearheaded a tunnel-hunting operation by the 1st Golani Infantry Brigade inside Kishta, one of Rafah's most dangerous neighborhoods. The team searched inside homes, in gardens, and underneath vehicles, until they discovered a large tunnel, responsible for the smuggling of explosives and weapons.

The extraordinary was simply part of the routine.

Unlike many of his contemporaries serving on the General Staff, Major General Dan Harel's CV was not filled with a career full of service in special operations. Harel was a gunner, an artilleryman, and his combat experience was in Lebanon supporting Israel's special operations forces as they waged a bitterly fought campaign against Hezbollah. Harel knew how difficult counterterrorism warfare was; Gaza was no different than Lebanon, Harel would learn. This form of warfare was exhausting and bloody. It was the type of warfare in which defeat or victory hinged on the action of small bands of men with boundless courage and endless resolve.

Harel arrived in Gaza in 2003, just as the intifada in Gaza was shifting from small-scale encounters to full-blown combat. His front was the most explosive of the entire intifada, and the costliest in terms of Israeli casualties. His front was also the only one that Israel unilaterally walked away from. In

August 2005, Harel commanded the pullout, the disengagement, from the Gaza Strip.

The very best units in the Israeli military carried out counterterrorist operations inside Gaza during General Harel's tenure at Southern Command, and some of the work they did—missions coined by one insider as super top-secret—were worthy of a Hollywood blockbuster. But of all the units that worked inside the fences, the Ya'mas stood out above all. Week in and week out reports came across Harel's desk detailing missions of great daring and extraordinary feats of courage. Since the effort was collective, it was impossible for Harel to pinpoint individuals for their heroism and dedication under fire, so General Harel decided to decorate the entire unit.

In 2005, the Gaza Ya'mas received a unit citation. In a ceremony where the news photographers were warned they couldn't publish the faces of the men in the room wearing the Border Guard green beret, Chief Superintendent Yehonatan received the award on behalf of his men.

Ostensibly, the award was for the bloody May in Rafah in 2004 and the rescue of the trapped Giva'ati soldiers. A senior IDF officer said, of that operation, "The operators displayed amazing courage entering the crowded Palestinian neighborhood despite the fire that was directed at them at the entrance to the house. The operation will be remembered and not only in the unit's combat log. There's good reason why they are embraced by the IDF and the security forces. They are humble operators that are considered the iron fist in the Strip."[11]

One operation, though, could not define the unit's legacy during the bitterly fought five-year campaign. The commendation issued to the Gaza Ya'mas was for a long list of heroic actions and for the redefinition and expansion of the unit's size and capabilities while at war. The decoration was for an endless number of remarkable moments of unit audacity, courage under fire, and playing so pivotal a role in the war against terror during the al-Aqsa intifada. During the conflict, the unit neutralized more than one hundred terrorists; many of those were killed in direct battles with the Ya'mas; others were killed while launching attacks against Israeli targets. The unit spearheaded the discovery and destruction of twenty tunnels. The Gaza Ya'mas unit captured arsenals full of AK-47s, RPKs, and RPGs, and seized enough explosives and ammunition to equip an army. The Ya'mas apprehended almost five hundred wanted terror suspects who hid in plain sight inside areas where the very best of Israel's special operations arsenal often feared to tread.[12]

The Gaza Ya'mas brought guerrilla warfare to the doorstep of those who were the grand masters of asymmetrical terror. They did so as scalpels, sharp and precise, and as absolute professionals—with great planning and incredible luck, the Ya'mas did not suffer a killed in action, or a serious injury, during its sixteen years inside Gaza and the five years of the intifada. This is a remarkable accomplishment for those who were in command, as well as for those who ventured deep into the darkness night after night.

The Ya'mas forced the Palestinian terror factions to abandon their strategy of crossing the wire, making them resort to tactics that were underground or launched over the horizon. The Gaza Ya'mas unit played a pivotal role in containing a wave of seemingly unstoppable violence that, as horrific as it was, could have been so very much worse. The small, rarely talked about unit of undercover operators turned commandos in Gaza made a monumental difference. Few units in the history of Israel's wars have ever had finer hours.

THE END

DAWN

CHAPTER TWENTY-THREE

Cutting the Grass

It seemed as if a day didn't pass without someone asking Yaakov Berman or Sa'ar Shine if there was any news on Ziad Musa. The Hamas operative wasn't the most dangerous terrorist lurking about in the West Bank, but he had shot and killed an Israeli soldier and that usually propelled anyone to the top of the Shin Bet's most-wanted list. On November 2, 2005, Musa had shot and killed Sergeant Yonatan Avron, a twenty-year-old commando in the IDF's super-secret Sayeret Magian long-range reconnaissance unit, during a nighttime arrest operation in Mirka, a small fortress-like village southwest of Jenin. The Shin Bet came to the Ya'mas for the arrest. Sa'ar Shine received the assignment. His team had earned the reputation of being one of the most effective counterterrorist squads in all of Israel.

Shine, now Berman's deputy, had been in the unit long enough to know that the question wasn't if the Shin Bet would locate Musa, but rather when; killing a soldier—from one of the most elite units in the IDF—made Musa a most-wanted man. And Shine had fought enough battles in the West Bank to know that men with a price on their head tended to hide inside cities where they could easily disappear. If Shine was a betting man, he would have bet a hefty sum that Musa had found shelter in Jenin. Still, his team donned the masquerade and reconnoitered the villages around the Dotan Valley—Zawiya, Jarba, Misilya, and Sanur, all places that barely warranted mention on a map, places that hadn't changed in a thousand years and whose roadways all flooded into muddy mires in the winter months. Still, Shine wagered on Jenin. And, in the end, Shine was right.

The Shin Bet agents assigned the Musa file pressed their sources throughout the West Bank with a heavy hand and hefty resources. Money changed hands, favors were promised, and cell phone traffic was monitored. The usual list of information peddlers who were both duplicitous and reliable were pressured for something. And the something always came. The word came down that Musa was hiding inside an apartment that had been rented for him inside the heart of Jenin. The update gave the mission its name: "Operation Apartment for Rent." Shine and his men waited for the Shin Bet to find the actual apartment and building, and then to locate the suspect inside at a specific time. Once Shine's men received the green light, they'd rush to Jenin and get him.

The green light came early on the morning of December 21—a source had pinpointed his location. The news summoned Shine's team out of their bunks. The Speakers attended to their undercover vehicles; the sergeants readied the maps and the Horses. Commander Levy faced little challenge in getting the mission approved by the IDF brigade commander, Colonel Herzl Halevi, who was in charge of the Jenin area, and having the CP and the backup resources assembled; Halevi, the former commander of Sayeret Mat'kal, was known as a creative thinker among Israel's military commanders, beloved for attending memorials for fallen soldiers,[1] a man whose DNA relished missions of surprise that achieved their objectives. Musa was considered high-risk, a shooter, so Shine's arrest team took a dog with it, a Belgian Malinois named Barry, for extra bite. Oketz, the IDF's K9 special operations force, had started coordinated operations with all three of the Ya'mas units toward the latter stages of the intifada, with impressive success.

Shine's arrest convoy set out north, across the West Bank, toward the frontier on the outskirts of Jenin. A Ya'mas backup force stood at the ready at the entrance to the city; a larger IDF rescue element parked their APCs and vehicles farther down the road. The drone had already cut a path high above the city.

The Speakers were the first in. Shine and Abu Ahmed followed in the Horse with additional men. It was 0930 and relatively cool on a Sunday morning. The morning traffic into Jenin was heavy, but the force reached the location without incident or suspicion. Quickly, almost as a course of second nature, the entry team emerged from the first Horse without making a sound. Barry the dog did not bark.

The apartment block was a four-story complex near the courthouse in the center of town, off of a side street shielded from view from the main avenues. Musa's flat, a second-floor two-bedroom, was to the left of the staircase. The entry team made its way up the tiled stairs, stepping slowly and quietly with their rubber-soled boots; M4s were raised toward any threats, ready to engage at a moment's notice. The men lined up outside Musa's flat in a stick, poised to burst in once the front door had been breached. Barry's handler struggled to keep the excited dog at bay. Sa'ar Shine had borrowed a twelve-gauge shotgun from an IDF unit so that the hinges of Musa's door could be blown off with specially designed rounds. The shotgun blasts were amplified inside the hallway, the sounds magnified by the open space of marble floor and concrete walls. One of the operators kicked in the door, already loosened off its mount. Barry's handler removed the dog's leather muzzle and sent the eager Belgian hound inside. Less than three seconds passed before a burst of fire was heard inside the apartment, and then a fusillade punctured the wall behind which the Ya'mas entry team was standing. Musa knew that the wall had been recently fixed and that it was nothing more than drywall.

One of Musa's rounds hit Shine's M4 thirty-round magazine. The impact pushed Shine back. He knew he had been hit, and he felt some warm liquid dripping down his back. He didn't feel pain, but he closed his eyes for a nanosecond and felt relief. Finally, he thought to himself, "I'm wounded—I'll finally get a few days of rest off the line."[2] But as the gunfire continued, Shine opened his eyes and realized that he was actually OK. Abu Ahmed, his trusted NCO, had suffered bullet and shrapnel wounds in his shoulder; the moisture that Shine felt was Abu Ahmed's punctured CamelBak, spraying water forward.

There was no need to play around anymore. Shine and his men removed grenades from their load-bearing gear and tossed them inside the apartment, seizing ground inside the fiery, smoky rooms once the explosions cleared. Musa should have surrendered, one of the operators thought, but he never had a chance. Musa had been killed by grenade and weapons fire; his body was found on the floor, his weapon and ammunition close to hand. Musa had managed to kill Barry the Belgian Malinois before being taken out. Barry's handler cradled the dog in his arms and rushed downstairs to the awaiting Horse. The dog would be buried later that day in the Oketz cemetery at the unit's base in central Israel with full military honors.[3]

Abu Ahmed was rushed to the hospital for surgery. Sa'ar Shine returned to the unit's base for the operational debrief and to clean himself off. Tomorrow would be another day at the office. The war went on.

In Jerusalem, Palestinian terrorists had returned to medieval warfare—sticks, stones, and knives—in the attempt to continue the conflict against Israel. In Gaza, the terrorist groups retreated and regrouped, choosing short-range homemade rockets in the continuation of hostilities against Israel, instead of in-your-face encounters. The last major suicide bombing perpetrated against Israel from the West Bank was on December 5, 2005, when five people were killed and fifty were wounded by a PIJ suicide bomber at the entrance to the Sharon Shopping Mall in Netanya,* but the Ya'mas campaign against the entrenched terrorist networks in the West Bank continued without respite.

In September 2006, on a warm fall morning, a Ya'mas task force entered Qabatiya to arrest a band of al-Aqsa Martyrs Brigade terrorists that the Shin Bet had learned were planning a suicide bombing in northern Israel. Sa'ar Shine led the operation. Twenty Ya'mas operators, consisting of Speakers and men crammed in Horses, entered the town from different directions through the main roads, all wide and beautifully paved, and some of the narrower unpaved gravel paths that the locals used. The town was relatively affluent; impressive mosques and schools, marble and stone landmarks dominated the landscape. Qabatiya had small residential plots on the outer periphery of the city limits and clusters of two- and three-story homes where multiple families in a larger clan lived throughout the city center. Shine's force of operators negotiated the twisting turns of the town, built around small hills and steep declines, and reached the targeted location. They had arrived at the location unnoticed. Officers at the CP were relieved that all was going according to plan.

The assault force closed in on the terrorists' house from all sides to secure the perimeter. A few stray dogs barked down the road. The sounds of women cooking could be heard coming from nearby kitchen windows. The entry team approached from the six o'clock side of the home, weapons at the ready, moving cautiously under the sunny skies. The force didn't make it to the top of the stairs before a thunderous burst of fire erupted at them from a nearby window. The perimeter teams too suddenly found themselves pinned down

---

* The mastermind of the bombing, Adham Muhammed Abdel Aziz Yunis, was arrested in the summer of 2007 by a Ya'mas arrest team in Jenin.

by gunfire pouring in from every angle. Four separate battles erupted. Shine radioed his situation back to the CP, but the raid took place in an area where the radio and cellular phone reception was blocked by the nearby hills. Under fire, Shine worked the radios and the mobile telephones while on his hands and knees. Because of the complexity of the operation, deep inside Palestinian territory, the Ya'mas backup was forty minutes away.[4]

Outnumbered and surrounded, Shine and his twenty operators fought several individually desperate battles around the besieged house. Some of the fighting was hand-to-hand; it was all at close range. Instead of retreating into a more easily defended perimeter, the operators continued with their mission, searching for the wanted men during the battle and searching the home for documents, explosives, and weapons. The Shin Bet intelligence had been spot-on—too accurate, perhaps. But the intelligence had failed to indicate that the location was a vibrant nerve center controlling all al-Aqsa Martyrs Brigade activity in the area.

By the time the main rescue force arrived, Sa'ar Shine and his men had killed five terrorists and wounded scores more. Smoke grenades had to be used to conceal the force's departure.

Shin Bet director Avi Dichter once addressed a group of Ya'mas operators during a lull in their operations to give the unit a pep talk and to brief them on the campaign against the Palestinian terror factions. Dichter likened the Israeli effort, one Ya'mas officer remembered, to "cutting the grass": Whenever the terrorists grew too large, too strong, and too present, the Israelis would cut them down to size.[5] Cutting the grass had worked. The terror cells in the West Bank were badly beaten; many had been destroyed. Many of the men who perpetrated bloodshed, planning and facilitating attacks against Israel's cities from their safe havens in Qalqilya, Tulkarm, Nablus, Hebron, and Jenin, were either dead, captured, or in hiding.

On February 21, 2007, a Ya'mas operator ventured into the Jenin refugee camp to hunt Ibrahim Qassam Obeid, the PIJ's military commander in the city, who was known by his nom de guerre of "Abu Jahim." Abu Jahim commanded the PIJ's entire terror apparatus in northern Samaria and was considered one of the organization's top bomb-making engineers.[6] He was also paranoid, and believed that the Israelis were never more than a trigger pull away from killing him. Abu Jahim never slept in the same bed twice; he carried his M16 at all times and always moved about with a team of bodyguards. Abu Jahim thought that if he remained mobile, moving about every few hours and living in and out of a variety of vehicles, he could outsmart the Shin Bet. But the Israelis had the make and model of his current car on this cold winter's morning. Master Sergeant Abdallah,* a Muslim from northern Israel who, at the age of twenty-eight, was one of the most decorated NCOs in the unit (and one of the most decorated soldiers in Israeli history),[7] was driving a white Volkswagen sedan, along with several other Speakers, right behind the PIJ commander's red Suzuki Grand Vitara. The undercover team were dressed as common laborers. The jackets worn were larger than normal size in order to conceal the body armor and extra ammunition each man wore underneath his disguise.

Abu Jahim sensed that the Israelis were following him. He ordered his driver to slam on the brakes and to make a U-turn just in front of Yehiya Ayyash Square. The PIJ commander rolled down his window and raised his M16 into the air, firing a burst of fire to sound the alarm inside the city. He then aimed his weapon at the white Volkswagen and ordered his driver to slow down. Abdallah didn't have time to reach for his concealed weapon, nor was his sedan armored. So he improvised. Abdallah whispered to the other two men in the car to raise their hands and smile. Without panicking or losing a beat, Abdallah slowly lowered his window and yelled in a perfectly accented Jenin Arabic, "What's wrong with you? I'm from here. I'm one of you." Abdallah's facial pantomime was a mixture of surprise and resigned indignation for even being suspected. Abu Jahim smiled, and approved. He pulled his M16 back into the vehicle and closed the windows. Close to ten Palestinian policemen stood nearby across the square. They didn't even bother to look up.

Once Abu Jahim's Suzuki had roared away in a show of power, Abdallah ordered his men to take the subject down. The Speakers' vehicle entered into a brief though high-speed pursuit of the Suzuki, while the Horse that was nearby rushed into position to block off any escape. Abu Jahim was blocked in. The Palestinians emerged from the SUV and fired. Several rounds sliced

---

* A pseudonym—true identity withheld for security considerations.

through the Volkswagen's windshield. The Ya'mas team exited their vehicle. Abdallah closed range by running toward the PIJ gunmen, firing his M4 as he ran a zigzag pattern. The two other Speakers followed close behind. Within seconds, Abu Jahim and his two bodyguards were dead, hit several times by M4 fire. Once again the Palestinian policemen thought it best not to intervene.

Abu Jahim's death came a day after one of his suicide bombers had been arrested in Tel Aviv hours before he was to have blown himself up inside Israel's largest city.[8]

The operation in Jenin would be one of the final missions during Uzi Levy's command of the unit. In March 2007, Levy was promoted to the rank of commander, akin to an army full colonel, and named the deputy commander of all Border Guard units operating in Judea and Samaria. Levy had been commander of the Ya'mas for a remarkable six-and-a-half years. Such a lengthy tenure at the helm of a top-tier unit was unheard of; unit commanders never remained at their post for more than three years. But Levy's unit was on a roll and it was deemed inadvisable to disrupt such a successful run at counterterrorist operations. During Levy's stretch in the unit, the Ya'mas carried out 1,215 operations. The unit arrested 610 high-value terrorist targets.[9] The men who were arrested were field commanders, the machinery that made the intifada so lethal. Each man that the Ya'mas brought into custody had the answers to unravel countless operations that were in motion or being planned, and these men knew the names of those responsible for many of the attacks that had already taken place. Many, of course, didn't surrender. During Levy's years in command, the Ya'mas neutralized 123 terrorists; 109 terrorists were seriously wounded in exchanges of gunfire.[10]

Uzi Levy's replacement, Chief Superintendent Gal,* was a straightforward by-the-book officer who had spent nearly twenty years in the Ya'ma'm before taking over the West Bank undercover unit. Gal wanted the job of Ya'mas commander. His last posting was that of squadron leader in the Ya'ma'm, and he had led many engagements against the most fanatical hardcore terrorists during the intifada. Gal inherited a unit that had been one of the most successful Israeli counterterrorist forces of that conflict. He also received a built-in cadre of heroic and capable officers and NCOs who possessed

---

* A pseudonym—true identity withheld for security considerations.

invaluable operational experience and who knew the terrain like the back of their hands. But there were many things that were lacking inside the force, as well. The Ya'mas had grown exponentially during the intifada, but its resources were still limited and its facilities sorely lacking. There had been no time for the operators to train properly during the intifada—there was barely enough time to sleep. The unit did not have proper training grounds, nor had there been time to embrace new technologies and absorb new equipment. During the five hard years of fighting, everything had been done on the fly; it was all improvised. There was no choice. Uzi Levy and his men had pulled off a remarkable success with the most Spartan of resources.

Gal was determined to change the molecular makeup of the force—especially in how it was perceived by the decision-makers who allocated materiel and funding. "In the past the unit received an armored vehicle, almost as a reward, for carrying out a successful mission," Gal recalled. "The unit had to demand resources that should have been available to you from the get-go. A unit cannot receive basic necessities as a reward or because it managed to kill a couple of terrorists. The Ya'mas deserved the same resources, the same equipment, and the same basic amenities as the other counterterrorist units."[11] Gal did not subscribe to the ethos that missions were worth any cost. The lives of his men were of paramount importance, and Gal was determined through his time at command to fight the powers that be with the same gusto as he would fight the terrorists, in order to get the men the tools they needed.

The armored undercover vehicles were especially needed. A few weeks after Gal became the unit commander, Sa'ar Shine led a force of operators on an arrest operation near Jenin in which terrorists opened fire on the Ya'mas operators with machine guns and RPGs. Shine didn't like to hear the generals or the politicians say that the intifada was over. "The volume of the violence was lower than before," he commented, "but you could still hear the noise."[12]

Operations in the West Bank continued.

CHAPTER TWENTY-FOUR

The Last Shot Fired

The sun set early in those fall days as winter neared. The evening sky had turned a blackened purple, a sign that the winter grasp was soon approaching. It had been a quiet day at the Ya'mas base in the central West Bank. Operations officers planned arrest strikes, training officers prepared days at the range and some large-scale urban warfare obstacle courses, and the operators prepared for dinner. Old-timers in the unit, men who had earned a chest full of medals and citations, relished the relative quiet. Newcomers, conscripts and officers alike, enjoyed hearing the war stories of shoot-outs in Jenin and Tulkarm. No one expected a call-out. When it came, they all rushed to their vehicles.

The Shin Bet had just learned that a suicide bomber had left Jenin and was making his way along the byroads of the surrounding hills to reach the Green Line and northern Israel. Sa'ar Shine summoned his squadron. His men suited up and grabbed their heavy vests and weapons. They would get additional instructions en route. The bomber, driven by a young bodyguard in a pickup truck, had to be stopped at all costs before he could enter Israel.

Shine set up his position at a junction near Kafr Dan, a small and isolated village northwest of Jenin. As he moved slowly along a dirt path, he noticed a vehicle fitting the Shin Bet description heading his way. The pickup noticed the Ya'mas vehicle, as well, and the driver floored the gas pedal. Shine's driver maneuvered the van so that the head-on impact was less severe than it could have been. The passenger emerged from his vehicle, attempting to flee into the darkness. Shine gave chase. It was 2008. Eight years after the intifada began, three years after the last suicide bombing, and a year since Israel and the Palestinian Authority had entered into an agreement where fugitives would not be targeted for death if they abandoned a terrorist operation, the rules governing the use of lethal fire had changed. A fleeing suspect couldn't be killed, so Shine aimed for his legs.

One round pierced the young man's left thigh, but the bullet ricocheted off his bones and up into his heart. Ya'mas paramedics worked feverishly to save him, but the bullet had done too much damage. Shine searched the young man's pants pockets and found a fifty-shekel note with a bullet hole through it.

The would-be suicide bomber was the last man that Sa'ar Shine shot and killed during his time with the Ya'mas. The intifada was over.

POSTSCRIPT FROM THE FIRST EDITION

There are no happily ever afters in the Middle East, only periods of not-so-violent remission. Politicians and pundits talk of peace; it's their job. Citizens can dream of peace; it's their right. But the men on the front lines, the soldiers and professional operators who fight terror for a living, don't have the luxury to think of long-term solutions to geopolitical issues with far-reaching regional repercussions. Their world is one of the fight before their eyes, the mission late into the dark hours before morning. Theirs is the world of kill and capture so that someone they don't know can get on a bus in their Jerusalem neighborhood and make it to work without being decapitated in a fiery explosion. During the intifada, Israel's military and security forces looked at their watches and counted the hours until tomorrow. That's as far as their peripheral vision allowed them to see. It was a horrible period in the country's violence-scarred history.

The three Ya'mas units—West Bank, Jerusalem, and Gaza—were part of the vanguard of counterterrorist units that took it upon their shoulders to stem the tide of unstoppable carnage. There were several commando and counterterrorist units that fought the Palestinian terrorist faction, but only the Ya'mas operated day in and day out inside enemy territory. The three Ya'mas units did not buy peace. But in the West Bank, in Jerusalem, and in Gaza, a small group of highly skilled and incredibly courageous men did buy peace and quiet by ending the campaign of the suicide bomber.

In the years since the intifada, Israel has fought a war in Lebanon, and several campaigns against Hamas in the Gaza Strip. Salafist terrorist groups have attempted to enter into Israeli territory through the Sinai Desert. The shrapnel of the Arab Spring, a civil war in neighboring Syria, and the emergence of an Islamic State movement, punches along Israel's frontiers. Yet the Palestinian terror factions inside the West Bank and Gaza have been unable—or, perhaps, unwilling—to repeat the suicide bombing campaign that killed and maimed so many Israeli citizens during those bloody years of indiscriminate violence.

The work of the undercover units during these most violent times can be defined by meticulous preparation and accurately flowing intelligence that, when combined with indefinable courage, enabled small teams to mount pinpoint operations where the enemy felt safest. These operations required a delicate balancing act of risk versus reward and target value. Living inside the veins of the enemy—entering a city, a village, or a market, in small teams against a determined and very dangerous foe—was perhaps one of the most isolated and dangerous aspects of Israel's brand of counterterrorism. The work wasn't for everyone; it required unique talents and unflinching determination. Few in Israel know what the Ya'mas did during the intifada. The work was bloody, dangerous, but many Israelis had the luxury to sleep safely in their beds and not think of what others were doing on their behalf alone and outnumbered inside the central nervous system of the terrorist armies.

The men who served inside the undercover units preferred working far from the spotlight. These men didn't do it for the money, even though counterterrorism was their profession. The salary was awful and their work conditions were treacherous. Many of the men look at pictures of themselves when the intifada began and then look at their reflections in a mirror and see men who were once young and who have now been aged thirty years in ten; hopes for longevity have probably been shortened irreversibly thanks to cigarettes, caffeine, high blood pressure, and exhaustion. The psychological scar tissue of wading through the endless muck of pressure and danger will remain with them for the rest of their lives.

More decorations of valor were awarded to the men of the three Ya'mas units than to any other unit during the intifada. Some of the operators, like Sa'ar Shine, have joined an elite class of national hero, earning multiple medals of valor from a nation that is incredibly stingy in bestowing recognition of extraordinary courage in battle. Still, even those who received what for Israel is a chest full of ribbons would give the medals back in a heartbeat in exchange for the time they can never have back with their wives and children. And, as much as these men have already sacrificed, most have continued to remain on the front lines of Israel's war on terror.

There are still those inside the three Ya'mas units who began their under-cover wars when the units were created, more than twenty-five years ago, and continue to work, day in and day out, inside the imminent danger of counterterrorist work. Undercover work is their specialty—their calling. A few of the team leaders and squadron commanders who played so pivotal a role leading these undercover forces in battle have left the front lines. Some of the men, like Yaakov Berman in the West Bank and Shimon in Gaza, went full circle with their careers in the Ya'mas—going from new teammate to unit commander in the span of remarkable careers and now in the "blue" police, promoted to positions where their rise up the chain of command is fast-tracked and secured. Nasser, the man who encountered the Jaradat clan in Jenin, is, at the time of this book's writing, now the commander of the Ya'mas unit that works along Israel's volatile border with Gaza and Egypt.

IDF chief of staff Lieutenant General Gadi Eisenkot, who commanded the Judea and Samaria Division from 2003 to 2005 at the height of the undercover war in the West Bank, once said that the job of the army, the security ser-vices, was to provide the political echelon the quiet and the capacity to make decisions from a position of strength. The Ya'mas fielded a greater burden. The three Border Guard undercover units played a pivotal role in preventing indiscriminate bloodshed. By doing so, they enabled Israel's political echelons to maintain the semblance of day-to-day normalcy inside a country merci-lessly under siege. The three Ya'mas units remain at the forefront of Israel's counterterrorist efforts precisely because there are never any happily-ever-after endings in the Middle East. For Israel, there are only prolonged periods of cherished quiet that are secured by those who operate in the darkness, strike from the shadows, and rush inside the danger.

The Road to an Unimaginable Horror

Peace in the Middle East, an Israeli counterterrorist commander would comment, "can only be defined as temporary lulls in between massacres and misery: a relatively quiet time to regroup, rearm, and reload." The end of the second intifada—the slow cessation of the suicide bombings and active shooter massacres—signaled the beginning of one of these gray periods of quiet when both sides reassessed and redefined their tactics and overall objectives.

Like any hope for a more peaceful future in a region where the horrors of the past are always more important than the promise of tomorrow, the respite and any hints of optimism would be short-lived. Hamas, the Palestine Islamic Jihad, and their benefactors in Iran never abandoned their plans to destroy the Jewish State. Israel never relinquished its responsibility to defend its citizens with proactive and preemptive intelligence-based special operations that captured or killed men who planned and tried to execute plans of mass carnage. Hamas took ownership of massive arsenals of new weapons. The group redesigned its operational networks and developed new tactics and technologies. So, too, did the Israelis. This is the DNA of the asymmetrical warfare fought between the Israelis and the Palestinian terror groups on the bloody chessboard battlefield until the unthinkable—and unimaginable—happened.

On the morning of October 7, 2023, 3,800 Hamas terrorists invaded southern Israel and captured and held twenty-two communities and military bases; an estimated 2,500 Gazans also crossed into Israel to join in on the savagery. The terrorists breached the border in 119 locations, and attacked overland, through fortified fences, under them through massive tunnels, by air utilizing motorized paragliders, and even from the sea. The terrorist blitz was supported by the launch of five thousand rockets against Israel's population centers in the south, which required the involvement of an additional one thousand terrorists.[1] The Shin Bet and A'man, the two agencies responsible for intelligence gathering inside the Gaza Strip, obtained the Hamas operational plans a few years earlier—codenamed Jericho Walls, the documents listed in great and frighteningly accurate details precisely what Hamas was planning.

Israel's political and military leadership never acted on the intelligence it held. Knowing what could be coming was different than knowing when it would arrive. The multiplatform Hamas operation on October 7 achieved complete surprise. By the end of that terrible day, over 1,200 Israeli men, women, and children lay dead—most butchered, raped, and mutilated in their own homes or at a desert music festival. Over 250 men, women, and children—Israelis and citizens from twenty-five nations—were dragged to Gaza and held hostage by Hamas and the PIJ. October 7 was the darkest day in the modern history of the Jewish people and the State of Israel. The Hamas attacks launched a war that still rages; the conflict sparked anti-Israel and antisemitic protests around the world, especially on American college campuses.

Israel—and the Middle East—will never and can never be the same.

For close to fifteen years before the October 7 Hamas invasion, the Israeli special operations units that were instrumental in ending the second intifada played a key role in stopping the outbreak of a third uprising. The terror dynamics changed after the unilateral Israel withdrawal from Gaza in 2005. Hamas seized political control of the Gaza Strip the following year and then took over from the Palestinian Authority in 2007 in a bloody coup. Hamas turned Gaza into a modern-day metamorphosis of Mogadishu in the early 1990s and what ISIS would build years later in Mosul in 2014. Gaza, the home of over two million people, became a terror hub and an Iranian proxy base of operations to be used for attacks against Israel. Hamas turned its tunnel-carving skills, having used them so effectively to bring in arms, money, and personnel in and out of the Sinai, particularly the Egyptian side of the city of Rafah, into a national industry. Tactical tunnels were constructed for terrorists to use as covert thoroughfares into Israel for kidnapping operations.

On June 25, 2006, a Hamas terror squad emerged from a terror tunnel it had dug underneath the Keren Shalom border crossing. They attacked a tank, killed several of the crew members, and dragged a wounded soldier, Gilad Shalit, into Gaza. Hamas held him captive, often under inhumane conditions, for over five years. On October 18, 2011, he was freed in a complex prisoner exchange in which Israel freed 1,027 imprisoned terrorists, including many with blood on their hands who were responsible for heinous acts of mass murder. One of the released terrorists was Yahya Sinwar, the "Butcher of Khan Younis," a Hamas enforcer sentenced to multiple life terms for the kidnapping and execution of two Israeli soldiers in 1989.[2]

Sinwar, who learned Hebrew and something about the Israeli mindset in prison, soon began his march toward seizing command of the terror group. He embarked on a massive armaments program to equip Hamas with home-made and Iranian-acquired short- and medium-range rockets and missiles. An army of burrowers began to dig hundreds of miles of tunnels underneath the Gaza Strip; some were as deep as eighty meters below ground and con-sisted of multistory subterranean complexes. Sinwar's dream was to hold Israel hostage and bring the region to a state of permanent war.

On the night of June 12, 2014, a three-man West Bank Hamas cell based in Hebron, masquerading as observant Jews, abducted three teenage yeshiva students, who attempted to hitch a ride home near their school in Gush Etzion. The kidnapping sparked a massive manhunt across the West Bank—the mission to locate the boys was called "Operation Brothers Keeper." Israel's top-tier special operations units—led by the Ya'ma'm and Ya'mas units—raided hundreds of locations and arrested over four hundred suspects; fifty-six of them were released three years earlier as part of the Gilad Shalit exchange. Israeli forces also captured extensive arsenals of weapons and bomb-building materials.[3] The bodies of the three boys were found eighteen days later; the terrorists buried them in a shallow ditch.*

---

* Bringing the three kidnappers responsible for the abduction and murder of the three teenagers to justice was a Shin Bet imperative. On August 5, Husam Kawasme was arrested in the Shu'afat section in East Jerusalem—he was captured hours before an attempt to escape to Jordan. On September 23, the Shin Bet tracked down the other two terrorists—Marwan Kawasme and Amar Abu Aysha—in a safe house in Hebron. The Ya'ma'm laid siege to the location, and in a pitched battle, the two were killed; bulldozers were summoned to make sure that the terrorists had been neutralized.

Hamas launched 4,500 rockets and missiles at Israel from Gaza to support its besieged cells in the West Bank responsible for the kidnapping and murder of the teenagers. Israel responded with air strikes and then with a limited ground incursion known as "Operation Protective Edge." Urban combat against an enemy that hid behind a population of human shields and booby-trapped buildings and street corners proved costly and sparked an international outcry against Israel for hitting civilians. Even the United States, Israel's main ally, was hyper-critical of the tactics that the IDF employed even though Hamas fired missiles from apartment complexes, United Nations schools, and hospitals.

The conflict ended after fifty days. It was a stalemate—a testament to the power of misplaced political pressure over military results against an entrenched terror army. Ironically, and quite hypocritically, the United States and a vast international coalition, would employ tactics identical to Israel in the war against the Islamic State in Iraq and Syria a few months later.

The war in the summer of 2014 was a dress rehearsal for October 2023. Hamas learned an invaluable lesson that summer about manipulating the news and the use of social media and propaganda to control international opinion. Sinwar ordered his legions to dig tunnels and stockpile weapons and ammunition for the permanent war he coveted.

When the fighting ended in Gaza at the end of the summer of 2014, the Ya'mas order of battle still consisted of the three regional units. The unit previously responsible for the Gaza Strip had been reorganized into the Ya'mas South. Since Israel was no longer responsible for the Gaza Strip nor the smuggling routes on the Philadelphi corridor, the Ya'mas South focused on new terrain and new threats: battling heavily armed violent criminal gangs in the Bedouin communities of southern Israel and working along the rest of the porous border with Egypt where a pro-ISIS Salafist terror underground had taken hold in the Sinai Peninsula. The West Bank and Jerusalem Ya'mas missions remained the same: assist the Shin Bet and the IDF commands in apprehending high-value terror suspects responsible for acts of murder and thwart those planning large-scale attacks inside Israel.

The second intifada had been an Aberdeen Proving Ground for the deployment of undercover assets deep inside areas held by heavily armed terror groups. The capabilities that the three Ya'mas squads developed in the fight against Hamas and the PIJ were not lost to the top-tier units of the IDF and the INP—especially the Ya'ma'm. The national hostage rescue force took great interest in developing in-house undercover capabilities that they could include in their tactical playbook.

The Ya'ma'm intended for this new tool in its arsenal to remain secret but it didn't last. On November 12, 2015, closed-circuit cameras captured a group of a dozen men and women entering Hebron's al-Ahli Hospital; one was even in a wheelchair, and another was dressed as a woman, complete with a black niqab. They belonged to a Ya'ma'm undercover squad sent into the medical center before dawn to arrest a wanted Hamas terror suspect who was hospitalized after having been shot by a young man he stabbed a week earlier.[4] "Small undercover units can today do the work that once required entire military divisions," Israeli defense minister Moshe Ya'alon, a former IDF Chief of Staff, claimed after the raid.[5]

Ya'alon was right. The officers who commanded the three Ya'mas units possessed unrivaled tactical counterterrorism experience, prompting exchanges with the U.S. military that suddenly found itself facing off against a determined enemy in Iraq and Syria that had perfected the use of subterranean attack tunnels and civilians as human shields. Veterans of the three Ya'mas units were promoted to district commander in the Border Guard, while some, like Yaakov Berman, lateraled over to the blue police where senior officers with skills for decisive strategic action under enormous tactical pressure were asked to fight crime in Israel's population centers. Patrol and detective units inside the INP were soon led by veteran undercover officers who were promoted. They looked at day-to-day challenges differently than other policemen.

In February 2016, Yaakov "Kobi" Shabtai was promoted to deputy commissioner and named commander of the Border Guard. Shabtai, who led Ya'mas Gaza in the 1990s, had a decisively tactical mindset to solving operational challenges—especially when small-man Special Forces units could be used to tackle large-scale strategic issues. Shabtai had a sixth sense about impending threats and felt that the country's paramilitary law enforcement

arm needed a boost against the growing threats emanating from the dangerous nexus between Hamas and the Islamic Jihad and organized crime rings in
the Arab sector, to the increasing capabilities of the terror groups to emulate
ISIS-like battlefield tactics to Israel. Organized crime, particularly in the Arab
sector, had turned into a violent epidemic plaguing the country. Murders and
robberies in the Arab communities throughout the country were alarming
and developed into a national security risk. These towns and villages were
rife with firepower and the local police precincts were undermanned and
ill-equipped to battle the heavily armed gangs.

Shabtai increased the budgets for his undercover and other tactical units:
new vehicles, weapons, optics for marksmen and long-range surveillance, and
advanced high-tech communications equipment. A year after taking charge
of the Border Guard, wanting to be prepared for what he feared would be an
intifada on steroids, Shabtai created the *Hativat Ha'Taktit*, or Tactical Brigade,
a dedicated on-call mobile special ops force team responsible for responding
immediately anywhere in Israel in cases of a national emergency.

The new brigade consisted of a Matilan (the Hebrew acronym for
Intelligence Gathering and Infiltrations Interception) force, a canine unit,
a mobile tactical team (equipped with dirt bikes and all-terrain vehicles), a
drone squad, and an indigenous intelligence-gathering force. The brigade was
built around a new Ya'mas, a fourth undercover unit, which spearheaded and
initiated operations across the country—primarily inside southern Israel's
Bedouin population where gun running and narcotics led to a violent epidemic of murders and gangland executions.

The Tactical Brigade's undercover unit utilized the same Arabic-speaking
infiltration techniques to raid the crime families with the same modus operandi that had been used against the terror factions during the second intifada, but now it openly recruited female operators. Shabtai appointed a
veteran undercover officer who served during the second intifada to lead
the tactical brigade. Also, long before female soldiers became full-fledged
members of IDF combat units, the Border Guard and especially the Tactical
Brigade incorporated them without issue. Chief Inspector N.* became the
first female undercover unit team leader in Israel's history.[6]

---

* Identity withheld for security considerations.

Shabtai was ideally suited to lead the Border Guard. His mindset—and organizational talents—were purely results-driven and tactically pragmatic. He had transformed Israel's paramilitary law enforcement arm into a vital cog of the country's internal security machinery, and in January 2021, parliament approved his selection as the Israeli police commissioner. Shabtai faced numerous challenges from day one—the COVID-19 pandemic and a disaster at a religious festival in northern Israel resulted in forty-five dead worshippers. Two years of massive political indecision and division resulted in Shabtai serving three prime ministers. The West Bank, one law enforcement official commented, was a "vat of high explosives and flammable liquid waiting for a spark to set the whole thing off."

The Palestinian Authority, corrupt and ineffective, had become increasingly unpopular inside the towns and cities under their control. Hamas and the PIJ prepared for the next intifada. The flow of top-grade black-market weapons that reached terror cells throughout the West Bank, especially stolen IDF assault and sniper rifles, was alarming. Explosives were stockpiled. The chatter picked up by the Shin Bet warned of a possible intifada.

The Ya'mas West Bank operated nightly, acting upon intelligence provided by the Shin Bet, and operating in conjunction with the IDF to develop an up-close-and-personal tactical assessment of what was transpiring inside the main thoroughfares of Jenin and the Kasbah of Nablus. Between 2021 and 2022, Ya'mas operations resulted in the arrests of 286 terrorists and operatives, and an additional twenty-three terrorists were killed in firefights with undercover forces.[7]

Jenin became ground zero. The PIJ upped the ante and changed their tactics. Rather than hide their activities and scatter when the undercover units approached, the terrorists took a page out of the Hezbollah playbook, planting powerful improvised devices alongside roadways that any responding Israeli force would have to cross. The devices were sophisticated and triggered to be detonated by remote control. In the predawn hours of June 19, 2023, after roadside bombs damaged several armored vehicles ferrying a Ya'mas team on a raid in Jenin, PIJ gunmen opened fire in a sophisticated ambush and then closed in on the Israeli force.[8] Seven Ya'mas operators were seriously wounded in the exchange, and a rescue force including D9 dozers and air cover had to be summoned. Even veteran Ya'mas officers, those with over twenty years of combat experience, were surprised by the sheer might of the PIJ devices and the tactics they employed in the ambush.

The game of cat-and-mouse between Israel's security and intelligence forces trying to contain the tensions, and the Palestinians hoping to ignite the territories, prompted the IDF to launch Operation House and Garden, a large-scale special operation inside Jenin and its refugee camp. The counterterrorist offensive involved the elite of the IDF's Order of Battle—fifteen hundred soldiers in all—and was one of the first times that unmanned aerial vehicles were used to bomb targets inside the West Bank. Elements of the Ya'ma'm and Ya'mas spearheaded the assault that resulted in thirteen terrorists killed, over three hundred suspects arrested, and arsenals of weapons, explosives, and cash seized.[9]

Shabtai faced an uphill struggle in his attempts to prepare the Israel National Police for the escalating terror violence he felt would erupt into a full-fledged conflagration. Many senior commanders in the regular blue police resisted his efforts while others, reportedly, undermined his vision. Itamar Ben-Gvir, the controversial ultra-right-wing Minister of Public Security, pushed Commissioner Shabtai to politicize the police, weakening its ability to protect and serve the country. Shabtai was criticized for spending far too much of his daily schedule—and department resources—on addressing the tactical threats that Israel was facing and not on the day-to-day administrative tasks that usually fell on the desk of the national police chief. Shabtai, his detractors claimed, spent more time thinking about new tools to help the Ya'ma'm and the Ya'mas carry out their missions than he did thinking about the less attractive aspects of the job like traffic enforcement.[10] But, after the bloody months in the West Bank and violent Palestinian protests in Jerusalem, Shabtai felt that something dangerous was on the horizon. It was an intangible feeling, like the realization that the Ya'mas officers in the West Bank felt in the months preceding the second intifada, that the terrorists were planning something major.

The Hamas invasion of October 7 took every piece of Israel's defense shield by complete surprise. It was Simchat Torah and a holiday weekend, but word spread quickly of the Hamas invasion by phone and WhatsApp. Residents of the south, besieged by the terrorists in their armored safe rooms, tried in vain to send out urgent SOS messages to anyone who could come and rescue them.

Messages raced back and forth among the units as well, in real time, with graphic photos and videos that detailed the ongoing attack. Soldiers and policemen on duty, on the front lines in Israel's south, were the first to withstand the worst of the terror blitzkrieg. Within two hours, organized elements from Israel's top-tier units—Sayeret Mat'kal, Flotilla 13, Shaldag—and the other elite formations mobilized in haste and headed toward the Gaza Envelope. The Ya'ma'm raced to Sderot and Ofakim to rescue communities seized by Hamas terrorists. In Sderot, the police station was overrun and a desperate point-blank firefight erupted inside the building after a Ya'ma'm task force arrived.

The terrorists drove into Israel in an armada of Toyota Pathfinders and other vehicles that ferried enough weapons, explosives, and antitank rockets to fight for days and last against forces ten times their size. The terrorists had been issued Captagon, an inexpensive amphetamine made in Lebanon and Syria, that had become a staple of jihadists fighting for ISIS and that produced feelings of superpowers allowing them to stay awake for days.[11] Israeli forces were locked in dozens of small, desperate battles against a drug-crazed fundamentalist suicidal army that was butchering, raping, and kidnapping the men, women, and children they encountered.

In the first few hours of the Hamas invasion, it was the police in Sderot and Ofakim who held the line—preventing the terrorists from making their way to the center of the country. Many of these officers were Ya'mas veterans armed with nothing more than their semiautomatic pistols and two magazines holding off truckloads of terrorists armed with RPGs and heavy machine guns. There are remarkable stories of courage and sacrifice emanating from the battles of that day including a Ya'mas veteran and officer in a motorcycle traffic unit who engaged an overwhelming force of terrorists, firing his weapon and zigzagging his bike between the bullets and grenades.

Unit 33, the Gidonim, and Ya'mas South were the first of the police undercover units to find themselves battling the terrorist onslaught that morning. Two of the kibbutzim where they fought were Kfar Aza and Nahal Oz—Kfar Aza was only a mile-and-a-half from Gaza; the gates of Nahal Oz were even closer to the frontier, only eight-tenths of a mile away.

Unit 33 officers encountered a massive terror presence near the Black Arrow Monument, between Sderot and Nir Am. The terrorists were eager to hold the strategic junction and set up a perimeter supported by RPGs. The Hamas Pathfinders had 12.7mm and 14.5mm Soviet-era heavy machine guns*—a weapon that could shoot down aircraft and penetrate vehicle armor. When the Unit 33 response force arrived, a massive firefight erupted. The policemen found themselves outnumbered, outgunned, and outflanked. The sheer number of terrorists that the Gidonim encountered and killed—and the fact that they carried enough firepower and ammunition to equip a conventional military battalion—daunted them to realize that they were in the center of an unprecedented moment where Israel's very existence was threatened. The realization motivated them to fight harder. The unit organized itself and, armed only with 5.56mm assault rifles, they engaged the terrorists in a courageous display of tactical prowess. They knew that unless they denied Hamas access to the strategic junction, the population centers of central Israel would be threatened.

When the situation at Black Arrow stabilized, Unit 33 split into two. One team, led by Chief Inspector L.,† rushed toward Kfar Aza. The kibbutz was overrun by over one hundred Nukhba force terrorists who killed and raped scores of men and women and then barricaded themselves inside people's homes. The Gidonim raced into the battle to join IDF units already on sight in a furious exchange of fire and did everything they could to make sure that the hostages—locked inside their safe rooms—made it out alive. Their tactical—and psychological—training played an integral role in their decision-making and combat battle plan. Joined by a joint Shin Bet and Unit 33 tactical team, they launched their rescue bid, fighting inside living rooms and kitchens. It lasted for hours.[12]

It is believed that seventy Hamas terrorists took over the kibbutz. It took the IDF and the police units two-and-a-half days to secure Kfar Aza,[13] but not before sixty-seven of the kibbutz's four hundred residents were murdered, raped, and mutilated. Others were kidnapped back to Gaza.

---

* These included Soviet-made DShK (Dushkas), Chinese and North Korean–produced Type 77s, and Hamas-built copies manufactured in underground factories under the Gaza Strip.

† Identity withheld for security reasons.

Members of the Ya'mas task force that headed to Kibbutz Nahal Oz thought that they were responding to an infiltration of three or four terrorists—not over one hundred. "We thought we were in a nightmare," a Ya'mas sniper would comment to Israel's Channel 13. "This was not something we expected." Hamas terrorists wearing green headbands and Islamic Jihad wearing black and yellow ones had breached the fortifications surrounding the kibbutz in several key locations, allowing dozens of heavily armed men to rush inside and storm the homes. At the same time, the local guard force, made up of residents, tried to stall and save their loved ones.

Many of the terrorists who stormed Kfar Aza and Nahal Oz, along with the other kibbutzim, wore IDF fatigues to sow confusion among the civilians they targeted and the forces they knew would respond. But the unit's desperate efforts to rescue the Israelis trapped inside their homes' safe rooms that horrible day were made somewhat easier by the Arabic language skills they possessed. Responding Ya'mas operators were able to yell at the terrorists in Arabic but few surrendered. The battles to save families and wounded soldiers who were cut down trying to save the kibbutz took hours. Twenty-three-year-old Staff Sergeant Yaakov Krasniansky was the sole Ya'mas casualty of the fight for Nahal Oz.

The battle to repel the terrorists had been costly: 689 Israeli soldiers and sixty-three police officers, including nine Ya'ma'm operators, were killed in the hundreds of other battles around the Gaza Envelope on October 7. It is estimated that the Ya'ma'm, Unit 33, and the four undercover units killed over five hundred terrorists that day.* Commissioner Shabtai's elite units saved southern Israel from being overrun.

The work of the specialized police units would not be restricted to the Israeli side of the frontier. When Israel went to war after October 7 to destroy Hamas and its vast military infrastructure—both above and below ground—returning the 251 kidnapped men, women, and children from the depths of a tunnel prison was a mission of the greatest national importance. Some of the hostages were released in December 2023 during a cease-fire,

---

* It took weeks before the last Hamas terrorists were located and neutralized in and around southern Israel—some had managed to evade the Israeli dragnet by hiding in the many agricultural communities that were abandoned after the attack.

but fourteen months after October 7, there were still ninety-six hostages unaccounted for in Gaza. It is not sure how many are still alive.

Hostage-rescue operations are the domain of the Ya'ma'm but operating in the confines of the densely populated rubble-strewn Gaza Strip, where buildings were booby-trapped and virtually every home hid a tunnel opening, required guile along with tactical prowess. Although information about methods employed by the Ya'ma'm and Shin Bet to locate and rescue the hostages are naturally classified, details have emerged indicating that "undercover" personnel played a critical role in the unit's June 8 rescue of four captives held in the Nuseirat refugee camp in central Gaza. According to accounts published in the Israeli daily *Yediot Aharonot*, Israeli operatives rented an apartment near the location where one of the hostages, Noa Argamani, was being held; the flat was also near where three other male hostages were imprisoned.[14] It was reported that the undercovers included women wearing dresses and hijabs.

When the Ya'ma'm rescue force received the green light to launch the operation, codenamed Summer Seeds,[15] the unit was reportedly ferried to the targeted locations by battered white trucks, some sporting commercial advertising and others carrying furniture.[16] The undercovers played an intrinsic role in gathering intelligence on the terrain and inserting the operators near the hostages. The mission, not the unit's first rescue during the war, was a brilliant success and considered one of the most spectacular and dangerous hostage rescue operations ever attempted in war.[*]

Some three hundred days after October 7, Israel's primary objective of destroying Hamas's military capabilities has resulted in fighting a war on five fronts: full-scale combat in Gaza, counterterrorist operations in the West Bank, rocket exchanges across the Lebanese frontier, containing terror Iranian proxies in Iraq and Syria, and missile and drone fire from the Houthis in

---

[*] The name of the operation was posthumously changed to Arnon in honor of Chief Inspector Arnon Zmora, a Ya'ma'm team leader, killed in the furious firefight that erupted after the rescue was launched.

Yemen. Preemptive deterrence has been a stop-gap strategy to contain the violence and prevent a third intifada.

The events of October 7 and the subsequent fighting across the region had proven that the current conflict has nothing to do with achieving a two-state solution, but rather an attempt to rewrite history by erasing the United Nations partition in 1947 and the very establishment of the Jewish State altogether. It is a strategy of pointless suffering and endless tragedy that all but guarantees a state of inescapable permanent war. For the Palestinians, this is a futile course of action that takes them further away from any hope of achieving their nationalistic aspirations. For Israel, the current fighting is a battle for national survival, one that will require its best and its bravest—especially those who are on the front lines in disguise and lurking in the shadows.

For almost forty years, Israel's undercover and special operations police units have played an integral role in the country's epic fight against terror. In the desperate and uncertain times that Israel faces in the future, that operational burden only grows greater.

ACKNOWLEDGMENTS

I wrote this book, first page to the very last (and not necessarily in that order . . .) over the course of a year. My journey with the Border Guard and their undercover units began many years earlier.

In April 1992, a year and a half before Arafat and Rabin shook hands on the White House lawn, I found myself working on a documentary covering an Israeli Border Guard bomb squad unit in Ramallah. The unit worked in one of the most dangerous precincts of the first intifada and rushed from call to call, working to render safe the volatile IEDs and the unexploded ordnance that was used by Palestinian terror factions against Israeli forces. At the end of a long day in the field, the film crew was invited to join in on a brief celebration as some of the officers at headquarters gathered to honor a comrade who had just been promoted. The officers smiled and joked among themselves as they raised a glass, ate some cake, and attempted to ignore the camera-carrying intruders in their midst. One officer, a slim man with a large smile who looked like he hadn't slept in a few days, came over to me with a slice of cake in one hand, a plastic cup with some wine in the other. "La'briut" ("To health"), he said, as he made sure I was looked after. I didn't ask his name, nor did I even think to query as to why some of the men he was with spoke Arabic and wore costumes to masquerade as the local Palestinians. I was simply struck by his kindness to make sure that a stranger, a guest in his home, was treated with such respect. That officer was Superintendent Eli Avram, the first commander of the West Bank Ya'mas unit.

I saw Superintendent Avram a few more times over the course of the week I spent in Ramallah. We smiled at each other in the mess hall and we exchanged the odd "Shalom." I regret not having had the chance to talk to him more; he probably couldn't—and wouldn't—have told me very much anyway. I saw his face again four months later. When he was killed on August 25, 1992, while leading an operation against terrorists in Jenin, his photo, along with a story about his life and final operation, was in every one of the Israeli newspapers. Reading the remarkable account of his short life, I began to think about that week in Ramallah and wondered what Eli and his men must have been working on. I was fascinated by the very notion of these men who ventured into very dangerous territory wearing nothing but a disguise and their wits, and I knew that one day I wanted to write about them.

In my career, now spanning close to forty years, I have always enjoyed working with the Border Guard; my work with this small and very professional force began years before I met Eli in Ramallah, and thankfully it continues to this day. I find the Border Guard to be a true mosaic of the modern State of Israel—a family of different accents, languages, cultures, complexions, and religions united by a green beret and driven by a very stoic approach to security operations. I have had the privilege to see the Border Guard in action in places like northern Israel and the Lebanese frontier, the West Bank, Jerusalem, and the Gaza Strip. I have had the honor to spend time with and write about many of this force's true elite units, especially the undercover forces.

Over the years, many of the operators and officers in the undercover units became very close friends of mine. They felt comfortable enough to open up to me about some of their exploits, yet they always downplayed the heroics of their work. They personified what quiet professionals were all about. This book is a testament to their tremendous skill and courage. I am honored to be the one to write their story.

Many of the individuals who helped me with this book—intelligence professionals, counterterrorist operators, and other men who work in the shadows—prefer to remain anonymous. Even though I cannot mention them by name, I am forever grateful to them for their service, their support, and their tolerance of the million and one questions I posed to them at all hours of the day and night. I would like to thank those members of the undercover units—past and present—who were generous with their time and their stories. I would like to offer a very special few words of gratitude to the veteran officer in this book known by his pseudonym of Yehonatan. "Yehonatan" is far more than just a friend—he became a brother. He is an incredible hero who, as I like to say, has forgotten more about special operations and counterterrorism than most experts will ever know.

Some deserving of gratitude can be named, and I am so thankful for everything that they have done for me. I would like to thank Major General Amos Yaakov, the Border Guard commander at the time of this book's writing, for his support and backing. A very special thanks goes to Superintendent Shai Hakimi, the Border Guard spokesman, for his intrepid efforts on my behalf and for spearheading the security review of the manuscript. I am also grateful to Chief Inspector Idan Aluz, and First Sergeant Ehud Dror for their Herculean work to see this project through.

I am grateful to Dr. Eldad Harouvi, the archive director at the Pal'mach Museum, for his invaluable assistance and research. I would also like to thank General (Ret.) Uri Bar-Lev, the first commander of the IDF's Duvdevan undercover unit and the police Unit 33 special operations and intelligence force, for his time and insight. And to thank Major General (Ret.) David Tzur, a former Ya'ma'm and Border Guard commander, and my brother-from-another-mother Superintendent (Ret.) Gil Kleiman, for their friendship and always going above and beyond the call of friendship on my behalf.

A book of this nature could never have been completed were it not for the help of very special friends, and I would like to offer my heartfelt gratitude to Ziv Koren. Ziv is one of Israel's top photographers, a true artist and master at his craft who continually breaches the envelope of low light and creative wonder. Ziv is also one of the world's foremost photographers of special operations units, and he has accompanied the best of them (the Ya'ma'm, Flotilla 13, and the army's undercover unit) on actual operations, many of them classified, behind enemy lines. It would be an understatement to say that this book could never have been completed were it not for Ziv's friendship and support. As a working partner, Ziv is second to none, and I look forward to working with him on numerous projects in the future. Ziv's work can be seen at www.zivkoren.com. Ziv ventured to the communities in the Gaza Envelope during the October 7 onslaught, risking his life to document the horrors of that day, the courage of those who repelled the Hamas attack as well as the resilience of those whose lives were shattered by the murders, destruction, and abduction. He is a witness to history.

I would like to offer a very special word of thanks to another one of Israel's top photographers—Nati Shohat. Nati, founder of Flash90, is one of Israel's preeminent news and combat photographers, whose brilliant eye and unique style paint a human and intimate, multilayered fabric of the men who venture deep behind enemy lines to keep Israel safe. Several of Nati's photographs are featured in this book, and I am grateful to him for his generosity. Nati's agency's website is www.Flash90.com.

I want to thank my dear friend and literary agent Doug Grad for going above and beyond to ensure that the story of the undercover operators who fought—and fight—evil will continue to be told.

Writers do not live and operate in a vacuum, and I would like to thank my three wonderful children for filling my life with endless pride and joy. The most important words of thanks belong to Sigi, my wife of thirty-nine years and counting. Sigi knows more about courage and character than anyone I have ever met, and she inspires me with her love, her devotion, and her ambitious pursuit of academic achievements and long-held dreams. She reminds me each and every day about all that is wonderful in this world. This book is for her.

GLOSSARY

A'man Hebrew acronym for *Agaf Mode'in* or IDF's Military Intelligence Directorate.

Duvdevan The IDF's undercover unit operating in the West Bank (Judea and Samaria).

Flotilla 13 The IDF/navy's commando force, known in Hebrew as *Shayetet* or *Shin* 13.

Grass Widow The Israeli tactic of seizing a building or a home, and securing the residents of that location, in order to pre-position snipers for an operation.

Horse The name in the Israeli security vernacular for the unmarked vehicles used to transport the operators on their missions.

IAF Acronym for Israel Air Force.

IDF Acronym for Israel Defense Forces. In Hebrew, the acronym is "Tzahal" for *Tzava Haganah Le'Yisrael*.

INP Acronym for Israel National Police.

Matilan Border Guard long-range reconnaissance and intelligence-gathering special operations counterterrorist unit.

Mishmar Ha'Gvul Hebrew for "Border Guard," the paramilitary arm of the Israel National Police.

Mossad *Ha'Mossad le'Modi'in ule'Tafkidim Meyuhadim* (or Institute for Intelligence and Special Tasks), better known simply as the Mossad, is Israel's intelligence service responsible for overseas intelligence-gathering and special operations in the protection of Israeli interests and national security around the world.

MOUT Acronym for Military Operations Urban Terrain.

Pressure Cooker The *Seer Lahatz*, or Pressure Cooker, is a tactic used by Israeli military and security forces to isolate and contain a terrorist inside a location (when no hostages are involved) and to increase pressure on the individual with overwhelming force and, often, the introduction of a D9 bulldozer to knock down the barricaded structure.

Sayeret Egoz The special operations counter-guerrilla reconnaissance commando unit of the 1st Golani Infantry Brigade. Formed in many ways from the veterans of the Samson undercover unit when that force was disbanded in 1996, the unit fought in southern Lebanon against Hezbollah, throughout the West Bank during the second intifada, and in Gaza in operations subsequent to the unilateral Israeli withdrawal in 2005.

Sayeret Giva'ati The reconnaissance force of the Giva'ati Infantry Brigade.

Sayeret Golani The reconnaissance force of the 1st Golani Infantry Brigade.

Sayeret Magian An IDF reconnaissance commando force tasked with top priority long-range special operations.

Sayeret Mat'kal Sayeret Mat'kal, or General Staff Reconnaissance Unit, is the IDF's premier special operations unit, which became operational in 1959 performing strategic long-range reconnaissance and intelligence-gathering and other operations on behalf of the General Staff; the unit was also known as the "Chief of General Staff's Boys." Modeled along the lines of the British Special Air Service, Sayeret Mat'kal adopted the "Who Dares Wins" motto of Britain's famed 22 Special Air Service (SAS) Regiment and became known as something of a king-maker, being led by men who would serve as prime minister and director of the Shin Bet and Mossad, including Ehud Barak (its most decorated officer and commander), Yonatan and Benjamin Netanyahu, Danny Yatom, Avi Dichter, and Moshe Ya'alon. The unit achieved legendary status in 1972 for rescuing hostages on board a hijacked Sabena Belgian Airlines jet that was seized by Black September and flown to Israel (the commandos masqueraded as airline mechanics to gain access to the aircraft); a 1973 raid against Beirut that targeted the top Black September leadership; and, most significantly, the July 1976 Entebbe rescue.

Sayeret Rimon The undercover counterterrorist force that operated in the Gaza Strip from 1970 to 1971.

Sayeret Tzanhanim The reconnaissance commando force of the IDF's conscript paratroop brigade.

Shimshon The IDF undercover unit for the Gaza Strip, disbanded in 1996.

Shin Bet Israel's domestic counterintelligence and counterterrorist agency, the Shin Bet is known in Hebrew as the *Sherut Ha'Bitachon Ha'Klali*, or General Security Service, and referred to often by its Hebrew acronym of Shabak. It is also known in some circles as the Israel Security Agency.

Speaker An undercover operator, usually someone from Israel's Arabic-speaking minorities, who is designated to be the lead member of the force to interact with local Palestinian security men—or civilians—during an operation.

Ya'ma'm The INP Border Guard national counterterrorist and hostage-rescue unit known by its Hebrew acronym for *Yechida Mishtartit Meyuchedet*, or Special Police Unit.

Ya'mas The INP Border Guard undercover units, known by their Hebrew acronym for *Yechidat Mista'aravim*, or Undercover Unit. Three regional Ya'mas units exist, one responsible for Judea and Samaria (West Bank); one responsible for Jerusalem; and one now known as Southern Ya'mas, responsible for southern Israel (formerly Ya'mas Gaza).

SELECT BIBLIOGRAPHY

Abu-Amr, Ziad. *Islamic Fundamentalism in the West Bank and Gaza*. Bloomington, Indiana: Indiana University Press, 1994.

Bechor, Guy. *Lexicon Ashaf: Ishi'im, Irgunim, Ve'Iru'uim*. Tel Aviv: Israel Ministry of Defense Publishing House, 1991.

Bergman, Ronen. *The Secret War with Iran: The 30-Year Covert Struggle for Control of a "Rogue State."* Oxford: Oneworld Publications, 2008.

Berko, Anat. *The Path to Paradise: The Inner World of Suicide Bombers and Their Dispatchers*. Westport, Connecticut: Praeger Security International, 2007.

Bethell, Nicholas. *The Palestine Triangle: The Struggle for the Holy Land, 1935-48*. New York: G.P. Putnam's Sons, 1979.

Black, Ian, and Benny Morris. *Israel's Secret Wars: A History of Israel's Intelligence Services*. New York: Grove Press, 1991.

Deflem, Mathieu. *The Policing of Terrorism: Organizational and Global Perspectives*. New York: Routledge, 2009.

Dror, Tzvika. *Ha'Mista'aravim Shel Ha'Pal'mach*. Bnei Brak: Ha'Kibbutz Ha'Me'uchad Publishing House Ltd. (*Sidrat Ha'Lochamim Al Shem Yigal Alon—Misrad Ha'Bitachon*), 1986.

Dzikansky, Mordecai, Gil Kleiman, and Robert Slater. *Terrorist Suicide Bombings: Attack Interdiction, Mitigation, and Response*. Boca Raton, Florida: CRC Press, 2012.

Falk, Ophir, and Henry Morgenstern (eds.). *Suicide Terror: Understanding and Confronting the Threat*. Hoboken, New Jersey: John Wiley and Sons, Inc., 2009.

Givati, Moshe. *Abir 21: Sipurav Shel Eli Avram Mefaked Yechidat Ha'Mista'aravim*. Jerusalem: Re'ut Publishing, 2003.

Katz, Samuel M. *The Hunt for the Engineer: How Israeli Agents Tracked the Hamas Master Bomber*. New York: Fromm, 1999.

Kershner, Isabel. *Barrier: The Seam of the Israeli-Palestinian Conflict*. New York: Palgrave MacMillan, 2005.

Levitt, Matthew. *Hamas: Politics, Charity, and Terrorism in the Service of Jihad*. New Haven, Connecticut: Yale University Press, 2006.

Schiff, Zeev, and Ehud Ya'ari. *Intifada: The Palestinian Uprising—Israel's Third Front*. New York: Simon and Schuster, 1991.

Shabi, Aviva, and Ronni Shaked. *Hamas: Mamuna Be'Allah Le'Derech Ha'Terror*.

Jerusalem: Keter Publishing House, Ltd., 1994.

Yousef, Mosab Hassan (with Ron Brackin). *Son of Hamas*. Carol Stream, Illinois: Tyndale House Publishers, Inc., 2010.

Zunder, Moshe. *Sayeret Mat'kal* Jerusalem: Keter Publishing House, Ltd., 2000.

NOTES

Chapter 1

1. Meir Tujeman, "*Mechasel Ha'Mechablim Ha'No'az Yefaked Al Mishteret Rechovot, Mista'ar Al Ha'Mishtara,*" *Yediot Aharonot,* December 27, 2013.
2. Oz Almog, *The Sabra; The Creation of the New Jew,* University of California Press, 2000, p. 198.
3. Esther Tomer, "*Ha'Machlaka Ha'Aravit Shel Ha'Pal'mach*" (http://www.misham.co.il /uploads/Magazines/Magazine9/magazine9_44_46.pdf).
4. Oz Almog, *The Sabra,* p. 199.
5. Tzvika Dror, *Ha'Mista'aravim Shel Ha'Pal'mach,* Israel Ministry of Defense Publishing House/Ha'Kibbutz Ha'Meuchad Publishers, Tel Aviv, 1986, p. 13.
6. Yossi Melman, "I'm Not Your Husband Ahmed, I'm Yossi from the Shin Bet," *Ha'aretz,* January 10, 1998.
7. Wael R. Ennab, *Population and Demographic Developments in the West Bank and Gaza Strip Until 1990,* United Nations Conference on Trade and Development, June 28, 1994, p. 12.
8. https://www.gvura.org/a4839-%D7%25Al%D7%A8%D7%9F-%D7%9E%D7%90.
9. Interview, Tel Aviv, January 4, 2014.
10. Amir Rappaport, "*Ha'Ragish Ve'Hanechush,*" *Ma'ariv,* September 16, 2005.
11. Documentary film, *Abir 21,* Nano 10, May 4, 2014.
12. Ibid.
13. Moshe Givati, *Abir 21: The Story of Eli Avram, Commander of the Undercover Unit,* Eli Avram Memorial Foundation/Hemed Publishing, Jerusalem, 2003, p. 91.
14. The account was quoted in the book *Suicide Terror: Understanding and Confronting the Threat* (John Wiley and Sons, Inc., Hoboken, New Jersey, 2009, p. 113), edited by Ophir Falk and Henry Morgenstern, as quoted originally by Yossi Kupperwasser, Israeli Institute for Democracy on October 31, 2004, in Dan Meridor and Haim Pass, eds., *21st Battle—Democracies Fight Terror* (Hebrew), the Israeli Institute for Democracy, Jerusalem, 2006, p. 251.
15. Amir Buhbut, "*Kach Po'alim Mista'arvei Magav: Mi'Yerushalayim ve'ad Ha'Negev,*" *Ma'ariv NRG,* October 4, 2008.
16. See Moshe Givati, *Abir 21,* p. 155.
17. Ibid., p. 171.
18. Doron Me'iri, "Hasifa Rishona: Ha'Mista'aravim Shel Magav Chislu 50 Mechablim," Yediot Aharonot, November 4, 1994, p. 3.
19. Ibid.
20. Yossi Klein Halevi, "I Have Two Nightmares About a Palestinian State," *New Republic,* August 27, 2014.

Chapter 2

1. Interview with Uzi Levy, Lod, March 27, 2014.
2. Ibid.
3. Dalia Shechori, "Cabinet Approves Dichter to Be the Shin Bet's Next Chief," *Ha'aretz*, May 8, 2000.
4. Peter Ford, "US Is Expected to Push Israel on Its Deportees," *Christian Science Monitor*, February 22, 1993.
5. Yoav Ze'evi and Yanki Galanti, "*Onat Ha'Duvdevnim Mesarevet Le'Higamer*," *Bamachne*, December 1, 1994, p. 23.
6. Ra'anan Ben-Tzur, Avi Tal, and Eli Senior, "*Hashavti She'hu Yihiye Batuach Be'Duvdevan*" Yediot/Ynet, August 27, 2000.
7. Yehudit Yechezkeli, "*Hizharnu She'yikre Ason*" *Yediot Aharonot*, August 29, 2000, p. 2.
8. Amos Harel, "Despite Failure, There Is Still No Substitute for Duvdevan," *Ha'varetz*, September 1, 2000.
9. Arieh O'Sullivan, "Inquiry: Duvdevan Raid Fatally Compromised," *Jerusalem Post*, September 8, 2000.
10. Interview, Ronen Goresh, Lod, February 6, 2014.

Chapter 3

1. Interview, Yaakov Berman, Rechovot, March 19, 2014.
2. Ze'ev Schiff, "Learning from the Disturbances," *Jerusalem Post*, October 27, 2000.
3. Ze'ev Schiff, "Analysis: Looking Back After Two Years," *Jerusalem Post*, September 29, 2002.
4. Zohar Palti and Matthew Levitt, "Assessing Hezbollah's West Bank Foothold," *Policy Watch* #463, June 18, 2004.
5. Anthony Cordesman, *Palestinian Forces: Palestinian Authority and Militant Forces*, Center for Strategic and International Studies, February 2006, p. 8.
6. Ibid.
7. Yoram Schweitzer, "The Rise and Fall of Suicide Bombings in the Second Intifada," *Strategic Assessment*, Volume 13, No. 3, October 2010.
8. "*Husal Ha'Mevukash Mispar Echad Be'Hamas*," *Ma'ariv*, November 24, 2001.
9. "Powell Says U.S. Opposes Targeted Israeli Killings," Reuters, July 5, 2001.
10. Interview, Tel Aviv area, March 18, 2014.
11. Margot D udkevitch, "Soldiers Kill Dov Drieben's Murderer," *Jerusalem Post*, November 8, 2001.
12. Interview with Uzi Levy, Lod, March 27, 2014.
13. Amir Oren, "IDF Sending Crack Units into W. Bank," *Ha'aretz*, May 31, 2001.
14. Amos Harel, "Elite Duvdevan Unit Commander Killed in W. Bank Operation," *Ha'aretz*, February 15, 2002.
15. Interview, central Israel, February 11, 2014.

Chapter 4

1. Roni Shaked, "*Ha'Sukariot Shel Mister Sataneli Me'Ha'CIA,*" Yediot Aharonot Ha'Mosaf Le'Shabbat, pp. 20–21.

2. Matthew Levitt, *Hamas: Politics, Charity, and Terrorism in the Service of Jihad*, Yale University Press/Washington Institute for Near East Policy, New Haven/Washington, D.C., 2006, p. 4.
3. Official declassified Israel Security Agency (Shin Bet) account of the Park Hotel bombing.
4. Interview, Yuri, February 9, 2014.
5. INP Border Guard film honoring Superintendent Patrick Pereg.
6. Death announcement, Israel National Police ("One Family Fund: Helping Israeli Victims of Terror"), April 2002.
7. Interview, Kfar Saba, March 19, 2014.
8. Avi Issacharoff and Amos Harel, "Recollections of Israel's Operation Defensive Shield, Ten Years Later," *Ha'aretz*, March 30, 2012.
9. Hanan Shlain and Yossi Levy, "*Ha'Mevukash Mispar Ehad Be'Hebron Husal Be'Makom She'Bo Ratzach Yisraelim*," *Ma'ariv*, June 30, 1995, p. 4.
10. Interview, Uzi Levy, Lod, March 27, 2014.
11. Amos Harel, "Slain Colonel Was Destined for Greatness," *Ha'aretz*, November 17, 2002.
12. Amir Buchbut, "*Tamid Amarta: Tov La'Mut Be'ad Artzeinu*," *Ma'ariv*, April 11, 2002.
13. Memorial Web Page for Border Police Superintendent Patrick Pereg, Israel Ministry of Foreign Affairs, April 4, 2002.
14. INP Border Guard film honoring Superintendent Patrick Pereg.
15. Interview, Uzi Levy, Lod, March 27, 2014.
16. Felix Frisch and Efrat Weiss, "*Ko'ach Tzahal Harag Shnei Ktzinim Palestina'im*," *Ma'ariv*, May 14, 2002.

Chapter 5

1. Shlomo Tzezna and Yoav Limor, "*Tevach Ha'Mishpacha*," *Ma'ariv*, June 21, 2002.
2. Peter Beaumont, "Children Shot Dead in Their Home," *Guardian*, June 21, 2002.
3. Interview, Yaakov Berman, Rechovot, March 20, 2014.
4. Interview, Northern Israel, February 25, 2015.
5. Interview, Sa'ar Shine, Lod, February 4, 2014.
6. Internal Border Guard reconstruction of the events at Itamar on June 20, 2002.
7. Interview, Lod, February 25, 2015.
8. Interview, Lod, February 4, 2014.
9. Internal Border Guard reconstruction of the events at Itamar.
10. Interview, Lod, February 25, 2015.
11. Interview, Sa'ar Shine, Lod, February 4, 2014.
12. Ibid.
13. Internal Border Guard reconstruction of the events at Itamar.
14. Interview, Lod, February 4, 2014.
15. Interview, Rechovot, March 20, 2014.
16. Shlomo Tzezna and Yoav Limor, "*Tevach Ha'Mishpacha*."

Chapter 6

1. As relayed in an interview with Chief Superintendent R., Lod, March 25, 2014.
2. Interview, Kfar Saba, May 30, 2014.

3. Amos Harel, *"Tzevet Shel Duvdevan Nichnas Le'Toch Ha'Binyan: Barghouti Hisgir EtAtzmo Be'Heder Ha'Madregot,"* *Ha'aretz,* April 16, 2002.

4. Isabel Kershner, "Barrier: The Seam of the Israeli-Palestinian Conflict," New York, Palgrave MacMillan, 2005, p. 96.

5. *"Ha'Eyin Shel Ha'Medina,"* *Makor Rishon,* July 16, 2006.

6. *"Ha'Mista'aravim Hitchapsu Le'Shotrei Ha'Reshut Ve'Chatfu Ish Hamas Be'Tulkarm,"* *Haaretz,* September 5, 2002.

7. Yossi Yehoshua and Reuven Weiss, *"Ha'Tzayad,"* *Yediot Aharonot,* April 8, 2005.

8. Interview, Uzi Levy, Lod, February 4, 2014.

9. *"Ha'Mista'aravim Hitchapsu Le'Shotrei Ha'Reshut Ve'Chatfu Ish Hamas Be'Tulkarm,"* September 5, 2002.

10. *"Ha'Eyin Shel Ha'Medina."*

11. Margot Dudkevitch, "Hamas Deputy Commander Grabbed in Tulkarm Raid," *Jerusalem Post,* September 5, 2002.

12. Ehud Ya'ari, "Three Cheers for the Spooks," *Jerusalem Report,* May 20, 2002.

13. Amos Harel, *"Ktzin Shayetet Ne'Herag Im Hitaklut Im Mevukash Le'Yad Tul Karem,"* *Ha'aretz,* September TJ, 2002.

14. Interview, Nasser, Lod, March 25, 2014.

15. Ehud Ya'ari, "Three Cheers for the Spooks."

16. Interview, Ya'mas officer (anonymous), March 20, 2014.

17. Interview, Yaakov Berman, Rechovot, March 20, 2014.

18. Interview, Chief Superintendent Micah, Tel Aviv, March 27, 2014.

19. Interview, Yaakov Berman, March 20, 2014.

20. *"Schem: Mista'arvei Magav Atzru Pa'il Fatah Be'Schem,"* Nano 10 News, September 26, 2002.

21. Baruch Kara, *"79 Palesteniyaim Ne'Hergu be'2002 Mi'yadei Ha'Yechidot Ha'Meyuchadot Shel Magav,"* *Ha'aretz,* March 12, 2003.

Chapter 7

1. "Background: Abu-Hanoud," *Haaretz,* November 24, 2001.

2. Mitch Ginsburg, "Saving Sergeant Netanyahu," *Times of Israel,* October 25, 2012.

3. Interview, Kfar Qassem, March 19, 2014.

4. Interview, Kfar Saba, June 27, 2014.

5. Interview, Israel, Rechovot, March 20, 2014.

6. Ibid.

7. As per the document http://www.mfa.gov.il/mfa/foreignpolicy/iran/supportterror/pages/iranian%20activities%20in%20support%20of%20the%20palestinian%20i.aspx.

8. As per www.gvura.org.

9. Interview, Rechovot, March 20, 2014.

Chapter 8

1. Vered Levy-Barzilai, "Ticking Bombs," *Ha'aretz,* October 13, 2003.

2. Ibid.

3. Interview, Rechovot, March 20, 2014.

4. Israel Ministry of Foreign Affairs, List of Victims of Terror (http://mfa.gov.il/MFA/ForeignPolicy/Terrorism/Victims/Pages/St-Sgt%20Liat%20Ben-Ami.aspx).

5. Interview, Tel Aviv, March 27, 2014.
6. Interview, Lod, February 4, 2014.
7. Interview, Tel Aviv, March 27, 2014.
8. Interview, Lod, March 26, 2014.
9. Yoni Fighel, "Palestinian Islamic Jihad and Female Suicide Bombers," ICT, October 6, 2003.
10. Interview, Lod, March 26, 2014.
11. Vered Levy-Barzilai, "Ticking Bombs," *Ha'aretz*, October 15, 2003.
12. Ibid.
13. Interview, Nasser, Lod, March 26, 2014.
14. Ibid.
15. Arnon Regular, "Mother of Two Becomes First Female Suicide Bomber for Hamas," *Ha'aretz*, January 16, 2004.
16. Arnon Regular, "Female Bombers Show Shift in Thinking," *Haaretz*, May 21, 2003.
17. According to noted terrorism expert Anat Berko, as quoted in the Israeli daily *Ha'aretz*, "When men become terrorists, the ideological motive is dominant. In contrast, women are pushed to carry out a terrorist attack and never choose to do so out of their own free will. There are always personal problems hidden in the background." Avi Issacharoff, "Femme Fatale, Jihad Style," *Ha'aretz*, April 5, 2010.
18. Yoni Fighel, "Palestinian Islamic Jihad and Female Suicide Bombers."
19. Amos Harel, "Security Forces Trace Haifa Bomber's Path," *Ha'aretz*, October 7, 2003.
20. Yoram Schweitzer (ed.), "Female Suicide Bombers: Dying for Equality?" The Jaffee Center for Strategic Studies (JCSS), August 2006, p. 20.
21. Interview, Lod, March 26, 2014.

Chapter 9

1. Samuel M. Katz, *Hunt for the Engineer: The Inside Story of How Israel's Counterterrorist Forces Killed the Hamas Master Bomber,* New York, Fromm, 2000.
2. Interview, Jerusalem, June 23, 2014.
3. Bruce Hoffman, "The Logic of Suicide Terrorism," *Atlantic Monthly,* June 2003, p. 43.
4. Ra'anan Ben-Zur and Avner Cohen, "*Ha'Pigu'a Be'Netanya: Hayal Niftza Kashe She'Nise La'atzor et Ha'Mechabel,*" *Ynet/Yediot Aharonot,* March 30, 2003.
5. Arieh O'Sullivan and Margot Dudkevitch, "Hamas Vows Revenge for Killing of Bomb Mastermind," *Jerusalem Post,* July 1, 2002.
6. Joel Leyden and Margot Dudkevitch, "Israeli Commando Killed in Nablus Raid," *Jerusalem Post,* August 9, 2003.
7. Yossi Yehoshua and Reuven Weiss, "Ha'Tzayad," *Yediot Aharonot,* April 8, 2005.
8. Ibid.
9. Interview, Beit Horon, Israel, March 25, 2014.
10. "*Husal Bachir Ba'Jihad be'Tulkarm She'Tichnen Pigu'im; Nichsafa Meconit Tofet Be'Shchem,*" *Globus,* October 2, 2003.
11. See "Ha'Tzayad."
12. Interview, northern Israel, July 1, 2014.
13. Ibid.
14. Ibid.
15. Interview, March 25, 2014.

16. Hillel Frisch, "Motivation or Capabilities? Israeli Counterterrorism Against Palestinian Suicide Bombings and Violence," The Begin-Sadat Center for Strategic Studies at Bar-Ilan University, *Mideast Security and Policy Studies,* No. 70, p. 4.
17. Ibid.

Chapter 10

1. Interview, Superintendent Salah, Lod, March 25, 2014.
2. Interview, Lod, February 4, 2014.
3. Interview, Lod, March 25, 2014.
4. Interview, Rechovot, Israel, March 20, 2014.
5. Arnon Regular, "*Koach Mista'aravim Harag Hamisha Pe'ilei Fatah Be'Jenin,*" *Ha'aretz,* March 10, 2004.
6. "*Jenin Birat Ha'Mitabdim,*" *Ha'Merkaz Le'Moreshet Ha'Mode'in erkaz Ha'Medida Le'Mode'in Ve'Terror.*
7. Ibid.
8. Amit Navon, "*Eich Po'el Mangenon Ha'Terror Shel Ha'Jihad Ha'Islami,*" *Maariv Sof Shavu'a,* June 14, 2002, p. 32.
9. "*Ko'ach Mista'aravim Harag Mevukash Me'Ha'Tanzim,*" *Walla Hadashot,* April 7, 2003.
10. Interview, northern Israel, March 22, 2014.
11. Interview, Rechovot, Israel, March 20, 2014.
12. Yossi Yehoshua and Reuven Veiss, "*Ha'Tzayad,*" *Yediot Aharonot,* April 8, 2005.
13. Uri Glickman and Marwan Ata'mna, "*Husal Mefaked Ha'Jihad Be'Jenin,*" *NRG Maariv,* July 13, 2004.

Chapter 11

1. "*Shkhem: Ko'ach Tzahal HaragMe'Vukash She'Patach Be'Yeri La'A'var Ha'Koach,*" Nana 10, April 14, 2005.
2. Sarah Liebovitch-Dar, "*Ha'Shikhrur Shel Rotzchei Ish Ha'Sha'bach Mas'ir Mishpachto,*" *NRG,* August 2, 2013.

Chapter 12

1. Amira Hass and Amos Harel, "Hamas Holiday Attack Averted," *Ha'aretz,* September 17, 2001.
2. Efrat Weiss, "16 Ma'asrei Olam Le'Mis'at Ha'Mechabel Shel Sbarro," Ynet, October 23, 2003.
3. Interview with al-Quds TV, date unknown, following her release from Israeli prison in the Gilad Shalit prisoner deal in October 2011.
4. Interview, Jerusalem, March 26, 2014.

Chapter 13

1. Interview, Israeli counterterrorist officer, Tel Aviv, December 29, 2013, and Sharon Ben Ami-Halevi, "*Har-Ha'Bayit Be'Yadeinu* (2000)," *Iton Yerushalayim,* October 13, 2000, p. 38.
2. Samuel M. Katz, "The Sword of Gideon: Unit 33—The Israel National Police Special Intelligence Unit," *Special Operations Report,* Vol. 17, Winter 2008, p. 34; as well as: http://mops.gov.il/Documents/Publications/InformationCenter/Innovation%20Exchange/Innovation%20Exchange%2014/New%20National%20Crime%20Unit%20

Inaugurated.pdf; https://www.police.gov.il/gius/FullMainSubject.aspxJidM9; and http://www.mako.co.il/men-magazine/firepower/Article-fac944d91119231006.htm.

3. Amir Ben-David, "*Chayav Shel Mista'arev*" *Ma'ariv,* October 20, 2000, p. 16.

4. Interview, central Israel, September 14, 2014.

5. Interview, northern Israel, July 1, 2014.

6. Serge Schmemann, "Bus Bombing Kills Five in Jerusalem; 100 Are Wounded," *New York Times,* August 22, 1995.

7. Israel Ministry of Foreign Affairs, "Pronouncement by Moslem Religious Leaders Defending Suicide Attacks," Communiqué, September 21, 1997.

8. In Dror Moreh's brilliant 2012 Academy Award–nominated documentary, *The Gatekeepers,* Shin Bet director Ayalon emphatically explained how Jibril Rajoub told him that the Palestinians did not work for the Israelis when they arrested Hamas terrorists or key operatives for the PIJ because the Israelis told them to. They (the Palestinians) did so because it was in their best—and immediate—interests to do so.

9. Interview with a Ya'mas operator, Jerusalem, March 26, 2014.

10. Sharon Ben Ami-Halevi, "*Har-Ha'Bayit Be'Yadeinu* (2000)," *Iton Yerushalayim,* October 13, 2000, p. 38.

11. Interview, Jerusalem, March 26, 2014.

12. Amir Ben-David, "*Chayav Shel Mista'arev,*" p. 16.

13. Ibid, p. 38.

Chapter 14

1. Limor Shmuel, Eitan Glickman, Amir Rappaport, Joel Beno, and Tzvi Zinger, "*Mirdafim Be'akvot Ptzatzot Mitaktekot,*" *Yediot Aharonot,* August 30, 2001.

2. Gali Tivon and Anat Ro'e, "*Nilkadu Havrei Ha'Huliya Be'Yerushalayim,*" *Ynet,* August 31, 2001.

3. Interview, Gil Kleiman, Tel Aviv, March 20, 2014.

4. Interview, Inspector Mike, Jerusalem, March 25, 2015.

5. Amir Rappaport, "*Ha'Mechablim Shel Ha'Yom Metuchkamim Yoter,*" *Israel Defense,* November 27, 2002.

6. Interview, Shai, Jerusalem, March 25, 2014.

7. Efrat Weiss, "*Toshav Mizrach Yerushalayim Hashud Be'Hasa'at Mechabel Le'Pigu'a,*" *Ynet,* May 5, 2003.

8. James Bennett, "At Least 10 Killed in Suicide Bombing of Jerusalem Bus," *New York Times,* November 21, 2002.

9. Haim Barvida and Amir Ben-David, "*SofMasa Ha'Retzach,*" *Yediot Aharonot,* August 22, 2002, p. 2.

10. Yossi Levi, "*Nilkadu Be'Derech Le'Pigu'a,*" *Ma'ariv,* August 22, 2002, p. 5.

11. Interview, Shai, March 25, 2014.

12. Ibid.

13. Hanan Greenberg, "*Me'Tchilat Ha'Shana Suklu 83 Pigu'ei Hitabdut,*" *Ynet,* July 18, 2004.

Chapter 15

1. Etgar Lefkovitz, "Waiter Foils Jerusalem Café Bombing," *Jerusalem Post,* March 8, 2002.

2. Efrat Weiss, "*Mehabel Mitabed Higi'ia Le'Beit Ha'kafe 'Kaffit' Ve'Hitharet,*" *Ynet,* July 18, 2004.

3. Interview, Western Africa, September 28, 2014.

4. Interview, New York City, August 19, 2014.
5. Interview, Jerusalem, March 26, 2014.
6. Interview, Jerusalem, March 26, 2014.
7. Ibid.
8. Efrat Weiss, "*Mehabel Mitabed Higi'ia Le'Beit Ha'kafe 'Kaffit' Ve'Hitharet.*"
9. John Ward Anderson and Molly Moore, "Suicide Bombings Kill 18 in Israel," *Washington Post,* September 1, 2004.
10. Hanan Greenberg and Ali Wakd, "*Hebron: Nilkad Ha'Ekhra'I Le'Pigu'a Be'Beer Sheva,*" *Ynet,* October 13, 2004.
11. Amos Harel, "*Mivtza Echad, Matarot Sotrot: Ha'Pe'ilot Neged Hamas 'Alula Lifgo'a Be'Itur Ha'Hotfim,*" *Ha'aretz,* June 20, 2014.

Chapter 16

1. Alan Cowell, "8 Killed and 17 Wounded in Raid on Bus of Israeli Tourists in Egypt," *New York Times,* February 5, 1990.
2. Felix Frisch and Efrat Weiss, "*12 Harugim, Be'Hem Mefaked Ha'Hativa, Be'Maarav Metuchkam,*" *Ynet/Yediot Aharonot,* November 16, 2002.
3. Ibid.
4. Felix Frisch and Efrat Weiss, "*4 Harugim Be'Hatkafa Al Ha'Yeshiva Be'Hitnahalut Otniel,*" *Ynet/Yediot Aharonot,* December 28, 2002.
5. Efrat Weiss, "*17 Maasrei Olam Le'Metchnen Ha'Pigu'a 'Be'Tzir Ha'Mitplalelim',*" *Ynet/Yediot Aharonot,* December 8, 2003.
6. Interview, Jerusalem, March 26, 2014.

Chapter 18

1. Wael R. Ennab, "Population and Demographic Developments in the West Bank and Gaza Strip Until 1990," study prepared for the United Nations Conference on Trade and Development (UNCTAD), June 28, 1994 (http://israelipalestinian.procon.org/view .resource.php?resourceID=000636).
2. Andrew Roberts, "From an Era of Refugee Millions, Only Palestinians Remain," *Wall Street Journal,* November 21, 2014.
3. Shiomi Tzipori, *Tzedek Mesuarav,* Tel Aviv, Agam Publishing, 2004, p. 51.
4. BBC 4 Dispatches, Profile of Samson unit, October 1991.
5. Robert Fisk, "Hamas Mourns Its Greatest Martyr: Robert Fisk in Marj al-Zohour, Southern Lebanon, Hears How a Palestinian Came to Die for the Islamic 'Revolution' in Israel," *Independent,* November 29, 1993.
6. http://www.izkor.gov.il/HalalKorot.aspx?id=514720.
7. BBC 4 dispatches.
8. http://www.yehida.co.il/index.php?option=com_content&view=artide&id=201.
9. Interview, Chief Superintendent Shimon, Lod, February 6, 2014.
10. Doug Struck and Dan Fesperman, "Arafat Returns in Victory," *Baltimore Sun,* July 2, 1994.
11. David Hirst, "Sheikh Ahmed Yassin," *Guardian,* March 22, 2004.

Chapter 19

1. Felix Frisch, "*Shnei Harugim Be'Pigua Be'Elei Sinai,*" *Ynet/Yediot Aharonot,* October 3, 2001.

2. Interview, Chief Superintendent O., Israel, Kfar Saba, March 6, 2014.
3. James Bennett, "Key Palestinian Security Posts Becoming Harder to Fill," *New York Times,* June 2, 2002.
4. Inigo Gilmore and Philip Jacobson, "Five Killed as Israeli Tanks Go Deep into Gaza," *Telegraph,* December 16, 2001.
5. Interview, Border Guard antiterrorism school, Israel, March 24, 2014.
6. Interview, Shimon, Lod, February 6, 2014.
7. Ibid.
8. James Bennett, "Seized Arms Would Have Vastly Extended Arafat Arsenal," *New York Times,* January 12, 2002.
9. Ibid.

Chapter 20

1. Inigo Gilmore, "Israel Kills 10 in Raid to Root Out Militants," *Telegraph,* December 7, 2002.
2. Ilan Goren, *"Pigu'im Neged Shirion: Lo Ha'Pa'am Ha'Rishona,"* Ma'ariv, May 11, 2004.
3. Interview, December 12, 2014.
4. Interview, Master Sergeant Vlad, March 24, 2014.
5. Chris McGreal, "Hamas Celebrates Victory of the Bomb as Power of Negotiation Falters," *Guardian,* September 12, 2005.
6. Interview, Ze'ev, Beit Horon, March 24, 2014.
7. Interview, Shimon, Lod, February 4, 2014.
8. Interview, Vlad, Beit Horon, March 24, 2014.
9. Felix Frisch, *"Khan Yunis: Pa'il Hamas TakafHayalim Ve'Nura LeMavet,"* Ynet/Yediot Aharonot, December 10, 2002.

Chapter 21

1. Associated Press, "Israeli Army Conducts Major Anti-Guerrilla Sweep," *Times Daily,* Sunday, December 3, 1989.
2. Associated Press, "Troops Kill 4 in West Bank's 'Black Panthers' Gang," *Los Angeles Times,* December 2, 1989.
3. Interview, Chief Superintendent A., New York, December 21, 2014.
4. Interview, Uri Bar-Lev, Tel Aviv, August 28, 2014.
5. Elhanan Miller, "Arafat Gave Us Arms for Second Intifada Attacks, Hamas Official Says," *Times of Israel,* December 16, 2014.
6. Ibid.
7. Margot Dudkevitch, "IDF Tunnel Ops to Continue," *Jerusalem Post,* October 13, 2003.
8. Interview, Chief Superintendent (Ret.) Yehonatan, New York, September 27, 2014.
9. Interview, Yaron, Lod, February 4, 2014.
10. Interview, September 28, 2014.
11. Ronen Bergman, *The Secret War with Iran: The 30-Year Covert Struggle for Control of a "Rogue" State,* London, One World Publications, 2008, p. 289.
12. Interview, Shimon, Lod, February 4, 2014.
13. Interview, Chief Superintendent Yehonatan.
14. Ibid.
15. Interview, Shimon, Lod, February 6, 2014.

16. Interview, Vlad, Beit Horon, March 24, 2014.

17. Interview, Chief Superintendent Yehonatan.

18. Ibid.

19. Ronen Bergman, *The Secret War with Iran*, pp. 287–288.

Chapter 22

1. Amir Buchbut, "*Ha'Matara Shelanu Brura: Le'Hisha'er Bnei Adam,*" *Ma'ariv NRG Hadashot,* December 4, 2004.

2. Interview, Chief Inspector Yaron, Israel, Lod, March 23, 2014.

3. http://www.izkor.mod.gov.il/HalalKorot.aspx?id=517054.

4. Hanan Greenberg, "*Ha'Pe'ilut Be'Philadelphi: Ha'Makom Ha'Chi Mafhid Be'Shtahim,*" *Yediot Aharonot/Ynet,* May 13, 2004.

5. Interview, Vlad, Beit Horon, March 24, 2014.

6. Interview, Yehonatan, September 28, 2014.

7. Interview, Yaron, March 23, 2014.

8. Interview, Yehonatan, December 24, 2014.

9. Interview, Yaron, Beit Horon, March 23, 2014.

10. Ibid.

11. Amir Buchbut, "*Ha'Matara Shelanu Brura: Le'Hisha'er Bnei Adam.*"

12. Interview, Superintendent, January 17, 2005.

Chapter 23

1. Jodi Rudoren, "To a Philosopher-General in Israel, Peace Is the Time to Prepare for War," *New York Times,* November 15, 2013.

2. Interview, Kfar Saba, March 20, 2014.

3. Amir Buchbut, "*Ha'Kelev Barry NeheragBe'At Milui Tafkido,*" *NRG Ma'ariv,* December 21, 2005.

4. Interview, Yehonatan, Israel, December 30, 2014.

5. Interview, Lod, March 25, 2014.

6. Tal Yamin-Wolvovitz, Amir Buchbut, and Amit Cohen, "*Ha'Echra'i Le'Nisayon Ha'Pigu'a Be'Tel Aviv Chusal Be'Jenin,*" *NRG Ma'ariv,* February 21, 2007.

7. Avi Ashkenazi, "*Ha'Tza'la'sh Ha'Hamishi Shel Ha'Mista'arevHa'Bedui,*" *NRG Ma'ariv,* September 13, 2009.

8. See Tal Yamin-Wolvovitz, Amir Buchbut, and Amit Cohen, "*Ha'Echra'i Le'Nisayon Ha'Pigu'a.*"

9. Yehonatan Lis, "*Harag Arba'a Bechirei Jihad Ve'Kibel Itur,*" *Ha'aretz,* April 25, 2007.

10. Ibid.

11. Interview, Israel, July 1, 2014.

12. Interview, Tel Aviv, December 30, 2014.

Epilogue

1. TOI Staff, "Report: New IDF Assessment Shows Some 6,000 Gazans Invaded Israel on October 7," *Times of Israel,* August 31, 2024.

2. Ayelett Shani, "'Sinwar Told Me: One Day I'll Be in Power – and You'll Be the One Interrogated,'" *Haaretz,* December 15, 2023.

3. IDF Editorial Team, "Operation Brother's Keeper," Israel Defense Force, October 30, 2017, https://www.idf.il/en/mini-sites/wars-and-operations/operation-brother-s-keeper /operation-brother-s-keeper/.

4. Yoav Zaitun and Elior Levi, "*Lohamei Ya'ma'm Mechupasim Le'Yoldot VeMishpacha A'tzru Mehabel Be'Beit Holim Ve'Hislu Et Korvo,*" Ynet/Yediot, November 12, 2015.

5. Josef Federman, "Hospital Raid Video Offer Rare Glimpse into Undercover Israeli Units," *Times of Israel*, November 13, 2015.

6. News 13, "Undercover in Israeli territory: This Is How the New Tactical Unit of the MGB Works" YouTube, July 11, 2023, https://www.youtube.com/watch?v=y94Lia-iDJE &t=206s.

7. "A Unitary Police Officer - The Undercover Unit of the IOSH Police Force," November 7, 2022. https://www.gvura.org/a349170-%D7%A6%D7%9C-%D7%A9-%D7%99%D7% 97%D7%99%D7%93%D7%AA%D7%99-%D7%99%D7%97%D7% 99%D7%93%D7%AA-%D7%94%D7%9E%D7%A1%D7%AA%D7%A2%D7%A8%D 7%91%D7%99%D7%9D-%D7%9E%D7%92-%D7%91-%D7%90%D7%99%D7%95- %D7%A9.

8. Amir Buchbut, Guy Alistar, Yoav Itiel, Eli Ashkenazi, and Uri Sela, "*Ko'ach Mista'arvim Nichsaf Be'Pe'ilut Be'Jenin – 7 Lohamim Nifga'u Be'Hilutz,*" Walla News, June 19, 2023.

9. Yoav Zaitun, "*Machane Refaim: 'Ha'Food Truck' Ha'Natush VeCrazot Ha'Shihadim – Divuach Meyuchad MiMachane Ha'Plitim Jenin,*" Ynet, July 4, 2023.

10. Guy Assif, "'*Hu Ala Al Tractor Ve'Ramas Et Ha'Bayit': Ha'Kadentziya Ha'So'eret Shel Ha'Maf'kal Shabtai,*" Ynet, August 2, 2024.

11. Sharon Packer, MD, "The Captagon Controversy and Why It Captivates," *Psychiatric Times*, December 26, 2023.

12. Ynet, "'In October It Didn't Surprise Me': The Commander of the Elite Unit of the Police Speaks," YouTube, October 31, 2023. https://www.youtube.com/watch?v=DThy FHjTEY8.

13. Steve Hendrix, "Scenes from a Massacre: Inside an Israeli Town Destroyed by Hamas," *Washington Post*, October 10, 2023.

14. "*Ha'Hachanot Le'Hilutz Arba'at Ha'Hatufim Nihsafot: 'Mistaarvim Sachru Dira Be'Nuseirat, Nashim Histovevu Im Smalot Ve'Hijab',*" Ynet/Yediot, June 14, 2024.

15. Israel Defense Force, X, June 8, 2024. https://x.com/idfonline/status/17994864982254 43216.

16. Dov Lieber, "Israel's Undercover Forces Emerge as Gaza's Newest Battlefield Player," *Wall Street Journal*, July 17, 2024.